CELESTIAL PHILOSOPHY,

OR

Genethliacal Astronomy,

CONTAINING

THE ONLY TRUE METHOD OF

CALCULATING NATIVITIES,

MADE PLAIN AND EASY.

By John Worsdale, Astronomer,
Near the Cathedral, Lincoln.

Published by Messrs. Longman, & Co. 47 Paternoster Row,
London; and may be had of the Author, or Printer,
and all Booksellers in the United Kingdom.

M. KEYWORTH, PRINTER, LINCOLN.

Price £1. 5s. *in Boards.*

**Kessinger Publishing's Rare Reprints
Thousands of Scarce and Hard-to-Find Books!**

We kindly invite you to view our extensive catalog list at:
http://www.kessinger.net

CONTENTS.

This Work contains an exposition of the Errors of all Ancient and Modern Authors, impartially stated, proving that no Original Works on this department of Astronomy, have been published in this Kingdom for several Centuries past, and that all Modern Publications on Nativities, which have yet been given to the World, are pirated from Ancient Authors, with a developement of their erroneous operations, and Judgment in Directional Motion, &c. including the Names of all piratical Authors, who have dishonored this CELESTIAL SCIENCE by their inexplicable principles and practice.

THE PRISTINE ELEMENTS OF CALCULATING NATIVITIES, and the true Method of delivering Judgment in all cases, are clearly demonstrated in this Work, divested of every fallacious hypothesis, with a concise illustration of the Computations of all MUNDANE DIRECTIONS, and Parallels by DIRECT, RAPT, and CONVERSE MOTION, comprising the most correct Rules, and demonstrable Examples for Computing all Arcs of Directions IN THE ZODIAC, which are proved in the Calculations of THIRTY REMARKABLE MODERN NATIVITIES, never before published; including the Geniture of the INFANT DUKE DE BORDEAUX. All those who are disposed to Study this department of Astronomy, may refer to the exemplary Computations given in full, by attending to which, they will be qualified to Calculate all the Arcs of Directions in any Nativity, with accuracy and expedition, and also ascertain their various Effects in the different Terms and Constellations, &c. by which all important Events, during any person's Life, are accurately discovered, and previously ascertained. Many Examples for practice are given in this Work, computed in full, from NEW ASTRONOMICAL TABLES, according to the present Ecliptical Obliquity, exemplifying the influence of the Celestial Bodies on Man, comprising the established Method of selecting, and directing the True Apheta, in any Nativity, in Examples of Life and Death. The Precepts are interspersed with copious strictures, practical and scientific, comprehending the Stellar Causes of the retardation, frustration, and acceleration of the Effects of all Primary Directions, with a dissertation on Directional Motion in all its parts, which may be proved by the use of the Celestial Globe, or Spherical Trigonometry. To which are added, concise Rules for delivering Judgment ON THE REVOLUTIONS OF KINGDOMS AND STATES; INCLUDING CORRECT PRECEPTS FOR COMPUTING SOLAR AND LUNAR ECLIPSES, for any number of Years past or to come, with Examples containing the Calculations; and also *the Elements of the great Eclipse of the Sun*, on the 15th of May 1836. NEW TABLES of the Poles of the Houses, and those of Declination, Right Ascension, and Ascensional Difference, are given in this Work, and likewise all those *new and valuable Tables of Oblique Ascension*, computed by the Author, according to the present Obliquity of the Ecliptic, from *one to sixty Degrees of Latitude*, comprising those Calculated for the principal Cities, and Towns in England, Scotland, France, Ireland, and North America, which were never before published in this Kingdom.

THE AUTHOR'S ADDRESS
TO
THE READER.

MANY improvements have been made in all ages, for promoting and advancing useful arts and sciences, which merit the approbation of an impartial community; but in the present age, the divine science of Genethliacal Astronomy has been neglected, and in a great measure discountenanced, in consequence of the numerous errors and notorious contradictions which are recorded in the pirated works of all Authors. Many have applied themselves to this Celestial Study, but have soon been defeated, because they were not able to obtain a competent knowledge of its primitive principles, having nothing to attend to but delusive Theorems, multifarious processes, and inexplicable Problems void of legal demonstration, which have plunged them into a Labyrinth of insurmountable error and confusion. Thus it becomes evident to every enlightened mind, that this sublime science, as it is now generally studied, and practised, must be considered as a most disgusting and contemptible study, because its advocates and professors have not produced any of those substantial and indubitable proofs, which are required to place this useful, and interesting branch of sacred literature, high in public estimation; for no modern examples have yet been given, which are deemed sufficient to establish the verity of Stellar power on mankind, neither are there any manifest facts on record, that are competent to convince the unbelievers, of the truth of Astronomical computations, and predictions; but in this work I presume I have unveiled all those flagrant abuses, and delusive chimeras, with which the Volumes of all piratical Authors abound, and having so done by authentic examples founded on facts, which cannot be confuted, I flatter myself that my feeble exertions, will be productive of establishing the truth and utility of this sacred and much injured science, and once more restore it to the summit of its ancient respectability and splendour.

It is well known that this branch of Astronomical literature, was sanctioned and practised in the earliest ages, by the most august and learned personages, whose works exhibit numerous interesting and important truths relative to the effects of Sideral power; but though the laudable and indefatigable researches, of those literary and scientific characters, were attended with consummate success, yet all those who are Students in this department of Astronomy, ought to know that there are several works, which if adhered to, will constantly mislead them in all their operations and judgment. The Authors of the works I allude to, are Gadbury, Coley, Parker, White and Sibly. These pirates have dishonoured this predictive science by the fallacious innovations, and notorious prevarications which pollute their pages; they have multiplied the most flagrant errors in directional motion and judgment, which ought to have been deposited in the confines of oblivion, for it is plain from their pirated works, that they were deficient in Astronomical calculations. The true method of directing a significator to its promittor in Mundo, by direct and converse motion, was unknown to them, because they did not understand the Rapt motion of the Earth, and doctrine of the sphere in all its parts. Their Tables and Arcs of directions are all incorrect, and their division of the Heavens are also false, delusive and undemonstrable, which I have proved by the examples given in this work. They have absurdly invented many vague motions of the Celestial Bodies that have no existence, being remote from truth, which the most correct Astronomical computations, and use of the Celestial Globe are incompetent to explain.

A Work entitled, "an illustration of Astrology", was *pirated* and published by Mr. E. Sibly, about thirty years ago, which has done incalculable injury to this noble science. In many cases he has given precepts for computing directions, which he has abandoned in his operations, he has also extracted most of the Nativities from Gadbury's collection; with all the erroneous calculations and judgment of that Author, which have been very ably exposed, and refuted, more than a century ago, by Mr. John Partridge, in his valuable English works called Opus Reformatum, and Defectio Geniturarum, the compilation of those volumes will immortalize his name, and exhibit his superior talents in this department of Astronomy, to generations yet unborn.

The Works of Mr. William Lilly on Horary questions, and on the subsequent mutations of the World, are interesting and of considerable importance to all genuine students in this celestial science, and though the Author was unacquainted with the true method of directional motion in Nativities, and the correct division of the Heavens by duplicate horary times, yet he certainly was the greatest professor of the Mundane, and Horary departments of this science, that ever wrote in the English language; his precepts and judgment prove his abilities to every unprejudiced reader. The Works of Mr. John Partridge, and Mr. William Lilly, are of more value than all others that have been published in this Kingdom; but if the industrious Students are disposed to purchase the works of other Authors, which are altogether a confused heap of rubbish, they are at liberty to do so, as Booksellers may always be found, who will be very ready and willing to supply their customers with works on Nativities, at enormous prices, if the deluded purchasers think proper to dispose of their cash for articles that are of no use, or value whatsoever.

About twelve years ago, Mr. Thomas White published a work called, "The Celestial Intelligencer," which is a wretched compilation of borrowed, and stolen trash, collected from the works of most of the pirates I have mentioned. The truth is, his work does not contain fifty pages of his own composition; his Arcs of directions are all notoriously false, and his judgment incoherent and absurd; he has given the most inconsistent examples to prove, that the Planets, after they have passed the Ascendant and Midheaven, return back, contrary to the regular order of nature, and the distance of the Stars from those Angles, he is pleased to stile Arcs of Directions; by these and other ridiculous, and whimsical notions, the industrious Students are misguided, and continually deceived in their practice, thus when a Man is disposed to transcribe and pirate the works of the living, or the dead, combined with new inventions void of truth, his own inability then becomes manifest to an impartial community and his works will ever record his ignorance and folly.

Mr. James Wilson has lately published a Dictionary of Astrology, in which he has given all the fallacious precepts, false terms, and preposterous innovations of the transcribers before quoted. The errors and contradictions which he has revived, ought to have been placed in obscurity, and not raked together to deceive the ignorant, and confound the Students in this Science; but I have given my opinion on his Dictionary more at large in another part of this work, hoping that my impartial admonitions will prove useful to those who are inclined to adhere to truth alone, founded on authentic examples and experience.

There are several other Authors who have written on Nativities, but I shall not notice the rubbish they have collected, and impudently foisted on the Public; but it is by no means sufficient for me to say that the works of the Authors I have mentioned are false, without producing satisfactory proofs of the truth of my assertions, which I presume I have done in the course of my calculations; all of which may be proved by the use of the Celestial Globe; for what can be more simple and plain than the examples I have given, or what more easy to be understood, than those invariable facts, proved by the clearest demonstration. In the compilation of this work, I have received no assistance from any Man living, but I anticipate that succeeding generations will return me grateful thanks for exposing the errors contained in this noble Science, and particularly those in directional motion. It is notorious to observe the villany which is practised by *numerous impostors*, who travel through the Country, and pretend to calculate Nativities, of which they know nothing; these

Jugglers, and artful deceivers, who are generally as ignorant as they are impudent, frequently attempt to perform many things, which are far beyond the extent of human comprehension; In many towns or villages of note, some of this *scandalous tribe* may be found, they often attract the attention of the vulgar, and to carry on their *villany* without control, pretend to *converse with Spirits,* and to have *Legions of Angels* at their command. Many of these *detestable impostors,* manufacture, and dispose of *Charms, Sigils* and *Lamens,* to make their poor deluded clients *rich* and *completely happy,* and thereby put their designs of *knavery* into execution, by which they impose on the credulous, and deceive the ignorant; but all these, and many other species of villany, (too odious, and contemptible to mention,) are by no means connected with the genuine principles of Genethliacal Astronomy, reduced to practice. There may be, and doubtless are some, who understand the primitive rudiments of this celestial science, but those literary characters are at present unknown to me. Every attentive observer may soon discover the numerous abuses practised under the name of this sublime study, which when attended to in its divine purity, is far superior to all the known arts and sciences in the World.

In this Work I have given the primitive elements of calculating Nativities, and the method of delivering judgment in all cases, which are clearly demonstrated and divested of every fallacious hypothesis, with an illustration of the projections of the Mundane Aspects of the significators and promittors in any Geniture, and in all parts of the Heavens, comprising the most correct rules and demonstrable examples for computing all Arcs of directions in the Zodiac, which are proved in the calculation of thirty remarkable modern Nativities, according to the doctrine of Ptolemy.

I have also given new Tables of Declination, computed according to the present obliquity of the Ecliptic, with those of right Ascension, and Ascensional difference, including new Tables of the Poles of the Houses, calculated by duplicate horary times; I have likewise given new Tables of oblique Ascension, computed according to the Ecliptical Angle of twenty three degrees, twenty eight minutes, from one to sixty degrees of latitude, among which are given, those calculated for the latitudes of several principal Towns and Cities in England, Scotland, France, Ireland and North America, which were never before published in this Kingdom.

Those who purchase this Work will not require any aid or assistance from any other Author, as I have not omitted any thing that is requisite to be understood, by the attentive practitioner. In erecting the first Figure in this Work, for the Latitude of the City of Lincoln, I have given the true method of placing the proper Signs, Degrees and

Minutes, on the Cusps of all the Houses, and have also given Rules how to place the Planets therein, so that without the least difficulty, a Figure of the Heavens may be truly erected for other Latitudes, according to the same rules and computations from the tables of Oblique Ascension at the end of this Work, as tables of Houses are unnecessary. I have likewise explained the method of calculating the true Geocentric places of the Planets from the Ephemeris, for the time of Birth, and have also given rules and examples in full, for computing the Latitudes, Declinations, Right Ascensions, Semidiurnal, Seminocturnal Arcs, and Ascensional Differences of the Planets, with their diurnal and nocturnal horary times, all of which I have endeavoured to make as plain and as easy as possible, in order that these operations may be perfectly understood by every Student in this science, before he proceeds to compute any Arcs of directions, either in the Zodiac, or in Mundo.

I have given the true computation of the place of the part of Fortune, and the method of directing it from the original Greek Quadripartite of the learned Claudius Ptolemy, which has never been published in the English Language. The Lunar Horoscope can only be directed in the World, having a regular and uniform motion through all the Houses, it is always found to preserve the same space from the Eastern Horizon, whether by day, or night, as the Luminaries are distant from each other; it does not depend on the Latitude and Declination of the Moon, as those numbers are only required in constituting the Moon's true distance from the Solar place, neither can it claim the horary times of the Moon, for certain and obvious reasons; for if the Moon and part of Fortune, were allowed to have the same Latitude and Declination in all parts of the Heavens, and in all cases, we should then to no purpose, endeavour to explain, what is impossible to be proved by human Literature. The calculation of this important point, as it is given by all Authors presents an entire mass of error and confusion; but as I have given all its Arcs of Directions in the Genitures calculated in this Work, it would be needless to dwell longer on this subject, which if duly investigated, will doubtless give the greatest satisfaction to all Students in this Celestial Science.

All Authors have given inaccurate methods for computing the Poles of the Planets, which I have proved by examples in this Work, for when the Student has used his best endeavours to ascertain his numbers and distances, &c., under incorrect polar Elevations, his Arcs of Directions then become entirely deficient, so that no events can be truly predicted from such false operations; but I have made all these subjects as plain as possible by my computations; I have also instructed the Student, (by the precepts I have recorded,) how to give immediate Judgment on any Nativity, respecting the propitious and malignant qualities of the Celestial bodies, from their different positions, and configurations in the Radix; so that when a figure is erected, the Student may examine the precepts I have given, and he will instantly discover, whether that Native, born under the power of those Elementary qualities will obtain Wealth and Preferment, or experience Poverty and Woe. I have likewise given many Arcs of Directions wrought in full, both in the Zodiac, and in Mundo, including Mundane Parallels, by Direct, Rapt and Converse Direction, so that the Student may soon become Master of the whole Art of directional Motion, without which, the time of any important Event during the Life of an individual, cannot be previously pointed out, and truly ascertained. But to instruct the Student still further in these Celestial enquiries, I have also given Rules by which I have explained the nature, power, and effects of all Directions and Parallels in the Zodiac, and in the World; so that when the Student has computed the Arcs of Directions in any Geniture, by the examples given, he may then refer to the Precepts, where he will instantly discover the nature of the Events portended by the quality and Effects of the different directions, whether they are good or evil.

The Rules which I have given for delivering judgment on the Revolutions of Kingdoms and States, War and Peace, Plenty and Scarcity, &c. may be depended on in all cases, and those who properly attend to them, will be amply rewarded for their exertions. The method of computing Solar and Lunar Eclipses I have also given in this Work, and have inserted the calculations in full, by a correct method, by which any Student may compute them with ease and accuracy, for any number of Years past, or to come.

In the Nativities calculated in this Work, I have explained the power of Progressions, Annual Revolutions and Secondary Directions by examples, so that the Student will be enabled to understand them by little application, and apply them in all cases in the calculation of other Genitures; but though I have recorded the most substantial truths relative to the verity of sideral prediction, which the testimony of many hundreds of respectable characters can substantiate, yet I am aware that the most flagrant and abusive arguments will be advanced against the utility of this venerable Science, by those, who are always ready to condemn what they are unable to define, or comprehend; if such characters are of a different opinion, and do not believe that the Heavenly Bodies have any influence on Mankind, they ought to avoid every portion of censure, and view those who Study the power, magnitude and motions of the Celestial Orbs, with pity and regret, for it is absurd and unjust to deny the truth of what they never proved; but Alas! in the present Age, when *bold Infidelity* is making *gigantic movements* in this once happy Land; even those sacred writings which contain GOD'S HOLY WORD, are frequently traduced, disregarded, and a considerable portion of odium, and ignominy levelled against them, but sacred and Celestial truth in its purity, will ever reign triumphant over vice, profaneness and immorality, Those who demand proof of Astral power on man, may observe, that I have furnished them with examples, over which contention, and hypocrisy are unable to prevail; if the difference between the *Cause* and the *Effect* is required, the most ample proofs are given throughout the Work which will repel every artful insinuation opposed to the Study of Stellar power, it would therefore be inconsistent to attend to arguments advanced by *Infidels*, *Deists*, and *Atheists*, who generally use their puny efforts, to stifle and traduce visible facts of every description, if those facts appear mysterious to their own comprehension. The untaught vulgar are generally enemies to Celestial truths; their impertinent, and *pitiful ribaldry* combined with a large portion of *low cunning*, in a moment proclaim an *ignoble origin*; but the ignominious conduct of such characters is beneath my notice. It is well known that there are some who remain of opinion, that allowing the time of every important Event of any person's Life, with the period of dissolution, to be previously ascertained with correctness and precision, by Astronomy, or any laudable Calculations whatsoever, it would prove injurious; and instead of administering comfort and consolation to an afflicted mind a perfect and previous knowledge of those Events, would be productive of unhappiness and misery. Such is the nature and extent of the ridiculous and absurd arguments, which some, who disbelieve the Occult power of Sideral agency on mankind, are disposed to produce, but the Royal Psalmist was of a different opinion, for his express and humble desire was, to know his end, and the number of his Days, that he might be prepared to meet his God; but the *hardened Infidels* generally condemn every contemplation of a solemn and instructive nature, and turn aside, and impiously spurn at all admonitions, which exhibit to them the period, when they must bid a final adieu to all alluring vices; then at last on a bed of sickness they appear conscious of their guilt, and wish in vain for the return of a few Years, that they might humbly reconcile themselves to an offended God, and receive spiritual consolation from every divine instruction, but Alas! the number of their Months are with THEE, they must go hence at the time appointed, unto that place, where the wicked cease from troubling, and where their impious Tongues will no more be able to utter daring eloquence, against the irresistable power of the wonderous Works of the MOST HIGH.

All those who are Students in this department of Astronomy, (in which the infinite Wisdom of the grand Architect of the Universe is so manifestly apparent in all his stupendous designs,) will soon be able to comprehend the primitive rudiments of this noble Science; they will not meet with any insurmountable difficulties in their practice, when they diligently apply themselves to directional Motion and Judgment, as I have used my best endeavours to make every thing as plain as possible, by the most familiar examples, The various opinions on FATE, and the freedom of the WILL, are here set at rest for ever, not by noisy arguments and contention destitute of proof, but by a combination of visible, and manifest facts which admit of no human contradiction. Religion in its *purity*, on which the Law of the Land is established, cannot unfold to human reason, more excellencies of the infinite Wisdom, Glory, and power of HIM, who is KING of KINGS, and LORD of LORDS, than a constant contemplation of the influence of those Celestial Bodies, which are the Works of his Hands, and by whose Almighty power, they are, and were created, for the use of mortal Man. Religion teaches us to worship the great Creator in Spirit, and in Truth; but the Study of Celestial Philosophy elevates our finite understanding still more, and displays to us the certain immortality of the Soul, and the boundless joys of eternal felicity, which are objects of the greatest importance; it also exhibits to us the unspeakable Love of the Lord of Hosts to mankind, and in a moment breaks all the forged *shackles of Priestcraft*, and liberates all those who are slaves to *refined Popery*; it exhibits to the rich Man the time when himself, his offspring, and relatives, must soon like shadows, vanish, and be no more: It teaches Kings, Princes and Emperors, that the silent Tombs wait for the reception of their earthly Tabernacles, which must shortly be dissolved; thus when the understanding of Man is soaring by contemplation above those Orbs of Light, we then reflect, that all Terrestrial objects are of small importance, when compared with even an imperfect view of those Celestial pleasures, which flow from the favour, mercy and goodness of the Almighty for evermore.

I now conclude, hoping that what I have developed by examples founded on the Basis of Truth, will ultimately prove of essential advantage to all genuine Sons of Urania, for whose Literary advancement I have unveiled and revived, the primitive principles of the venerable Science of Genethliacal Astronomy.

Laudate Deum in sanctitate eius; Laudate cum in firmamento fortitudinis eius.

TO THE MEMORY

OF THE IMMORTAL PTOLEMY.

BY THE AUTHOR.

Immortal Teacher of this Art divine,
Thy rules on record, most refulgent shine;
To thee alone we owe what we profess,
Though other Sages toil'd without success;
But now we daily prove, that by thy aid,
This Art in darkness, is no longer laid;
Those Myst'ries now unveil'd, are all as clear
As Light that floweth from each glitt'ring Sphere:
By thy assistance, we may always find,
Important Lessons, for the human mind:
All gloom is now dispell'd, and Man may show,
The certain Fate of Mortals here below,
As in a Glass we view the human face,
So by thy Lectures, all these things we trace;
Those who may cavil at this Learning; stand
Amaz'd to see its progress in this Land;
Thy precepts just, for ever will impart
Truth to each Student in this noble Art,
By which all Facts unfolded to our Eyes,
Are oft survey'd with wonder and surprise;
Through thee, the power of each Star we know,
Though far from all observers here below;
Strange then it must appear, that things now plain,
Should very oft be treated with disdain;
Those Orbs of Light, which roll in order, prove

XX

That all events on Earth, are from above;
Solemn the thought! such contemplation, brings
Us near to him, who is the *King of Kings*;
Thou learned Sage, hast taught us to explain,
Those Signs on High, which are not set in vain;
The tokens lately view'd in yonder sky,
Are seldom to be seen by human Eye;
Thou art no more, yet thy immortal Name,
Will soar triumphant on the Wings of Fame,
And though insulting Feet may on thee tread,
Now thou hast long been number'd with the dead;
Yet all thy Rules which infidels surprise,
Are daily proved in the boundless Skies,
Sages unborn, thy learning will adore,
'Till Sun and Moon and Stars, shall shine no more.

CELESTIAL PHILOSOPHY,

OR

GENETHLIACAL ASTRONOMY.

THE TRUE METHOD OF ERECTING A

FIGURE OF THE HEAVENS.

A Male Child was Born in the City of Lincoln, near the House in which I now live, on the first of October 1817, at for'y five minutes past four o'Clock in the Afternoon; the Latitude of the place of Birth is 53° 15' North. Now in this example as well as all others, the Sun's true Longitude at the time of Birth must be first ascertained, and then his Right Ascension, which must be added to the Right Ascension of the time of Birth, when converted into Degrees and Minutes, and then the true Right Ascension of the Midheaven will be found which is proved by the following computation.

In White's Ephemeris for the Year 1817, on the first of October, the Sun's place at Noon, is 7° 55' of Libra, and on the second day at Noon, his Longitude is 8° 54' of the same Sign, omitting seconds, the difference is 59', which is the Sun's motion in 24 Hours, but as the time of Birth is 4H. 45M. after the Noon of the first of October, I now say, if 24 Hours require 59', then 4H. 45M. will give 12', which added to the Sun's place at the Meridian of that day 7° 55', the true Longitude of the Sun at the time of Birth will be 8° 7' of Libra.

Now to find the true Right Ascension of the Sun, I look in the Table of Right Ascension in this Work, and in the first column opposite 8° of Libra, I find 187° 21', and opposite to 9° of the same Sign, the number is 188° 16', the difference is 55'; then if 1°, or 60' give 55', the 7' of Longitude will require 6', which added to 187° 21', the sum will be 187° 27', which is the Sun's Right Ascension at the time of Birth; I now refer to the Table in this Work, for converting Hours and Minutes into Degrees and Minutes; then consequently 4h. 45m. will produce 71° 15', which added to the Sun's Right Ascension before found, which is 187° 27', and the true Right Ascension of the Midheaven will be 258° 42'; now to find the true Degrees and Minutes of the sign corresponding with the above Right Ascension of the Medium Celi, the operation is thus; I look in the Table of Right Ascension, and seek the nearest number which is 258° 2', opposite to 19° of Sagittary, and even with 20°, of the same sign, I find 259° 7', the difference is 1° 5'; then if 65' require 60', what will the difference between the Right Ascension of the Midheaven, and the Right Ascension of 19° of Sagittary, (being 40') give? the number thus obtained by proportion, is 37', omitting Fractions; so that 19° 37' of that sign are on the Midheaven at the time of Birth. Then to the Right Ascension of the Medium Celi 258° 42', I add 30°, which make 288° 42', this number is the oblique Ascension of the eleventh House, and by looking in the Tables of the Poles of Position in this Work, and computing the proportional part for the elevations of the eleventh and third, twelfth and second Houses for the 15' of Latitude which exceed 53°, the former will become 25° 20', and the latter 42° 49'; I then look in the Table of Oblique Ascension for the Latitude of 25°, omitting the 20', and seek the number 288° 42', which as I have said before, is the Oblique Ascension of the Eleventh House, and the nearest number is 288° 8', opposite to 6° of Capricorn, and even with 7° of the same Sign I find 289° 12', the difference is 1° 4': I now subtract the Oblique Ascension corresponding with 6° of Capricorn from the Oblique Ascension of the Eleventh House 288° 42', and the difference is 34', then if 64' require 60', the above 34', will give 32'; so that 6° 32' of Capricorn must be placed on the cusp of the eleventh House; **then to the Oblique Ascension of the eleventh 288° 42', I** again add 30°, and the sum is 318° 42', which is the oblique Ascension of the twelfth, this number I seek in the Table of Oblique Ascension for the Latitude of 43°, which is the nearest to the required polar elevation, and opposite to 25° of Capricorn I find 318° 6', and even with 26° of the same sign, I find 318° 58', the difference is 52', and the difference between the Oblique Ascension of 25° of Capricorn, and the Oblique Ascension of the twelfth, 318° 42', is 36'; I now say, if 52' require 60', what will 36' require, the answer will be, 42', so that 25° 42' of Capricorn are to be placed on the cusp of the twelfth House. Now to the Oblique Ascension of the twelfth 318° 42', I add 30°, and the sum is 348° 42', which is the Oblique Ascension of the Ascendant, I then refer to the Table of Oblique Ascension for the Latitude of 53° 15', and seek the number 348° 42', and opposite to 1° of Pisces, I find 348° 20' and even with 2° of the same sign, I find 348° 46', the difference between these numbers is 26'; I then subtract the Oblique Ascension of 1° of Capricorn, which is 348° 20', from the Oblique Ascension of the Ascendant, being 348° 42', and the difference is 22', then if 26' require 60', the above number, which is 22' will produce 51', so that 1° 51' of Pisces must be placed on the cusp of the Ascendant. I then add 30° more to the Oblique Ascension of the Ascendant as above, which is 348° 42', and the sum will be 378° 42', but as this number exceeds the Circle, I subtract 360° from it, and the remainder 18° 42' will be the Oblique Ascension of the second, which I look for in the table of Oblique Ascension under the Pole of 43°, and opposite to 2° of Taurus I find 18° 12', and even with 3° of that sign stand 18° 48', then by subtraction the difference becomes 36', and by subtracting 18° 12' from 18° 42' there will remain 30'; therefore if 36' require 60', then the difference between the Oblique Ascension of 2° of Taurus, and the Oblique Ascension of the second, being 30' as above, will produce 50', so that 2° 50' of Taurus are to be placed on the cusp of the second; I then add 30° more to the Oblique Ascension of the second, and the Oblique Ascension of the third will be 48° 42′, this sum I seek for in the Table of Oblique Ascension under the Latitude of 25°, and even with 0° of Gemini I find 47° 56′, and opposite to 1° of that Sign stand 48° 52′, the one number being too little, and the other too much, the difference between them is 56′, then by subtracting the Oblique Ascension of 0° of Gemini 47° 56′ from the Oblique Ascension of the third 48° 42′, there will remain 46′; I now say, if 56′ require 60′, then 46′ will produce 49′; so that 0° 49′ of Gemini must be placed on the Cusp of the third House.

In these computations it must be observed that the Signs, Degrees, and Minutes, occupying the Cusps of the oriental and occidental Houses stand as follow.

Oriental Houses.	°	′		Occidental Houses.	Opposite Signs, degrees & minutes.
10	19	37	♐	4	19 37 ♊
11	6	32	♑	5	6 32 ♋
12	25	42	♑	6	25 42 ♋
1	1	51	♓	7	1 51 ♍
2	2	50	♉	8	2 50 ♏
3	0	49	♊	9	0 49 ♐

The sign Aries is intercepted in the Ascendant, and Libra in the Seventh; Aquarius is also intercepted in the twelfth, and Leo in the sixth.

The Geocentric Longitudes of the Planets at the time of Birth, are calculated as follow.

The diurnal motion of Saturn in the Ephemeris is 3′; but as the proportional part for the time of Birth amounts only to seconds; I take the place of that Planet in 0° 13′ of Pisces, Retrograde.

The Longitude of Jupiter on the first of October, is 6° 41′ of Sagittary, and on the second, his place is 6° 51′ of that Sign, then by subtraction his daily Motion is 10′; I now say if 24 Hours require 10′, the time of Birth 4H. 45M. will require

2′, which being added to the place of Jupiter on the first of October, his true Longitude at the time of Birth will be 0° 43′ of Sagittary.

By the same method the diurnal motion of Mars will be 20′; for if 24 Hours give 20′, then 4H. 45M. will produce 4′, which added to 20° 36′ of Gemini, his Longitude is 20° 40′ of that Sign.

The daily motion of Venus by subtraction as in the above Examples, is 1° 11′; then if 24 Hours require 71′; the time of Birth 4H. 45M. will give 14′, which added to 9° 4′, the true place of Venus will be 9° 18′ of Virgo.

The diurnal motion of Mercury is 27′; now if 24 Hours give 27′, then the time of Birth 4H. 45M. will give 5′, which must be *subtracted* from the place of Mercury on the first of October, because he is Retrograde, and his true Longitude at the time of Birth will be 24° 34′ of Libra.

The Longitude of the Moon on the first of October, is 14° 32′ of Gemini, and on the second, her place is 26° 28′ of that sign; now by subtraction, as in all the above examples, her diurnal motion becomes 11° 56′; then if 24 hours require 11° 56′, what will 4H. 45M. the time of Birth give? the answer will be 2° 22′, which added to 14° 32′, the true Longitude of the Moon at the time of Birth will be 16° 54′ of Gemini.

The computation of the Latitudes of the Planets, at the time of Birth.

As there is not more than one Minute in the variation of the Latitude of Saturn in the space of six days, and the same with respect to Jupiter's Latitude, I take 1° 49′ South for the Latitude of Saturn, and that of Jupiter 0° 28′ North.

The Latitude of Mars on the first of October is 0° 30′ South, and on the seventh of the same Month it is 0° 19′ South, the difference is 11′ in six days, therefore by proportion the time of Birth 4H. 45M. will not produce any number, so that the Latitude of Mars will be 0° 30′ South.

Then by subtraction according to the above method, the

E

variation of the Latitude of Venus in six days is 18′, therefore 4H. 45M. will produce nearly one Minute, which must be added to 0° 36′, and the Latitude of Venus at the time of Birth will be, 0° 37′ North.

The Latitude of Mercury on the first day of the above Month is 3° 34′ South, and on the seventh it is 2° 33 ; the difference then produced is 1° 1′ in six days ; then if six days or 144 Hours require 61′, what will 4H. 45M. the time of Birth require? the answer will be 2′ omitting seconds, which I subtract from 3° 34′, and the true Latitude of Mercury will be 3° 32′ South.

The difference in the Moon's Latitude, between the first and second of October, is by subtraction, 55′; then by the rule of proportion, if 24 Hours require 55′, what will 4H. 45M. give? the Answer is 11′, which being added to 2° 17′, the true Latitude of the Moon will be 2° 28′ North. The Dragon's head at the time of Birth, is 19° 56′ of Taurus.

From the new Tables of Declinations contained in this Work, the true Declinations of the Planets are computed, which are more correct than taking them from White's Ephemeris.—The operations are as follow.

The Declination of Saturn is thus calculated. His Longitude is 0° 13′ of Pisces, in which place he has 1° 49′ South Latitude :—I now refer to the Tables of Declination, and opposite 0° of Pisces at the bottom of the Table, with 1° South Latitude, I find 12° 24′, and even with 1° of the same sign with 1° South, the number is 12° 4′, and the difference 20′ ; then if 60′ require 20′, what will 13′ of Longitude give? Answer 4′, which subtracted from 12° 24′, there will remain 12° 20′ :—I now equate for 49′ of Latitude thus :—opposite 0° of Pisces with 1° of Latitude I find 12° 24′, and even with 0° of the same Sign, with 2° of Latitude, the corresponding number is 13° 20′, thus by subtraction the difference is 56′ :— Now if 60′ give 56′, then 49′ of Latitude will produce 46′, which added to 12° 20′ as above, the true Declination of Saturn at the time of Birth will be 13° 6′ South.

The Declination of Jupiter is computed as follows.
The Longitude of Jupiter is 6° 43' of Sagittary, with 0° 28' North Latitude;—I now turn to the Tables of Declination, and opposite 6° of Sagittary with 0° North Latitude, stand the number 21° 20', and even with 7° of the same sign under 0°, I find 21° 30'; the difference will be 10':—Then if 60' require 10', what will 43' of Longitude give? Answer 7' which added to 21° 20', and the sum is 21° 27':—I now compute for 28' of Latitude; opposite 6° of Sagittary with 0° North, I find 21° 20', and even with 6° of the same sign with 1° of Latitude, the number is 20° 21'; the difference will be 59', then if 60' require 59', what will 28' of Latitude give? Answer 28', which I subtract from 21° 27', and the true Declination of Jupiter at the time of Birth is 20° 59' South.

The Declination of Mars is found as follows.
The Longitude of Mars is 20° 40' of Gemini, in which place he has 0° 30' South Latitude;—I again refer to the Tables of Declination, and opposite 20° of Gemini with 0° South Latitude, the number is 23° 5', and even with 21° of the same sign, and under the same Latitude I find 23° 10' the difference is 5'—Now if 60' give 5', then 40' of Longitude will require 3', which must be added to 23° 5', and the number is 23° 8'. I now compute for 30' of Latitude:—opposite 20° of Gemini with 0° of Latitude I find 23° 5', and even with 20° of the same sign, and with 1° of Latitude stand 22° 5':—Then by subtraction the difference is 1°:—I now say, If 60' require 1° then 30' of Latitude will consequently produce 30', this last number obtained I subtract from 23° 8' as before found, and the true Declination of Mars will be 22° 38' North.

The Calculation of the Sun's Declination.
The Longitude of the Sun is 8° 7' of Libra, I then refer to the Tables of Declination, and even with 8° of Libra I find 3° 11', and under 9° of the same sign the number is 3° 34':— The difference is 23':—Now if 60' require 23', then 7' of Longitude will produce 3', which added to 3° 11', the sum thence arising will be 3° 14' South, which is the true Declination of the Sun in the Geniture.

The following is the computation of the Declination of Venus. In the Nativity, the place of Venus is 0° 18' of Virgo, and her Latitude 0° 37' North :—I again turn to the Tables of Declination, and opposite 0° of Virgo, with 0° North Latitude, I find 11° 29', and even with 1° of the same sign and under the same Latitude, stand 11° 8' :—I now subtract the lesser number from the greater, and the remainder will be 21' :—I then say, If 60' give 21' what will 18' of Longitude require? the answer will be 6', which I subtract from 11° 29', (because the Declination is *decreasing* by Latitude, which must be attended to in all similar cases,) and the remainder will be 11° 23' :—I now equate for 37' of Latitude ; even with 0° of Virgo with 0° of Latitude, I find 11° 29', and opposite 0° of the same sign, with 1° of Latitude, the number is 12° 24', the difference is 55' :—Then if 60' require 55', the above 37' of Latitude will produce 34', which added to 11° 23', then consequently the true Declination of Venus will be 11° 57' North.

The Calculation of the Declination of Mercury is thus wrought. The Longitude of Mercury is 24° 34' of Libra, in which place he has 3° 32' South Latitude :—I again refer to the Tables of Declination, and opposite 24° of Libra, with 3° South Latitude I find 12° 6', and even with 25° of the same sign with 3° of Latitude, the number is 12° 30' ; then by subtraction the difference is 24' :—I now say, If 60' require 24' ; what will 34' of Longitude give? the answer will be 14', which added to 12° 6' the sum will be 12° 20' :—I now equate for 32' of Latitude :—even with 24° of Libra with 3° of Latitude, I find 12° 6', and opposite to 24° of Libra under 4° of Latitude, the number is 13° 2' ; I subtract the lesser number from the greater and the difference is 56' :—I then say, If 60' give 56' what will 32' require, the answer is 30', which added to 12° 20', the sum then obtained, is 12° 50', which is the true South Declination of Mercury.

The computation of the Declination of the Moon, is as follows. The Geocentric longitude of the Moon at the time of Birth is 16° 54' of Gemini, where she has 2° 28' North latitude: Then in the Tables of Declination, even with 16° of Gemini, with 2° North latitude, I find 24° 43', and opposite 17° of the same sign, under the same latitude, the number is 24° 50': the difference is 7':—Then if 60' give 7', what will 54' of longitude require? the answer will be 6', which I add to 24° 43', and the sum is 24° 49':—Then to obtain the requisite number for 28' of latitude, I proceed in the same manner as in the operations before wrought; opposite 16° of Gemini, with 2° of latitude, I find 24° 43'; and even with 16° of the same sign, with 4° of latitude, the number is 25° 43'; the difference is 1°:—Then if 60' require 1°, consequently, 28' will produce 28', which I add to 24° 49', and the sum will be 25° 17', which is the true North declination of the Moon, at the time of birth.

The Calculation of the Right Ascensions of the Planets, with their Latitudes.

The longitude of Saturn is 0° 13' of Pisces, where he has 1° 49' South latitude;—I look in the tables of right ascension, under Pisces, with South latitude, and even with 0° in the first column, and under 1° of latitude, I find 332° 28'; and opposite 1°, on the left hand, and under 1° of latitude, I find 333° 25' the difference is 57':—Then if 60' require 57', the longitude of Saturn, 13', will require 12', which, added to 332° 28' make 332° 40', being the true right ascension of Saturn, with 1° South latitude. But to equate for the 49' of latitude, I take the difference between 332° 28', under 1°, and 332° 49', under 2° of latitude, which is 21':—Then, if 60' require 21' what will 49' require? the answer will be 17', which, added to 332° 40', the true right ascension of Saturn with his latitude will be 332° 57'.

The place of Jupiter is 6° 43' of Sagittary, and his latitude 28' North:—In the Tables of Right Ascension under Sagittary North Latitude, and opposite 6° on the left hand under 0° of Latitude I find 244° 6', and opposite 7° under the above 0° of latitude, I find 245° 9', the difference is 1° 3':—Then if

60′ require 63′ the above 43′ of Jupiters longitude will require 45′, which added to 244° 6′, the Right Ascension of Jupiter without latitude, will be 244° 51′ :—I then subtract 244° 6′ from 244° 17′ under 1° of latitude, and the difference is 11′, then if 60′ require 11′, Jupiter's latitude being 28′ will require 5′, which must be added to 244° 51′ and the true Right Ascension of Jupiter will be 244° 56′.

The longitude of Mars is 20° 40′ of Gemini, and his latitude 0° 30′ South, his right Ascension is thus computed. I look in the Tables of Right Ascension, and opposite to 20° of Gemini under 0°, I find 79° 7′, and the next number even with 21°, is 80° 12′, the difference is 1° 5′ :—Then if 60′ give 65′ what will 40′ give? Answer 43′, which added to 79° 7′, the sum will be 79° 50′ :—the difference between 79° 7′ and 79° 12′ is 5′ :—Then if 60′ require 5′, the above 30′, the latitude of Mars will give 3′, which with the above 79° 50′, the true Right Ascension of Mars will be 79° 53′.

The Right Ascension of the Sun has been computed, and was found to be 187° 27′.

Venus is in 0° 18′ of Virgo, with 0° 37′ North latitude, the difference between 152° 6′ and 153° 4′ in the Tables of Right Ascension under Virgo is 58′ :—Then if 60′ give 58′, the longitude of Venus being 18′ will give 17′, which I add to 152° 6′ and the sum is 152° 23′ :—Now for the latitude which is 0° 37′, the difference between 152° 6′ and 152° 27′ under 1° of latitude, is 21′ :—Then if 60′ require 21′ what will 37′ give? Answer 13′, which I add to 152° 23′, and the true Right Ascension of Venus will then become 152° 36′.

The place of Mercury is 24° 34′ of Libra, Retrograde, and his latitude 3° 32′ South :—In the Tables of Right Ascension under 3° South latitude, and even with 24° on the left hand I find 201° 5′, and under the same latitude opposite to 25° stand 202° 2′, by subtraction there remains 57′ :—Then if 60′ require 57′, the remaining minutes of Mercury's longitude being 34′, will give 32′, which added to 201° 5′ the sum will be 201° 37′: The difference between 3° and 4° of latitude opposite 24° of

Libra is 23': —Then if 60' give 23', the 32' of Mercury's Latitude will give 12'; which I subtract from the above sum 201° 37', because the Right Ascension decreases by South Latitude, and the Right Ascension of Mercury will be 201° 25'.

The longitude of the Moon is 16° 54' of Gemini, where she has 2° 28' North latitude:—Then in the Tables of Right Ascension North latitude, opposite to 16° to the left hand, and under 2° of latitude I find 74° 33', and even with 17° under the same latitude, stand 75° 39', the difference between these numbers is 1° 6':—Then if 60' require 66' what will 54' give? Answer 59', which added to 74° 33' the sum is 75° 32':—Now opposite 16° and under 2° of latitude I find the number 74° 33', and under 3° of Latitude stand 74° 27', the difference is only 6':—Then if 60' require 6' what will 28' require? Answer 3' (omitting fractions in all cases,) which I subtract from 75° 32', and the Moon's Right Ascension in the Nativity will be 75° 29'.

The following is the calculation of the Ascensional Difference of the Planets, by which their Semidiurnal and Seminocturnal Arcs are ascertained, with the Diurnal and Nocturnal horary times at the time of Birth, under the Latitude of 53° 15' North.

The Declination of Saturn is 13° 6', I look for 13° in the Tables of Ascensional Difference, and even with that number under 53° of Latitude I find 17° 50', and opposite to 14° under the same Latitude stand 19° 19', the difference is 1° 29':—Then if 60' require 89', the 6' of Saturn's Declination will give 9', which I add to 17° 50' and the sum is 17° 59': The difference between 53° and 54° of Latitude opposite to 13° on the left hand is 42':—Then if 60' give 42' the 15' of Latitude which exceed 53°, will give 10', which I add to 17° 59', and the ascensional Difference of Saturn will be 18° 9': Now having found this number, I subtract it from 90° because the Declination of Saturn is *South*, and I then obtain the Semidiurnal Arc of Saturn 71° 51', this number I divide by 6, and I obtain his diurnal horary times 11° 58':—I then subtract

12   CELESTIAL PHILOSOPHY,

the Semidiurnal Arc 71° 51' from 180°, and the number remaining, being 108° 9', will then be the correct Seminocturnal Arc of the Planet, which also divided by 6, the nocturnal horary times will be 18° 2'.

Jupiter's Declination is 20° 59':—In the Tables of Ascensional Difference as before, I look for 20° on the left hand, and under 53° of Latitude even therewith I find 28° 53', and opposite 21° the number is 30° 37', by subtraction the difference will be 1° 44':—Then if 60' give 104' what will 59' give? Answer 1° 42', which added to 28° 53', the number is 30° 35'; the difference between 53° and 54° of Latitude opposite 20° on the left hand I find to be 1° 11':—Then if 60' give 71', the 15' of Latitude will produce 18', which added to 30° 35', the Ascensional Difference of Jupiter will become 30° 53', which I subtract from 90°, because the Declination is *South*, and Jupiter's Semidiurnal Arc will be 59° 7' which divided by 6 give his diurnal horary times 9° 51':—Then I subtract the above Semidiurnal Arc 59° 7' from 180°, and the Seminocturnal Arc will be 120° 53', which divided by 6 the nocturnal horary times thus produced will be 20° 9'.

The Declination of Mars is 22° 38', then in the Tables of Ascensional Difference I observe 22° and under 53° the number is 32° 25', and even with 23° I find 34° 17', the difference is 1° 52'; then if 60' give 112', the 38' of Declination will give 71' or 1° 11', which I add to 32° 25', and the number will be 33° 36', the difference between 53° and 54° even with 22° on the left hand as in the foregoing Examples, will become 1° 22':—I now say, if 60' give 82' what will 15' of Latitude give? Answer 20', which being added to 33° 36', the number thence arising will be the true Ascensional Difference of Mars 33° 56':—Now as Mars has *North* Declination, I add the Ascensional Difference thus found to 90°, and the Semidiurnal Arc of Mars will be 123° 56' which I divide by 6, and I then obtain the diurnal horary times 20° 39', I now subtract the above Semidiurnal Arc from 180°, and the Seminocturnal Arc will be 56° 4', which divided by 6,

OR GENETHLIACAL ASTRONOMY, 13

will give 9° 21', being the nocturnal horary times of Mars.

The Sun's Declination is 3° 14': Now in the above Tables opposite 3°, and under the elevation of the Pole 53°, I find 3° 59', and even with 4° under the same Latitude, stand 5° 19', the difference is 1° 20'; then if 60' give 80', the 14' of the Sun's Declination will give 19', which with 3° 59' make 4° 18', then the difference between 53° and 54° of Latitude even with 3° on the left hand, will be 9':—therefore if 60' give 9', the 15' above the Latitude of 53°, will produce 2'; which added to 4° 18', make the Ascensional Difference of the Sun, 4° 20', which I subtract from 90°, because the Sun has *South* Declination, and his Semidiurnal Arc will be 85° 40', this number by being divided by 6, will give his diurnal horary times, 14° 17'; then by subtracting the above Semidiurnal Arc from 180°, there remains the Seminocturnal Arc 94° 20', which I again divide by 6, and his nocturnal horary times will be 15° 43'.

The Declination of Venus is 11° 57'; I enter the Tables of Ascensional Difference with 11° on the left hand, then under 53°, I find 14° 57', and opposite 12° the number is 16° 23', and the difference 1° 26':—Now if 60', give 86', then 57' will give 1° 22', which I add to 14° 57', and the number will be 16° 19'; then by subtraction, the remaining difference opposite 11° under 53° and 54° will become 34':—Thus the proportional part for 15' of Latitude will be 8', which I add to 16° 19', and the Ascensional Difference of Venus will be 16° 27', which being added to 90°, because the Declination is *North*, will produce her Semidiurnal Arc 106° 27', this number divided by 6, will give the diurnal horary times 17° 44', and the Seminocturnal Arc by subtraction as before, 73° 33', which again divided by 6, the nocturnal horary times of Venus will be 12° 16'.

The Declination of Mercury being 12° 50', I look in the Table even with 12°, and I find 16° 23', under the elevation of the Pole 53°, the next number below is 17° 50', the difference is 1° 27'; the proportional part obtained as in the foregoing Examples, is 1° 12', which I add to 16° 23', and the number will become 17° 35'; the difference between 53° and 54°, opposite 12° on the left hand, is 37';—Then if 60' give 37', the 15' of Latitude will give 9', which added to 17° 35', will produce the Ascensional Difference of Mercury 17° 44':—I subtract this number as before, from 90° because the Declination is *South*, and the Semidiurnal Arc is 72° 16', and the diurnal horary times 12° 3'; consequently the Seminocturnal Arc will be 107° 44', and the Nocturnal horary times 17° 57'.

The Moon's Declination is 25° 17';—In the Table opposite 25° on the left hand, and under 53° of Latitude I find 38° 14', and opposite 26° stand 40° 20', the difference is 2° 6':—then if 60' give 126' what will 17' give? Answer 36', which I add to 38° 14', and it makes 38° 50'; then for the 15' of Latitude; the difference under the elevation of the Pole of 53° and 54° opposite 25°, is 1° 45'; then by the rule of proportion, if 60', give 105', the 15' of Latitude which exceed 53° will give 26', which added to 38° 50' will produce the Ascensional Difference of the Moon 39° 16' under the Latitude of 53° 15':—Now as the Moon's Latitude is *North*, I add the Ascensional Difference above computed to 90°, and I make the true Semidiurnal Arc of the Moon 129° 16', which divided by 6, her diurnal horary times will be 21° 33';—then consequently the above Semidiurnal Arc taken from 180°, the remainder, which is 50° 44' will be the Moon's Seminocturnal Arc, this number I also divide by 6, and I obtain the nocturnal horary times of the Moon 8° 27'.

It is to be observed in all cases, that when a Planet has *North* Declination, the Ascensional Difference must *always be added to* 90°, which will produce the Semidiurnal Arc, but when the Declination is *South*, the Ascensional Difference must then be *subtracted from* 90°, and the remainder will be the Semidiurnal Arc required.

The only correct Method of computing the Poles of the

OR GENETHLIACAL ASTRONOMY

Planets, with their Oblique Ascensions, and Oblique Descensions in the Radix, which ought to be attended to in all Nativities.

The Sun's true Polar Elevation is thus calculated.

	°	′
As one third part of his Semidiurnal Arc.	28	33
Is to his distance from the Medium Celi,	71	15
So are thirty Degrees,	30	0
To the proportional part.	74	52
Which must be subtracted from the Right Ascension of the Midheaven, (because the Sun has passed that Angle in the World.)	258	42
And the Oblique Descension of the Sun under his own Pole will be.	183	50
The Right Ascension of the Sun is.	187	27
Subtract his Oblique Descension under his own Pole.	183	50
Sun's Ascensional Difference under his own circle of Position.	3	37

	°	′	
Then from Sine with Radius.	3	37	= 18,79989
Subtract Tangent of the Sun's Declination.	3	14	= 8,75199
Tangent of the Sun's Pole	48	9	= 10,04790

The computation of the Moon's Circle of Position.

	°	′
As one third part of her Seminocturnal Arc.	16	54
Is to her distance from the Imum Celi.	3	13
So are thirty degrees.	30	0
To the part proportional.	5	42
Which must be subtracted from the Right Ascension of the Northern Angle, (because the Moon has seperated therefrom in Mundo.)	78	42
And the Oblique Ascension of the Moon under her own Pole is.	73	0

Right Ascension of the Moon. 75 29
Subtract her Oblique Ascension under her own Pole. 73 0

Moon's Ascensional Difference under her own Polar Elevation. } 2 29

Then from sine with Radius. 2 29 = 18,63677
Subtract tangent of the Moon's declination 25 17 = 9,67426

Tangent of the Moon's true Pole 5 14 = 8,96251

From these plain and easy calculations, the Poles of the other Planets stand as follow.

The Pole of Saturn ....52 39, Oblique Ascension 350 42
Jupiter's Polar Elevation ..18 6, Oblique Descension 237 44
Mars' Circle of Position ... 1 43, Oblique Descension 80 36
The Pole of Venus ....53 9, Oblique Descension 169 0
The Polar Elevation of Mercury } 46 51, Oblique Descension 187 21

There are several Methods of computing and directing the Part of Fortune, all which differ materially from each other, being false and groundless; for it is certain that this point, (which can only be directed in Mundo,) will continually be found to preserve the greatest order and regularity in its movements, being always as far from the Eastern Horizon, as the Moon is distant from the Sun in the various parts of the Heavens. Nothing can be more absurd than allowing it to claim the same Latitude and Declination as the Moon for by the false Methods that are used, the Moon may be posited in the middle of the Tropical Sign Cancer, and the Part of Fortune near the end of the opposite Sign Capricorn, and yet many would allow them both to have North Declination, which in several other similar cases, are inconsistent and undemonstrable. Now if the Moon was posited in twelve degrees of Virgo, and the Part of Fortune in twenty two Degrees of Libra; then if the Moon in that place had no Lati-

OR GENETHLIACAL ASTRONOMY, 17

tude, most practitioners would allow her to have the same Declination, when it is evident that one point is North, and the other South of the Equator; and then if we were to allow five degrees of North Latitude to each of those places, it would augment the Declination of the one point, and reduce that of the other. I have plainly stated these observations that the Student may no longer be deluded by those false Rules, which I am certain will deceive him in all his calculations.

The true computation of the Part of Fortune in this Nativity.

From the Oblique Descension of the Sun before calculated.	183-50
Subtract the Oblique Ascension of the Moon.	73 0
Remains the distance between the Sun and Moon.	110 50
Subtract ninety Degrees.	90 0
And the distance of the Part of Fortune from the Medium Celi will be.	20 50
Its distance from the Southern Angle as above, subtract from.	30 0
And its distance from the ninth becomes.	9 10

I now add the distance of the Part of Fortune from the ninth to the Oblique Descension of the ninth, being 228° 42′, which is found by adding 60° to the Oblique Descension of the seventh, and the Oblique Descension of the Part of Fortune will be 237° 52′, which points to 10° 26′ of Sagittary, where its Declination is 22° 2′ *South*; and its Right Ascension 248° 49′: its Ascensional Difference then consequently will be 32° 49′, that number being subtracted from 90°, leaves its Semidiurnal Arc 57° 11′, which divided by 6, its diurnal horary times become 9° 32′:—I then subtract its Semidiurnal Arc from 180°, and the remainder will be the Seminocturnal Arc 122° 49′, which also divided by 6, will produce its nocturnal horary times 20° 28′. The Pole of the Part of Fortune is never required, because it can only be directed in the Mundane Circle.

In all computations when the Degrees and Minutes of a Planets Longitude exceed those of the House where it claims its position, it must then be placed past the cusp, according to the regular succession of the Signs in the Zodiac: but when the Degrees and Minutes of the Stars Geocentric Longitude, are less than those of the House to which it belongs, then the reverse Rules must be uniformly attended to, without the least variation.

I have not noticed the difference between the Meridian of Greenwich, and that of Lincoln in this Geniture, because it is very small, but when the difference in time is more considerable, then it must be attended to in all Nativities, by adding it to the correct time of Birth if the Longitude be West, and subtracting it if the Longitude be East of the given place of Birth.

From the foregoing Calculations, the true Celestial Figure of Birth, including the requisite numbers for computing all the Arcs of Directions in the Zodiac and Mundo, stand as follow.

OR GENETHLIACAL ASTRONOMY.

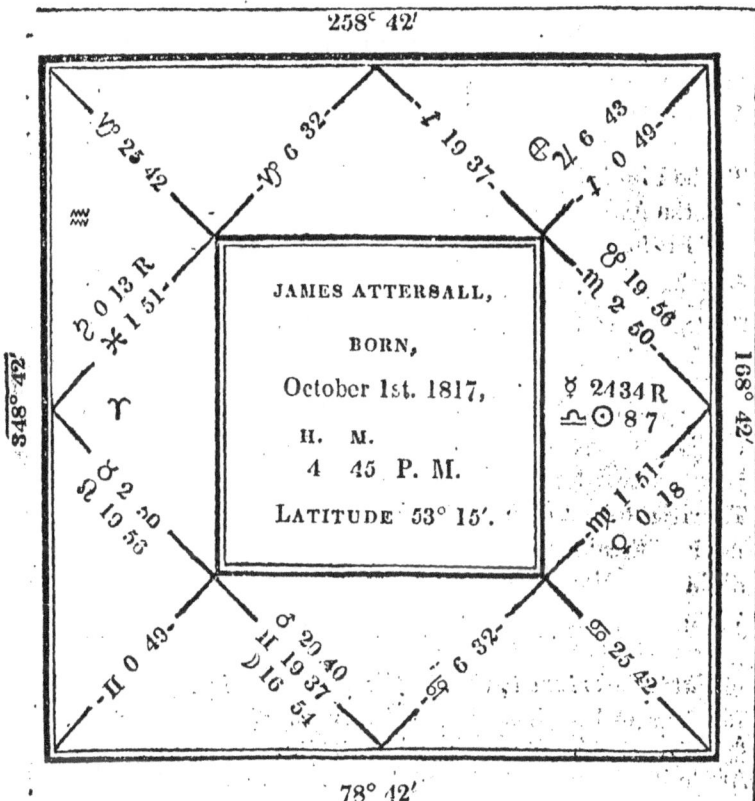

258° 42′

♑ 25 42
♑ 6 32
♐ 19 37
⊕ 2⃞ 6 43
♐ 0 49
♄ 0 13 R
♓ 1 51
♂ 19 56
♏ 2 50

JAMES ATTERSALL,

BORN,

October 1st. 1817,

H. M.
4 45 P. M.

LATITUDE 53° 15′.

☿ 24 34 R
♎ ☉ 8 7

♃ 2 30
♌ 19 56
♍ 1 51
♀ 0 18

♊ 0 49
♂ 20 40
♊ 19 37
☽ 16 54
♋ 6 32
♋ 25 42

78° 42′
348° 42′
168° 42′

	LAT.	DEC.	R. A.	S D A.	D H T.	S N A.	N H T.	A. D.
	° ′	° ′	° ′	° ′	° ′	° ′	° ′	° ′
♄	1 49 s.	13 6 s.	332 57	71 51	11 58	108 9	18 2	18 9
♃	0 28 N.	20 59 s.	244 56	59 7	9 51	120 53	20 9	30 53
♂	0 30 s.	22 38 N.	79 53	123 56	20 39	56 4	9 21	33 56
☉		3 14 s.	187 27	85 40	14 17	94 20	15 43	4 20
♀	0 37 N.	11 57 N.	152 36	106 27	17 44	73 33	12 16	16 27
☿	3 32 s.	12 50 s.	201 25	72 16	12 3	107 44	17 57	17 44
☽	2 28 N.	25 17 N.	75 29	129 16	21 33	50 44	8 27	39 16
⊕		22 2 s.	248 49	57 11	9 32	122 49	20 28	32 49

THE DIRECTIONS ARE ASTRONOMICALLY COMPUTED IN FULL, AND ARRANGED IN PROGRESSIVE ORDER AS FOLLOW.

Ascendant to the Opposition of Venus in Mundo.

	° ′
To the Right Ascension of Venus.	152 36
Add the Ascensional Difference under the Pole of Birth.	16 27
Oblique Descension of Venus.	169 3
Subtract the Oblique Descension of the Western Horizon.	168 42
Arc of Direction.	0 21

ANOTHER WAY.

	° ′
The Right Ascension of Venus added to her Semidiurnal Arc.	259 3
Right Ascension of the Midheaven subtract.	258 42
Remains the Arc of Direction.	0 21

Part of Fortune to the Sextile of the Sun in Mundo.

	° ′
As the horary times of the Part of Fortune,	9 32
Are to its distance from the ninth,	9 10
So are the horary times of the Sun,	14 17
To the proportional part.	13 44
Primary distance of the Sun from the West,	14 25
Above part proportional subtract	13 44
And the remainder is the Arc of Direction.	0 41

Sun to the Sextile of Jupiter in the Zodiac, Converse Direction,

	° ′
From the Oblique Descension of the Sun's sextile which falls in 8° 7′ of Sagittary.	238 52
Subtract the Oblique Descension of Jupiter	237 44
Direction's Arc	1 8

OR GENETHLIACAL ASTRONOMY, 21

Midheaven to the Opposition of Mars in Mundo.

               °   ′

Right Ascension of Mars.............................79 53
Subtract the Right Ascension of the Northern Angle. 78 42

And the Arc of Direction will be..................... 1 11

Moon to the Quintile of Venus in the Zodiac.

This Direction falls in 18° 18′ of Gemini, where the Moon has 2° 35′ North Latitude. From the Oblique Ascension of the Quintile of Venus under the Pole of the Moon.   74 32

Subtract the Oblique Ascension of the Moon...........73 0

     Arc of Direction..................... 1 32

Ascendant to the Body of Saturn in Mundo.

               °   ′

Right Ascension of Saturn...........................332 57
Add his Seminocturnal Arc...........................108 9

    And the sum is.....................441 6
    The Circle Subtract.................360 0

     Remains..................... 81 6

From which subtract the Right Ascension of the Imum Celi............................... 78 42

    And the Arc of Direction is............... 2 24

OR THUS.

               °   ′

To the Right Ascension of Saturn........................332 57
Add the Ascensional Difference under the Pole of Birth.18 9

   And the Oblique Ascension will be...............351 6

From which subtract the Oblique Ascension of the Eastern Horizon............................... 348 42

   Remains the Arc of Direction.................. 2 24

22   CELESTIAL PHILOSOPHY,

Sun to the Body of Mercury in Mundo by Direct Motion

                                                                            °   ′

As the horary times of the Sun..............................14 17
Are to his distance from the Seventh......................14 25
So are the horary times of Mercury.........................12 3
To his secondary distance from the West................12 10
Primary distance of Mercury from the Western Horizon 14 59
From which subtract the secondary........................12 10
                  Arc of Direction............................. 2 49

Moon to the Trine of Mercury in Mundo, Converse Direction.

                                                        °   ′

As the horary times of Mercury..............................12 3
Are to his distance from the Seventh......................14 59
So are the horary times of the Moon....................... 8 27
To the part proportional..10 30
Primary distance of the Moon from the third...........13 41
The above proportional part subtract.....................10 30
              And the Arc of Direction is. 3 11

Part of Fortune to the Sextile of Mercury in Mundo.

                                                        °   ′

As the horary times of the Part of Fortune. 9 32
Are to its distance from the ninth. 9 10
So are the horary times of Mercury.........................12 3
To his secondary distance from the seventh. 11 35
Primary distance of Mercury from the West. 14 59
From which subtract the secondary........................11 35
                  Direction's Arc............................3 24

Sun to the Sesquiquadrate of Saturn in the Zodiac.

                                                        °   ′

From the Oblique Descension of the Sesquiquadrate of Saturn, in 15° 13′ of Libra, under the Pole of the Sun. } 187 16

Subtract the Oblique Descension of the Sun. 183 50

Remains the Arc of Direction..................... 3 26

Sun to the Semiquartile of Venus in the Zodiac.
This Direction falls in 15° 18' of Libra.

                                                                               °   '

The Oblique Descension of the Semiquartile of Venus under the Pole of the Sun is.   187 19

From which subtract the Oblique Descension of the Sun, under his own Circle of Position.   183 50

Arc of Direction............................. 3 29

Moon to the Body of Mars in the Zodiac.

                                                                     °   '

From the Oblique Ascension of Mars in the Radix under the Pole of the Moon.   77 4

Subtract the Oblique Ascension of the Moon, under the same Pole.   73 0

And the Arc of Direction is................ 4 4

Sun to the Trine of the Moon in the Zodiac.

                                                                     °   '

The Oblique Descension of the Trine of the Moon, in 16° 54' of Libra, under the Pole of the Sun is.   188 6

Subtract the Oblique Descension of the Sun, under his own Polar Elevation.   183 50

And the remainder is the Arc of Direction. 4 16

Moon to the Body of Mars in Mundo, Direct Direction.

                                                                    °   '

As the horary times of the Moon. 8 27
Are to her distance from the Imum Celi. 3 13
So are the horary times of Mars. 9 21
To his secondary distance from the fourth. 3 33
Primary distance of Mars from the Imum Celi add.......1 11

24   CELESTIAL PHILOSOPHY,

    Arc of Direction. 4 44

Moon to the Square of Venus in Mundo, Direct Direction.

               ° '

As the horary times of the Moon. 8 27
Arc to her distance from the fourth. 3 13
So are the nocturnal horary times of Venus, (as
 she will be below the Earth when the Direction is finished.)   12 16
To her secondary distance from the Seventh............. 4 40
Primary distance of Venus from the West, add.......... 0 21

    And the Arc of Direction will be.......... 5 1

Sun to the Trine of the Moon in Mundo, by Direct Motion.

               ° '

As the horary times of the Sun. 14 17
Arc to his distance from the seventh. 14 25
So are the horary times of the Moon. 8 27
To the proportional part. 8 32
Primary distance of the Moon from the third. 13 41
Above part proportional subtract. 8 32

    Arc of Direction. 5 9

Part of Fortune to the Opposition of the Moon in Mundo.

               ° '

As the horary times of the Part of Fortune. 9 32
Arc to its distance from the ninth, ... 9 10
So are the horary times of the Moon. 8 27
To her secondary distance from the third. 8 7
The primary distance from the third is. 13 41
From which subtract the secondary. 8 7

    Direction's Arc. 5 34

Moon to the Quintile of Saturn in Mundo Converse Direction.

               ° '

As the horary times of Saturn. 18 2

Are to his distance from the ascendant	2 24
So are the horary times of the Moon	8 27
To her secondary distance from the third	1 7
Primary distance from the third is	13 41
From which subtract the secondary	1 7
Remains the sextile's Arc of Direction	12 34
Subtract four-fifths of the horary times of the Moon below the Earth	6 46
And the Arc of Direction is	5 48

Sun to the Sextile of Jupiter in Mundo, by Converse Motion.

As the horary times of Jupiter	9 51
Are to his distance from the ninth	5 56
So are the horary times of the Sun	14 17
To the proportional part	8 36
The primary distance of the Sun from the seventh	14 25
Above part proportional subtract	8 36
Arc of Direction	5 49

Sun to the Semiquartile of Jupiter in Mundo, Direct Direction.

As the horary times of the Sun	14 17
Are to his distance from the seventh	14 25
So are the horary times of Jupiter	9 51
To his secondary distance from the Western horizon	9 57
The primary distance from the seventh, is	45 21
From which subtract the secondary	9 57
And the Sun to the Body of Jupiter, is	35 24
Subtract half his Semidiurnal Arc	29 33
Remains the Arc of Direction	5 51

26 CELESTIAL PHILOSOPHY,

Ascendant to the Trine of Jupiter in Mundo.

	° ′
The Oblique Ascension of Jupiter under the Pole of the Horoscope.	275 49
Add four-thirds of his Semidiurnal Arc.	78 49
The sum.	354 38
From which subtract the Oblique Ascension of the Ascendant.	348 42
Arc of Direction	5 56

ANOTHER METHOD.

	° ′
From the duplicate horary times of Jupiter	19 42
Subtract his distance from the Southern angle.	13 46
And the remainder is the Arc of Direction.	5 56

Sun to the Trine of Mars in the Zodiac.

	° ′
From the Oblique Descension of the Trine of Mars, in 20° 40′ of Libra, taken under the Pole of the Sun.	189 56
Subtract the Oblique Descension of the Sun under the same Pole of Position.	183 50
And the Arc of Direction is.	6 6

Sun to the Virgin's Spike in the Zodiac.

	° ′
From the Oblique Descension of the Virgin's Spike, in 21° 19′ of Libra, under the Sun's Pole.	190 17
Subtract the Oblique Descension of the Sun.	183 50
Direction's Arc.	6 27

Sun to the Semiquartile of Jupiter in the Zodiac.
This Direction falls in 21° 43′ of Libra.

	° ′
From the Oblique Descension of the Semiquartile of Jupiter, under the Sun's Pole.	190 30

OR GENETHLIACAL ASTRONOMY. 27

	° ′
Subtract the Oblique Descension of the Sun, under his own Polar Elevation.	183 50
Arc of Direction.	6 40

Sun to the Parallel of Venus in Mundo, by the Rapt Motion.

	° ′
Right Ascension of the Opposition of Venus.	332 36
Right Ascension of the Sun, subtract.	187 27
Distance of the Sun and Venus in Right Ascension.	145 9
Diurnal horary times of the Sun.	14 17
Nocturnal horary times of Venus.	12 16
The sum	26 33

Then, by the Rule of Proportion,

	° ′
As the sum of both the horary times.	26 33
Is to the horary times of Venus.	12 16
So is the difference in Right Ascension, as above.	145 9
To the proportional part.	67 4
The distance of Jupiter from the Imum Cœli.	73 52
Proportional part, subtract.	67 4
And the Arc of Direction is.	6 48

ANOTHER METHOD BY WHICH THIS DIRECTION MAY BE COMPUTED.

	° ′
As the Sum of the horary times of the Sun and Venus.	26 33
Is to the horary times of Venus.	12 16
So is the difference in Oblique Descension between the Sun and Venus.	14 4
To the proportional part	6 30
Add the primary distance of Venus from the seventh.	0 21
Arc of Direction.	6 51

Ascendant to the Quintile of the Moon in Mundo.

	°	′
The distance of the Moon from the third, is.	13	41
Subtract four-fifths of her horary times below the Earth.	6	46
Remains the Arc of Direction.	6	55

OR THUS,

	°	′
From the Oblique Ascension of the Moon under the Pole of Birth, with the circle.	396	13
Subtract four-fifths of her Seminocturnal Arc.	40	35
Remains.	355	38
Oblique Ascension of the Ascendant, subtract.	348	42
Direction's Arc.	6	56

ANOTHER WAY.

	°	′
From one-fifth part of the Moon's Seminocturnal Arc.	10	9
Subtract the distance of the Moon from the fourth.	3	13
Arc of Direction.	6	56

Moon to the Square of Saturn in Mundo, Direct Direction.

	°	′
As the horary times of the Moon.	8	27
Are to her distance from the Imum Cœli.	3	13
So are the diurnal horary times of Saturn, (as the Direction is finished above the Earth.)	11	58
To the proportional part.	4	33
Primary distance of Saturn from the Ascendant, add.	2	24
And the Arc of Direction will be.	6	57

OR GENETHLIACAL ASTRONOMY.   29

Moon to the Square of Saturn in the Zodiac, by Converse Motion.

	° ′
From the Oblique Ascension of the Square of the Moon, in 16° 54′ of Pisces, with 1° 51′, South Latitude under the Pole of Saturn.	357 45
Subtract the Oblique Ascension of Saturn under the same Pole,	350 42
Arc of Direction.	7 3

Sun to the Parallel of Saturn in Mundo, by the Rapt Motion.

	° ′
As the Sum of the horary times of the Sun and Saturn.	26 15
Is to the horary times of Saturn, diurnal, (as he will be above the Earth when the direction is finished.)	11 58
So is the distance in Oblique Descension between the Sun and Saturn in opposition.	12 1
To the part proportional.............................	5 29
Primary distance of Saturn from the Horoscope, add.	2 24
Direction's Arc.	7 53

OR THUS.

	° ′
As the Sum of both the horary times................	26 15
Is to the Diurnal horary times of Saturn.	11 58
So is the difference in Right Ascension between the Sun and Saturn.	145 30
To the proportional part.	66 19
Primary distance of Saturn from the Medium Celi...	74 15
Subtract the above part proportional.	66 19
Remains the Arc of Direction.	7 56

A small variation is visible in the different operations, owing to the superlative numbers being used with the same horary times, and Fractional parts in the Radix.

Moon to the Square of Venus in the Zodiac, Converse Direction.

	° ′
This Direction falls in 16° 54′ of Virgo, with 1° 14′ North Latitude, From the Oblique Descension of the Square of the Moon, under the Pole of Venus.	176 57
Subtract the Oblique Descension of Venus under the same Circle of position.	169 0
And the Arc of Direction is..............	7 57

Sun to the Body of Mercury in the Zodiac.

	° ′
The Oblique Descension of Mercury in the Radix, under the Pole of the Sun, is.	191 57
Oblique Descension of the Sun, subtract.	183 50
Arc of Direction.	8 7

Moon to the Trine of Mercury in the Zodiac.

	° ′
The Oblique Ascension of the Trine of Mercury, (in 24° 34′ of Gemini, where the Moon obtains 3° 3′ North Latitude,) under the Pole of the Moon, is.	81 20
Subtract the Oblique Ascension of the Moon, under her own polar elevation.	73 0
Direction's Arc.	8 20

Moon to the Opposition of Jupiter in Mundo, Converse Motion.

	° ′
As the horary times of Jupiter.	9 51
Are to his distance from the ninth, ...	5 56

So are the horary times of the Moon.................. 8 27
To her secondary distance from the third............ 5 5
The primary distance from the third is................ 13 41
From which subtract the secondary................... 5 5

   Remains the Arc of Direction............... 8 36

Moon to the Opposition of Jupiter in the Zodiac, by Converse Direction.

From the Oblique Descension of the opposition
of the Moon, under the Pole of Jupiter.......} 248 2
Subtract the Oblique Descension of Jupiter
under the same Pole. ....} 237 44

   Arc of Direction................................. 10 18

Sun to the Trine of Mars in Mundo, Direct Motion.

As the horary times of the Sun......................... 14 17
Are to his distance from the seventh.................. 14 25
So are the horary times of Mars....................... 9 21
To the proportional part................................. 9 26
Primary distance of Mars from the third............. 19 53
Above part proportional subtract...................... 9 26

   Direction's Arc................................... 10 27

Part of Fortune to the Opposition of Mars in Mundo.

As the horary times of the Part of Fortune........... 9 32
Are to its distance from the ninth...................... 9 10
So are the horary times of Mars....................... 9 21
To the proportional part................................. 8 59
Primary distance of Mars from the third............. 19 53
The above part proportional subtract................. 8 59

   Arc of Direction................................. 10 54

Sun to the Trine of Saturn in the Zodiac.

From the Oblique Descension of the Trine of Saturn, in 13′ of Scorpio, under the Pole of the Sun.	194 54
Subtract the Oblique Descension of the Sun under the same Pole.	183 50
Remains the Arc of Direction.	11 4

Sun to the Sextile of Venus in the Zodiac.

Oblique Descension of the Sextile of Venus which falls in 18′ of Scorpio, taken under the Sun's Polar Elevation.	194 58
Subtract the Oblique Descension of the Sun.	183 50
Direction's Arc.	11 8

Moon to the Sesquiquadrate of Mercury, in the Zodiac, Converse Direction.

The Oblique Descension of the Sesquiquadrate of the Moon, in 1° 54′ of Scorpio, with 1° 38′ North Latitude, under the Pole of Mercury is.	198 44
Subtract the Oblique Descension of Mercury under his own Pole of position.	187 21
And the Arc of Direction is.	11 23

Moon to the Sesquiquadrate of Mercury in Mundo, by Converse Motion.

The Moon to the Trine of Mercury in the World, Converse Direction, is.	3 11
Add the horary times of the Moon below the Earth.	8 27
And the Arc of Direction will be.	11 38

OR GENETHLIACAL ASTRONOMY.

ANOTHER METHOD.

From the Moon to the Opposition of Mercury, in Mundo, Converse Direction. .... } 37 1
Subtract half the seminocturnal Arc of the Moon. 25 22

Arc of Direction. 11 39

Sun to the Parallel of Venus in the Zodiac.

From the Oblique Descension of the zodiacal Parallel of Venus, which falls in 1° 20' of Scorpio, taken under the Sun's Pole. } 195 31
Subtract the Oblique Descension of the Sun under his own Pole. } 183 50

And the remainder is the Arc of Direction. 11 41

A TABLE OF THE DIRECTIONS WITH THEIR ARCS AND MEASURES ADJUSTED BY THE SUN'S GEOCENTRIC MOTION IN THE ECLIPTIC.

	ARC. D. M.	TIME. years months
Ascendant to the Opposition of Venus in Mundo.	0 21	0 4
Midheaven to the Square of Venus in Mundo.	0 21	0 4
Part of Fortune to the Sextile of the Sun in Mundo.	0 41	0 8
Sun to the Sextile of Jupiter in the Zodiac, Converse Direction.	1 8	1 3
Midheaven to the Opposition of Mars in Mundo.	1 11	1 4
Ascendant to the Square of Mars in Mundo.	1 11	1 4
Moon to the Quintile of Venus in the Zodiac.	1 32	1 8
Ascendant to the Body of Saturn in Mundo.	2 24	2 8
Midheaven to the Square of Saturn in Mundo.	2 24	2 8
Sun to the Body of Mercury in Mundo, by Direct Motion	2 49	3 1
Moon to the Trine of Mercury in Mundo, Converse Direction.	3 11	3 6
Part of Fortune to the Sextile of Mercury in Mundo.	3 24	3 9
Sun to the Sesquiquadrate of Saturn in the Zodiac.	3 26	3 9
Sun to the Semiquartile of Venus in the Zodiac.	3 29	3 10
Moon to the Body of Mars in the Zodiac.	4 4	4 6
Sun to the Trine of the Moon in the Zodiac.	4 16	4 9

34 CELESTIAL PHILOSOPHY,

	ARC. D. M.	TIME. Years Month
Moon to the Body of Mars in Mundo, Direct Direction.	4 44	5 2
Moon to the Square of Venus in Mundo Direct Direction	5 1	5 6
Sun to the Trine of the Moon in Mundo, by Direct Motion.	5 9	5 8
Part of Fortune to the Opposition of the Moon in Mundo	5 34	6 1
Moon to the Quintile of Saturn in Mundo, Converse Direction.	5 48	6 5
Sun to the Sextile of Jupiter in Mundo, by Converse Motion.	5 49	6 5
Sun to the Semiquartile of Jupiter in Mundo, Direct Direction.	5 51	6 6
Ascendant to the Trine of Jupiter in Mundo.	5 56	6 7
Sun to the Trine of Mars in the Zodiac.	6 6	6 9
Sun to the Virgin's Spike in the Zodiac.	6 27	7 1
Sun to the Semiquartile of Jupiter in the Zodiac.	6 40	7 4
Sun to the Parallel of Venus in Mundo, by the Rapt Motion.	6 51	7 6
Ascendant to the Quintile of the Moon in Mundo.	6 56	7 7
Moon to the square of Saturn in Mundo, Direct Direction	6 57	7 7
Moon to the square of Saturn in the Zodiac, by Converse Motion.	7 3	7 9
Sun to the Parallel of Saturn in Mundo, by the Rapt Motion.	7 56	8 8
Moon to the Square of Venus in the Zodiac, Converse Direction.	7 57	8 8
Sun to the Body of Mercury in the Zodiac.	8 7	8 10
Moon to the Trine of Mercury in the zodiac.	8 20	9 1
Moon to the Opposition of Jupiter in Mundo Converse Motion.	8 36	9 5
Moon to the Opposition of Jupiter in the zodiac, by Converse Direction.	10 18	11 3
Sun to the Trine of Mars in Mundo, Direct Motion.	10 27	11 5
Part of Fortune to the Opposition of Mars in Mundo	10 54	11 10
Sun to the Trine of Saturn in the zodiac.	11 4	12 1
Sun to the Sextile of Venus in the zodiac.	11 8	12 2
Moon to the Sesquiquadrate of Mercury in the zodiac, Converse Direction.	11 23	12 5
Moon to the Sesquiquadrate of Mercury in Mundo, by Converse Motion.	11 39	12 9
Sun to the Parallel of Venus in the zodiac.	11 41	12 9

OR GENETHLIACAL ASTRONOMY. 35

The foregoing Nativity is that of James, the Son of William Attersall, who was Born in the City of Lincoln. When this Child was about twelve Months old, and in good health, its Parents applied to me for the purpose of receiving my Judgment on its Geniture, which I gave them in few words, as it is my practice in all cases, not to write long Epistles, when short and concise observations are sufficient.

As soon as I had attentively investigated the positions of the Celestial Bodies at the time of Birth, with their various qualities, and configurations, &c. I was convinced that a *violent Death* was certain and inevitable, which was not in the power of any human efforts to prevent. I then delivered my impartial Judgment, which was, that dissolution would take place at, or before the Age of two years, and as the Child's Father was then constantly engaged in attending one of the Packets on the River Witham, I considered it a duty incumbent on me to admonish its Parents, never to suffer the Child to go on board the Packet, in consequence of the mortal Configurations then fast approaching without relief; they promised to attend to the solemn, and previous warning I had given, and certainly acted according to my request having informed them that Death would take place suddenly, either by a fall, or wound from a Horse, and as Horses were (in the course of Business,) frequently taken on board the Packet, I conceived his Death might arise from violence of that nature; the fact is, the Child was never suffered to go on board that or any other Packet, agreeable to my advice. But mark the UNCHANGEABLE DECREE OF THE OMNIPOTENT CREATOR, the unfortunate Child was kept as much as possible in the House, and was not suffered to approach any Horse, nor go on any Navigable Vessel. About ten days prior to its dissolution, I went to the abode of its Parents, and told them that manifest danger was at hand; there were several persons present, who replied, that if Death by violence should take place, as I had publicly declared, it could not be for want of sufficient warning. On the day of Death, the Child went into the Street unobserved by any one, and immediately accompanied several other Children who were playing very near a Horse that was feeding a short distance from the Door, near the side of the River. The Horse was always considered to be a very quiet Animal, but in the fatal Hour, he kicked at the Children, yet none were injured, except the unfortunate Child, who received the stroke in its forehead, which proved instantly Mortal; his Death happened on the 22nd. of September, 1819, near three o'Clock in the Afternoon, Aged one Year, eleven Months, and twenty days. This prediction obtained publicity near a Year previous to the time of Death, and there are many persons of respectability in this place, and its Vicinity, who will prove what I have here asserted to be correct, and beyond the bounds of contradiction, and if any doubts remain as to the verity of what I have related, I request that application may be made to the Parents in this City, who will establish the truth of what I have recorded.

But though I have given the hostile primary Directions in this Geniture, with their true computation as far as the orbs of the benign Stars are in operation, (which ought to be strictly regarded in all Nativities,) yet I would not have the Students to entertain Ideas, that all Children who die in their infant state, are destroyed by violent Directions to the giver of Life, &c; for those who die in infancy, or before the end of the fifth Year, are generally destroyed by those malignant and destructive positions that are formed in the Heavens at the time of Birth; as Ptolemy clearly informs us, and not by Directions, which was the case in this unfortunate Geniture, there are also other sideral causes of the utmost consequence, which have great and manifest power in destroying Life within the above period; for when the significators of Children are weak and afflicted in the Genitures of the Parents, it will require but little violence in the Nativity of the offspring to cut off Life. The great disproportion in the occult power of the Elementary qualities, with the evil testimonies predominating in the Radix, as well as the Mundane stations of the Stars, with their *heating, drying, cooling,* and *moistening* qualities, in the various *signs, and parts of the Heavens* in which they are posited; are all subjects which require serious consideration, chiefly when death occurs naturally, and must in all cases be attended to, before final Judgment is given, concerning the period of personal extinction.

The Astral causes that produced the sudden and violent Death of this Child, are plainly visible; the Ascendant is afflicted by the Body of Saturn, and Square of the Moon, and Mars in Mundo; the Moon is conjoined with Mars among evil Stars in the Northern Angle, approaching the Terms of Saturn, without any relief, and that Luminary is applying to the Mundane Square of Saturn, by direct motion. The Part of Fortune is afflicted by the opposition of the Moon and Mars; but I judged the work of Mortality to arise chiefly from the uninterrupted communication of those violent rays of Mars and the Moon from the Imum Celi, to the Sun, who is the true Apheta, or giver of Life, particularly because the Hyleg is near the Body of Mercury, and Rapt Parallel of Saturn; and I shall here observe that Mercury is of the nature of the enemies in the Celestial constitution.

Thus you see all the vital significators were afflicted at the time of Birth, and no intervening Rays of a benevolent nature, could break their force, or counteract their fury; for Jupiter is posited near the Heart of the Scorpion, and afflicted by the Quartile of Saturn, and Venus by the opposition of that Malefic, and also by the square of Mars in Mundo, so that all benign influence was destroyed, and could be of no avail whatever, in supporting the Life of the Native.

At the return of the Sun to his radical place, on the first of October 1818, we find many furious and alarming motions of the Stars, which augment in a great measure, the Effects of the other malignant positions in the Radix. At the above time, Saturn was Retrograde, and posited in the Ascendant, in Square to the Moon in the Nativity, and that Luminary and Mars who were in conjunction in the Imum Celi at Birth, were conjoined in the Western Angle, on the place of Mercury in the Geniture, who was near the Sun's place in the Nativity. Jupiter was in Square to the Sun's position in the Radix, and Mercury was in opposition to the radical Ascendant, having lately separated from the opposite rays of Saturn. Venus was in a violent part of the Heavens, and afflicted by the evil Rays of Mercury from zodiacal stations, being at the same time injured by the hostile beams of Saturn and his Terms. These positions of the Stars are astonishing, and certainly prove the great and manifest power of such motions, when rightly compared with the true places of the superior significators that have dominion in the Geniture. In fine, such furious irradiations were assured testimonies of approaching dissolution by *violence*, but the Mundane and zodiacal stations of the Stars at the time of Death, were still more remarkable, when compared with the Anaretic positions of the Planets in the Radix:—there was a new Moon three Days previous to his dissolution, when both the Luminaries were in opposition of Saturn, and also in square to the place of the Moon and Mars in the Nativity. Venus had the Declination of Saturn, and was combust: the Moon was also cadent in the terms of Saturn at the time of Death, and Jupiter was nearly on the radical place of that Malefic. When he received the mortal wound, the Sun was afflicted by the opposition of Saturn, who was Retrograde, and under the Earth; such a train of evil testimonies, united with those corresponding positions, and primary Directions of an Anaretical nature in the Radix, are worthy of admiration. These things every attentive student ought to attend to, as well as all the powerful motions of the malignant Stars in the zodiac and Mundo, with their occult qualities, as they afflict the

Lights, or the most principal, and superior places of the Luminaries, or their Rulers, with other significators in the Geniture, and also the progressions and powerful secondary Directions then in operation; for when the corroborating testimonies of the Enemies are violent, and are likewise multiplied at the same time by other applications of an inimical power, without any benevolent assistance, they then, (as in this Example,) never fail to destroy Life.

All those litigious traducers (who condemn the Study of second causes,) may observe, that the FATE of this Child was clearly visible in the Heavens at the time of Birth, and that no human endeavours could alter, prevent, or control the *immutable* DECREE of the MOST HIGH. The FREE WILL of the Parents was previously used a long time, in a solemn and indefatigable manner for the preservation of their offspring, but in vain, which is well known to the Public. These facts are too obvious to be denied. The *Infidel*, the *Deist*, the *Atheist*, and the *Critic*, (who endeavour to turn every Sacred subject into ignominy and reproach,) may sneer at these remarks, but let such characters advance what scurrilous arguments they please, against this Sacred Science, yet they are, in their minds convinced by daily experience, that there is an *impending* FATE, or a SOMETHING that frustrates, defeats, and counteracts our actions, and engagements, during Life, let us endeavour as we may, for in numberless cases we may observe, that when our premeditated projects appear successful, and even infallible, according to human reason, yet in the execution of those Acts, SOMETHING overturns our flattering schemes, and renders our exertions ineffectual. By these manifest Facts we may be convinced, (as an eminent writer observes,) that if all men could arrive at affluence by their earnest endeavours, more would probably attain to it, than what at present are seen to do so.

"————*And this should teach us,*
There's a Divinity that shapes our ends;
Rough-hew them how we will."

The next is the Nativity of a Lady, who is now living, and in good Health. The estimate time of Birth, (which is given in the following Figure of the Heavens,) was extracted from the written documents of her Parents, and I am induced to believe it is correct, because the benign and hostile Effects of the antecedent Directions, with their sideral cause, and periods of operation, correspond with the past occurrences of Life. I have computed and arranged the Directions from the Tables contained in this Work, by which the Reader may observe that the methods I use in calculation, and Judgment, are invariably the same in all Nativities, and may be depended upon without error, when they are properly applied, and rightly understood, according to the Examples I have plainly developed in Directional motion, on which the foundation of this Sacred Science depends. The true distance between the Apheta and the Anaretical Promittors, ought first to be computed in all Genitures; for it is certainly contradictory to the established principles of this department of Astronomy, when Judgment is pronounced on the Events of the Life of an Individual, (whether good, or evil, with the time thereof,) from the Effects of subsequent Directions, &c. at those remote periods, after the Prorogator to the mortal train has completed its final course. There are many, who being ignorant of the true motions of the Heavens, mistake the *first* and chief essential cause which offers itself for consideration, and absurdly attend to those vague, and unintelligible Directions, which were to produce Effects after the Native's Demise; for if those *arrogant pretenders* to these Astronomical Calculations are unacquainted with the time, and quality of Death, from a true Nativity, when the Native is living, I am confident they know nothing of it after dissolution, though they may vainly attempt to invent *something* as the probable cause of personal extinction, when the Native is no more.

OR GENETHLIACAL ASTRONOMY.

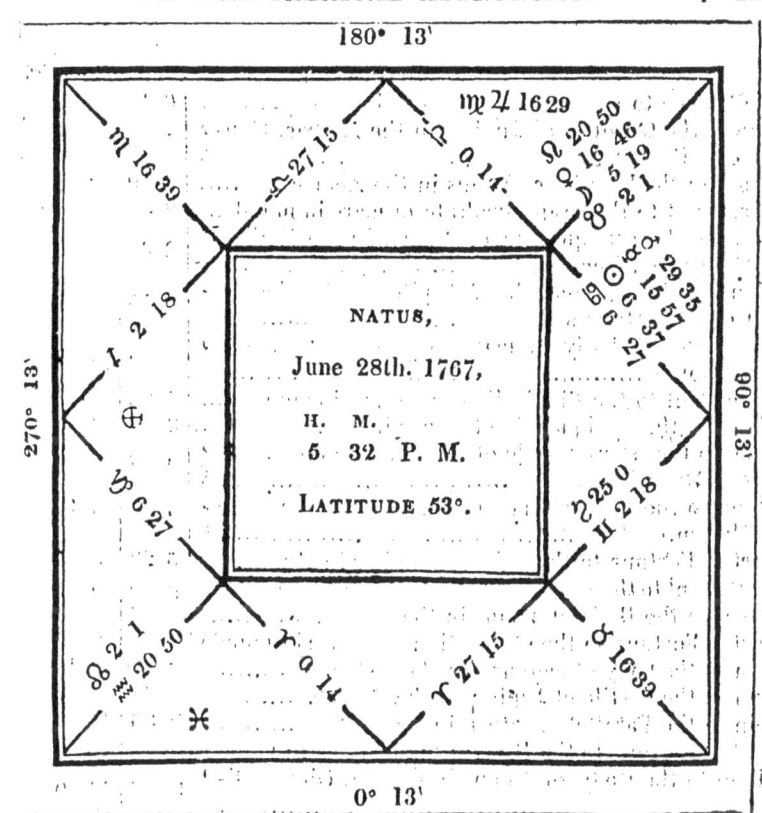

NATUS,
June 28th, 1767,
H. M.
5 32 P. M.
LATITUDE 53°.

LAT.	DEC.	R. A.	S D A.	D H T.	S N A.	N H T.	A D.
° ′	° ′	° ′	° ′	° ′	° ′	° ′	° ′
♄ 1 3 s.	22 19 N.	84 35	123 0	20 30	57 0	9 30	33 0
♃ 14 N.	6 29 N.	168 4	98 41	16 27	81 19	13 33	8 41
♂ 1 12 N.	21 25 N.	122 2	121 22	20 14	58 38	9 46	31 22
☉	23 18 N.	97 13	124 52	20 49	55 8	9 11	34 52
♀ 1 47 N.	17 31 N.	139 48	114 46	19 8	65 14	10 52	24 46
☿ 1 46 N.	24 15 N.	107 33	126 43	21 7	53 17	8 53	36 43
☽ 0 24 s.	18 35 N.	127 36	116 30	19 25	63 30	10 35	26 30
⊕	22 48 s.	255 25	56 2	9 20	123 58	20 40	33 58

CELESTIAL PHILOSOPHY,

A TABLE OF THE DIRECTIONS.	ARC. D. M.	TIME. Years Months.
Midheaven to the sextile of the sun in mundo.	0 14	0 3
Sun to the Quintile of Jupiter in the Zodiac, Converse Direction.	1 9	1 1
Moon to the Parallel of Venus in the Zodiac.	2 10	2 1
Ascendant to the sesquiquadrate of mars in mundo.	2 30	2 5
Sun to the semiquartile of Venus in the Zodiac, Converse Direction.	2 32	2 5
Moon to the semiquartile of Jupiter in the Zodiac, Converse Direction.	3 15	3 2
Moon to the Body of mars in mundo, Converse Motion.	3 15	3 2
Ascendant to the Biquintile of mercury in mundo.	3 22	3 3
Moon to the semiquartile of saturn in the Zodiac.	3 30	3 5
Sun to the semiquartile of Jupiter in mundo, Direct Direction.	4 7	4 1
Moon to the Body of mars in the Zodiac, Converse Motion.	4 58	4 11
Part of Fortune to the Trine of Jupiter in Mundo.	5 29	5 5
Ascendant to the sesquiquadrate of the moon in mundo.	5 38	5 7
Moon to the Body of Venus in the Zodiac.	8 19	8 1
Part of Fortune to the Opposition of saturn in mundo.	8 21	8 1
Sun to the body of mercury in the zodiac.	9 9	8 10
Sun to the sextile of Jupiter in the Zodiac.	9 40	9 4
Sun to the Parallel of saturn in the Zodiac.	10 36	10 3
Part of Fortune to the Biquintile of Venus in mundo.	10 42	10 4
Moon to the Body of Venus in mundo, Direct Direction.	11 24	11 0
Sun to the Body of mercury in mundo, Direct motion.	11 35	11 2
Moon to the Semiquartile of the Sun in the Zodiac.	11 44	11 4
Midheaven to the sextile of mercury in mundo.	11 49	11 5
Moon to the sextile of saturn in the Zodiac.	13 59	13 7
Sun to the Body of saturn in the Zodiac, Converse Direction.	14 0	13 7
Sun to the Body of saturn in mundo, Converse motion.	14 5	13 8
Moon to the Body of mercury in mundo, Converse Direction.	14 11	13 9
Sun to the sextile of Venus in the Zodiac, by Converse motion.	14 16	13 10
Ascendant to the Biquintile of mars in mundo.	14 38	14 2
Ascendant to the scorpion's Heart in mundo.	14 45	14 4
Moon to the Lion's Heart in the Zodiac.	15 31	15 1

OR GENETHLIACAL ASTRONOMY. 43

THE DIRECTIONS CONTINUED.	ARC. D. M.	TIME. Years Months.
Sun to the sextile of Jupiter in mundo, Converse Direction.	15 36	15 2
Sun to the Parallel of mars in the Zodiac.	15 58	15 6
Moon to the sextile of Jupiter in the Zodiac, Converse motion.	16 0	15 6
Sun to the square of Jupiter in the Zodiac, Converse Direction.	16 30	16 0
Sun to the semiquartile of mars in the Zodiac, by Converse motion.	16 40	16 2
Moon to the Body of mercury in the Zodiac, Converse Direction.	16 53	16 5
Midheaven to the Quintile of the sun in mundo.	16 54	16 5
Ascendant to the sesquiquadrate of Venus in mundo.	16 57	16 6
Moon to the semiquartile of mercury in the Zodiac.	17 55	17 6
Midheaven to spica Virginis in mundo.	18 42	18 3
Ascendant to the Biquintile of the moon in mundo.	19 17	18 9
Moon to the semiquartile of Jupiter in mundo, by Converse Motion.	19 58	19 5
Ascendant to the Trine of Jupiter in mundo.	20 44	20 2
Sun to the Body of mars in the Zodiac.	21 4	20 6
Moon to the Parallel of Jupiter in the Zodiac.	21 11	20 7
Moon to the semiquartile of saturn in mundo, Direct Direction.	21 25	20 10
Moon to the Sextile of the sun in the Zodiac.	21 31	20 11
Moon to the Quintile of saturn in the zodiac.	21 45	21 2
Part of Fortune to the sesquiquadrate of Jupiter in mundo.	21 57	21 5
Sun to the Body of mars in mundo, Direct Direction.	22 30	22 0
Part of Fortune to the Opposition of the sun in mundo.	22 34	22 1
Midheaven to the sextile of mars in mundo.	22 43	22 3
Sun to the Quintile of Venus in the zodiac, by Converse Motion.	23 11	22 9
Sun to the semiquartile of Venus in mundo, Converse Direction.	23 23	23 0
Moon to the semiquartile of Venus in the zodiac, Converse motion.	24 38	24 3
Sun to the Body of the moon in mundo, Direct Direction.	24 50	24 5
Midheaven to the sextile of the moon in mundo.	25 3	24 8
Sun to the Body of the moon in the zodiac.	25 35	25 2
Moon to the Quintile of Jupiter in the zodiac, Converse motion.	26 22	25 11

CELESTIAL PHILOSOPHY,

THE DIRECTIONS CONTINUED.	ARC. D. M.	TIME. Years Months
Moon to the semiquartile of mars in the zodiac.	26 31	26 1
Sun to the Parallel of the Moon in the zodiac.	26 40	26 4
Sun to the semiquartile of mercury in the zodiac, Converse Direction.	27 9	26 8
Ascendant to the Opposition of saturn in mundo.	27 22	26 11
Midheaven to the square of saturn in mundo.	27 22	26 11
Moon to the sextile of mercury in the zodiac.	27 23	26 11
Sun to the sextile of mars in the zodiac, by Converse motion.	27 23	26 11
Moon to the Body of Jupiter in the zodiac.	27 42	27 3
Ascendant to the Biquintile of Venus in mundo.	28 27	28 0
Midheaven to the Quintile of mercury in mundo.	28 43	28 3
Moon to the Quintile of the sun in the zodiac.	29 2	28 7
Sun to the semiquartile of saturn in the zodiac.	29 6	28 8
Sun to the Parallel of Venus in the zodiac.	29 42	29 3
Moon to her own semiquartile in the zodiac.	30 4	29 7
Part of Fortune to the Biquintile of Jupiter in mundo.	31 49	31 5
Sun to the Parallel of saturn in mundo, by the Rapt motion.	31 55	31 6
Sun to the Quintile of Jupiter in mundo, Converse Direction.	32 15	31 10
Moon to the Body of Jupiter in mundo, Direct motion.	32 25	32 0
Moon to the square of saturn in the zodiac.	33 0	32 8
Sun to the Body of Venus in the zodiac.	33 49	33 6
Moon to the sextile of saturn in mundo, Direct Direction.	34 7	33 10
Moon to the sextile of Venus in the zodiac, Converse motion.	34 24	34 1
Part of Fortune to the Opposition of mercury in mundo.	34 28	34 2
Moon to the Quintile of mercury in the zodiac.	34 49	34 6
Sun to the Quintile of mars in the zodiac, Converse Direction.	35 28	35 2
Moon to the semiquartile of the sun in mundo, Direct Motion.	35 50	35 6
Moon to the sextile of mars in the zodiac.	35 51	35 6
Sun to the Body of Venus in Mundo, Direct Direction	35 52	35 6
Midheaven to the sextile of Venus in mundo.	36 5	35 10
Part of Fortune to the Parallel of saturn in mundo.	36 11	35 11

OR GENETHLIACAL ASTRONOMY.

THE DIRECTIONS CONTINUED.	ARC. D.M.	TIME. Years Months.
Sun to the square of Venus in the Zodiac, Converse Direction.	36 17	36 0
Sun to the semiquartile of saturn in mundo, Direct motion.	36 40	36 6
Sun to the sextile of mercury in the Zodiac, by Converse Direction.	37 6	36 10
Sun to his own semiquartile in the Zodiac.	37 6	36 10
Moon to the semiquartile of Venus in the Zodiac.	37 10	36 11
Ascendant to the sesquiquadrate of Jupiter in mundo.	37 11	36 11
Moon to the semiquartile of mars in the Zodiac, Converse motion.	37 35	37 4
Moon to the Body of saturn in mundo, Converse Direction.	37 58	37 9
Midheaven to the Quintile of mars in mundo.	38 55	38 8
Sun to the sextile of saturn in the Zodiac.	39 17	39 2
Moon to the Parallel of saturn in mundo, by the Rapt motion.	39 22	39 3
Moon to the sextile of Jupiter in mundo, by Converse Direction.	39 23	39 3
Moon to her own sextile in the Zodiac.	39 25	39 3
Moon to the Parallel of Jupiter in the Zodiac.	39 27	39 4
Moon to the Body of Saturn in the Zodiac, Converse Direction.	39 31	39 5
Moon to the square of the sun in the Zodiac.	40 15	40 2
Midheaven to the Quintile of the moon in mundo.	40 35	40 6
Sun to the semiquartile of mars in mundo, by Converse motion.	40 44	40 8
Sun to the Lions' Heart in the Zodiac.	40 45	40 8
Part of Fortune to the Biquintile of saturn in mundo.	41 21	41 4
Moon to the Quintile of saturn in mundo, Direct Direction.	41 43	41 9
Ascendant to the Opposition of the sun in mundo.	41 52	41 11
Midheaven to the square of the sun in mundo.	41 52	41 11
Moon to the Quintile of Venus in the Zodiac, by Converse motion.	42 4	42 1
Moon to the square of Jupiter in the Zodiac, Converse Direction.	42 10	42 2
Sun to the Trine of Jupiter in the Zodiac, Converse motion.	42 51	42 11
Sun to the sextile of Venus in mundo, Converse Direction.	42 54	43 0

K

CELESTIAL PHILOSOPHY.

THE DIRECTIONS CONTINUED.	ARC. D. M.	TIME. Years Months
Sun to the semiquartile of mercury in the Zodiac.	43 0	43 1
Moon to the semiquartile of mercury in the Zodiac, Converse motion.	43 24	43 6
Part of Fortune to the opposition of mars in mundo.	44 25	44 6
Sun to the Quintile of mercury in the Zodiac, Converse Direction.	44 32	44 7
Sun to the Parallel of mercury in mundo, by the Rapt motion.	45 34	45 8
Part of Fortune to the Opposition of the moon in mundo.	47 53	46 0
Sun to the semiquartile of mercury in mundo, by Converse motion.	45 55	46 0
Sun to the sextile of saturn in Mundo, Direct Direction.	46 16	46 4
Moon to the square of mercury in the Zodiac.	46 17	46 4
Midheaven to the Trine of saturn in mundo.	46 22	46 5
Sun to his own sextile in the Zodiac.	46 23	46 5
Sun to the Parallel of saturn in mundo, Direct Direction.	46 29	46 7
Sun to the Quintile of saturn in the Zodiac.	46 36	46 9
Moon to the semiquartile of Venus in mundo, Converse motion.	46 39	46 10
Moon to the sextile of Venus in the Zodiac.	46 50	47 1
Part of Fortune to the sesquiquadrate of saturn in mundo.	47 3	47 4
Ascendant to the Biquintile of Jupiter in mundo.	47 4	47 4
Moon to her own Quintile in the Zodiac.	47 11	47 5
Sun to the square of mars in the Zodiac, Converse Direction.	47 16	47 6
Moon to the sextile of mars in the zodiac, by Converse motion.	47 17	47 6
Moon to the semiquartile of mercury in mundo, Direct Direction.	47 56	48 2
Moon to the sextile of the sun in mundo, Direct Direction.	48 23	48 8
Sun to the Parallel of mars in mundo, by the Rapt motion.	48 31	48 10
Sun to the square of Jupiter in mundo, by Converse motion	48 39	48 11
Sun to the Parallel of the moon in mundo, by the Rapt motion.	48 56	49 4

OR GENETHLIACAL ASTRONOMY. 47

THE DIRECTIONS CONTINUED.	ARC D M.	TIME. Years Months.
Sun to the semiquartile of saturn in the zodiac, Converse Direction.	49 24	49 10
Moon to spica Virginis in the zodiac.	49 54	50 4
Sun to the sextile of mars in mundo, Converse motion.	49 55	50 4
Ascendant to the Biquintile of saturn in mundo.	50 10	50 8
Sun to the Quintile of Venus in mundo, Converse Direction.	50 14	50 9
Part of Fortune to the Parallel of the sun in mundo.	50 23	50 10
Sun to the Parallel of Jupiter in the zodiac.	50 24	50 10
Sun to his own semiquartile in mundo.	50 56	51 5
Sun to the semiquartile of mars in the zodiac.	51 1	51 6
Midheaven to the Quintile of Venus in mundo.	51 24	51 11
Sun to the sextile of mercury in the zodiac.	51 45	52 3
Sun to the Body of Jupiter in the zodiac.	52 3	52 8
Moon to the Trine of saturn in the zodiac.	52 22	53 0
Sun to the Parallel of Venus in mundo, by the Rapt motion.	52 24	53 0
Moon to the square of saturn in mundo, Direct Direction.	53 7	53 9
Sun to his own quintile in the zodiac.	53 16	53 11
Sun to the Body of Jupiter in mundo, Direct Direction.	53 27	54 1
Moon to the square of Venus in the zodiac, by Converse Motion.	53 28	54 1
Midheaven to the sextile of Jupiter in mundo.	53 38	54 3
Sun to the Quintile of saturn in mundo, Direct Direction.	53 52	54 7
Ascendant to the Opposition of mercury in mundo.	54 3	54 10
Midheaven to the square of mercury in mundo,	54 3	54 10
Sun to the Parallel of saturn in mundo, Converse Direction.	54 7	54 11
Sun to the semiquartile of the moon in the zodiac.	54 12	55 0
Moon to the Quintile of Jupiter in mundo, by Converse Motion.	54 55	55 9
Sun to the Sextile of mercury in mundo, Converse Direction.	55 6	55 11
Moon to the Quintile of Venus in the zodiac.	55 7	55 11
Moon to the Quintile of mars in the zodiac, Converse motion.	55 7	55 11
Sun to the square of mercury in the zodiac.	55 22	56 2
Part of Fortune to the Biquintile of the sun in mundo.	55 22	56 2
Moon to the square of mars in the zodiac.	55 43	56 6

CELESTIAL PHILOSOPHY,

	ARC.	TIME.
THE DIRECTIONS CONTINUED.	D. M.	Years Month
Moon to the Quintile of the sun in mundo, Direct Direction.	55 54	56 6
Ascendant to the sesquiquadrate of saturn in mundo.	55 52	56 8
Moon to the sextile of mercury in the zodiac, Converse Direction.	56 16	57 1
Part of Fortune to the Trine of saturn in mundo.	56 33	57 4
Part of Fortune to the Opposition of Venus in mundo.	56 36	57 5
Sun to the square of saturn in the zodiac.	56 51	57 8
Sun to the sesquiquadrate of Jupiter in the zodiac, Converse motion.	56 58	57 11
Moon to the semiquartile of Jupiter in the zodiac.	57 6	58 2
Moon to the Parallel of mercury in mundo, by the Rapt motion.	57 8	58 2
Sun to the Quintile of mars in mundo, by Converse Direction.	57 16	58 4
Moon to the semiquartile of mars in mundo, Direct Direction.	57 19	58 5
Sun to the sextile of saturn in the zodiac, Converse motion.	57 51	58 11
Sun to the Parallel of Jupiter in mundo, by the Rapt motion.	57 52	58 11
Moon to her own semiquartile in mundo.	58 15	59 5
Sun to the Quintile of mercury in the zodiac.	58 28	59 8
Moon to the Parallel of saturn in mundo, Direct Direction.	58 37	59 10
Sun to the Trine of Venus in the zodiac, by Converse motion.	59 1	60 3
Sun to the sextile of mars in the zodiac.	59 23	60 7
Moon to the Parallel of Venus in the zodiac.	59 28	60 8
Moon to her own square in the zodiac.	59 55	61 2
Sun to his own sextile in mundo,	60 8	61 5
Midheaven to the Trine of the sun in mundo.	60 14	61 6
Moon to the sextile of mercury in mundo, Direct Direction.	60 21	61 7
Sun to the semiquartile of Venus in the zodiac.	60 34	61 10
Moon to her own Parallel in the zodiac.	60 36	61 10
Moon to the Trine of the sun in the zodiac.	60 54	62 2
Part of Fortune to the sesquiquadrate of the sun in mundo.	60 54	62 2
Sun to the square of Venus in mundo, by Converse motion.	61 16	62 7

OR GENETHLIACAL ASTRONOMY. 49

THE DIRECTIONS CONTINUED.	ARC. D. M.	TIME. Years Months.
Midheaven to the Biquintile of saturn in mundo.	61 34	62 11
Part of Fortune to the Parallel of mercury in mundo.	62 17	63 8
Sun to the Quintile of mercury in mundo, Converse Direction.	62 27	63 11
Sun to the Sextile of the Moon in the zodiac.	62 32	64 0
Moon to the Quintile of Mercury in the zodiac, Converse Motion.	62 55	64 6
Ascendant to the Opposition of Mars in Mundo.	63 11	64 10
Midheaven to the Square of Mars in mundo.	63 11	64 10
Sun to his own square in the zodiac.	63 16	64 11
Moon to the Parallel of Mars in mundo, by the Rapt Motion.	63 25	65 1
Moon to the Sesquiquadrate of saturn in the zodiac.	63 30	65 2
Ascendant to the Opposition of the Moon in Mundo.	63 53	65 7
Midheaven to the square of the Moon in mundo.	63 53	65 7
Ascendant to the Biquintile of the Sun in Mundo.	63 55	65 7
Sun to the Quintile of saturn in the zodiac, Converse Direction.	64 4	65 9
Moon to the Quintile of mars in the zodiac.	64 46	66 6
Moon to the sextile of Venus in Mundo, by Converse Motion.	65 4	66 10
Sun to the square of Saturn in Mundo, Direct Direction.	65 16	67 3
Ascendant to the Trine of Saturn in Mundo.	65 22	67 4
Sun to the Parallel of Saturn in Mundo, by Converse motion.	65 23	67 4
Sun to the Biquintile of Jupiter in the zodiac, Converse Direction.	65 51	67 9
Sun to the Quintile of Mars in the zodiac.	66 4	68 0
Moon to the square of the sun in mundo, Direct Direction.	66 45	68 8
Midheaven to the Quintile of Jupiter in mundo.	66 48	68 8
Sun to the Trine of Jupiter in Mundo, by Converse motion.	67 1	68 11
Part of Fortune to the Biquintile of Mercury in mundo.	67 9	69 1
Moon to the Quintile of Mercury in Mundo, Direct Direction.	67 28	69 5
Sun to his own quintile in Mundo.	67 29	69 5
Moon to the semiquartile of Saturn in the Zodiac, Converse motion.	67 33	69 6
Moon to the square of Mars in the Zodiac, by Converse Direction.	67 34	69 6

L

CELESTIAL PHILOSOPHY,

THE DIRECTIONS CONTINUED.

	ARC. D. M.	TIME. Years Months.
Moon to the Parallel of Venus in Mundo, by the Rapt Motion.	67 37	69 6
Sun to the Trine of Mars in the zodiac, Converse Direction.	67 54	69 10
Sun to the square of Mars in mundo, Converse Motion.	68 17	70 3
Moon to the Parallel of Mars in the Zodiac.	68 18	70 3
Moon to the Trine of Mars in the zodiac.	68 19	70 3
Sun to the square of Mercury in the zodiac.	68 30	70 6
Moon to the sextile of Jupiter in the zodiac.	68 43	70 10
Sun to the Parallel of Jupiter in the zodiac.	68 49	70 11
Sun to the sextile of Venus in the zodiac.	68 59	71 3
Moon to the square of Venus in the Zodiac.	68 59	71 3
Sun to the Quintile of the Moon in the Zodiac.	69 17	71 7
Ascendant to the Sesquiquadrate of the Sun in Mundo.	69 25	71 9
Part of Fortune to the Trine of the Sun in mundo.	70 5	72 5
Moon to the sextile of Mars in Mundo, Direct Direction.	70 9	72 6
Sun to the Parallel of Mars in Mundo, by Converse Motion.	70 32	72 11
Moon to the Biquintile of Saturn in the Zodiac.	70 50	73 3
Moon to the Trine of Jupiter in the zodiac, Converse Direction.	70 50	73 3
Moon to the Parallel of Saturn in the Zodiac.	70 52	73 3
Part of Fortune to the Opposition of Jupiter in mundo.	71 17	73 9
Moon to her own sextile in mundo.	71 24	73 11
Sun to the sesquiquadrate of Venus in the zodiac, by Converse motion.	71 35	74 1
Sun to Spica Virginis in the Zodiac.	71 36	74 1
Moon to the square of Jupiter in mundo, Converse Direction.	71 42	74 2
Midheaven to the Trine of Mercury in mundo	71 49	74 4
Sun to the Parallel of mercury in mundo, Direct Direction.	71 55	74 5
Sun to the Parallel of the moon in mundo, Converse motion.	72 5	74 7
Moon to the Trine of Saturn in mundo, Direct Direction.	72 7	74 8
Part of Fortune to the Parallel of Mars in mundo	72 14	74 10

OR GENETHLIACAL ASTRONOMY.

THE DIRECTIONS CONTINUED.	ARC D M	TIME. Years Months
Part of Fortune to the sesquiquadrate of Mercury in Mundo.	72 29	75 1
Moon to the Parallel of Jupiter in mundo, by the Rapt motion.	72 45	75 4
Moon to the sesquiquadrate of the Sun in the zodiac.	73 0	75 8
Sun to the square of Saturn in the Zodiac, Converse Direction.	73 3	75 8
Moon to the square of mercury in the Zodiac, by Converse Motion.	73 14	75 10
Sun to the square of mercury in mundo, Converse Direction.	73 28	76 1
Moon to the Quintile of Venus in mundo, Converse motion.	73 32	76 2
Part of Fortune to the Parallel of the Moon in mundo.	73 42	76 4
Sun to the Trine of saturn in the Zodiac.	73 48	76 5
Ascendant to the Opposition of Venus in mundo.	74 21	77 3
Midheaven to the square of Venus in mundo,	74 21	77 3
Moon to the Parallel of the Sun in the zodiac.	74 26	77 4
Sun to the Trine of mercury in the Zodiac, Converse Direction.	74 27	77 4
Midheaven to the Biquintile of the Sun in mundo.	74 57	77 10
Ascendant to the Biquintile of mercury in mundo.	75 22	78 4
Moon to the sextile of saturn in the Zodiac, by Converse motion.	75 24	78 4
Part of Fortune to the square of saturn in mundo.	75 33	78 6

The positions of the Planets in this Nativity, are of an unpropitious Nature, and as their various configurations to each other, are also of an inimical power, I shall therefore make a few *plain* observations on their effects, that those who apply themselves to this Sacred Study, may form a decisive and impartial Judgment on other Genitures, in which similar positions and Directions are frequently apparent, which when diligently attended to, will give pleasure and satisfaction to every industrious Student in the noble Science of prognostic Astronomy.

The Celestial Sign Sagittarius occupies the oriental Horizon, and Jupiter Lord of the Ascendant, and significator of the Native, is posited in the Ninth House, cadent, and in his detriment, near violent fixed Stars; he is likewise applying to the square of Saturn in the Western Angle, without any assistance from benign Rays, or propitious terms, either in the Zodiac, or in the World. Mercury who disposes of Jupiter in the Radix, is combust, and besieged between the bodies of the Sun and Mars in the descending part of the Heavens, where the evil power of the Malefic Stars is augmented by the Rapt Motion of the Earth. The Moon and Mars, which are the chief *Mortal promittors*, are very violently conjoined, and as they approach their subterraneous positions, they consequently increase their baneful rays to each other; the part of Fortune is afflicted by the opposition of Saturn, Lord of the second, and its dispositor is weak, and deprived of all his dignities in the Radix; these positions and violent motions of the Stars, combined with the evil stations of the Satellites of the Luminaries, will (notwithstanding the mundane Sextile of the Sun to the Midheaven, and the Trine of Venus ruler of the supreme Southern Angle to the Ascendant in the World,) always produce sorrows, and many difficulties, with various calamities during the whole period of the Native's Life; and I shall further observe, that in all Genitures, (whether Male or Female,) where such hostile positions, and configurations as the above are discovered, those persons will be subject to contempt, and reproach; innumerable troubles, and losses, with dangers to Life will surround them, and in the end they will always descend below the sphere of Life in which they were Born.

There are many methods invented for the purpose of ascertaining the true Hour, and Minute of a Nativity, from the estimate, or given time of Birth. I have tried all the rules, both Ancient and Modern, in an impartial manner, that have been published; and in many hundreds of Nativities which I have calculated, they have generally deceived me in my computations, and I am certain they will deceive every practitioner who may think proper to rely on such preposterous inventions, which can neither be supported by proof, nor illustrated by proper Examples, and Experience: The truth is, *there is but one true Method* for correcting the given time of any Birth, and that method will never fail, when properly understood, and rightly practised; and when the estimate time does not exceed its reasonable limits. The Method I allude to, is the computation of the Arcs of Directions to the *Ascendant* and *Midheaven*, which are the two superior Angles of the Figure, so that when the time of any important Events, (whether good or evil,) are given, the true time of Birth may be readily discovered, by comparing the Numbers arising from the computed Arcs, with the Years, and Months of the Native's Life, when the corresponding occurrences took place; thus by adjusting the Directions, according to the nature, and power of the promittors, &c. in the manner above described, the true time of Birth will visibly appear without the least confusion or error, but when the time of any Nativity is truly taken from a corrected Clock, or Watch, no rectification will be required. I have recorded these important subjects in this place, because by the above Method, (which I daily use in my practice,) I have proved the time of the foregoing Nativity correct, as will appear from the Nature of the following Directions; the Effects of which perfectly correspond with the periods of the given Events of Life.

At the Age of twenty-seven Years, the Life of the Native was in imminent danger from a lingering Illness, which continued upwards of six months. She also suffered much injury by a fall from a Horse. The Ascendant was then directed to the Opposition of Saturn.

Aged forty-one Years and ten Months, she was not expected to survive the Effects of an intermitting Fever, which attacked her with unusual violence, during several weeks; this Direction at the same time produced several other calamities, and troubles. The Ascendant at that period was directed to the Opposition of the Sun.

When the Native was nearly fifty-five years of age, she was afflicted with another violent Illness, accompanied with delirium, and hysteric affections, which according to the opinion of her Medical attendants, had every appearance of terminating in death; but after two Months severe sickness, she was restored to her former state of Health. The Effects of the Ascendant to the Opposition of Mercury, were in operation at that period.

These three directions of Saturn, the Sun, and Mercury to the Ascendant, were those which I previously selected for the purpose of proving the correctness of the given time of Birth, before I commenced the calculation. The Ascendant is certainly the giver of Life; according to the Rules I have given in this Work, for selecting the true prorogator in all Genitures, and at the Age of sixty-four Years and ten Months, that Aphetical point will be directed to the opposition of Mars and the Moon, without assistance, the Effects of which will certainly destroy the Native's Life.

OR GENETHLIACAL ASTRONOMY.

But though I have stated the time of Dissolution, to prove the important use of the true Prorogator, I shall observe, that the power of the Anaretic Directions will be considerably increased and accelerated under their horary Circles of position; for before the mortal promittors descend the Western Horizon, the Terms of both the Malefics, and their Parallels under the Motion of the Primum Mobile, set, with two Degrees fifty Minutes of Leo, and consequently precede the deadly train at the age of sixty years and nine months: at which time, Life will be exposed to the most alarming danger by a violent sickness, from which the Native will never perfectly recover. The Mortal disease will be violent palpitations of the Heart, with difficulty of breathing, pains and inflamations in the Breast, and a putrid Fever; such will be the Nature and Effects of the disease, which will terminate the Native's existence in this earthly World.

I have not made any comments on the Events produced by the Effects of those Directions that are Tabulated in this Geniture, from the time of Birth, to the present period of the Native's Life, except a few of those computed to the Oriental Horizon, having omitted such observations to avoid repetition, as the practitioner will find the Rules for Judgment with the EFFECTS OF ALL DIRECTIONS in any Nativity, progressively arranged in another part of this Publication.

I have calculated all the preceding Arcs of Directions in this, and all other Nativities in this Work, from Tabular numbers, being *the only true Method*, though the Planisphere is used by some, who *falsely* and *impudently* affirm, that for accuracy and expedition, it is far superior to any other invention; I have had one of those Instruments in my possession, with all its *pretended* improvements, several years, and I flatter myself, that I understand its use as well as any of those Teachers. This *paltry thing* at first sight appears *beautiful to behold*, in consequence of the *various*

Colours with which the *Signs* and *Planets*, &c, are ornamented; but the more it is attentively surveyed, the more *disgusting* it appears, with all its *visible imperfections*, Most Students are disposed to attend to any inventions which appear likely to prove advantageous to their pursuits, but I will ask, Why is so much time sacrificed in *Mapping, Colouring*, and *Ornamenting* a piece of Cardboard, before the Compass, &c. are applied, and which is good for nothing at last, and why are the *Stars* and *Constellations whimsically embellished* with most of the *Colours*, which the understanding of man can devise ? Surely this is not the right way to instruct the ingenious Students, but it certainly is the Method which *Planispheric Teachers* (as they call themselves), adopt to *please the Eyes and tease the Pockets* of those, to whom they give *artful Lessons* of improvement, Lessons which I am certain many of the *deluded* Students will never forget. Some who are advocates for the use of this instrument, *gravely* say, that it saves much time and trouble, which is a most *notorious* and *false* assertion, for the time taken up in *Mapping, Colouring*, and *Ornamenting*, is much more than able calculators require in computing the whole of the Directions in any Geniture whatsoever; and when the Arcs of Directions are numerous in a Nativity, *this thing* altogether becomes *useless*, as well as the *childish Speculum* which is generally attached to it; I have made these remarks, by which the Reader may observe, that I do not sanction the use of this Instrument, (which is only a Globe delineated on a Plane,) because it is deficient in all those parts where true Calculations are required, though it is *artfully* contrived to attract the notice of the innocent, and delude the ignorant, and un wary,

There has been much contention among many who pretend to calculate Nativities, concerning the power of the Georgian Planet, and the other four, which have been re-

OR GENETHLIACAL ASTRONOMY. 57

cently discovered, I have omitted them in all my computations, being convinced that we have not had any Examples sufficient to prove the existence of their power, for plain and manifest reasons, The *true* and *correct* places and Revolutions, &c, of these Planets, are unknown to us at present; so that if we were to notice them in our Calculations and Judgment, we should soon be convinced of our Errors. I know some will say they have discovered many of their Effects in Nativities, but those who entertain an opinion of that nature, ought to produce *substantial proofs* of their discoveries, which I am certain they are unable to explain, tho' if such persons are inclined to discountenance what I have here stated, I entreat them not to stand any longer at a distance but come forward and publish to the world, the result of their observations, founded on legal examples, and experience.

☞ *The Reader will observe, that as there was not sufficient room to contain the Characters, Degrees, and Minutes of the Moon, Venus, and the Dragon's Head, in the eighth House, in which they claim their true position; the compositor has unavoidably placed them as they now appear in the preceding Figure of Birth*

This is the Nativity of Mr. Thomas Willoughby, a young Gentleman, with whom I was acquainted, and owing to his request, and the desire of some of his Friends, when he was in perfect health, I calculated his Geniture, and immediately observed, that there were many Anaretical Directions following each other, in regular succession to the Moon, the giver of Life, which would show their Mortal Effects, early in the month of August, 1822, agreeable to the most accurate computations; and which, according to my judgment, would produce personal dissolution, as there were no benevolent directions to give the least support, or assistance to the true Prorogator, when those powerful Directions were in operation. My previous prediction was verified; as the time of Birth was taken with the greatest care. He was born at Hull, in Yorkshire, at the time given in the following Figure; and departed this life on the 26th of July, 1822, at eleven o'clock in the evening, aged twenty-two years, seven months and five days.

OR GENETHLIACAL ASTRONOMY.

193° 12'

♏ 26 22
♂ 20 30

☿ 12 48
8 26
♃ 48
♏

♎ 14 21
☽ 16 35

♍ 7 5

♐ 11 0
☉ 29 30

⊕

♌ ☊ 9 21 R
♋ 19 23

NATUS,

December 20th, 1799,

H.   M.
18 55 P. M.

LATITUDE 53 45.

♄ 10 52 R
♅ 19 23

♑

♃ 26 4 R
♓ 11 0

♒

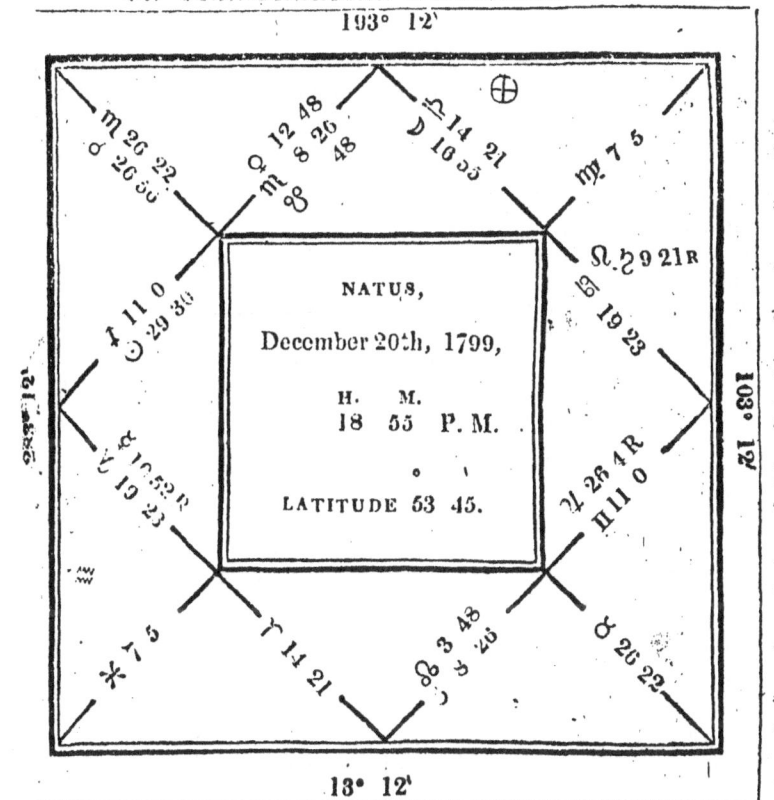

♓ 7 5

♈ 14 21

♉ 3 48
♀ 20

♉ 26 22

283° 12'

103° 12'

13° 12'

LAT.	DEC.	R. A.	S D A	D H T	S N A	N H T	A D.
° ′	° ′	° ′	° ′	° ′	° ′	° ′	° ′
♄ 0 38 N	18 32 N.	131 59	117 12	19 32	62 48	10 28	27 12
♃ 0 21 S.	23 4 N.	85 43	125 31	20 55	54 29	9 5	35 31
♂ 0 14 N.	19 16 S.	234 40	61 32	10 15	118 28	19 45	28 28
☉	23 28 S.	269 27	53 42	8 57	126 18	21 3	36 18
♀ 3 9 N.	12 41 S.	221 19	72 7	12 1	107 53	17 59	17 53
☿ 0 49 N.	22 13 S.	281 45	56 9	9 21	123 51	20 39	33 51
☽ 1 37 N.	5 8 S.	196 11	82 57	13 49	97 3	16 11	7 3
⊕	0 11 S.	180 26	89 45	14 57	90 15	15 3	0 15

A TABLE OF THE DIRECTIONS

	ARC. D. M.	TIME. Years Months
Midheaven in the sextile of Mars in Mundo.	0 28	0 4
Moon to the Quintile of the sun in the Zodiac.	0 33	0 5
Sun to the Quintile of Venus in mundo, Direct Direction	0 50	0 9
Part of Fortune to the Semiquartile of Venus in Mundo.	2 20	2 2
Moon to the sextile of Mars in mundo, by Converse motion.	2 21	2 2
Sun to the Semiquartile of Venus in the Zodiac, Converse Direction.	2 43	2 6
Midheaven to the body of the moon in mundo.	2 59	2 9
Ascendant to the square of the moon in mundo.	2 59	2 9
Sun to the sesquiquadrate of Saturn in the Zodiac Converse motion,	3 20	3 1
Moon to Spica Virginis in the Zodiac.	4 5	3 8
Ascendant to the sextile of Venus in mundo,	4 5	3 8
Moon to the quintile of Saturn in the Zodiac.	4 6	3 8
Sun to the Biquintile of Saturn in the Zodiac.	4 7	3 9
Sun to the Opposition of Jupiter in mundo, Converse Direction.	4 24	3 11
Moon to the Semiquartile of Saturn in mundo, by Converse motion.	4 49	4 2
Midheaven to Spica Virginis in mundo.	5 43	5 4
Moon to the sextile of Saturn in the Zodiac, Converse Direction.	6 5	5 6
Moon to the Semiquartile of Mars in the Zodiac, by Converse motion.	6 26	5 10
Moon to the square of Mercury in the Zodiac, Converse Direction.	7 24	6 9
Moon to the Quintile of Jupiter in mundo, Converse motion.	7 39	7 0
Moon to the semiquartile of Mars in mundo, Direct Direction.	8 29	7 8
Moon to the trine of Jupiter in the Zodiac.	8 31	7 8
Part of Fortune to the trine of Mercury in Mundo.	8 46	7 11
Moon to the trine of Mercury in Mundo, by Converse motion.	8 56	8 1
Ascendant to the Biquintile of Saturn in Mundo,	9 6	8 3
Part of Fortune to the sextile of Mars in Mundo.	9 14	8 5
Sun to the sextile of Mars in Mundo, Direct Direction	9 50	9 0
Sun to the Body of Mercury, in Mundo, Direct motion	10 17	9 8

OR GENETHLIACAL ASTRONOMY.

THE DIRECTIONS CONTINUED.	ARC. D. M.	TIME. years months.
Ascendant to the semiquartile of Mars in Mundo.	10 43	9 8
Sun to the parallel of Jupiter in the Zodiac.	11 4	10, 0
Moon to the Quintile of Mercury in the Zodiac.	11 9	10 1
Sun to the body of Mercury in the Zodiac.	11 40	10 7
Moon to the Sextile of the Sun in the Zodiac.	11 44	10 8
Moon to the Semiquartile of Venus in Mundo, by Converse Motion.	12 6	10 11
Sun to the semiquartile of Mars in the Zodiac.	12 41	11 6
Moon to the sextile of Saturn in Mundo, Direct Direction.	12 42	11 6
Moon to the quintile of Mars in Mundo, Converse Motion.	13 24	12
Sun to the sextile of Venus in the Zodiac.	13 30	12 2
Moon to the square of Jupiter in Mundo, Direct Direction.	13 31	12 2
Ascendant to the quintile of Venus in Mundo.	13 42	12 4
Part of Fortune to the semiquartile of Saturn in Mundo.	14 5	12 9
Sun to the Trine of Saturn in the Zodiac, by Converse Motion.	14 9	12 10
Part of Fortune to the Body of the Moon in Mundo.	14 48	13 6
Sun to the square of Venus in Mundo, Direct Direction.	15 15	13 9
Sun to the Sextile of Venus in Mundo, Converse Motion.	15 24	13 11
Sun to the Trine of the Moon in Mundo, Direct Direction.	15 49	14 4
Moon to the Parallel of Venus in the Zodiac.	15 51	14 4
Moon to the Parallel of Venus in Mundo, by the Rapt Motion.	16 26	14 10
Midheaven to the Sextile of Saturn in Mundo.	16 55	15 4
Sun to the Square of the Moon in the Zodiac.	17 14	15 7
Moon to the Semiquartile of Saturn in the Zodiac, Converse Direction.	17 17	15 7
Part of Fortune to the Parallel of Venus in Mundo.	17 51	16 1
Moon to the square of the Sun in Mundo, Direct Direction.	18 0	16 3
Ascendant to the Opposition of Jupiter in Mundo.	18 2	16 3
Midheaven to the Square of Jupiter in Mundo.	18 2	16 3
Sun to the Quintile of mars in mundo, by Direct motion	18 11	16 5

M

CELESTIAL PHILOSOPHY,

THE DIRECTIONS CONTINUED.	ARC. D. M.	TIME. Years Months
Sun to the Parallel of Mercury in the Zodiac.	18 24	16 8
Moon to the Sextile of Jupiter in Mundo, Converse Direction.	18 42	16 11
Part of Fortune to the Semiquartile of mars in Mundo.	19 29	17 8
Ascendant to the Sextile of Mars in Mundo.	20 58	18 11
Moon to the square of Saturn in the Zodiac.	21 7	19 1
Moon to the square of Jupiter in the Zodiac, by Converse Motion.	21 48	19 9
Moon to the Semiquartile of Venus in the Zodiac, Converse Direction.	21 54	19 10
Ascendant to the Body of the Sun in Mundo.	22 33	20 5
Midheaven to the square of the Sun in Mundo.	22 33	20 5
Moon to the Sextile of Mercury in the Zodiac.	22 37	20 6
Moon to the Sesquiquadrate of mercury in mundo, Converse Motion.	22 45	20 7
Moon to the Sesquiquadrate of Jupiter in the Zodiac.	22 50	20 8
Sun to the Quintile of Venus in the Zodiac.	23 50	21 7
Moon to the Body of Venus in the Zodiac.	24 32	22 2
Moon to the Parallel of mars in mundo, by the Rapt Motion.	25 5	22 8
Moon to the Sextile of mars in the zodiac, Converse Direction.	25 16	22 10
Sun to the Sextile of Mars in the Zodiac.	25 30	23 1
Moon to the Body of Venus in mundo, Direct motion.	25 31	23 1
Sun to the Parallel of mercury in mundo, by the Rapt motion.	25 32	23 1
Part of Fortune to the square of Jupiter in mundo.	25 48	23 4
Moon to the Sextile of Venus in mundo, Converse Direction.	25 55	23 6
Moon to the Semiquartile of the Sun in the zodiac.	26 13	23 10
Moon to the Square of mercury in mundo, Direct motion.	27 56	25 4
Sun to the Semiquartile of mercury in the zodiac, Converse Direction.	28 3	25 6
Midheaven to the Body of Venus in mundo.	28 7	25 7
Ascendant to the square of Venus in mundo.	28 7	25 7
Moon to the Quintile of Saturn in mundo, Direct Direction.	28 20	25 10

OR GENETHLIACAL ASTRONOMY, 63

	ARC.	TIME.
THE DIRECTIONS CONTINUED.	D. M.	Years Months.
Sun to the Semiquartile of Venus in mundo, Converse motion.	28 27	25 11
Ascendant to the Quintile of mars in mundo.	29 10	26 7
Sun to the Biquintile of Jupiter in the Zodiac.	29 19	26 9
Sun to the Sesquiquadrate of the moon in mundo, Direct Direction.	29 38	27
Moon to the Square of mars in mundo, by Converse motion.	29 59	27 5
Sun to the Biquintile of Jupiter in mundo, Direct Direction.	30 6	27 6
Part of Fortune to the Square of the Sun in mundo.	30 12	27 8
Moon to the Parallel of Saturn in the zodiac.	30 24	27 11
Sun to the Square of mars in mundo, Direct Direction.	30 29	28 0
Ascendant to the Trine of the moon in mundo.	30 37	28 1
Moon to the Parallel of Venus in mundo, Direct motion.	30 43	28 2
Sun to the Parallel of mars in the zodiac.	30 44	28 2
Moon to the Biquintile of mercury in mundo, Converse Direction.	31 2	28 5
Moon to the Quintile of the Sun in mundo, Direct motion.	31 21	28 8
Moon to the Biquintile of Jupiter in the zodiac.	31 49	29 1
Ascendant to the Body of mercury in mundo.	32 24	29 7
Midheaven to the Square of mercury in mundo.	32 24	29 7
Moon to the Trine of mercury in the zodiac, Converse Direction.	32 31	29 8
Moon to the Semiquartile of Jupiter in mundo, by Converse motion.	32 31	29 8
Moon to the Parallel of mars in the zodiac.	32 41	29 10
Sun to the Trine of Saturn in mundo, Converse Direction.	32 42	29 10
Part of Fortune to the Parallel of mars in mundo.	32 42	29 10
Sun to the Parallel of Saturn in the zodiac.	32 48	29 11
Sun to the Parallel of Saturn in mundo, by the Rapt motion.	33 3	30 2
Midheaven to the Quintile of the Sun in mundo.	33 17	30 5
Sun to the Square of Saturn in the zodiac, Converse Direction.	33 36	30 9
Part of Fortune to the Sextile of Saturn in mundo.	33 37	30 9
Sun to the Quintile of mars in the zodiac.	34 2	31 1

CELESTIAL PHILOSOPHY,

THE DIRECTIONS CONTINUED.	ARC. D.M.	TIME. years months
Moon to the Trine of Jupiter in mundo, Direct motion.	34 14	31 3
Sun to the Opposition of Saturn in the zodiac.	34 19	31 4
Sun to the Opposition of Saturn in mundo, Direct Direction.	35 4	32 2
Moon to the Parallel of Venus in mundo, by Converse motion.	35 18	32 5
Sun to the Semiquartile of mercury in mundo, Converse Direction.	35 21	32 5
Sun to the Sesquiquadrate of Jupiter in the zodiac.	35 24	32 6
Sun to the Sesquiquadrate of Jupiter in mundo, Direct Direction.	35 33	32 8
Sun to the Biquintile of Jupiter in the zodiac, Converse motion.	35 51	32 11
Midheaven to the Trine of Jupiter in mundo.	36 12	33 3
Sun to the Biquintile of Jupiter in mundo, Converse Direction.	36 19	33 4
Moon to the Quintile of Jupiter in the zodiac, Converse motion.	36 28	33 6
Sun to the Square of Venus in the zodiac.	36 29	33 6
Sun to the Parallel of mercury in mundo, by Converse Direction.	36 35	33 7
Moon to the Quintile of Venus in mundo, Converse motion.	36 58	33 11
Sun to the Sextile of mercury in the zodiac, Converse Direction.	37 11	34 2

The Tabulated Directions preceding, are those which I computed for this Gentleman two Years before his demise, which several of his Friends now living, well know; but there is something remarkable in the quality of his Death, therefore it is my wish that all Students in this Science may properly attend to the Rules I have laid down in this Work, concerning the nature, and quality of dissolution in any Nativity; for the same *Causes* will invariably produce the same *Effects*, when the Heavens are accurately divided by duplicate horary times, and the Arcs of Directions truly calculated, from the new Astronomical Tables contained in this Publication.

The Moon is certainly the giver of Life in this Nativity, and though the Sun is in an Aphetical position, yet he can by no means claim the prorogatory power, according to the established precepts and Examples which I have given for selecting the true Hyleg. This Gentleman was dangerously indisposed at the Age of Nineteen Years, and I am of opinion that many pretenders to this Science, would have judged inevitable Death at that time, because the Hyleg was then directed to the Square of Saturn in the Zodiac, that promittor being in the eighth House, which is considered to be their favourite killing Mansion in all Genitures. I certainly admit that the Effects of the Direction of the Apheta to the quartile Rays of that Malefic, were of a dangerous nature, but had not power to destroy Life, because when that Direction was in operation, the Moon was received in the terms of Jupiter, and his orbs, and was also directed to his Square, by Converse Motion, she afterwards applied to the Body of Venus in the Zodiac, which must appear evident to the Judgment of those who are masters of directional motion; but though the above Direction of the Moon to Saturn's quartile was deprived of its mortal influence, yet it clearly shewed the quality of Death: for Venus in Scorpio, indicates poison, both by position, and Direction, as she is in square to Saturn in the Radix, and both their Directions fall in the Mortal train to the giver of Life; therefore my previous and impartial Judgment was, that the Native's Death would be occasioned, either by the baneful Effects of improper Medicine, or, by poisonous Effluvia, received by respiration into the Lungs, which would corrupt the Blood, and ultimately produce Death, the latter of which was the case, for Venus, though she cannot save, yet she transmits Saturn's malignant Rays to the Hyleg, and joins at the same time in the Anæretical train of Directions, which clearly prove the nature and quality of Death, as specified above.

The Directions which destroyed the Life of this Native, were the Moon to the Parallel of Mars in Mundo, by the Rapt Motion, followed by the semiquartile of the Sun in the Zodiac, the square of Mercury, in Mundo, by a right Motion, and by a Converse Direction, the Hyleg was directed to the Mundane square of Mars, succeeded by the Parallel of Saturn's Declination, and also by the zodiacal Parallel of Mars; and though the sun was directed to violent promittors near the same period, which doubtless increased the Effects of the mortal train to the true prorogator, yet he had no power of himself to destroy Life, because the Aphetical dignity is claimed by the other Luminary in this Example; such Directions as the above will always destroy Life in any Nativity in which such corresponding positions, and configurations of the Celestial Bodies, appear to our view, for it is certain that in every Geniture, when the true significator of Life is strongly dignified, and free from the contact of inimical beams, one violent Direction to the Apheta cannot produce dissolution, but when all the vital significators are at the same time united with baneful Directions, without any assistance from benign rays, &c. then, and then only, the Effects of one Direction of a violent nature to the Hyleg, will cut off Life.

In the secondary Directions, the sun was in square to the moon's place in the Nativity, and the Hyleg was likewise conjoined with saturn, near his station at the time of Birth, and was declining from an opposition to the sun by those motions, which increased the Effects of the corresponding primary Directions to the giver of Life, when they were in operation; and in the Revolutional Figure for the twenty second Year, the moon was posited on the place of mars in the Geniture, and saturn and Jupiter were in opposition to the Radical position of the Prorogator. Venus was then separating from the opposite place of Saturn at the time of Birth, and mars was in square to mercury, they being both promittors in the mortal train; but in the Progression, the applications of the chief significators were still more violent; for the Luminaries were both afflicted by the stations of the malefics from the superior places, and were also superseded by their terms in those parts of the Heavens where no benign rays could interpose to counteract their baneful powers; and what is more remarkable, that in all these motions, the antecedent parallels of the Declination of the promittors, minutely correspond with the nature and Effects of the primary Directions in the mortal train, which not only prove the truth of the computations, but also confirm the cause of the acceleration, and retardation of the *Effects* of all those Directions to the giver of Life, which have power to produce the work of mortality.

At the time of his Death, Saturn was on the Ascendant in opposition with the moon giver of Life in the

Nativity, and had descended below the Western Horizon at the time of his departure. The sun was in quartile with saturn, and near the Radical place of that malefic; mercury was then in exact zodiacal square to the place of the Hyleg in the Geniture, and was also in direct opposition to the place of that Luminary in mundo at the time of Birth; I have thus given a brief illustration of all these corresponding motions of the Planets in their moveable stations, which perfectly represent the plain, and easy method of discovering the difference between the important *Causes* and *Effects* in any Geniture, which relate to directional motion, and which when properly understood, will amply compensate every attentive student, for his researches in this department of Astronomy.

OR GENETHLIACAL ASTRONOMY,

The estimate time of the following Geniture, was February 5th 1802, 9H. 40M. P. M. Latitude 53° North; it was carefully taken by the Accoucher, who was a Man of the strictest Virtue, and Fidelity, so that owing to his attention in recording the Hour, and Minute of Birth, there is sufficient reason to believe, that the time given is near truth; for it cannot be supposed that a Man, on whose Character and Reputation, the malignant Breath of slander had never blown, would give a false time to deceive the Calculator. The Natives Relatives and Friends, (acting under the *polluted* Banners of *Priestcraft:*) are enemies to these Astronomical enquiries, and do not believe that the Celestial Bodies, as second *causes*, have any influence on the Actions, and affairs of Mankind; so that they at once deny the existence of those things, which *they, and their Offspring daily see, and feel*, and which are proved to be *continually visible* by numberless Examples. It must appear ridiculous, and contemptible, in this enlightened Age, when such characters, *(not mutilated by the profound Literature they possess,)* endeavour to traduce the common rules of Arithmetic, on which the immoveable foundation, and admirable structure of this venerable Science depend. How wretched and superficial must the minds of those persons be, who, impiously condemn what they cannot comprehend; they insolently slander the works of the Creator, and treat their power and operation with ridicule and disdain, because they are unable to define the *Sideral Causes* which forebode, and produce the various, and *visible Effects* on the Life of Man; thus being foiled in their superficial researches, they then have recourse to *visionary Themes*, which they adopt to amuse the credulous, and impose on the unlettered part of Mankind. Some of these pitiful *deceivers*, and *licentious impostors pretend* to know the state of Mortal Man *after dissolution, and impudently affirm* that they are qualified to ascertain those who are objects of Divine displeasure: but I am not disposed to sanction any of those *Chimeras* which degrade the human understanding; for how can I depend on the judgment of those, who are *unable to prove one single Fact* to the satisfaction of any rational inquirer. It is much to be regretted that many are to be found, who pretend to resolve those Mysteries which relate to a *Life immortal*, and which the feeble, and finite imagination of Man, is unable to comprehend.

> The *Popish Priests*, when in their sables clad,
> Would prove their TRADE, but proof cannot be had;
> With hands *unclean*, to *Metaphors* they fly,
> To solve their *Chimeras*, beyond the Sky;
> But all in vain, *their Tricks* now old and stale,
> Are disregarded as an *idle Tale*:
> O *irksome Priestcraft*, hide thy *guilty head*,
> There is ONE GOD, the Judge of quick and dead.

But though it may be considered that I have made a digression in this place, yet I shall not apologise for so doing, for the *well known* subjects which I have here introduced, are of *recent date*, and ought to be faithfully handed down to future Generations. The Study of Genethliacal Astronomy, shews forth the incomprehensible WISDOM, POWER, and GLORY of ONE OMNIPOTENT CREATOR in his wonderous Works, and is far superior to those debased principles of *refined Popery*, which are now become a Stalking-horse, to answer every vile, and nefarious purpose that human reason can devise. Such feigned delusion and detestable duplicity, *(being pious Mockery in its odious garb,)* are frequently practised by such as are GUILTY OF CRIMES NOT FIT TO BE NAMED. Many of those *cold blooded* MONSTERS of iniquity, (who reside *near the place* where this Native was Born,) are well known to the Public, their Names are already written with *human gore*, which will not be obliterated by time. We have viewed those *immaculate Cannibals*, and *their Offspring*, in the act of *devouring* the *Flesh* of their *fellow Mortals*, and have seen them *quaff the blood of innocent* and *defenceless Orphans*. These well known *facts* clearly prove, that there are Beings yet *prowling* on the Earth in the human form, who have bid adieu to Morality, humanity, and honesty, having *artfully destroyed those* whom they ought to have protected, in *open violation* of the SACRED TRUST reposed in them. It is notorious to observe, that under the Mask of *prostituted Piety, Priestcraft*, and *hypocritical Friendship*, the most atrocious Acts of premeditated *Murder, Plunder*, and *Villany*, have been accomplished, which will ever disgrace the human Character, in an enlightened and civilized Nation.

But though we cannot view such diabolical actions as those above recorded without indignation and horror, yet there is a *crime* of a more heinous Nature committed by *those* who have *yet* escaped the hand of the Executioner. The Sacred writings inform us, that the Almighty destroyed two of the most magnificent Cities in the World, by Fire and Brimstone from Heaven, because there were not ten righteous persons to be found therein. All were *guilty* of the most horrid, *unnatural*, and detestable Crimes. Those personages who assume the presumptious habit of Piety, and who are *now* moving in apparent affluence, ought to reflect, that there is an Eye that never slumbereth, and the time is fast approaching, when DIVINE VENGEANCE will overtake them. It is certainly the duty of an Author to *expose* by every just, and proper means in his power, and in the *strongest Language*, the Malignancy of a crime of this description, which is making considerable progress in this Nation, with all its horrid, and dreadful consequences. The *treacherous* and *blood thirsty* PETTIFOGGER, and the POLLUTED POPISH PRIEST, dare not appear before the Bar of an Earthly tribunal, to answer the *horrid charges* exhibited against them; but they put a period to their existence, and thereby evaded the presence of a Mortal Judge, to appear before HIM WHO IS IMMORTAL; and who will "Judge the World in righteousness, and the People with Equity".

OR GENETHLIACAL ASTRONOMY, 73

103° 57'

♃ 2 41 R
♍ 17 26 R
♉ 22 29 41

♌ 18 47

♋ 12 50

♊ 5 26

♀ 9 39

♂ 4 8

NATUS,

February 5th, 1802,

H. M.
9 40 P. M.

LATITUDE 53°

♏ 4 8

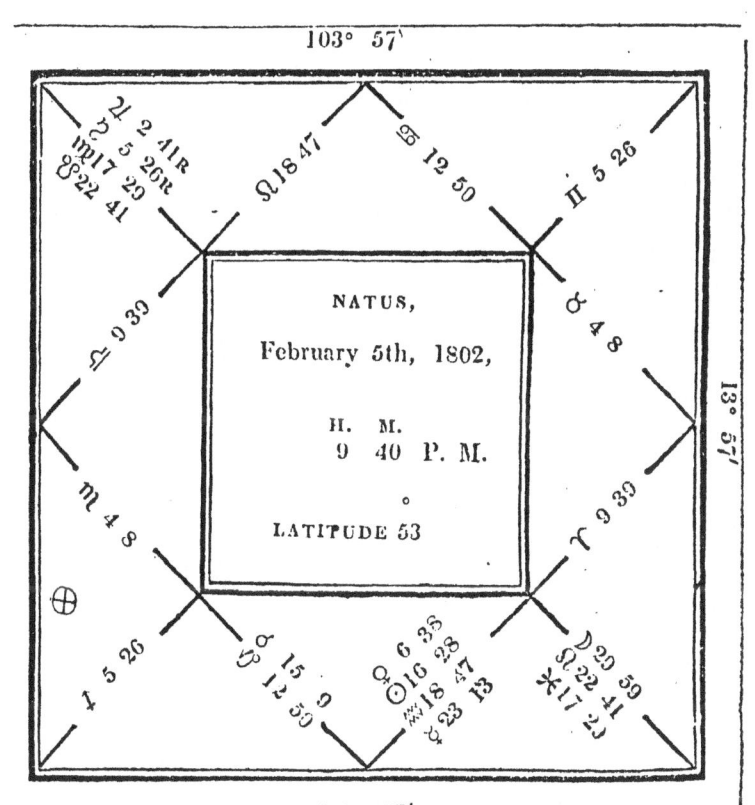

⊕

♐ 5 26

♂ 15 9
☿ 12 30

☿ 6 35
☉ 16 28
♒ 18 47
♄ 23 13

☽ 20 59
♌ 22 41
♓ 17 23

♈ 9 39

13° 57'

283° 57'

LAT.	DEC.	R. A.	S D A.	D H T.	S N A.	N H T.	A D.
° '	° '	° '	° '	° '	° '	° '	° '
♄ 1 50 N	11 16 N.	157 57	105 20	17 33	74 40	12 27	15 20
♃ 14 N.	11 41 N.	155 6	105 56	17 39	74 4	12 21	15 56
♂ 0 44 s.	23 20 s.	236 32	55 55	9 11	124 55	20 49	34 55
☉	15 55 s.	318 57	67 46	11 18	112 14	18 42	22 14
♀ 0 55 s.	19 32 s.	309 18	61 55	10 19	118 5	19 41	28 5
☿ 1 45 s.	15 25 s.	326 10	68 32	11 25	111 28	18 35	21 28
☽ 0 50 N.	0 46 N.	359 40	91 1	15 10	88 59	14 50	1 1
⊕	17 19 s.	225 53	65 33	10 55	114 27	19 5	24 27

CELESTIAL PHILOSOPHY,

A TABLE OF THE DIRECTIONS.

	ARC. D. M.	TIME. Years Months
Ascendant to the semiquartile of Saturn in Mundo.	1 21	1 5
Part of Fortune to the Quintile of Mercury in Mundo.	1 24	1 5
Sun to the Parallel of Mercury in the Zodiac.	1 52	1 11
Moon to the Semiquartile of the Sun in the Zodiac.	2 4	2 1
Midheaven to the Opposition of Mars in Mundo.	2 35	2 7
Ascendant to the Square of Mars in Mundo.	2 35	2 7
Moon to the quintile of Mars in Mundo, Converse Direction.	2 41	2 8
Moon to the Semiquartile of mercury in mundo, Direct motion.	3 7	3 2
Moon to the Quintile of mars in the Zodiac, by Converse Direction.	3 7	3 2
Moon to the Biquintile of Jupiter in mundo, Direct Direction.	3 26	3 6
Sun to the Semiquartile of the moon in mundo, Direct Direction.	3 37	3 6
Moon to the Sextile of Venus in mundo, Direct Direction.	3 27	3 8
Ascendant to the Trine of mercury in mundo.	5 3	5 1
Moon to the Biquintile of Saturn in mundo, by Direct motion.	6 32	6 7
Sun to the body of mercury in mundo, Direct Direction.	7 26	7 6
Sun to the Body of mercury in the zodiac.	7 36	7 8
Part of Fortune to the Sextile of the Sun in mundo.	8 53	9 0
Moon to the Semiquartile of Venus in the Zodiac Converse Motion.	9 12	9 4
Moon to the Sextile of Venus in the Zodiac.	9 20	9 6
Sun to the Body of Venus in the zodiac, Converse Direction.	10 50	11 0
Sun to the Body of Venus in mundo, by Converse motion.	10 55	11 1
Moon to the Semiquartile of Mercury in the Zodiac.	11 34	11 9
Moon to the Semiquartile of Venus in Mundo, Converse Direction.	12 8	12 4
Moon to the Biquintile of Jupiter in the Zodiac.	12 14	12 5
Moon to the Sesquiquadrate of Jupiter, in mundo, Direct Direction.	14 1	14 4
Moon to the Sextile of the Sun in mundo, Direct Direction.	14 21	14 8

	ARC.	TIME.
THE DIRECTIONS CONTINUED.	D. M.	Years Months.
Sun to the Parallel of Jupiter in the zodiac.	14 31	14 10
Moon to the Sextile of mars in mundo, Converse Direction.	14 33	14 10
Sun to the Semiquartile of mars in the zodiac.	15 19	15 8
Ascendant to the Sextile of Jupiter in Mundo.	15 51	16 2
Sun to the Parallel of Saturn in the zodiac.	15 51	16 2
Moon to the Sextile of mars in the zodiac, Converse motion.	15 56	16 3
Moon to the Biquintile of Saturn in the Zodiac.	16 3	16 5
Part of Fortune to the Sextile of mercury in mundo.	16 16	16 8
Midheaven to the Trine of the Moon in Mundo.	16 23	16 9
Moon to the Sesquiquadrate of Saturn in mundo. Direct Direction.	17 4	17 6
Part of Fortune to the semiquartile of Venus in Mundo.	17 34	18 0
Sun to the Opposition of Jupiter in the zodiac.	18 1	18 6
Sun to the Opposition of Jupiter in mundo, Direct Direction.	18 7	18 7
Ascendant to the Spica Virginis.	18 50	19 4
Ascendant to the Sextile of Saturn in mundo.	18 54	19 5
Moon to the Quintile of Venus in mundo, Direct Direction.	19 22	19 11
Sun to the Parallel of mars in mundo, by the Rapt motion.	19 39	20 2
Sun to the Biquintile of Saturn in the zodiac, Converse motion.	20 56	21 7
Sun to the Opposition of Saturn in mundo, Direct Direction	21 9	21 10
Sun to the Opposition of Saturn in the zodiac	21 11	21 10
Moon to the Square of mars in mundo, Direct Direction.	21 14	21 11
Moon to the square of mars in the Zodiac.	21 19	22 0
Moon to the Sextile of mercury in mundo, Direct Motion.	21 42	22 5
Ascendant to the Biquintile of the moon in Mundo.	22 29	23 1
Sun to the Biquintile of Saturn in mundo, Converse Direction.	22 21	23 1
Moon to the Sextile of the Sun in the Zodiac.	23 11	24 0
Sun to the Biquintile of Jupiter in the zodiac, Converse Direction.	23 43	24 7

CELESTIAL PHILOSOPHY,

THE DIRECTIONS CONTINUED.	ARC. D. M.	TIME. years month
Moon to the Sesquiquadrate of Jupiter in the zodiac.	24 53	25 10
Part of Fortune to the Square of the Moon in Mundo.	25 20	26 4
Midheaven to the Opposition of Venus in mundo.	25 21	26 4
Ascendant to the square of Venus in mundo.	25 21	26 4
Sun to the Biquintile of Jupiter in Mundo, by Converse Motion.	25 41	26 8
Sun to the Semiquartile of mars in mundo, Direct Direction.	26 5	27 1
Moon to the Quintile of Venus in the Zodiac.	20 15	27 3
Part of Fortune to the Trine of Jupiter in mundo.	26 30	27 7
Ascendant to the Quintile of mars in mundo.	27 34	28 9
Part of Fortune to the semiquartile of the Sun in Mundo.	27 35	28 9
Moon to the Sesquiquadrate of Saturn in the Zodiac.	28 49	30 0
Moon to the Quintile of the Sun in mundo, Direct Direction.	29 19	30 7
Moon to the Opposition of Saturn in the Zodiac, Converse Direction.	29 22	30 7
Moon to the Semiquartile of mars in mundo, Converse motion.	29 23	30 8
Part of Fortune to the Trine of Saturn in mundo.	29 30	30 9
Ascendant to the Quintile of Jupiter in Mundo.	29 58	31 4
Moon to the Opposition of Saturn in mundo, Converse motion.	30 4	31 5
Sun to the Parallel of Venus in mundo, by the Rapt motion.	30 18	31 8
Part of Fortune to the Parallel of the moon in mundo.	30 35	31 11
Ascendant to the Sesquiquadrate of the moon in mundo.	31 13	32 8
Moon to the Semiquartile of mars in the Zodiac, Converse Direction.	31 28	32 11
Sun to the Sesquiquadrate of Saturn in the Zodiac, Converse Motion.	31 38	33 1
Moon to the Trine of Jupiter in mundo, Direct Direction.	31 40	33 1
Moon to the Parallel of Saturn in the zodiac.	31 42	33 2
Sun to the Sextile of Mars in the Zodiac.	31 49	33 4
Moon to the Opposition of Jupiter in the zodiac, Converse Direction.	32 19	33 10
Sun to the Body of mars in the Zodiac by Converse motion.	32 39	34 2

OR GENETHLIACAL ASTRONOMY.

	ARC.		TIME.	
THE DIRECTIONS CONTINUED.	D.	M.	YRS.	MO.
Sun to the Body of Mars in Mundo, Converse Direction	32	41	34	2
Moon to the Opposition of Jupiter in Mundo, Converse Direction.	32	44	34	3
Moon to the Sextile of Mercury in the Zodiac.	32	48	34	4
Ascendant to the Quintile of Saturn in Mundo.	32	56	34	6
Moon to the Parallel of Jupiter in the Zodiac.	33	5	34	8
Sun to the Sesquiquadrate of Saturn in Mundo, Converse Direction	33	34	35	2
Sun to the Sesquiquadrate of Jupiter in the Zodiac, by Converse Motion.	34	18	36	0
Moon to the Trine of Saturn in Mundo, Direct Direction.	34	37	36	4
Part of Fortune to the Semiquartile of Mercury in Mundo.	34	51	36	7
Ascendant to the Square of the Sun in Mundo.	35	0	36	9
Midheaven to the Opposition of the Sun in Mundo.	35	0	36	9
Moon to the Quintile of Mercury in Mundo, Direct Direction.	36	34	38	6
Sun to the Sesquiquadrate of Jupiter in Mundo, by Converse Motion.	36	54	38	10
Sun to the Parallel of Mars in Mundo, Converse Direction.	37	19	39	4
Sun to the Parallel of Mercury in Mundo, by the Rapt Motion.	38	37	40	9
Sun to the Semiquartile of Venus in the Zodiac	38	54	41	1
Midheaven to the Biquintile of the Moon in Mundo.	40	7	42	5
Sun to the Parallel of Mars in Mundo, Direct Direction.	41	32	43	11
Moon to the Body of Mercury in the Zodiac, Converse Motion.	41	46	44	2
Moon to the Body of Mercury in Mundo, Converse Direction	42	1	44	6
Ascendant to the Square of Mercury in Mundo.	42	13	44	8
Midheaven to the Opposition of Mercury in Mundo.	42	13	44	8
Moon to the Square of Venus in Mundo, Direct Direction.	42	59	45	6
Part of Fortune to the Quintile of the Moon in Mundo.	43	8	45	9
Sun to the Parallel of Jupiter in Mundo, by the Rapt Motion.	43	19	45	11
Sun to the Semiquartile of Mercury in the Zodiac, Converse Direction.	43	38	46	3
Part of Fortune to the Sesquiquadrate of Jupiter in Mundo.	44	9	46	10

N

CELESTIAL PHILOSOPHY,

THE DIRECTIONS CONTINUED.	ARC. D. M.	TIME. yrs. mo.
Ascendant to the Sextile of Mars in Mundo	14 13	16 11
Moon to her own Semiquartile in Mundo.	14 30	17 2
Sun to the Parallel of Saturn in Mundo, by the Rapt Motion.	14 48	17 6
Sun to the Quintile of Mars in the Zodiac.	14 53	17 7
Moon to the Parallel of Mars in Mundo, by the Rapt Motion.	15 16	18 0
Moon to the Parallel of Mercury in the Zodiac	15 45	18 6
Midheaven to the Lion's Heart.	15 45	18 6
Sun to the Parallel of the Moon in the Zodiac.	15 54	18 9
Ascendant to the Trine of the Moon in Mundo.	16 3	8 11
Moon to the Trine of Jupiter in the Zodiac.	16 25	19 4
Sun to the Sextile of Mars in Mundo, Direct Direction.	16 54	19 10
Part of Fortune to the Sesquiquadrate of Saturn in Mundo.	17 3	50 0
Moon to the Parallel of the Sun in the Zodiac	17 29	50 5
Sun to the Semiquartile of Venus in Mundo, Direct Direction	17 34	50 6
Sun to the Body of the Moon in Mundo, by Direct Motion	17 57	51 0

In taking a view of the Significators of Riches in the foregoing Geniture, we find strong, and powerful testimonies, which show a sufficient portion of Wealth.— The Lord of the second, is in his exaltation, angular, and applying by a Mundane sextile to the Cusp of the second, and its dispositor is in the Northern Angle, in his dignities, and in the Cardinal Sign Capricorn, disposed of by Saturn, ruler of the Imum Cœli, who is conjoined with Jupiter above the Earth, and free from all affliction; these positions, without the aid of other concurring testimonies, clearly denote a competent property, which the Native will enjoy, during the short period of Life.

I shall make a few observations on the Religion of this Native. The general significator of Piety, and Virtue, is Jupiter, who is Retrograde, in his detriment, and afflicted by the Body of the greater Malefic, who is also Retrograde, and afflicting the Ascendant. Mercury Lord of the Ninth, is combust of the Sun, in a violent sign, and his dispositor, as well as himself, are deprived of all their powerful Dignities; from which it is plain that the Religion of the Native is a deceitful, vain, and fanciful show, let the Native's pretensions in society be what they may; and as the Ascendant is afflicted by the Mundane square of Mars, united with the baneful rays of Saturn, and Mercury, they instil a considerable portion of pride and insolence into the Native's Mind, which is further proved by the ruler of the Ascendant applying to the Rapt Parallel of Mars, in the Radix; thus it becomes obvious, that such *feigned Religion* is a *something* that wants a name, set forth to *pick* the *pocket* of the *simple,* and to show the Native's *Vanity, Hypocrisy, Insincerity, Superstition and Folly,*

In this Geniture the Ascendant is the giver of Life, as all the Planets are under the Earth, except Saturn, and Jupiter, and neither of them can claim the Aphetical power; therefore the Eastern Horizon is the point which must be selected to determine the time of the Native's Death.

The ridiculous, vain, and romantic Hypothesis given by Mr. Wilson, who, in his DICTIONARY OF ERRORS AND CONTRADICTIONS, page 311, says, that both the Luminaries under the Earth, in the Nativity of Philip the 3rd were Hylegiacal, he also informs us, that the Moon on the Cusp of the third House, was Hyleg in the Nativity of the Child who was drowned, about the age of three years; these Genitures he has selected from Placidus, to prove his GROUNDLESS OPINION, that the Luminaries under the Earth are Hyleg in any Geniture, and he further observes, " nor will all the crude formal dogmas of Ptolemy persuade me to the contrary", but he has left the subject in *obscurity*, without any proofs whatsoever; then in page 308, he mentions the "foolish doctrine of Ptolemy', yet after all the *unbecoming insult* levelled against the *dumb ashes of the dead,* he has in page 159, (and in *direct contradiction* to his former assertions,) affirmed, that "amidst this vast heap of incongruities, I would advise the Student to confine himself chiefly to the Rules laid down by Ptolemy, which are by far the most rational."

The learned Cardan strictly adhered to the genuine principles of Ptolemy, and acknowledged that whenever he deviated from his Doctrine, he was placed in confusion, and error. The precepts delivered by Ptolemy, for selecting the Prorogator, which I have given in this work, are clearly illustrated by examples, and those who attend to their application, will soon discover the luminous Facts they unfold to the Students in this Science. Mr. Wilson is, I believe, the only Author, who has the *effrontery* to affirm, that the Luminaries, under the Earth, are Hylegiacal, contrary to the Rules of Ptolemy, and repugnant to Reason, and daily experience. I have made these remarks that the Student may not be led astray by those fanciful innovations, promulgated to DECEIVE, ANNOY, CONFOUND, AND MISLEAD all those who adhere to such FALSE, and delusive Notions. In the preceding Geniture, the Student may observe, that both the Luminaries are under the Earth, and at the Age of twenty one years and ten months, the

Sun was directed to the opposition of Saturn, followed by the Moon to the Square of Mars in Mundo, and also by his quartile in the Zodiac, which ought, (if the Luminaries under the Earth are Hylegiacal,) to have given dangerous Sicknesses, and misfortunes, but no such Events took place, as *he* then enjoyed a good state of Health. I could produce more than one hundred examples of a similar nature, to prove, that the Luminaries, when in a subterranean position, cannot possess the Aphetical power to destroy Life, even when they meet a train of violent Directions, except when the Lights are within the prescribed limits of the Eastern, and Western Horizon, by which they then claim the Hylegiacal Dignity.— But some will probably ask, if I allow the Directions of the Luminaries under the Earth, to the baneful configurations of the Malefics, to give dangerous Sicknesses, Accidents, and other misfortunes? I certainly admit that such Directions, when they shew their effects, will produce diseases, troubles, and Losses, &c. when the Malefics possess their *own Nature* in the places where those violent Directions finish their course; but when the reverse takes place, and the obnoxious rays of the Promittors become considerably diminished, by the Terms of the Benefics, & their directions, then their malignant power becomes weak, and unable to produce any serious injury to the Health, and affairs of the Native, so that in many cases they pass over, and cannot produce any visible effects whatsoever.

I have observed before that the Ascendant is the giver of Life in this Nativity, and therefore in few words I shall inform the Reader, that when that point of the Heavens is directed to the Sesquiquadrate of the Moon in Mundo, at the Age of thirty two years, and eight months, followed by the Mundane square of the Sun, Life will be destroyed, as there is then no benign assistance that can impede the violence of their Anaretical power, for I consider the Luminaries, and also the benevolent Planets in this Geniture to be *weak*, as well as those parts of the Heavens where they exercise their dominion over Life, but it is not from the

Effects of the above Directions *alone* that I award this Judgment, but from the combined power of other Motions, which not being remote, co-operate with the destructive positions, and directions of the Mortal Promittors from the Oriental Horizon, and Supreme Southern Angle. Now the Nature and quality of Death must be defined from the active power of those Directions that follow in the train, and as the Sun, and Mars, have considerable dominion in those places, it is certain that the dissolution of the Native will be occasioned by a violent Fever, with pains at the Heart, disorders in the Reins, and Mesentery, and as the Lungs will be considerably affected at the same time, it further shows, that the powerful Effects of such diseases, cannnot be alleviated in the least degree by the most judicious assistance of the Medical practitioner.

The following Nativity is that of Joseph Kent; this Child lived with his Parents, in the City of Lincoln, and on the twelfth of July, 1824, in consequence of his not returning home from school at the usual time in the Evening, his Relatives were alarmed for his safety, and applied to me, on the morning of the following day, requesting my Judgment, whether he was living, or dead; they informed me that he was born at Liverpool, on the 6th of June, 1817, at half past eleven at night, and further observed I might depend that the time of his Birth, was exact, being taken by his Father, (who is now living,) with the greatest care and attention; As soon as I had observed that the Effects of the mortal Directions to the true Hyleg were then in operation, and that all the secondary significators of Life were likewise afflicted, both by position, and Direction, without any relief from benefic irradiations, the giver of life being angular, in Pisces, a sign of the watery Trigon, with Saturn, & applying to the Body of that Malefic by a converse Motion, and also to the Zodiacal Parallel, and conjunction of Mars, by a direct Direction; I then delivered my Judgment, that the Child was drowned, and told those who applied to me on this melancholy occasion, that the River, which had been superficially examined, ought to be more diligently explored, which was accordingly done, and the Body was found near the Swivel Bridge, though all signs of Life had disappeared; these facts are well known to the Inhabitants of Lincoln. I have inserted this Nativity with the following directions, & judgment, which will doubtless be considered as an interesting Example, by all those who are seriously inclined to investigate, and prove the true principles of this Heavenly Science,

84   CELESTIAL PHILOSOPHY,

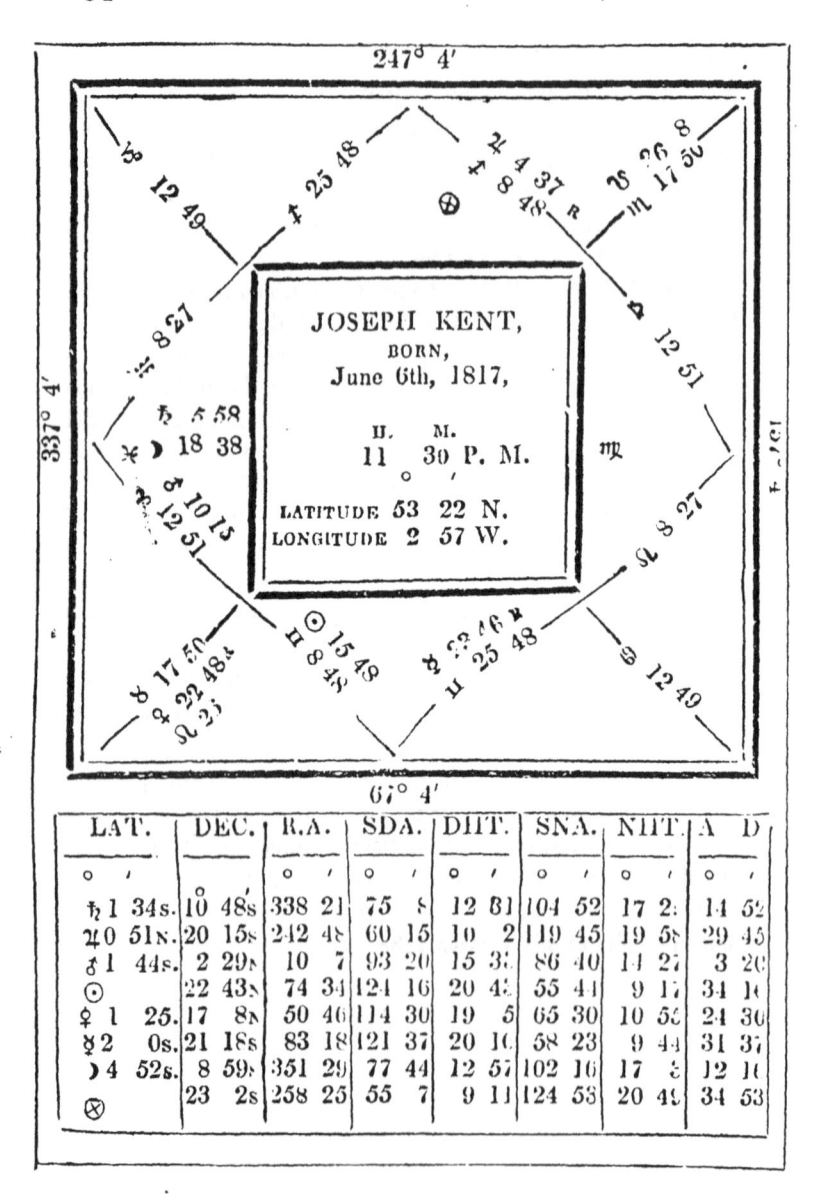

247° 4'

JOSEPH KENT,
BORN,
June 6th, 1817,

H.   M.
11   30 P. M.

LATITUDE 53 22 N.
LONGITUDE 2 57 W.

Chart positions:
- ♃ 25 48 ♐
- ♅ 12 49
- ♄ 4 37, ♀ 8 48 ℞
- ⊕
- ♑ 26 8, ♏ 17 50
- ♒ 8 27
- ♎ 12 51
- ♄ 5 52, ☽ 18 38 ♓
- ♏ 8 27
- ♂ 10 15, ♓ 12 51
- ♊ 15 48 ☉
- ♂ 22 46, ♊ 25 48 ☿
- ♂ 17 50, ♀ 22 48, ♌ 25
- ♍ 12 49

337° 4'   157° 4'
67° 4'

	LAT.	DEC.	R.A.	SDA.	DHT.	SNA.	NHT.	A D
	° '	° '	° '	° '	° '	° '	° '	° '
♄	1 34s.	10 48s	338 21	75 8	12 31	104 52	17 28	14 52
♃	0 51n.	20 15s	242 48	60 15	10 2	119 45	19 58	29 45
♂	1 44s.	2 29s	10 7	93 20	15 33	86 40	14 27	3 20
☉		22 43s	74 34	124 16	20 43	55 44	9 17	34 16
♀	1 25.	17 8s	50 46	114 30	19 5	65 30	10 55	24 30
☿	2 0s.	21 18s	83 18	121 37	20 16	58 23	9 44	31 37
☽	4 52s.	8 59s	351 29	77 44	12 57	102 16	17 3	12 16
⊕		23 2s	258 25	55 7	9 11	124 53	20 49	34 53

OR GENETHLIACAL ASTRONOMY.

A TABLE OF THE DIRECTIONS.

	ARC. D. M.	TIME. YRS. MO.
Moon to the Trine of Jupiter in Mundo, Direct Direction.	0 6	0 1
Sun to the Quintile of Mars in Mundo, Direct Directon.	0 43	0 9
Midheaven to the Trine of Mars in Mundo.	0 49	0 10
Sun to the Sextile of Mars in the Zodiac, by Converse Motion.	0 55	0 11
Moon to the Semiquartile of Venus in Mundo, Converse Direction.	0 59	1 0
Moon to the Square of Mercury in Mundo, Direct Motion.	1 0	1 0
Moon to the Sextile of Venus in the Zodiac.	1 59	2 0
Sun to the Square of Saturn in Mundo, Direct Direction.	2 1	2 0
Sun to the Square of Saturn in the Zodiac, by Converse Motion.	2 24	2 5
Moon to the Square of Mercury in the Zodiac.	2 27	2 5
Part of Fortune to the Sesquiquadrate of Venus in Mundo.	2 58	2 10
Sun to the Square of the Moon in the Zodiac.	3 8	3 0
Sun to the Parallel of Jupiter in Mundo, Converse Direction.	3 33	3 5
Sun to the Parallel of Jupiter in Mundo, Direct Direction.	3 50	3 8
Moon to the Quintile of the Sun in Mundo, by Direct Motion.	4 6	3 11
Part of Fortune to the Opposition of Mercury in Mundo.	4 12	4 0
Ascendant to the Sextile of Venus in Mundo.	5 32	5 4
Part of Fortune to the Square of the Moon in Mundo.	5 37	5 5
Moon to the Body of Saturn in the Zodiac, Converse Motion.	6 35	6 5
Moon to the Quintile of the Sun in the Zodiac.	6 55	6 9
Sun to the Sextile of Mars in Mundo, by Converse Direction.	6 58	6 10
Moon to the Parallel of Mars in the Zodiac.	6 59	6 10
Moon to the Body of Mars in Mundo, Direct Direction.	7 6	7 0
Sun to the Quintile of Mars in the Zodiac.	7 7	7 0
Moon to the Trine of Jupiter in the Zodiac.	7 16	7 2
Ascendant to the Square of the Sun in Mundo.	7 30	7 5
Midheaven to the Opposition of the Sun in Mundo.	7 30	7 5
Sun to the Semiquartile of Venus in Mundo, Direct Motion.	7 38	7 6
Sun to the Body of Mercury in Mundo, by Direct Direction.	8 22	8 1
Moon to the Semiquartile of Venus in the Zodiac.	8 41	8 5

CELESTIAL PHILOSOPHY,

THE DIRECTIONS CONTINUED.	ARC. D. M.	TIME YRS. MO.
Sun to the Body of Mercury in the Zodiac.	8 47	8 6
Moon to the Quintile of Venus in the Zodiac, Converse Motion.	8 52	8 7
Sun to the Semiquartile of Mars in the Zodiac, Converse Direction.	9 40	9 4
Moon to the Body of Mars in the Zodiac.	9 45	9 5
Midheaven to the Biquintile of Venus in Mundo.	9 54	9 7
Sun to the Quintile of Saturn in Mundo, by Converse Motion.	10 4	9 9
Moon to the Sesquiquadrate of Jupiter in Mundo, Direct Direction.	10 8	9 10
Moon to the Quintile of Mercury in the Zodiac.	10 26	10 2
Sun to the Quintile of Saturn in the Zodiac, Converse Direction.	10 43	10 5
Moon to the Body of Saturn in Mundo, by Converse Motion.	10 56	10 8
Sun to the Opposition of Jupiter in Mundo, Converse Direction.	11 27	11 1
Sun to the Opposition of Jupiter in the Zodiac, Converse Motion.	11 29	11 1
Moon to the Sextile of the Sun in Mundo, Direct Direction.	11 32	11 2
Moon to the Parallel of Mars in the Zodiac.	11 37	11 3
Sun to the Parallel of Mercury in Mundo, by the Rapt Motion.	11 46	11 5
Sun to the Biquintile of Jupiter in Mundo, Direct Direction.	11 46	11 5
Part of Fortune to the Square of Mars in Mundo.	11 52	11 6
Moon to the Sextile of the Sun in the Zodiac.	12 15	11 10
Moon to the Quintile of Mercury in Mundo, Direct Motion.	12 41	12 3
Sun to the Square of the Moon in Mundo, Direct Direction.	12 54	12 6
Part of Fortune to the Semiquartile of Jupiter in Mundo.	13 29	13 0
Moon to the Semiquartile of Mars in the Zodiac, Converse Motion.	13 36	13 1
Part of Fortune to the Trine of Venus in Mundo.	13 53	13 5
Moon to the Sesquiquadrate of Jupiter in the Zodiac.	13 59	13 6
Moon to the Semiquartile of Saturn in the Zodiac.	14 29	13 11
Moon to the Square of Jupiter in the Zodiac, Converse Direction.	14 35	14 0
Part of Fortune to the Quintile of Saturn in Mundo.	15 42	15 1

THE DIRECTIONS CONTINUED.	ARC. D. M.	TIME. YRS.MO.
Ascendant to the Trine of Jupiter in Mundo.	15 48	15 2
Moon to the Sextile of Mercury in the Zodiac	15 52	15 3
Ascendant to the Body of Saturn in Mundo.	16 9	15 6
Midheaven to the Square of Saturn in Mundo.	16 9	15 6
Moon to the Biquintile of Jupiter in Mundo Direct Motion.	16 9	15 6
Midheaven to the Opposition of Mercury in Mundo.	16 14	15 7
Ascendant to the Square of Mercury in Mundo.	16 14	15 7
Sun to the Semiquartile of Mars in Mundo. Converse Motion.	16 15	15 7
Sun to the Sextile of Saturn in the Zodiac, Converse Direction.	16 19	15 8
Ascendant to the Semiquartile of Venus in Mundo.	16 27	15 10
Sun to the Sextile of Saturn in Mundo, Converse Motion.	17 30	16 10
Sun to the Sesquiquadrate of Jupiter in Mundo, Direct Motion.	17 47	17 1
Moon to the Sextile of Venus in Mundo by Converse Direction.	18 2	17 4
Sun to the Square of Mars in Mundo, Direct Direction.	18 3	17 4
Moon to the Biquintile of Jupiter in the Zodiac.	18 5	17 5
Sun to the Sextile of Venus in Mundo, by Direct Motion.	18 33	17 11
Ascendant to the Quintile of the Sun in Mundo.	18 39	18 0
Part of Fortune to the Parallel of the Sun in Mundo.	18 58	18 4
Moon to the Semiquartile of the Sun in the Zodiac.	19 12	18 6
Sun to the Semiquartile of Mercury in Mundo, Converse Motion.	19 52	19 2
Moon to the Sextile of Mercury in Mundo, Direct Direction.	20 28	19 8
Moon to her own Semiquartile in the Zodiac.	20 34	19 9
Moon to the Parallel of Saturn in Mundo, by the Rapt Motion.	20 37	19 9
Moon to the Semiquartile of the Sun in Mundo, Direct Direction.	20 49	20 0

Those who will take the trouble to examine the Rules I have laid down in this work, relative to violent Deaths, and apply them in a proper manner in the Nativity of this Child, will immediately discover, that the obnoxious positions of the Celestial Bodies minutely correspond with the quality of the Native's dissolution. The Moon who claims the Aphetical power is posited between the Bodies of both the Malefics, in the Ascendant, in a Watery Sign, and in that station she is deprived of sufficient support from the Benefics, both of which are afflicted in their radical stations; the giver of Life is in square to the Sun, and Mercury in the Zodiac, and applying to the Mundane quartile of the Sun by Converse Motion, that Luminary being posited in the Northern Angle, among violent Stars, in which place he becomes configurated with Saturn, by a baneful square in the World. The Ascendant is also afflicted by the quartile of the Sun in Mundo, and the Part of Fortune is in opposition to the Sun and Mercury, and in mundane Square of the Moon, and Mars in the Nativity; thus we may clearly observe that both the Luminaries, the Ascendant, and Part of Fortune, are all afflicted in this Geniture, which forebode a sudden, and violent Death, by suffocation or drowning, which happened as I have before related.

This Child was drowned at the Age of seven years, one Month, and six days, and the Directions that destroyed Life, (which shewed their effects at the time of Death,) were the Moon Hyleg, to the Body of Saturn, by Converse Motion, and also the parallel Declination of Mars, and body of that Malefic in the Zodiac, and Mundo; those Directions, with all others may be seen in the preceding Table, and though the giver of Life applied to the sextile of Venus, and trine of Jupiter, yet those applications could not produce any important assistance, because both the benefics were afflicted in the Nativity; for Jupiter is retrograde, near the Heart of the Scorpion, in square of Saturn, and in mundane Parallel with the Sun, and applying to his opposition, Venus is also Retrograde, near the Pleiades, and in exact parallel with Mercury in Mundo, where she becomes posited in the terms of both the Enemies; thus we may observe that though the apparent benign rays of Jupiter and Venus could not preserve Life, neither by position, or direction, yet owing to their Motions the fury of the Mortal Directions to the Hyleg were retarded for a time in producing their Effects, which will always be found to occur, wherever such configurations are prevalent in any Geniture whatsoever.

By Secondary Motion the Sun was in conjunction with Mercury, and the Moon the giver of Life, had nearly arrived at the place of the Sun in the Nativity, and was applying to the Square of her radical position, and likewise to the rays of Mars, the chief mortal promittor in the Geniture, these obnoxious applications, compared with the violence of the Progression, considerably increase the baneful power of the Anaretical Directions to the Prorogator. In the Revolutional Figure for the seventh Year of the Native's age, the Moon was in a violent part of the Heavens, and separating from the opposite place of Mars in the Nativity; Jupiter was also in Square to the place of Mars, and that Malefic was applying to the opposition of his own radical station. Saturn and Venus were conjoined in a subterranean position, among violent fixed Stars; those Planets, with Mercury, having nearly the same Declination; all these testimonies fully corroborate the Mortal power of the primary Directions to the giver of Life, as well as the correctness of all the corresponding calculations. At the time he was drowned, the Sun, Jupiter, and Venus were in conjunction in the watery sign Cancer, and descended below the Western Horizon, with Castor, and Pollux; they were likewise in Square to Mars, who was separating from the Opposition of his place in the Nativity, and Saturn had then returned to the quartile of his own position at the time of birth. The giver of Life was also near the radical Horizon, afflicted by the baneful stations of the Enemies, at the time of his death.

Samuel Portwood was Born at Donington near Spalding, Lincolnshire, on the 5th of June 1790, 18ʜ. 55ᴍ. P. M. he was the Son of William Portwood, Farmer of that place. In the month of October 1821, this young Man (with whom I was well acquainted,) applied to me. and gave me the above time of his Birth, requesting me to calculate his Nativity, which I performed, and delivered the Figure, and Directions to him including my impartial Judgment thereon; he had a little knowledge of this Science, which he had obtained from my Books. and Papers, and appeared confident that the given time of his Birth was correct, of which I have no doubt, as the nature of the primary Directions is confirmed by the preceding events of his Life. He told me that he had gained considerably by *Land jobbing*, and was *very lucky*, though the Moon, and Saturn, in the Midheaven, he thought, *should* have given something *far different*, according to the Works of all those Authors he had read on this Science; he further observed with a smile, that the evil conjunction of the Moon, and Saturn in the Zenith, could do him *no harm*, because by their different Latitude, they were far distant from each other, and Jupiter was posited in the second House, with the Lion's Heart; I told him that all his observations were founded on error, as other Astral Causes of a different nature, were the Auxiliaries of his success, which would continue but a *short time*, when *Land jobbing*, and Life would be no more, for I never knew the least portion of *durable good* to flow from a *Treasury of evil*; I also informed him that though he had many Books, Papers, and documents of *mine* in his possession, which I expected he would peruse to the time of his Death, yet there was one that surpassed all others, on which the following words were written.—"*Prepare to meet thy God, for soon thou shalt surely Die.*"

I quickly discovered that my admonitions were but little regarded, I then told him he was not aware that the Moon was Hyleg, or giver of Life, and would encounter those terrible Anaretical Directions in the Summer of 1824, which would cut off Life, to which he replied, that as the Birth was by Day, the Sun, he believed was the true Prorogator, because he was posited in the Eleventh House; I informed him that according to the Sun's *position*, he certainly was *not qualified* to claim the Aphetical power, which a short time would prove, because that Luminary had not arrived at that part of the Eleventh, where he claims his full, and perfect Hylegiacal Dignity; I further observed that there were other arguments to prove, that the Sun could not be the Prorogator, for if that had been the case, his Direction to the squares of the Moon, and Saturn in the Zodiac, united with the Sextile of Mars, in Signs of long Ascensions, followed by the body of Mercury, and all in Cardinal Signs, would have destroyed Life several Years ago, instead of which, those Directions when they shewed their effects, produced only a dangerous fall from a Cart, with a few bruises, including troubles at the same time. The Figure of Birth with the Directions follow, according to true Astronomical Calculation.

92 CELESTIAL PHILOSOPHY,

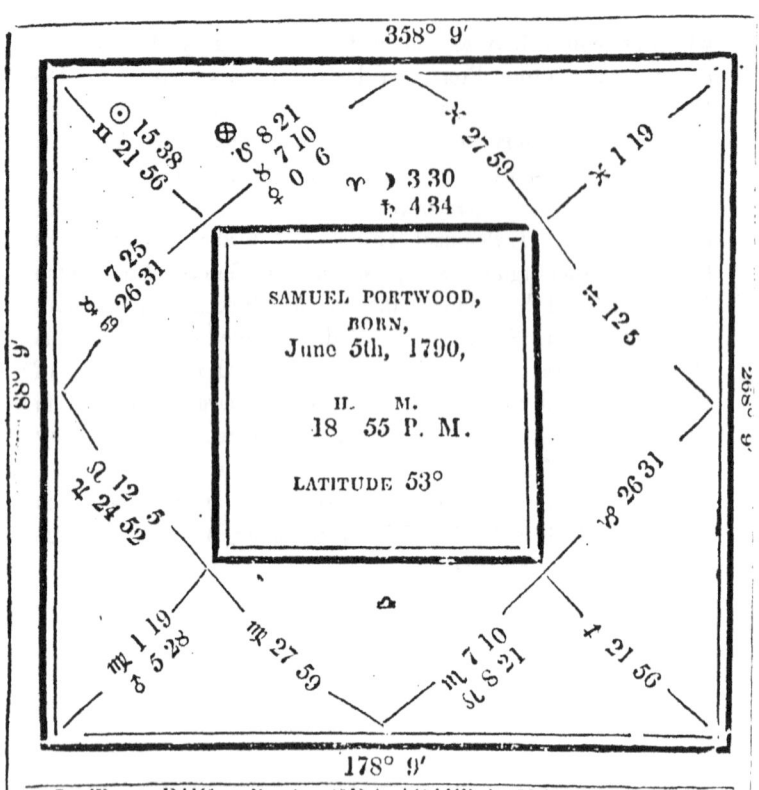

SAMUEL PORTWOOD,
BORN,
June 5th, 1790,

H. M.
18 55 P. M.

LATITUDE 53°

358° 9' (top)
178° 9' (bottom)

☉ 15 38 ♊ 21 56
⊕ 8 21 ☿ 7 10 ☿ 0 6
♈ ☽ 3 30
♄ 4 34
♓ 27 59
♓ 1 19
♉ 7 25 ♉ 26 31
♒ 1 25
♒ 26 31
♌ 12 5 ♃ 24 52
♏ 1 19 ♀ 5 28
♍ 27 59
♏ 7 10 ♐ 8 21
♐ 21 56

	LAT.	DEC.	R. A.	SDA.	DHT.	SNA.	NHT.	A. D.
	° ′	° ′	° ′	° ′	° ′	° ′	° ′	° ′
♄	2 14s.	0 14s.	5 4	89 41	14 57	90 19	15 3	0 19
♃	1 3n.	14 13n.	147 32	109 39	18 16	70 21	11 44	19 39
♂	1 10n.	10 37n.	157 44	104 24	17 24	75 36	12 36	14 24
☉		22 41n.	74 24	123 41	20 37	56 19	9 23	33 41
♀	2 26s.	9 15n.	28 52	102 29	17 5	77 31	12 55	12 29
☿	0 26n.	23 41n.	98 7	125 36	20 56	54 24	9 4	35 36
☽	3 4n.	4 13n.	2 0	95 37	15 56	84 25	14 4	5 37
⊕		16 55n.	44 27	113 48	18 58	66 12	11 2	23 48

OR GENETHLIACAL ASTRONOMY. 93

	ARC.	TIME.
A TABLE OF THE DIRECTIONS:	D. M.	YRS. MO.
Moon to the Quintile of the Sun in the Zodiac	0 8	0 2
Sun to the Quintile of Saturn in the Zodiac	0 53	0 10
Moon to the Body of Saturn in the Zodiac	0 59	0 11
Moon to the Sesquiquadrate of Jupiter in Mundo, Direct Direction	1 42	1 7
Moon to the Biquintile of Jupiter in the Zodiac, by Converse Motion	3 7	3 0
Moon to the Body of Saturn in Mundo, Direct Direction	3 18	3 2
Sun to the Quintile of Jupiter in the Zodiac, Converse Direction	3 29	3 4
Moon to the Square of Mercury in the Zodiac	3 39	3 6
Midheaven to the Body of the Moon in Mundo	3 51	3 8
Ascendant to the Square of the Moon in Mundo	3 51	3 8
Moon to the Quintile of Mercury in Mundo, Converse Motion	4 15	4 1
Ascendant to the Semiquartile of Jupiter in Mundo	4 32	4 4
Ascendant to the Sextile of Mars in Mundo	4 47	4 7
Sun to the Semiquartile of Saturn in Mundo, Converse Direction	4 53	4 8
Moon to the Parallel of Saturn in Mundo, by the Rapt Motion	5 26	5 3
Moon to the Sesquiquadrate of Jupiter in the Zodiac	5 55	5 9
Sun to the Square of Jupiter in Mundo, by Converse Motion	6 27	6 2
Moon to the Biquintile of Mars in Mundo, Direct Direction	6 46	6 6
Midheaven to the Body of Saturn in Mundo	6 55	6 8
Ascendant to the Square of Saturn in Mundo	6 55	6 8
Moon to the biquintile of Jupiter in Mundo converse direction	7 15	7 0
Moon to the Biquintile of Mars in the Zodiac	7 25	7 2
Sun to the Quintile of Mars in the Zodiac	7 49	7 7
Sun to the Square of Mars in Mundo, Direct Direction	8 35	8 3
Sun to the Sextile of the Moon in Mundo, Direct Direction	8 39	8 4
Sun to the Sextile of Saturn in the Zodiac, Converse Motion	8 51	8 6
Sun to the Sextile of Jupiter in the Zodiac	9 17	8 11
Moon to the Semiquartile of the Sun in Mundo, Direct Direction	9 26	9 1
Midheaven to the Biquintile of Mars in Mundo	9 49	9 6
Ascendant to the Quintile of Venus in Mundo	10 13	9 10
Sun to the Quintile of Jupiter in Mundo, Direct Direction	10 25	10 0
Moon to the Parallel of Saturn in Mundo, by Direct Motion	10 32	10 1
Sun to the Square of Mars in the Zodiac, Converse Direction	10 54	10 6
Moon to the Sextile of Mercury in Mundo, Direct Direction	11 10	10 9
Part of Fortune to the Square of Jupiter in Mundo	11 13	10 10
Moon to the Parallel of Saturn in Mundo, Converse Motion	11 13	10 10

P

CELESTIAL PHILOSOPHY,

THE DIRECTIONS CONTINUED.	ARC. D. M.	TIME. Yrs.Mo.
Moon to the Sextile of the Sun in the Zodiac.	11 21	10 11
Sun to the Sextile of Saturn in Mundo, Direct Direction.	11 25	11 0
Part of Fortune to the Semiquartile of the Moon in Mundo.	12 56	12 5
Moon to the Trine of Jupiter in Mundo, Direct Direction.	13 26	12 11
Moon to the Sesquiquadrate of Mars in Mundo, by Direct Motion.	14 20	13 9
Ascendant to the Semiquartile of the Sun in Mundo.	14 24	13 10
Sun to the Sextile of Venus in the Zodiac.	14 51	14 4
Moon to the Parallel of Venus in the Zodiac.	14 54	14 5
Part of Fortune to the Semiquartile of Saturn in Mundo.	15 27	14 10
Moon to the Semiquartile of Venus in the Zodiac, Converse Direction.	15 34	14 11
Moon to the Sesquiquadrate of Mars in the Zodiac.	15 56	15 1
Midheaven to the Sextile of Mercury in Mundo.	16 14	15 7
Midheaven to the Trine of Jupiter in Mundo.	16 16	15 7
Moon to the Parallel of Venus in Mundo, by the Rapt Motion.	16 49	16 1
Ascendant to the Semiquartile of Mars in Mundo.	17 23	16 8
Sun to the Square of the Moon in the Zodiac.	18 38	17 11
Sun to the Semiquartile of Venus in Mundo, Direct Direction.	18 47	18 1
Moon to the Parallel of Mars in the Zodiac.	19 27	18 8
Sun to the Sextile of Jupiter in Mundo, Direct Direction.	19 48	19 0
Sun to the Square of Saturn in the Zodiac.	19 50	19 0
Moon to the Trine of Jupiter in the Zodiac.	20 9	19 5
Moon to the Quintile of Mercury in the Zodiac.	20 42	19 11
Sun to the Sextile of Mars in the Zodiac.	20 50	20 0
Sun to the Quintile of the Moon in Mundo, Direct Motion.	21 24	20 7
Sun to the Body of Mercury in Mundo, Direct Direction.	22 33	21 8
Sun to the Semiquartile of Saturn in the Zodiac, Converse Motion.	22 34	21 8
Moon to the Semiquartile of Venus in Mundo, Converse Direction.	23 0	22 1
Sun to the Body of Mercury in the Zodiac.	23 4	22 2
Moon to the square of Mercury in Mundo, Converse Motion	23 22	22 5
Sun to the Quintile of Saturn in Mundo, Direct Direction.	23 22	22 5
Sun to the Quintile of Mars in Mundo, Direct Direction.	23 42	22 9
Sun to the Square of Jupiter in the Zodiac, Converse Motion.	24 26	23 7
Part of Fortune to the Square of Mars in Mundo,	24 34	23 8
Moon to the Body of Venus in the Zodiac.	25 12	24 4
Part of Fortune to the Quintile of Jupiter in Mundo	25 17	24 5
Moon to the Semiquartile of the Sun in the Zodiac.	25 45	24 11

THE DIRECTIONS CONTINUED.

	ARC. D. M.	TIME. YIS. M.
Sun to the Semiquartile of Jupiter in the Zodiac........	25 53	25 0
Part of Fortune to the Body of the Sun in Mundo........	26 9	25 2
Moon to the Body of Venus in Mundo, Direct Direction.	26 35	25 7
Moon to the Trine of Mars in Mundo, by Direct Motion.	26 56	25 11
Sun to the Trine of Mars in Mundo, Converse Direction...	27 11	26 2
Sun to the Quintile of Venus in the Zodiac.............	28 30	27 6
Part of Fortune to the Sextile of the Moon in Mundo,....	28 52	27 10
Moon to the Sextile of Venus in the Zodiac, Converse Direction..	29 4	28 0
Moon to the Opposition of Mars in Mundo, Converse Motion	29 40	28 7
Sun to the Semiquartile of Mercury in the Zodiac, Converse Direction..................................	29 50	28 9
Moon to the Opposition of Mars in the Zodiac, Converse Direction..................................	29 55	28 10
Midheaven to the Trine of Mars in Mundo.............	29 59	28 11
Part of Fortune to the Sextile of Saturn in Mundo.......	30 24	29 4
Moon to the Trine of Mars in the Zodiac................	30 33	29 6
Midheaven to the Body of Venus in Mundo..	30 43	29 8
Ascendant to the Square of Venus in Mundo...........	30 43	29 8
Sun to his own Parallel in the Zodiac.................	31 12	30 2
Sun to the Semiquartile of Jupiter in Mundo, Direct Motion...	31 32	30 6
Moon to the Semiquartile of Mercury in Mundo, Direct Direction..	32 6	31 0
Moon to the Sextile of Mercury in the Zodiac..........	32 27	31 4
Moon to the Parallel of Venus in Mundo, by Converse Motion...	32 30	31 4
Moon to the Trine of Mercury in the Zodiac, Converse Direction..	32 44	31 7
Moon to the Parallel of Jupiter in the Zodiac...........	32 44	31 7
Sun to the Sextile of Mars in Mundo, Direct Direction...	33 47	32 7
Part of Fortune to the Sextile of Jupiter in Mundo......	34 41	33 6
Moon to the Parallel of Venus in Mundo, Direct Motion	34 51	33 8
Ascendant to the Sextile of the Sun in Mundo...........	35 1	33 10
Moon to the Parallel of the Sun in Mundo, by the Rapt Motion..	35 25	34 3
Ascendant to the Trine of the Moon in Mundo.........	35 43	34 6
Sun to the Sextile of Venus in Mundo, Direct Direction...	35 52	34 7
Sun to the Parallel of Saturn in Mundo, by the Rapt Motion..	36 4	34 9
Ascendant to the Trine of Saturn in Mundo.............	36 49	35 7

CELESTIAL PHILOSOPHY.

THE DIRECTIONS CONTINUED.	ARC. D. M.	TIME. YRS. MO.
Moon to the Square of Jupiter in Mundo, Direct Direction.	36 54	35 8
Ascendant to the Semiquartile of Mercury in Mundo.	37 10	36 0
Sun to the Semiquartile of Mars in the Zodiac.	38 35	37 4
Moon to the Sextile of Venus in Mundo, Converse Motion.	38 56	37 8
Sun to the Body of Venus in Mundo, Converse Direction.	39 11	37 11
Sun to the Body of Venus in the Zodiac, Converse Motion.	39 34	38 3
Sun to the Semiquartile of Mercury in Mundo, Converse Direction.	39 39	38 4
Part of Fortune to the Quintile of Mars in Mundo.	39 41	38 4
Ascendant to the Body of Jupiter in Mundo.	39 44	38 5
Midheaven to the Square of Jupiter in Mundo.	39 44	38 5
Moon to the Semiquartile of Saturn in the Zodiac, Converse Motion.	40 23	39 1
Part of Fortune to the Semiquartile of Venus in Mundo.	40 28	39 2
Moon to the Square of the Sun in Mundo, Converse Direction.	40 31	39 3
Moon to the Quintile of Venus in the Zodiac, Converse Motion.	40 37	39 4
Sun to the Square of Saturn in Mundo, Direct Direction.	41 19	40 0
Part of Fortune to the Quintile of the Moon in Mundo.	41 37	40 4
Part of Fortune to the Quintile of Saturn in Mundo.	42 22	41 1
Sun to the Trine of Mars in the Zodiac, Converse Direction.	42 50	41 6
Moon to her own Semiquartile in the Zodiac.	43 32	42 3
Moon to the Semiquartile of Saturn in Mundo, Converse Motion.	44 17	43 0
Moon to the Semiquartile of Saturn in the Zodiac.	44 37	43 4
Moon to the Opposition of Jupiter in the Zodiac, Converse Direction.	44 58	43 8
Moon to the Parallel of Mercury in Mundo, by the Rapt Motion.	45 23	44 1
Moon to the Opposition of Jupiter in Mundo, Converse Direction.	45 30	44 2
Sun to the Semiquartile of Mars in Mundo, Direct Direction.	46 23	45 1
Moon to the Semiquartile of Mercury in the Zodiac.	47 33	46 3

This Native lived at Donington, where he was Born, and for some years previous to his Death, was a writer to Benjamin Smith, an Attorney at Law, at Horbling, near Folkingham, Lincolnshire. Those who view the malignant conjunction of the Moon, and Saturn in the Zenith, in Square to Mercury, in Cardinal Signs, will instantly discover circumstances of a most *remarkable Nature*. When in Health, he witnessed the *destruction* of the *Foes* of a *certain individual*; he was *cut down* in the early part of Life like a *Flower of the Field*, according to the Judgment I had given three Years prior to his demise, the truth of which can at any time be proved; but though he had obtained MY DOCUMENTS which showed that the *King of Terrors*, was nearly at the Door of his dwelling, to execute his final summons, yet he would not be convinced that the Moon was Hyleg, he therefore paid but little attention to my Judgment, strictly, and absurdly depending on the Sun as the right prorogator, which he vainly believed, promised him Health, and old Age, though that Luminary was certainly the chief mortal Promittor in the Radix, and thus instead of producing long Life to the Native, he ushered in Death at a period but little thought of, and by no means expected, according to all human appearance. Several *unbelievers* in this Science whose true Nativities I have in my Possession, and who are yet living near the same place, must with their Offspring, suffer severe calamities, and in a *few Years*, " pass that Bourn from whence no Travellers return", leaving their SANGUINE DEEDS to be had in remembrance, by Generations yet unborn.

Both the Luminaries, and Ascendant are afflicted in the Radix, and the Stars that assume the Dominion of the Lights, and Eastern Horizon, are not Dignified, so that they were unable to produce any *durable* Prosperity, what they give by the impotence of their power, show Life, and every object however desirable, to be of short duration, and had not the ruler of the Part of Fortune been strong, and beheld by Jupiter with other benign testimonies, the Native would have been involved in great troubles, and misfortunes;

the weakness of the Moon the giver of Life, and her affliction without Auxiliaries, convinced me, that when that Luminary was directed to the Rapt Parallel of the Sun, followed by his Mundane Square, Converse Motion, with the other vital significators afflicted at the same time by Malefic Directions, the Native would exchange this mortal Life, for a state of immortality, the truth of which was verified, for though the Directions of Jupiter, and Venus are conjoined, yet they could not save, owing to the Terms of the Enemies being united near the Anaretical places; it must also be further observed, that when the Moon was directed to the mundane Square of Jupiter, and also to the Parallels of Venus in Mundo, by Direct, and Converse Motion, their apparent benign power became null, and void, because they were both afflicted by the same Directions of Saturn in the World, and by Mars also in the subsequent Motions. THIS EXAMPLE, (which I have handed down to posterity, with others, for the Instruction of the Students in this Sublime Science,) clearly prove, that it is the true Prorogator alone, that must be strictly attended to in all cases of Life and Death. The Native died on the 16th of October. 1824; Aged thirty four Years, four months, and ten days.

By Secondary Direction, the significators of Life, and Death were violently disposed, which may be seen by comparing them with the mortal Directions that were in action at the time of dissolution. The Progression also corresponded with the Effects of the hostile Motions, and concurring Declinations, and Terms; the Moon separated from the quartile of Mars, and applied to the Body of Mercury, and also to the Square of Saturn from Cardinal Signs, by the other subsequent stations; thus by the preceding applications, Mars had returned to the place of the moderator in the Nativity, and both the Luminaries were also in obnoxious places without any relief from benevolent applications, either in the Zodiac, or in the World. The Revolutional Figure for his thirty fourth Year was violent, the Sun being within the Orbs of a conjunction with Saturn, and that Malefic was among violent stars conjoined with Venus; the Moon the giver of Life was afflicted by the body of Mars, and had returned to the opposition of her own Radical place, Saturn, Venus, and Mercury having the same declination, and Mars was at the same time posited in the Nadir, in opposition to the place of the Prorogator at the time of Birth, and was also in Mundane Square to the Radical Ascendant.

A short time after I had Calculated the Geniture of this Native, he requested me to make a few observations on the Nativity of his Daughter, Melicent, who is now living at Donington, I therefore complied with his request; he told me that the time of her Birth was carefully taken by himself, and might be depended on as correct; he also said that I was welcome to make what remarks I thought proper upon it, for the benefit of the Science, but owing to his engagements, he had but little time to apply himself to the Study of its principles; he requested me *repeatedly*, to be as particular as possible in my calculations, relative to the length of Life, for it appeared to him that both the Luminaries contended for the Aphetical Dominion, which is by no means the case, for as the Birth is diurnal, the Sun being in an Hylegiacal station is certainly the legal, and true Prorogator, and supporter of Life, until his power becomes destroyed by the mortal union, and Directions of the Anaretical Promittors without assistance, which will appear evident from the following display of the Celestial Bodies at the time of Birth, united with the Tabulated Arcs of Directions.

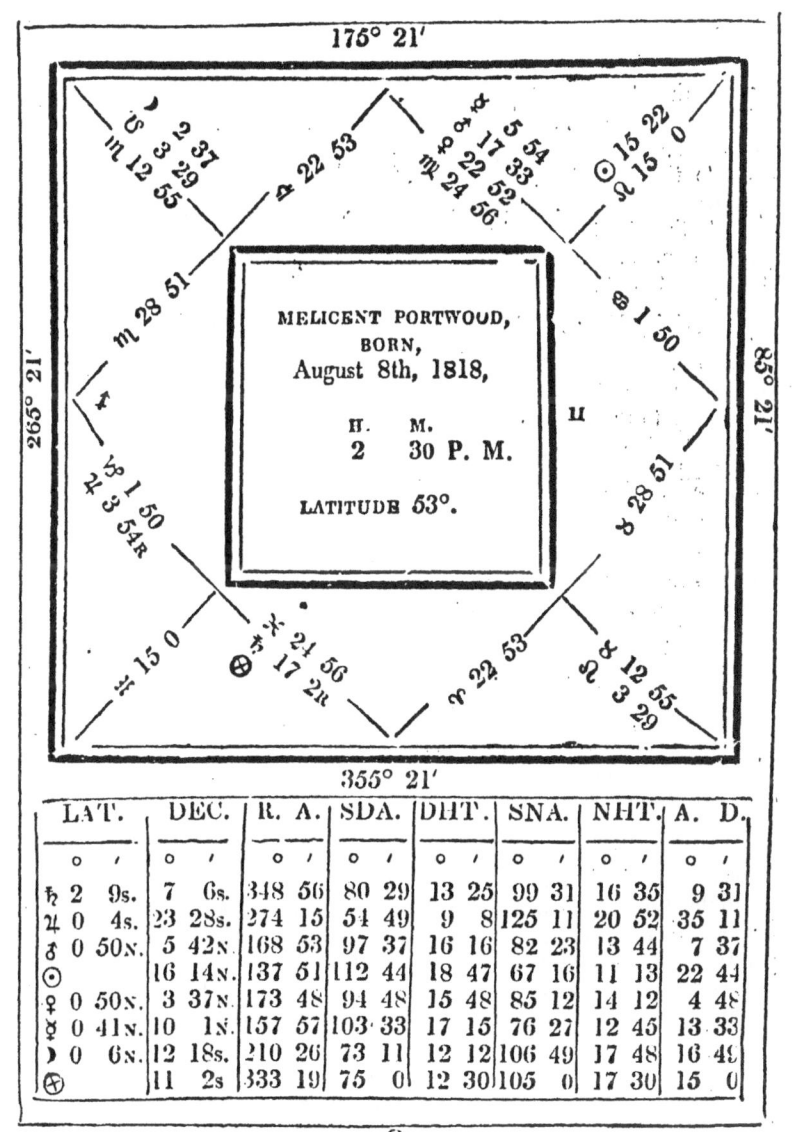

CELESTIAL PHILOSOPHY. 101

175° 21'

☽ ♌ 2 37
♏ 12 55 3 29
♎ 22 53
♏ 28 51

♂ ☿ ♍ 5 54
17 33
22 52
24 56

☉ 15 22
♌ 15 0

⊕ 1 50

MELICENT PORTWOOD,
BORN,
August 8th, 1818,

H. M.
2 30 P. M.

LATITUDE 53°.

♃

♐
♑ 1 50
2 3 54 R

♒ 15 0

⊕ ♓ 21 56
17 2 R

♈ 22 53

♉ 28 51

♉ 12 55
3 29

265° 21'

85° 21'

355° 21'

	LAT.	DEC.	R. A.	SDA.	DHT.	SNA.	NHT.	A. D.
	° ′	° ′	° ′	° ′	° ′	° ′	° ′	° ′
♄	2 9s.	7 6s.	348 56	80 29	13 25	99 31	16 35	9 31
♃	0 4s.	23 28s.	274 15	54 49	9 8	125 11	20 52	35 11
♂	0 50n.	5 42n.	168 53	97 37	16 16	82 23	13 44	7 37
☉		16 14n.	137 51	112 44	18 47	67 16	11 13	22 44
♀	0 50n.	3 37n.	173 48	94 48	15 48	85 12	14 12	4 48
☿	0 41n.	10 1n.	157 57	103 33	17 15	76 27	12 45	13 33
☽	0 6n.	12 18s.	210 26	73 11	12 12	106 49	17 48	16 49
⊕		11 2s	333 19	75 0	12 30	105 0	17 30	15 0

Q

A TABLE OF THE DIRECTIONS.

Direction	ARC. D. M.	TIME Yrs. Mo.
Moon to the Semiquartile of Mars in the Zodiac, Converse Direction.	0 4	0 1
Ascendant to the Trine of the Sun in Mundo.	0 6	0 1
Moon to the Sesquiquadrate of Saturn in the Zodiac, Converse Motion.	0 25	0 5
Moon to the Semiquartile of Venus in Mundo, Direct Direction.	0 25	0 5
Sun to the Quintile of the Moon in Mundo, by Direct Motion.	0 51	0 11
Part of Fortune to the Trine of the Moon in Mundo.	1 29	1 6
Moon to the Sextile of Jupiter in the Zodiac.	1 35	1 7
Moon to the Sextile of Mercury in Mundo, Direct Direction	2 3	2 2
Midheaven to the Trine of Jupiter in Mundo.	2 21	2 6
Sun to the Biquintile of Saturn in the Zodiac, Converse Direction.	2 49	3 0
Sun to the Sesquiquadrate of Jupiter in the Zodiac.	2 59	3 2
Moon to the Sesquiquadrate of Saturn in Mundo, by Converse Motion.	3 13	3 4
Moon to the Semiquartile of Mars in Mundo, Converse Direction.	3 20	3 5
Moon to the Sextile of Mercury in the Zodiac.	4 1	4 3
Part of Fortune to the Opposition of Mercury in Mundo.	4 9	4 5
Sun to the Quintile of the Moon in the Zodiac.	4 25	4 8
Sun to the Biquintile of Jupiter in the Zodiac, Converse Direction.	5 34	5 10
Moon to the Semiquartile of Venus in the Zodiac.	6 24	6 9
Sun to the Semiquartile of Venus in the Zodiac, by Converse Motion.	6 28	6 10
Part of Fortune to the Semiquartile of Jupiter in Mundo.	7 30	7 11
Moon to the Biquintile of Saturn in the Zodiac, Converse Direction.	8 25	8 11
Moon to the Quintile of Jupiter in Mundo, Direct Direction.	9 7	9 9
Moon to the Semiquartile of Mercury in the Zodiac, Converse Motion.	9 16	9 11
Moon to the Square of Jupiter in Mundo, Converse Direction.	9 19	9 11
Sun to the Lion's Heart in the Zodiac.	9 53	10 6
Sun to the Parallel of the Moon in the Zodiac.	10 8	10 9
Sun to the Biquintile of Jupiter in Mundo, Direct Direction	10 35	11 2
Sun to the Sextile of the Moon in Mundo, by Direct Motion.	10 37	11 2

THE DIRECTIONS CONTINUED.	ARC. D. M.	TIME. Yrs. Mo.
Ascendant to the Sextile of the Moon in Mundo..........	10 41	11 3
Sun to the Sesquiquadrate of Saturn in the Zodiac, Converse Direction..	10 46	11 4
Moon to the Semiquartile of Mercury in Mundo, Converse Motion.......................................	10 48	11 5
Sun to the Semiquartile of Mars in the Zodiac, by Converse Direction...................................	10 56	11 7
Moon to the Quintile of Jupiter in the Zodiac, Converse Direction..	1 0	11 8
Moon to the Parallel of the Sun in the Zodiac........	11 50	12 6
Moon to the Sextile of Mars in Mundo, by Direct Motion.	11 50	12 6
Moon to the Trine of Saturn in Mundo, Direct Direction.	12 15	13 0
Moon to the Parallel of Mercury in Mundo, by the Rapt Motion...	13 21	14 3
Ascendant to the Quintile of Saturn in Mundo..........	13 30	14 5
Part of Fortune to the Sesquiquadrate of the Moon in Mundo...	13 41	14 7
Part of Fortune to the opposition of Mars in Mundo.....	13 50	14 9
Sun to the Sextile of the Moon in the Zodiac..........	14 4	15 0
Part of Fortune to the Body of Saturn in Mundo.........	14 16	15 3
Sun to the Biquintile of Saturn in Mundo, by Converse Motion...	14 53	15 11
Sun to the Trine of Jupiter in the Zodiac............	15 2	16 1
Sun to the Parallel of Mercury in the Zodiac..........	15 11	16 3
Moon to the Square of the Sun in the Zodiac.........	15 45	16 10
Moon to the Quintile of Mercury in Mundo, Direct Direction..	15 51	16 11
Moon to the Sextile of Venus in Mundo, by Direct Motion.	16 13	17 4
Sun to the Body of Mercury in the Zodiac............	16 37	17 9
Sun to the Body of Mercury in Mundo, Direct Direction.	17 3	18 3
Ascendant to the Trine of Mercury in Mundo..........	17 9	18 4
Moon to the Parallel of Mars in Mundo, by the Rapt Motion...	17 17	18 6
Moon to the Parallel of Saturn in Mundo, by the Rapt Motion...	17 30	18 9
Moon to the Trine of Saturn in the Zodiac............	17 50	19 1
Part of Fortune to the Opposition of Venus in Mundo...	18 9	19 5
Moon to the Sextile of Mars in the Zodiac............	18 28	19 9
Ascendant to the Sesquiquadrate of the Sun in Mundo...	18 53	20 2
Moon to the Quintile of Mercury in the Zodiac........	18 54	20 2

	ARC.		TIME.	
THE DIRECTIONS CONTINUED.	D.	M.	YRS.	MO.
Moon to the Parallel of Venus in Mundo, by the Rapt Motion.	19	7	20	6
Part of Fortune to the Parallel of the Moon in Mundo.	19	43	21	2
Sun to the Semiquartile of Mercury in the Zodiac, Converse Direction.	20	1	21	6
Moon to the Semiquartile of Jupiter in the Zodiac.	20	9	21	8
Sun to the Sextile of Venus in the Zodiac, Converse Direction.	20	11	21	8
Ascendant to the Quintile of the Moon in Mundo.	20	27	21	11
Sun to the Semiquartile of Venus in Mundo, by Converse Motion.	20	41	22	3
Part of Fortune to the Biquintile of the Moon in Mundo.	21	0	22	6
Moon to the square of the Sun in Mundo, Direct Direction	21	13	22	9
Sun to the Parallel of Saturn in the Zodiac.	21	15	22	10
Moon to the Parallel of Mercury in Mundo, Converse Direction.	22	47	24	6
Sun to the Semiquartile of the Moon in Mundo, Direct Motion.	22	49	24	6
Sun to the Sesquiquadrate of Jupiter in Mundo, Direct Direction.	23	6	24	9
Midheaven to Spica Virginis in Mundo.	23	31	25	5
Sun to the Parallel of Mars in the Zodiac.	23	59	25	11
Sun to the Trine of Saturn in the Zodiac, Converse Motion	24	5	26	0
Sun to the Sextile of Mars in the Zodiac, Converse Direction.	24	14	26	2
Moon to the Quintile of Mars in Mundo, Direct Direction	24	51	26	10
Sun to the Opposition of Saturn in the Zodiac.	25	5	27	1
Moon to the Sextile of Venus in the Zodiac	25	9	27	2
Sun to the Body of Mars in the Zodiac.	25	27	27	6
Sun to the Semiquartile of the Moon in the Zodiac.	25	30	27	7
Moon to the Sextile of Jupiter in Mundo, Direct Direction.	25	49	27	11
Sun to the Body of Mars in Mundo, Direct Direction.	26	0	28	1
Ascendant to the Trine of Mars in Mundo.	26	5	28	2
Sun to the Sesquiquadrate of Saturn in Mundo, Converse Motion.	26	9	28	3
Sun to the Semiquartile of Mars in Mundo, Converse Direction.	26	21	28	6
Sun to the Opposition of Saturn in Mundo, Direct Motion.	26	41	28	10
Moon to the square of Jupiter in the Zodiac, Converse Direction.	26	45	28	11
Ascendant to the Sextile of Saturn in Mundo.	26	46	28	11

CELESTIAL PHILOSOPHY,

THE DIRECTIONS CONTINUED.

	ARC. D. M.	TIME YRS. MO.
Sun to the Parallel of Venus in the Zodiac	27 56	30 3
Part of Fortune to the Sextile of Jupiter in Mundo	28 22	30 8
Moon to the Quintile of Venus in Mundo, by Direct Motion	28 51	31 2
Sun to the Body of Venus in the Zodiac	29 25	31 10
Sun to the Body of Venus in Mundo, Direct Direction	29 58	32 4
Ascendant to the Trine of Venus in Mundo	30 3	32 5
Ascendant to the Biquintile of the Sun in Mundo	30 9	32 6
Moon to the Parallel of Mars in Mundo, Converse Direction	30 14	32 7
Moon to the Parallel of Saturn in Mundo, by Converse Motion	30 22	32 9
Sun to the Quintile of Venus in the Zodiac Converse Direction	31 20	34 0
Moon to the Parallel of Mercury in Mundo, Direct Motion	32 12	34 11
Sun to the Sextile of Mercury in the Zodiac, Converse Direction	32 28	35 2
Moon to the Quintile of Mars in the Zodiac	33 33	36 6
Moon to the Trine of Jupiter in Mundo, Converse Motion	33 43	36 8
Moon to the Parallel of Venus in Mundo, Converse Direction	33 53	36 10
Ascendant to the Sesquiquadrate of Mercury in Mundo	34 24	37 5
Sun to his own Semiquartile in the Zodiac	34 58	38 0
Sun to the Quintile of Mars in the Zodiac, Converse Direction	35 4	38 2
Midheaven to the Body of the Moon in Mundo	35 5	38 2
Ascendant to the Square of the Moon in Mundo	35 5	38 2
Sun to the Opposition of Jupiter in Mundo, Converse Motion	35 33	38 8
Sun to the Opposition of Jupiter in the Zodiac, Converse Direction	35 51	39 1
Moon to the Body of Venus in Mundo, by Converse Motion	36 17	39 6
Moon to the Square of Mercury in Mundo, Direct Direction	36 33	39 9
Moon to her own semiquartile in Mundo	36 35	39 9

This Native's Father, as I have said before, had a little knowledge of this Science; and as he had previously investigated the Geniture of his Daughter, by position, (not being able to compute Directions,) there is no doubt that he observed the Moon was posited in that part of the Heavens, which would have qualified her to receive the Prorogatory Dignity, if the Sun had been posited at a more remote distance from the Zenith; for if the time of Birth had been twenty-five minutes later, then it is certain that the Moon would become the giver of Life, and that no Directions, however Malefic to the Sun, could produce dissolution, though their Effects would be attended with dangerous consequences; these considerations induced him to be more urgent to receive my Judgment; I told him that as he wished to have the Directions computed with accuracy and precision, he might depend that my exertions should be used to give him satisfaction, respecting the length of Life in particular, which *he received from me*, and which he appeared remarkably *anxious* to ascertain.

The distance of the Moon from the Meridian, is 35° 5', and her Semidiurnal Arc, 73° 11', consequently her distance from the Oriental Horizon, becomes 38° 6', these numbers produce her distance from the Eleventh, 10° 41', and her true Polar Elevation 32° 43', under which her Oblique Ascension is 218° 29', these distances manifestly show, that though the Moon is in an Aphetical position, yet according to the given time of Birth, no Malefic Directions to that Luminary can produce Death.

That the Sun is the true Prorogator, or giver of Life in this Nativity, does not admit of any doubt whatever; therefore it is from his Directional Motion, that the length of Life must be ascertained; his true distance from the Zenith, is 37° 30', and his distance from the West, 75° 14', which give his Pole of Position 24°, and his Oblique Descension, 145° 18'. Now the first Direction that the Hyleg meets with, that will *put Life in danger*, is the Parallel of Saturn's Declination, which the Sun encounters in 11° 58' of Virgo, the Oblique Descension of that point, under the Sun's circle of position, is 166° 33', from that sum the Sun's Oblique Descension under his own Pole being subtracted, the Arc of Direction will be 21° 15'; by the same method, the Sun to the zodiacal Parallel of Mars, opposition of Saturn, Body of Mars, Semiquartile of the Moon, with the zodiacal Parallel, and Body of Venus, may be easily, and correctly computed, without much trouble, or difficulty; for by turning to the Tables at the end of this Work, and taking out the proper numbers, and using them according to the given precepts, the Directions will then be immediately discovered, not by *chance*, or any *juggling Art*, but by the true, and unerring principles of the Noble, and incomparable Science of Astronomy.

From the Nature and Effects of those violent primary Directions to the Prorogator before mentioned, united with the powerful secondary Motions, &c., it is evident that they will produce (by their furious velocity,) THE GREATEST DANGERS TO THE NATIVE'S LIFE which human aid cannot prevent, at the Age of twenty-five, Years, and eleven Months; there are also other Malefic Directions, that will be in operation to the Hyleg, upwards of two years prior to the above period, which will increase the power of the baneful applications in those Terms, and parts of the Heavens, where the Progressive Directions correspond.

Objection. You inform us in your Work, that the Directions of Jupiter, and Venus, when they are joined in a violent train to the giver of Life, will impede the fury of the evil Effects portended; how is it then that you do not notice the *power* of Venus in this Nativity, she being in conjunction with Mars, and Opposition of Saturn at the time of Birth, and as her parallel of Declination, and conjunction to the Hyleg follow in Directional Motion, why ought she not to dissolve some part of the evil, and save the Native from those *dangers to Life*, which you have so *positively predicted?*

Answer. I do affirm that the Directions of Jupiter, and Venus, will certainly impede the power of a violent train of Directions to the giver of Life, *in any Nativity*, when they are *strong, free from affliction*, and joined with them, either in the *Zodiac*, or in *Mundo*, but though these are my rules, which will not deceive the practitioner, yet from the same precepts sufficient is recorded to prove, that when the Benefics are unable to produce assistance, in consequence of their impotence, and affliction in the Radix, or in those places where the Directions fall, they then show the *nature, and quality of the disease, or Death*, which is frequently of a violent nature; therefore in this Geniture, though Venus is joined in the train with Saturn, and Mars, and is also afflicted by both the Malefics by position, and near violent fixed Stars, she is qualified to produce a considerable portion of Evil, for being overcome by the Enemies, she will protract the nature of the calamity, and produce diseases of the *Liver*, &c, and *injury by Medicine*; so that she cannot sufficiently counteract the impending violence of the dreadful train to the giver of Life.

I have omitted some observations on the Effects of several Directions that come up at an earlier period in Life, some of which will give injury to Health, but as I do not see any thing remarkable in the Figure, I have not noticed those subjects that appear to be of little advantage to the improvement of the Students in this Science.

As a further proof of the Truth of these Astronomical Calculations, I now lay before the public, the Nativity of Mr. Richard White, Hair-Dresser, who resided in Lincoln. On Monday the 8th of September, 1817, he requested me to Calculate his Nativity, which I undertook to convince him of the Truth of this venerable Study, being at the same time *aware*, that no Man was a greater *enemy* to this Science than himself, neither could any persons pass more *scurrilous reflections*, and *unbecoming Language* on the power of the Celestial Hosts, than himself, and his Relatives. The time of his birth, which he delivered to me from an indisputable document, was April 25th, 1792, 3H. 45M. A M.   My previous Judgment on the period of his demise, was truly verified, which is well known to the Public.

> By PROOFS like these, this Noble Science show,
> The FATE of ev'ry Mortal here below;
> *Those Starry Infidels, puff'd up with pride,*
> If they would suffer TRUTH to be their guide,
> They then by *Sacred thought*, would keep in view,
> The *solemn time*, when they must bid adieu
> To *Mortal objects*, with all *Terrene things*,
> AND VIEW THE GLORY OF THE KING OF KINGS.

110   CELESTIAL PHILOSOPHY,

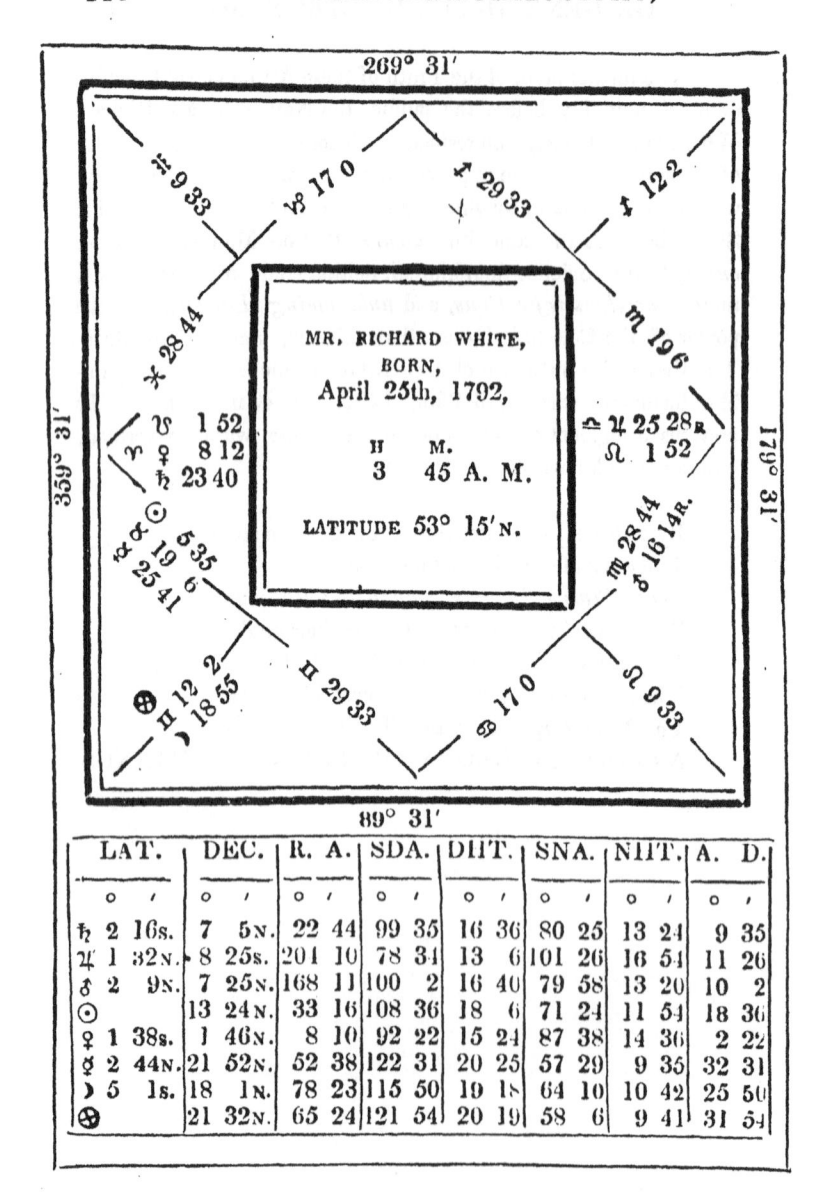

```
                269° 31'
         ♒ 9 33   ♑ 17 0   ♐ 29 33   ♐ 12 2
      ♓ 28 44                              ♏ 1 9 6

   ♈ 1 52                                 ♎ 25 28 ℞
   ♀ 8 12         MR. RICHARD WHITE,      ♌ 1 52
   ♄ 23 40              BORN,
359° 31'          April 25th, 1792,              179° 31'
   ♉ ☉                  H.  M.
     19 6               3   45 A. M.      ♏ 28 44
     25 41                                ♐ 16 14 ℞
                 LATITUDE 53° 15' N.
   ⊕ ♊ 12 2
     ☽ 18 55    ♊ 29 33   ♋ 17 0   ♌ 9 33
                 89° 31'
```

	LAT.	DEC.	R. A.	SDA.	DHT.	SNA.	NHT.	A. D.
	° ′	° ′	° ′	° ′	° ′	° ′	° ′	° ′
♄	2 16s.	7 5n.	22 44	99 35	16 36	80 25	13 24	9 35
♃	1 32n.	8 25s.	201 10	78 34	13 6	101 26	16 54	11 26
♂	2 9n.	7 25n.	168 11	100 2	16 40	79 58	13 20	10 2
☉		13 24n.	33 16	108 36	18 6	71 24	11 54	18 36
♀	1 38s.	1 46n.	8 10	92 22	15 24	87 38	14 36	2 22
☿	2 44n.	21 52n.	52 38	122 31	20 25	57 29	9 35	32 31
☽	5 1s.	18 1n.	78 23	115 50	19 18	64 10	10 42	25 50
⊕		21 32n.	65 24	121 54	20 19	58 6	9 41	31 54

OR GENETHLIACAL ASTRONOMY. 111

A TABLE OF THE DIRECTIONS.	ARC. D. M.	TIME. Yrs. Mo.
Moon to the Trine of Jupiter in Mundo, Direct Direction..................................	0 41	0 9
Moon to the Sextile of Saturn in Mundo, Direct Direction..................................	0 49	0 10
Moon to the Quintile of Venus in the Zodiac.........	1 21	1 6
Midheaven to the Trine of Mercury in Mundo.......	1 26	1 7
Ascendant to the Quintile of the Moon in Mundo......	1 42	1 10
Moon to the Semiquartile of the Sun in the Zodiac.....	1 45	1 10
Sun to the Biquintile of Mars in the Zodiac, Converse Motion..................................	1 50	1 11
Moon to the Semiquartile of Mercury in Mundo, Direct Direction..................................	1 51	1 11
Sun to the Body of Saturn in Mundo, Converse Motion.	3 3	3 3
Sun to the Body of Saturn in the Zodiac, Converse Direction..................................	3 6	3 3
Sun to the Opposition of Jupiter in Mundo, Converse Motion..................................	3 9	3 4
Sun to the Opposition of Jupiter in the Zodiac, Converse Direction..................................	3 11	3 4
Moon to the Sextile of the Sun in Mundo, by Direct Motion..................................	3 46	3 11
Moon to the Sesquiquadrate of Jupiter in the Zodiac, Converse Direction..................................	3 55	4 1
Moon to the Sextile of Venus in the Zodiac, Converse Motion..................................	4 40	4 11
Moon to the Sextile of Saturn in the Zodiac..........	4 56	5 2
Moon to the Semiquartile of Saturn in the Zodiac, Converse Direction..................................	5 25	5 8
Moon to the Sextile of Venus in Mundo, by Converse Motion..................................	5 38	5 11
Ascendant to the Body of Venus in Mundo..........	6 17	6 7
Midheaven to the Square of Venus in Mundo.........	6 17	6 7
Sun to the Trine of Mars in the Zodiac.............	6 33	6 10
Moon to the Trine of Jupiter in the Zodiac...........	6 48	7 1
Sun to the Semiquartile of the Moon in Mundo, Direct Motion..................................	7 20	7 8
Sun to the Parallel of Mars in Mundo, by the Rapt Motion..................................	7 22	7 8
Sun to the Body of Mercury in Mundo, Direct Direction..................................	8 24	8 10

THE DIRECTIONS CONTINUED.	ARC. D. M.	TIME. YRS. MO.
Moon to the Biquintile of Jupiter in the Zodiac, Converse Motion	8 51	9 4
Moon to the Trine of Mars in the Zodiac, Converse Direction	8 59	9 5
Sun to the Parallel of the Moon in the Zodiac	9 41	10 2
Sun to the Body of Venus in the Zodiac, Converse Motion	9 57	10 5
Sun to the Body of Venus in Mundo, Converse Direction	10 2	10 6
Moon to the Semiquartile of Saturn in Mundo, Converse Motion	10 4	10 6
Moon to the Sesquiquadrate of Jupiter in Mundo, Converse Direction	10 9	10 7
Ascendant to the Sextile of the Moon in Mundo	10 14	10 8
Sun to the Semiquartile of Venus in the Zodiac	11 15	11 9
Moon to the Trine of Mars in Mundo, Converse Motion	11 17	11 9
Sun to the Parallel of Venus in Mundo, by the Rapt Motion	11 17	11 9
Moon to the Sextile of Mercury in Mundo, Direct Direction	11 26	11 11
Moon to the Semiquartile of Venus in the Zodiac, Converse Motion	11 32	12 0
Moon to the Square of Mars in Mundo, Direct Direction	12 35	13 2
Sun to the Body of Mercury in the Zodiac	13 2	13 7
Ascendant to the Opposition of Jupiter in Mundo	13 13	13 9
Midheaven to the Square of Jupiter in Mundo	13 13	13 9
Ascendant to the Body of Saturn in Mundo	13 38	14 2
Midheaven to the Square of Saturn in Mundo	13 38	14 2
Sun to the Biquintile of Mars in Mundo, Direct Direction	13 42	14 3
Sun to the Pleiades in the Zodiac	13 45	14 3
Part of Fortune to the Sextile of Venus in Mundo	13 47	14 4
Sun to the Parallel of Mars in Mundo, Converse Motion	13 59	14 7
Sun to the Parallel of Jupiter in Mundo, by the Rapt Motion	14 21	15 0
Midheaven to the Biquintile of the Moon in Mundo	14 31	15 2
Sun to the Parallel of Saturn in Mundo, by the Rapt Motion	14 31	15 2

OR GENETHLIACAL ASTRONOMY.

	ARC.		TIME.	
THE DIRECTIONS CONTINUED.	D.	M.	Yrs.	Mo.
Moon to the Sesquiquadrate of Mars in the Zodiac, Converse Direction..................................	15	5	15	8
Ascendant to the Body of the Sun in Mundo..........	15	9	15	9
Midheaven to the Square of the Sun in Mundo........	15	9	15	9
Part of Fortune to the Body of the Moon in Mundo..	15	27	16	0
Sun to the Parallel of Mars in Mundo, Direct Motion...	15	40	16	3
Part of Fortune to the Semiquartile of Mercury in Mundo	15	41	16	3
Moon to the Quintile of Mars in the Zodiac...........	16	1	16	8
Moon to the Semiquartile of Venus in Mundo Converse Motion.................................	16	20	17	0
Sun to the Opposition of Mars in Mundo, Converse Direction.................................	16	55	17	7
Sun to the Opposition of Mars in the Zodiac, Converse Motion.................................	17	6	17	9
Sun to the Biquintile of Jupiter in the Zodiac........	17	22	18	0
Moon to the Sextile of the Sun in the Zodiac..........	17	27	18	1
Ascendant to the Pleiades in Mundo..................	17	30	18	2
Moon to the Quintile of Saturn in the zodiac.........	17	31	18	2
Moon to her own Parallel in the Zodiac..............	17	55	18	7
Sun to the Parallel of Mercury in Mundo, by the Rapt Motion.................................	18	43	19	5
Moon to the Biquintile of Mars in the Zodiac, Converse Direction.................................	19	18	20	0
Moon to the Square of Venus in the Zodiac...........	20	12	20	11
Ascendant to the Body of Mercury in Mundo........	20	36	21	4
Midheaven to the Square of Mercury in Mundo........	20	36	21	4
Ascendant to the Semiquartile of the Moon in Mundo..	20	56	21	8
Part of Fortune to the Trine of Jupiter in Mundo......	21	27	22	2
Sun to the Sesquiquadrate of Mars in Mundo, Direct Motion.................................	21	42	22	5
Part of Fortune to the Sextile of Saturn in Mundo..	21	43	22	5
Moon to the Sesquiquadrate of Mars in Mundo, Converse Direction.................................	21	59	22	8
Sun to Aldebaran in the Zodiac....................	22	4	22	9
Moon to the Square of Venus in Mundo, by Direct Motion.................................	22	21	23	0
Moon to the Semiquartile of Mercury in the Zodiac....	22	50	23	6
Sun to the Sextile of Venus in the Zodiac...........	22	50	23	6
Sun to the Parallel of Venus in Mundo, Converse Motion.................................	22	56	23	7

CELESTIAL PHILOSOPHY.

	ARC.		TIME.	
THE DIRECTIONS CONTINUED.	D.	M.	YRS.	MO.
Sun to the Semiquartile of Saturn in the Zodiac	23	15	24	0
Sun to the Parallel of Mercury in the Zodiac	23	49	24	7
Part of Fortune to the Sextile of the Sun in Mundo	23	58	24	9
Midheaven to the Quintile of Venus in Mundo	24	46	25	6
Sun to the Sesquiquadrate of Jupiter in the Zodiac	24	48	25	6
Moon to the Body of Mercury in the Zodiac, Converse Motion	25	9	25	10
Midheaven to the Trine of Mars in Mundo	25	20	26	0
Sun to the Semiquartile of Mercury in the Zodiac, Converse Direction	25	42	26	4
Sun to the Parallel of Venus in Mundo, Direct Motion	25	53	26	6
Part of Fortune to the Quintile of Venus in Mundo	26	6	26	10
Sun to the Biquintile of Jupiter in the Zodiac, Converse Motion	28	18	29	0
Moon to the Biquintile of Mars in Mundo, by Converse Direction	28	24	29	1
Moon to the Quintile of Mars in Mundo, Direct Motion	28	35	29	3
Moon to Sextile of Mars in the Zodiac	28	46	29	5
Moon to the Parallel of Mars in Mundo, by the Rapt Motion	28	50	29	6
Sun to the Square of Mars in the Zodiac	29	59	30	8
Moon to the Body of Mercury in Mundo, Converse Motion	30	2	30	8
Moon to the Quintile of the Sun in the Zodiac	30	11	30	10
Part of Fortune to the Sextile of Mercury in Mundo	30	33	31	2
Sun to the Semiquartile of Mercury in Mundo, Converse Motion	30	33	31	2
Ascendant to the Biquintile of Mars in Mundo	30	40	31	3
Moon to the Square of Jupiter in Mundo, Direct Direction	30	51	31	5
Moon to the Square of Saturn in Mundo, Direct Motion	30	58	31	6
Midheaven to the Trine of the Moon in Mundo	31	38	32	3
Part of Fortune to the Square of Mars in Mundo	31	50	32	5
Moon to her own Semiquartile in Mundo	32	5	32	8
Sun to the Biquintile of Jupiter in Mundo, Direct Motion,	32	16	32	10
Sun to the Body of the Moon in the Zodiac	32	34	33	2
Sun to the Semiquartile of Venus in Mundo, Direct Direction	32	53	33	6
Sun to the Parallel of Jupiter in Mundo, Converse motion,	33	24	34	1
Midheaven to the Quintile of Saturn in Mundo	33	32	34	3
Sun to the Parallel of Saturn in Mundo, Converse Direction	33	34	34	3
Sun to the Quintile of Venus in the Zodiac	33	48	34	6

OR GENETHLIACAL ASTRONOMY.

THE DIRECTIONS CONTINUED.	ARC. D. M.	TIME. YRS. MO.
Moon to the Parallel of Venus in mundo, by the Rapt motion	33 52	34 6
Moon to the square of the Sun in Mundo, Direct Direction	34 3	34 8
Sun to his own Semiquartile in the Zodiac	34 10	34 9
Sun to the Parallel of Jupiter in Mundo, Direct Motion	34 44	35 4
Sun to the Parallel of Saturn in Mundo, Direct Direction	34 46	35 4
Part of Fortune to the Quintile of Saturn in Mundo	35 0	35 7
Sun to the Trine of Mars in Mundo, Direct Motion	35 2	35 7
Moon to the Opposition of Jupiter in the Zodiac, Converse Direction	35 45	36 4
Sun to the Semiquartile of Saturn in the Zodiac, Converse Motion	36 32	37 2
Sun to the Sesquiquadrate of Jupiter in the Zodiac, Converse Direction	36 38	37 3
Moon to the Square of Saturn in the Zodiac	36 40	37 3
Midheaven to the Quintile of the Sun in Mundo	36 52	37 6
Moon to the Body of Saturn in the Zodiac, Converse Motion	36 52	37 6
Midheaven to the Sextile of Venus in Mundo	37 5	37 8
Sun to the Sextile of Saturn in the Zodiac	37 16	37 10
Moon to the Parallel of Saturn in Mundo, by the Rapt motion,	37 35	38 2
Moon to the Parallel of Jupiter in mundo, by the Rapt motion.	37 36	38 2
Part of Fortune to the Quintile of the Sun in mundo	38 27	39 0
Moon to the Square of Jupiter in the Zodiac	38 36	39 2
Ascendant to the Sesquiquadrate of mars in mundo	38 40	39 3
Moon to the Sextile of mercury in the zodiac	38 49	39 4
Sun to the Parallel of the moon in mundo, by the Rapt motion.	38 58	39 6
Sun to the Trine of Jupiter in the zodiac	39 7	39 8
Moon to the Sextile of mars in mundo, Direct Direction	39 15	39 10
Sun to the Body of the moon in mundo, Direct motion	39 25	40 0
Sun to the Biquintile of Jupiter in mundo Converse Direction.	40 20	40 10
Moon to the Body of Venus in the zodiac, Converse motion	40 26	40 11
Sun to the Sextile of mercury in the zodiac, Converse Direction.	41 47	42 3
Moon to the Square of mercury in mundo, Direct Direction.	41 55	42 5
Moon to the Body of Saturn in mundo, Converse motion	42 9	42 7

	ARC.	TIME.
THE DIRECTIONS CONTINUED.	D. M.	YRS. MO.
Moon to the Opposition of Jupiter in mundo, Converse Direction.	42 15	12 8
Sun to the Semiquartile of Saturn in mundo, Direct Direction.	42 18	42 9
Sun to the Sesquiquadrate of Jupiter in mundo, Direct motion....................	42 24	42 10
Moon to her own Sextile in mundo..................	42 48	13 3
Ascendant to Aldebaran in mundo..................	44 6	44 5
Part of Fortune to the Square of Venus in mundo.......	44 35	44 11
Moon to the Semiquartile of mars in the zodiac.........	44 44	15 1

When this Native was sixteen Years of Age, he suffered severely by a violent nervous Fever, which continued almost two Months, during which time he was not expected to survive; the Directions of the Ascendant to the Body of the Sun, and the Hyleg to the Mundane Parallel of Mars, by Direct Motion, then shewed their Effects; for if the distance of Mars with his Latitude from the Nadir, be subtracted from his Seminocturnal Arc, his true distance from the Western Horizon, below the Earth, will be 1° 18', so that by these numbers, the Parallel of Mars, by the Motion of the Primum Mobile, may soon be discovered, and computed; the above Directions were preceded by the Sun to the Parallel of Mars in Mundo, Converse Direction, and the Rapt Parallel of Saturn, the superior Malefic being conjoined with the giver of Life in the Eastern angle, at the time of Birth.

At the Age of twenty-one Years, and a half, the Native entered into Business for himself, and was successful in his Profession, according to his station in Life; he also entered into the state of Matrimony near the same time; the Directions then in operation were the Ascendant to the Body of Mercury, the Part of Fortune to the Trine of Jupiter, the Sun to the Sextile of Venus in the Zodiac, and her Parallel in Mundo, by Converse Motion, all of which are benevolent, and agree with those Events; but the influence of the subsequent Directions was retarded, owing to the impotence of the Promittors in the Figure, and the depression of the Pole of the Sun in those places, and Terms, where both the Malefics, (by the frigidity of their nocturnal applications,) project their beams with increased power to the significators; it is necessary that these things should be properly considered, and understood by all Students in this incomparable Science, as the acceleration of the Effects of all Directions in the Zodiac, and Mundo, with their retardation, &c., chiefly depend on those Motions, and Terms, with which they continue in Direction, by their stations, and applications through all parts of the Heavens.

As soon as I had observed those Directions above, with their corresponding Effects, I then computed the time when the Native's Death might be expected, but in pointing out that solemn period, my Judgment was traduced, by the *hardened Infidel,* the *censorious Critic,* and the *Vulgar.* The Sun is the giver of Life, and as the position is weak, and both the Benefics, Ascendant, and Luminaries are all afflicted in the Geniture, I judged that at the Age of thirty-three Years, the Native would depart this Life, as the Hyleg was then directed to the Body of the Moon, Mundane Parallel of Saturn by Converse Direction, and also to the square of the Moon in Mundo, by Converse Motion, succeeded by the Apheta to his own Semiquartile in the Zodiac, and Parallel of Saturn in the World, by Direct Direction, and likewise to the Moon's Parallel in Mundo, by the Rapt Motion, these were the principal Directions that caused his Death, according to the Judgment I publicly delivered seven Years before his demise, the truth of which can at any time be proved; he died on the 18th of April, 1825, at Noon, aged thirty-three Years nearly.

I have now stated the Mortal Directions to the Hyleg which cut off Life, and whenever similar Anaretical Directions are observed in other Nativities to the Moderators, without sufficient assistance, they will not fail to destroy. The Hyleg was directed to the Quartile of Mars in the Zodiac, at the Age of thirty Years, and eight Months, the Effects of which could not produce any sudden, or serious injury to the Native's Life, owing to the powerful Terms of Jupiter, and Venus, in which that Direction completed its course; but as it was near the beginning of the deadly train, it caused a slow Fever, with a gradual diminution of strength, until the Apheta arrived at the Body of the Moon, and though the Directions of Jupiter were united to the giver of Life, yet they could not save, for as he was in the Western Angle at the time of Birth, and afflicted by the Opposition of Saturn, he shewed a *diseased Viscera* by position, and that an inflamation, and decay of the Lungs, (being that part which Jupiter governs,) would be the cause of the Native's Death.

Those who think proper to examine all the Primary Motions &c., and compare them with each other, will find that they display their baneful influence in producing dissolution; for when the Polar Elevations of the significators, and Promittors are considered, with their augmented strength as they ascend the superior Angles, it is evident that a sufficient portion of benign aid could not be received by the giver of Life, in his nocturnal station. The Secondary Directions were also of a violent nature, as well as the positions of the principal rulers in his last Revolution. At the time he died, there was a New Moon in the Zenith, on the place of Saturn in the Nativity, Venus was in conjunction with that Malefic, and Mars was on the radical place of the Sun, the giver of Life.

The next Geniture is that of Mary Dickinson, this young Woman lived in the service of Mr. Nathan Clayton, owner of one of the Steam Packets in the City of Lincoln. On the fifth of August, 1822, she, (in company with some of her Female Friends,) came to my House, and requested me to answer a few questions on her Nativity, she produced the correct time of her Birth, and observed, that she did not place confidence in such things, as she had never known any *proof* to give satisfaction; she asked me if I could inform her of the time of her Marriage, and whether she was likely to live happy in that state, to which I answered, that I was confident she would never enter into the Matrimonial Union; she said she was sorry that I should give such false Judgment, as she expected to Marry in the ensuing Spring; my reply was, that I had substantial reasons, (though they were of an *important and delicate nature,*) to prove the truth of my affirmation, which in a few Months would be verified; as she was anxious to know what my *delicate reasons* were, which caused me to withhold the principal part of my Judgment, I then informed her that *something* of an *awful nature* would occur, before the Month of March, then next ensuing, which would destroy Life. As soon as I had mentioned these things, including my reasons for giving this Judgment, she *laughed immoderately*, and said, she placed no confidence in my observations; I told her it was with *deep regret* that I beheld the *terrific Astral Causes* in her Geniture, the *Effects* of which were fast approaching, but none of my admonitions had any influence on her Mind; I endeavoured in vain, to inform her, that "HEAVEN IS THE BOOK OF GOD," in which we may clearly read the DIVINE ORDINANCES of the MOST HIGH; she said she believed that all things in the Science were *guessed at*, and if they happened right, it was all by *chance*; but before she left me she said in a *jocular way*, that as I had given my Judgment on the shortness of her Life, (if she thought proper to believe it,) she wished to be informed of the quality of Death; I told her it appeared to me, that *Drowning* would be the cause of her dissolution, at which she *laughed*, and said, that was impossible, for though Mr. Clayton, (with whom she had lived several Years,) had a Steam Packet, yet as she did not go on Board, she considered herself perfectly safe from any danger of that nature; her remarks were such as excited *pity*, rather than contempt; she then left me, and I saw her no more, though I sent some of her Friends about a fortnight afterward, to admonish her of the *formidable* danger approaching, but she treated them with derision, and endeavoured to depreciate my previous Judgment. As she had engaged to go to a Village near Boston, she went on Board the Packet, and in the act of leaning over the side of the Vessel, she was precipitated into the River, near the town of Bardney, and when taken out, Life was extinct; her Death happened on the 7th of January, 1823, at half past eleven o'Clock in the Morning, Aged twenty-four Years, eleven Months, and six days. The awful Figure of the Heavens, at the true time of her Birth, including the Directions, and Judgment, I have inserted in the following order.

122   CELESTIAL PHILOSOPHY,

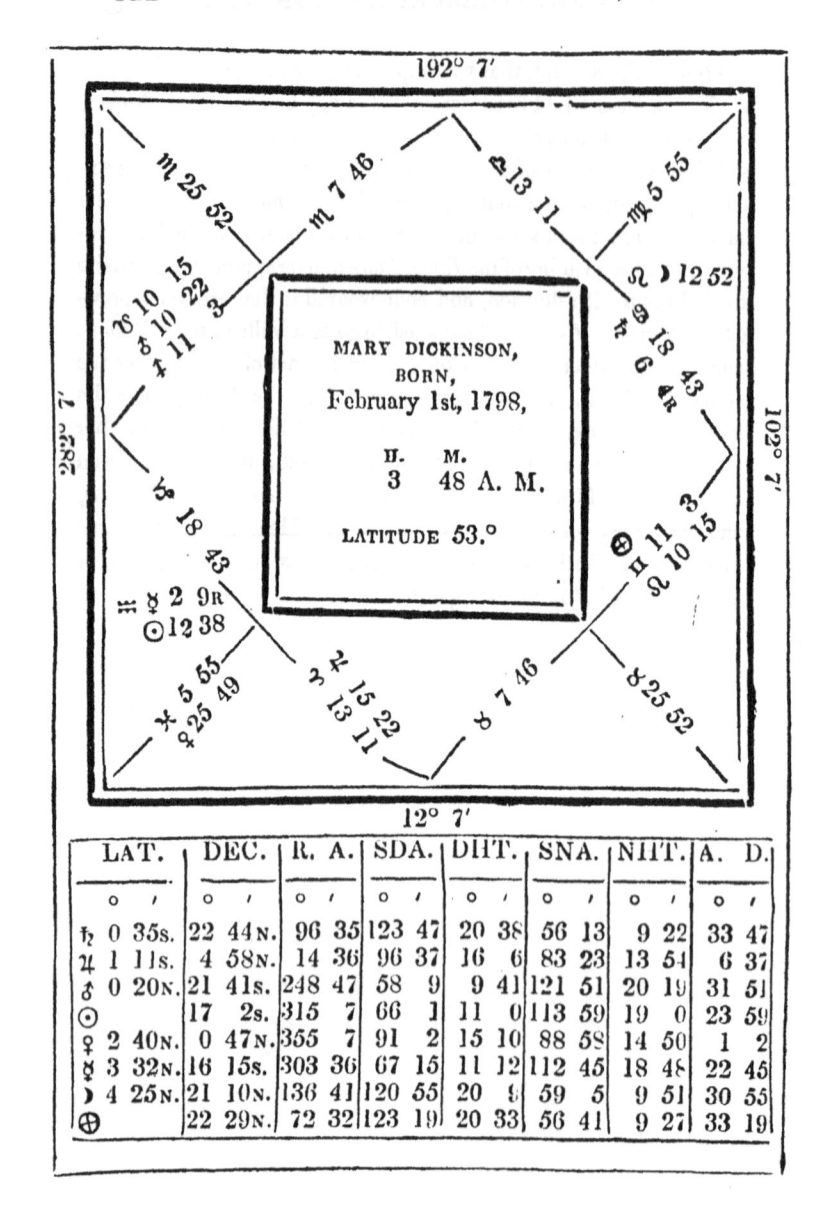

192° 7'

♏ 25 52 ♏ 7 46 ♎ 13 11 ♏ 5 55
♈ 10 15 ♎ 10 22 ☊ ☽ 12 52
♐ 11 ♎ 3 ♄ 18 43 ♂ 6 ℞

282° 7'   **102° 7'**

♑ 18 43   ♁ 11 3 ♊ 10 15

♒ ☿ 2 9℞
☉ 12 38

MARY DICKINSON,
BORN,
February 1st, 1798,

H.   M.
3   48 A. M.

LATITUDE 53.°

♓ 5 55 ♃ 15 22 ♉ 7 46 ♉ 25 52
♀ 25 49 ♎ 13 11

12° 7'

	LAT.	DEC.	R. A.	SDA.	DHT.	SNA.	NHT.	A. D.
	° ′	° ′	° ′	° ′	° ′	° ′	° ′	° ′
♄	0 35s.	22 44n.	96 35	123 47	20 38	56 13	9 22	33 47
♃	1 11s.	4 58n.	14 36	96 37	16 6	83 23	13 54	6 37
♂	0 20n.	21 41s.	248 47	58 9	9 41	121 51	20 19	31 51
☉		17 2s.	315 7	66 1	11 0	113 59	19 0	23 59
♀	2 40n.	0 47n.	355 7	91 2	15 10	88 58	14 50	1 2
☿	3 32n.	16 15s.	303 36	67 15	11 12	112 45	18 48	22 45
☽	4 25n.	21 10n.	136 41	120 55	20 9	59 5	9 51	30 55
⊕		22 29n.	72 32	123 19	20 33	56 41	9 27	33 19

OR GENETHLIACAL ASTRONOMY.

A TABLE OF THE DIRECTIONS.	ARC. D. M.	TIME. YRS. MO.
Sun to the Opposition of the Moon in the Zodiac	0 11	0 2
Ascendant to the Quintile of Venus in Mundo	0 46	0 9
Moon to the Sesquiquadrate of Venus in the Zodiac, Converse Motion	1 18	1 4
Part of Fortune to the Semiquartile of the Moon in Mundo	1 22	1 5
Moon to the Sesquiquadrate of Jupiter in Mundo, Converse Direction	1 26	1 6
Sun to the Parallel of Mercury in the Zodiac	2 7	2 1
Sun to the Sextile of Jupiter in the Zodiac	2 8	2 1
Moon to the Trine of Jupiter in the Zodiac	2 8	2 1
Midheaven to the Opposition of Jupiter in Mundo	2 29	2 5
Ascendant to the Square of Jupiter in Mundo	2 29	2 5
Sun to the Semiquartile of Jupiter in Mundo, Direct Direction	2 30	2 5
Sun to the Semiquartile of Mars in Mundo, Converse Motion	2 54	2 10
Sun to the Semiquartile of Venus in the Zodiac, Converse Direction	3 8	3 1
Moon to the Trine of Mars in the Zodiac, Converse Motion	3 26	3 5
Midheaven to the Quintile of Saturn in Mundo	3 30	3 6
Sun to the Sextile of Mars in the Zodiac, Converse Direction	3 33	3 7
Ascendant to the Sesquiquadrate of the Moon in Mundo	5 2	5 0
Sun to the Opposition of the Moon in Mundo, Direct Motion	5 3	5 0
Moon to the Biquintile of Venus in the Zodiac	5 46	5 9
Moon to the Trine of Mars in Mundo, Direct Direction	5 50	5 10
Sun to the Sesquiquadrate of Saturn in the Zodiac	6 29	6 5
Midheaven to the Trine of Mercury in Mundo	6 38	6 7
Moon to the Semiquartile of Saturn in the Zodiac	6 44	6 8
Midheaven to Spica Virginis	6 48	6 9
Sun to the Quintile of Mars in the Zodiac	7 25	7 5
Moon to the Sesquiquadrate of Mars in Mundo, Converse Motion	8 7	8 1
Sun to the Sextile of Mars in Mundo, by Direct Direction	8 16	8 3
Sun to the Quintile of Jupiter in the Zodiac, Converse Motion	8 24	8 5
Part of Fortune to the Trine of Venus in Mundo	9 56	9 11
Midheaven to the Quintile of Mars in Mundo	10 11	10 2

CELESTIAL PHILOSOPHY,

THE DIRECTIONS CONTINUED.

	ARC. D. M.	TIME. Yrs. Mo.
Moon to the Lion's Heart	11 32	11 7
Sun to the Body of Mercury in the Zodiac, Converse Motion	12 14	12 3
Sun to the Body of Mercury in Mundo, Converse Direction	12 17	12 3
Ascendant to the Sextile of Venus in Mundo	12 38	12 8
Sun to the Semiquartile of Jupiter in the Zodiac	13 10	13 3
Moon to the Opposition of Mercury in the Zodiac, Converse Motion	13 28	13 7
Moon to the Sesquiquadrate of Jupiter in the Zodiac	13 48	13 11
Sun to the Sextile of Venus in the Zodiac, Converse Direction	15 26	15 7
Sun to the Sextile of Jupiter in Mundo, by Converse Motion	15 35	15 9
Sun to the Quintile of Mars in Mundo, Direct Direction	16 1	16 2
Moon to the Biquintile of Venus in Mundo, Converse Motion	16 6	16 3
Moon to the Trine of Venus in the Zodiac, Converse Direction	16 34	16 9
Ascendant to the Biquintile of the Moon in Mundo	17 7	17 4
Sun to the Trine of Saturn in the Zodiac	17 8	17 4
Moon to the Sextile of Saturn in the Zodiac	17 55	18 1
Midheaven to the Sextile of Mars in Mundo	17 56	18 1
Moon to the Opposition of Mercury in Mundo, Converse Motion	18 4	18 3
Midheaven to the Biquintile of Venus in Mundo	18 31	18 9
Midheaven to the Trine of the Sun in Mundo	18 59	19 2
Ascendant to the Quintile of Jupiter in Mundo	19 10	19 5
Moon to the Biquintile of Mercury in the Zodiac	19 23	19 8
Part of Fortune to the Biquintile of Mars in Mundo	20 2	20 4
Sun to the Square of Mars in the Zodiac	20 3	20 4
Moon to the Biquintile of Mars in Mundo, Converse Motion	20 12	20 6
Moon to the Biquintile of Jupiter in the Zodiac	20 13	20 6
Moon to the Square of Mars in the Zodiac	20 54	21 3
Moon to the Trine of Jupiter in Mundo, Converse Direction	21 35	22 0
Sun to the Semiquartile of Venus in Mundo, Converse Motion	21 48	22 3

OR GENETHLIACAL ASTRONOMY.

THE DIRECTIONS CONTINUED.	ARC. D. M.	TIME. YRS. MO.
Sun to the Semiquartile of Mars in the Zodiac, by Converse Direction....................	21 50	22 3
Moon to the Sesquiquadrate of Mars in the Zodiac, Converse Motion.................	22 11	22 7
Moon to the Semiquartile of Saturn in Mundo, Direct Direction.......................	23 6	23 6
Moon to the Opposition of Venus in Mundo, by Direct Motion........................	23 46	24 3
Part of Fortune to the Body of Saturn in Mundo....	24 30	25 0
Sun to the Semiquartile of Mercury in the Zodiac......	24 32	25 0
Sun to the Parallel of Jupiter in the Zodiac...........	24 43	25 3
Part of Fortune to the Sesquiquadrate of Venus in Mundo	24 46	25 3
Midheaven to the Sextile of the Moon in Mundo......	25 11	25 9
Moon to the Square of Mars in Mundo, Direct Direction.	25 12	25 9
Sun to the Quintile of Venus in the Zodiac, Converse Motion................................	25 28	26 1
Moon to the Sesquiquadrate of Mercury in the Zodiac...	25 31	26 1
Sun to the Biquintile of the Moon in the Zodiac........	25 40	26 3
Part of Fortune to the Sesquiquadrate of Mars in Mundo.	25 51	26 6
Sun to the Square of Jupiter in the Zodiac, Converse Direction.............................	26 3	26 9
Moon to the Quintile of Saturn in the Zodiac.........	26 8	26 10
Moon to the Biquintile of the Sun in the Zodiac......	26 30	27 3
Moon to the Square of Jupiter in the Zodiac, Converse Motion................................	26 33	27 3
Ascendant to the Semiquartile of Venus in Mundo.....	27 28	28 3
Sun to the Body of Venus in Mundo, by Direct Direction.	27 29	28 3
Ascendant to the Semiquartile of Mars in Mundo.....	27 37	28 5
Sun to the Square of Mars in Mundo, Direct Motion...	27 38	28 5
Part of Fortune to the Trine of Jupiter in Mundo.....	27 46	28 7
Moon to the Sesquiquadrate of Venus in Mundo, Converse Direction...........................	28 11	29 0
Ascendant to the Opposition of Saturn in Mundo....	28 15	29 1
Midheaven to the Square of Saturn in Mundo.........	28 15	29 1
Sun to the Sesquiquadrate of Saturn in Mundo, Direct Motion................................	28 16	29 1
Part of Fortune to the Parallel of Saturn in Mundo....	29 57	30 10
Sun to the Body of Venus in the Zodiac.............	30 11	31 1
Ascendant to the Sextile of Jupiter in Mundo........	30 17	31 2
Sun to the Quintile of Jupiter in Mundo, Converse Direction................................	30 47	31 8

T

THE DIRECTIONS CONTINUED.

	ARC. D. M.	TIME. Yrs. Mo.
Sun to the Opposition of Saturn in Mundo, Converse Motion	30 58	31 11
Sun to the Opposition of Saturn in the Zodiac, Converse Direction	31 12	32 2
Sun to his own Semiquartile in the Zodiac	31 22	32 4
Sun to the Sesquiquadrate of the Moon in the Zodiac	31 31	32 6
Sun to the Parallel of Venus in the Zodiac	31 38	32 7
Moon to the Biquintile of Mars in the Zodiac, Converse Motion	32 8	33 3
Moon to the Sesquiquadrate of the Sun in the Zodiac	32 20	33 6
Moon to her own Semiquartile in the Zodiac	32 29	33 8
Moon to the Body of Saturn in the Zodiac, Converse Motion	32 33	33 9
Moon to the Quintile of Mars in the Zodiac	32 45	34 0
Moon to the Parallel of Jupiter in the Zodiac	32 53	34 2
Part of Fortune to the Biquintile of Venus in Mundo	33 40	34 11
Sun to the Parallel of Venus in the Zodiac	34 8	35 5
Sun to the Sextile of Mercury in the Zodiac	34 15	35 6
Moon to the Trine of Mercury in the Zodiac	35 11	36 6
Moon to the Sextile of Saturn in Mundo, Direct Motion	35 17	36 7
Part of Fortune to the Trine of Mars in Mundo	35 32	36 10
Midheaven to the Biquintile of Jupiter in Mundo	35 51	37 2
Sun to the Square of Saturn in the Zodiac	36 49	38 3

The foregoing Genethliacal display of the Celestial Bodies, and Directions, are the same as those that I used when this unfortunate Native applied to me. As soon as I had viewed the alarming testimonies that were prevalent, and presented themselves in every part of the Heavens, I was then convinced that a *violent Death* was apparent, and that there was nothing that could possibly mitigate the fury of those inimical configurations, that were conjoined with the Anaretical Directions, in their corresponding places, and Mortal stations. The Ascendant is afflicted by the Body of Mars (who is near the Heart of the Scorpion,) and also by the Semiquartile of the Sun, and that important Angle is likewise afflicted by the Moon's Mundane Sesquiquadrate, to which that Luminary is applying: the two Lights of the World are also in opposition to each other, and Mars, who has just risen at the time of Birth, is afflicting the Sun, and Moon, from obnoxious places and Terms, all of which portend a *violent Death*. The Part of Fortune claims the prorogatory Dignity, as a full Moon preceded the Nocturnal Birth, and neither the Ascendant, or any Planet, could claim the Hylegiacal power, the affliction of that Aphetical point by the Opposition of Mars, his Mundane Parallel, and also by the Semiquartile of the Moon, and Sesquiquadrate of the Sun in the World, are all strong, and additional arguments of a *sudden Death by violence*. The position of Jupiter in the Imum Cœli, afflicted by the quartile of Saturn in the Zodiac, and Mundane Square of Mars, applying, has a baneful appearance when compared with the Motions of the other Stars in their Longitudinal places. Venus is also applying to the Square of Saturn, therefore from these observations it will plainly appear, that both the benefics are deprived of their natural, and benign qualities, both by *position and Direction*, and consequently cannot render any support, either to the true Hyleg, or the other inferior Vital places, which have co-signification of Life. Some may probably observe, that as the giver of Life is in a Mundane Square to Jupiter, and near the Trine of Venus in the World, the affliction of the Prorogator in the Genethliacal Constitution is much reduced, and the violence thereof considerably dissolved; but those who are inclined to state such insignificant, and puny propositions, know nothing of the true principles of this Science, either by Theory, or Practice. I affirm that the Part of Fortune is the giver of Life, and it was from the Directions of that point to the Body of Saturn, Sesquiquadrate of Mars in Mundo, and Parallel of Saturn in the World, (he being posited in Cancer, a violent Cardinal Sign of the watery Trigon, and in the Western Angle,) that I foretold the Death of this Native by *Drowning*, five Months before that Event took place, which is well known to the Public. The true Calculations of those Directions to the Hyleg, or giver of Life, are as follow.

The true Pole of the Sun, is thus computed.

	°	′
As his duplicate nocturnal horary times.	38	0
Are to his distance from the Nadir.	57	0
So are thirty Degrees.	30	0
To the proportional part.	45	0
Which must be subtracted from the Right Ascension of the Northern Angle, with the Circle added.	372	7
And the Oblique Ascension of the Sun, under his Pole, is.	327	7
From which subtract his Right Ascension.	315	7
Ascensional Difference of the Sun, under his Polar Elevation.	12	0

	°	′	
Then from Sine, with Radius.	12	0 =	19,31787
Subtract Tangent of the Sun's Declination.	17	2 =	9,48624
Tangent of the Sun's Pole.	34	10 =	9,83163

The Moon's Polar Altitude, is thus calculated.

	°	′
As one third part of her Semidiurnal Arc.	40	18
Is to her distance from the Zenith.	55	26
So are thirty Degrees.	30	0

OR GENETHLIACAL ASTRONOMY.

	°	′
To the proportional part.	41	16
Which being subtracted from the Right Ascension of the Meridian.	192	7
The Oblique Descension of the Moon will be.	150	51
Subtract the Right Ascension,	136	41
Remains the Ascensional Difference, under her Pole.	14	10

	° ′	
Then from Sine, with Radius.	14 10 =	19,38871
Subtract Tangent of the Moon's Declination.	21 10 =	9,58794
Tangent of the Moon's Pole.	32 17 =	9,80077

	°	′
Then from the Oblique Ascension of the Moon's Opposition.	330	51
Subtract the Oblique Ascension of the Sun.	327	7
And the distance of the Part of Fortune from the West will be.	3	44
To which add the Oblique Descension of the Seventh, (as the Moon has passed the Opposition of the Sun, by Longitude, and Latitude,)	102	7
And the sum is the Oblique Descension of the Part of Fortune.	105	51

From the above Numbers its true Place is equal to 13° 54′ of Gemini, consequently its Declination will be 22° 29′ *North*, its Right Ascension 72° 32′, and its diurnal horary times 20° 33′.

The Part of Fortune to the Body of Saturn is thus computed.

	°	′
As the diurnal horary times of the Part of Fortune.	20	33
Are to its distance from the West.	3	44
So are the diurnal horary times of Saturn	20	38

To his secondary distance from the Seventh............	3 45
Which subtract from his Primary distance from the West.	28 15
Remains the Arc of Direction.	24 30

Part of Fortune to the Sesquiquadrate of Mars.
The operation to the Square, is thus wrought.

As the horary times of the Part of Fortune.............	20 33
Are to its distance from the Seventh.	3 44
So are the diurnal horary times of Mars..............	9 41
To the proportional part,...........................	1 46
Which subtracted from his Primary distance from the Zenith..	56 40
And the Arc of Direction to the Mundane Square will be.	54 54
From which subtract the triplicate diurnal horary times of Mars.....................................	29 3
Arc of Direction..	25 51

The Computation of the Part of Fortune, to the Parallel of Saturn.

As the horary times of the Part of Fortune............	20 33
Are to its distance from the West....................	3 44
So are the *Nocturnal* horary times of Saturn, (as he will be below the Earth, when the Direction is finished.)	9 22
To his secondary distance from the Seventh...........	1 42
Which added to his Primary distance from that Angle...	28 15
And the sum will be the Arc of Direction.	29 57

These were the Directions that I judged would produce Death, and when they shewed their Effects, I was not disappointed in my expectation, I do not deny that the Ascendant, and Luminaries, were afflicted by primary Directions, which succeeded those to the Hyleg that destroyed Life, and which doubtless increased the *sudden power* of the killing train to the Moderator; but though I have made these observations in this place, yet I positively say, that if the legal Prorogator had not encountered those Mortal Directions, which I have computed in full, the others of an inferior power that followed, could not have destroyed Life. I mention these things that the Students may observe, that no violent Directions can produce Death, except they are made to the *true giver of Life*, though they will, (when the Enemies possess their *own nature*,) give Sickness, Troubles, and Accidents, according to their power in the Radix, and in the places where the Promittors, &c. have dominion, when the Directions are finished. I trust I shall be excused for making repetition, yet the subject I am now discussing, demands the strictest attention, and ought to be laid down in *plain terms*, and not left in obscurity. The Students must always remember, that when a *sudden Death* is visible, they will then discover, that many violent Directions of different denominations, will generally be united with, or near those that are in operation to the Prorogator, though it is from the Anaretical power of the *latter alone*, that personal extinction is produced.

I conceive I have said sufficient on this Nativity, and hope from the EXAMPLES preceding, that the Students will readily understand how to judge of all the other Motions, and applications in the Zodiac, and Mundo, whether they are of an hostile, or benign power. In the Native's last Revolution, the Moon was just setting, in square to Mars, and in Opposition to the place of that Malefic, in the Nativity, being among violent fixed Stars, and near the place of the giver of Life in the Radix; she was also applying to the Mundane Squares of Saturn and Jupiter. At the exact time she was Drowned, the Moon, was in the watery Sign Scorpio in the Western Angle, in opposition to Saturn, and on the Mundane place of the Part of Fortune in the Geniture; Saturn, and Mars, the two Mortal Promittors, were also in quartile to each other, and conveyed their destructive power to the significator of Life, at the time of her expiration.

The time of the Birth of a Female, Born in Lincoln, was given to me about five Years ago, by one of her Relatives, now living, who informed me, that I might rely on the correctness thereof; which was, September 3rd, 1801, 0h. 35m. P. M. From the following Figure of the Heavens, and the Directions, it is well known to many, that I foretold the time of the dissolution of this Native, which clearly demonstrate the essential use, power, and sole dominion of the giver of Life, when properly chosen according to the Rules I have given; but though the Sun is certainly the Prorogator in this Nativity, yet as some of the Directions that assisted in destroying the Life of the Native, differ from the general precepts, and as these Examples clearly develope the true *Terms* of the Planets, in the most conspicuous manner, with their *saving*, and *destroying* power, I have taken the trouble, by true Calculation, to prove, that the *Terms, which ought to be used,* are wholly unconnected with any of those degrees in the Signs of the Zodiac, which the pretenders to this Science sanction, and admire without examination. I have tried them all in the Calculation of several hundreds of Nativities, as they are erroneously given in the Works, of Ancient, and Modern *Pirates*, and have discovered, that there is *no truth* in them whatever; therefore as they are not to be depended on in any Computations, as they are *now generally used*, all those who rely on their assumed power, which cannot be demonstrated, will remain in a labyrinth of confusion, so long as they suffer any of those false, and ostentatious innovations, to operate as a barrier to their progress in this Celestial Study.

It is extraordinary to observe, with what avidity the Students in general, adhere to the superficial, and preposterous notions, which have been falsely disseminated by various Authors. Many are so ardently attached to Ancient errors, (which the *Tables* of the *Terms* of the Planets, and *many other spurious inventions,* fully explain,) that they are not inclined to discountenance them, even when *Truth* makes its brilliant appearance to aid and faciliate them in their researches in the paths of Science. With some it is a matter of little consequence, whether the instructions they receive from an Author, are true, or false, as they seldom call them in question, if they appear sufficiently *prolix*, and originate from *Ancient Authority*; therefore *Truth*, (which ought to be esteemed as the most essential criterion) does not become their primary object, but is considered as a subject of minor importance; to what use then are false Rules, and fabricated Examples given by *Pirates*, which upon minute examination, are found to be deficient, and will not stand the test of impartial proof, when opposed to *Truth*, *Reason*, and *Experience*, which I have evinced in this Publication. The injury done to this Science by such *Pirates*, is incalculable; they have promulgated the most inconsistent, and superfluous Precepts, contrary to the true Motions of the Heavens, which mislead the Students, and cause them to imbibe *plausible Chimeras*, instead of those profound, and substantial Theorems, which cannot be refuted. An Author who intends that the Students should receive advantage from his labors, will always make his Rules, and instructions as clear as the nature of the subjects will admit, and deliver his sentiments in a plain, concise, and intelligent manner; for when irrefutable computations, (combined with Judgment which exhibit the true *Causes*, with their *Effects*,) are introduced in his Work, the Students will then attend with pleasure to the Proofs he has unveiled, by which the most *luminous Truths* become Publicly corroborated, and established beyond the bounds of contradiction. I hope I have sufficiently explained my instructions, and confirmed the Judgment I have given, not only from authentic demonstration, but also from the most respectable evidence, which neither the WISEACRES OR SCEPTICS, are able to refute; for it cannot be supposed that any *Infidel* can be found, who dare deny, or oppose those public, and *ocular* FACTS, contained in this Work, which are confirmed, and proved by the testimony of many hundreds of surviving witnesses. With respect to the *Terms* of the Celestial Bodies, I shall not trouble the Students with additional observations thereon, as Examples are far superior to comments, on subjects which require the most serious attention. I shall now proceed to illustrate, and explain those *Terms*, with their natural Effects by Directions to the Sun, who is the presiding Moderator, including his power in that part of the Heavens, in which he is posited, as the true giver of Life in this Geniture. The Native died on the 28th of June, 1825; Aged twenty three Years, nine Months, and twenty four Days.

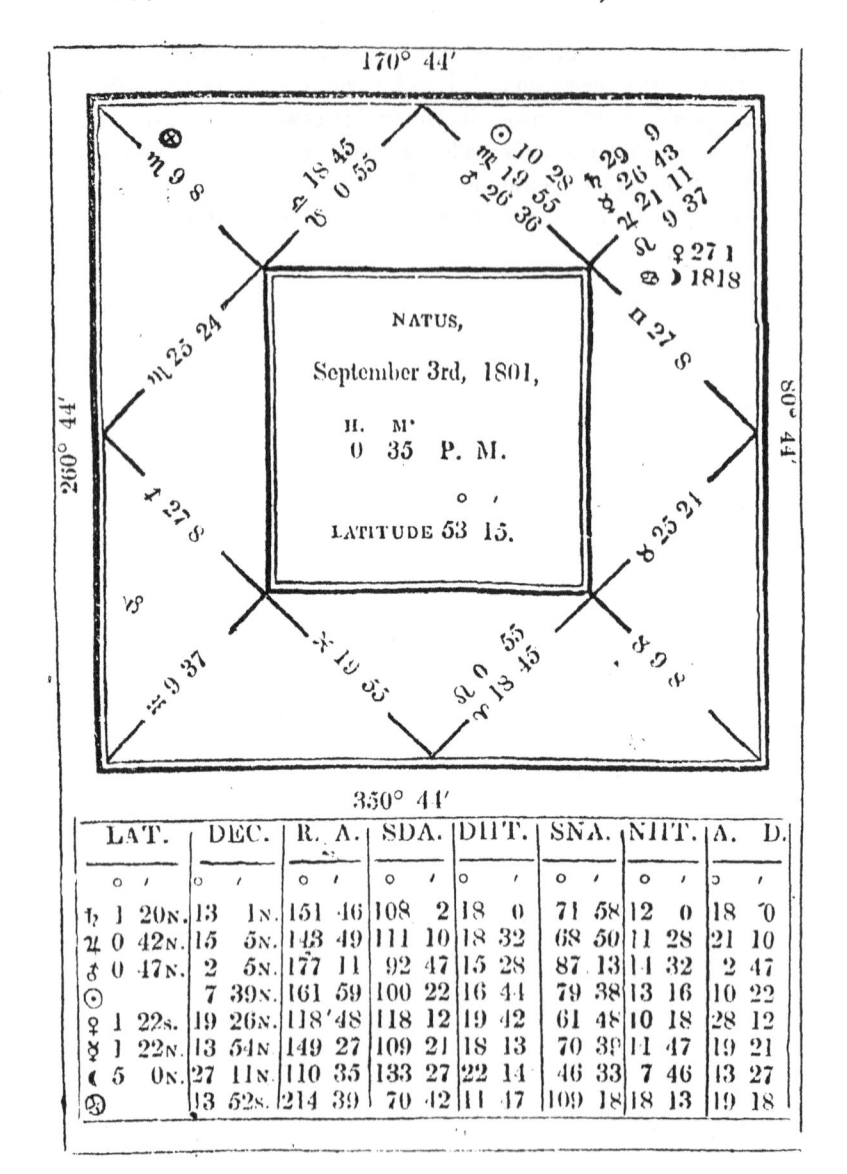

CELESTIAL PHILOSOPHY,

NATUS,

September 3rd, 1801,

H. M'
0 35 P. M.

° '
LATITUDE 53 15.

Top: 170° 44'
Left: 260° 44'
Right: 80° 44'
Bottom: 350° 44'

	LAT.	DEC.	R. A.	SDA.	DHT.	SNA.	NHT.	A. D.
	° '	° '	° '	° '	° '	° '	° '	° '
♄	1 20N.	13 1N.	151 46	108 2	18 0	71 58	12 0	18 0
♃	0 42N.	15 5N.	143 49	111 10	18 32	68 50	11 28	21 10
♂	0 47N.	2 5N.	177 11	92 47	15 28	87 13	14 32	2 47
☉		7 39N.	161 59	100 22	16 44	79 38	13 16	10 22
♀	1 22s.	19 26N.	118 48	118 12	19 42	61 48	10 18	28 12
☿	1 22N.	13 54N.	149 27	109 21	18 13	70 39	11 47	19 21
☽	5 0N.	27 11N.	110 35	133 27	22 14	46 33	7 46	43 27
⊕		13 52s.	214 39	70 42	11 47	109 18	18 13	19 18

OR GENETHLIACAL ASTRONOMY. 137

A TABLE OF THE DIRECTIONS.	ARC. D. M.	TIME. YRS. MO.
Sun to the Semiquartile of Venus in the Zodiac.......	1 22	1 6
Moon to the Semiquartile of Mars in Mundo, Direct Motion..	1 53	2 0
Moon to the Semiquartile of Saturn in the Zodiac, Converse Direction................................	3 37	3 11
Moon to the Semiquartile of Mercury in the Zodiac, by Converse Motion.............................	5 52	6 6
Midheaven to the Body of Mars in Mundo...........	6 27	7 1
Ascendant to the Square of Mars in Mundo.........	6 27	7 1
Moon to the Semiquartile of the Sun in the Zodiac.....	6 32	7 2
Ascendant to the Sesquiquadrate of the Moon in Mundo.	6 36	7 3
Sun to the Sextile of the Moon in the Zodiac........	6 53	7 8
Ascendant to the Sesquiquadrate of Venus in Mundo...	7 10	7 11
Moon to the Sextile of Mars in the Zodiac..........	7 33	8 4
Moon to the Body of Venus in the Zodiac...........	7 55	8 8
Part of Fortune to the Quintile of the Sun in Mundo...	8 33	9 6
Sun to the Body of Saturn in Mundo, Converse Motion.	8 49	9 9
Sun to the Body of Saturn in the Zodiac, Converse Direction...	8 53	9 10
Part of Fortune to the Sextile of Mars in Mundo.....	10 5	11 2
Ascendant to the Trine of Jupiter in Mundo.........	10 7	11 2
Moon to the Semiquartile of Jupiter in the Zodiac, Converse Motion.................................	10 21	11 5
Sun to the Body of Mercury in Mundo, by Converse Direction...	10 43	11 10
Sun to the Body of Mercury in the Zodiac, Converse Motion..	10 49	12 0
Sun to the Parallel of Mars in the Zodiac............	12 33	13 11
Sun to the Body of Mars in the Zodiac.............	14 7	15 8
Part of Fortune to the Square of Jupiter in Mundo...	14 28	16 0
Sun to the Sextile of Venus in the Zodiac..........	14 29	16 0
Sun to the Body of Mars in Mundo, Direct Direction.	14 32	16 1
Ascendant to the Trine of Mercury in Mundo.......	15 12	16 10
Sun to the Body of Jupiter in Mundo, Converse Motion.	15 33	17 2
Sun to the Body of Jupiter in the Zodiac, Converse Direction...	15 35	17 2
Moon to the Sextile of Saturn in the Zodiac, Converse Motion..	16 34	18 5
Ascendant to the Trine of Saturn in Mundo.........	17 4	18 11
Sun to the Quintile of the Moon in the Zodiac........	17 20	19 3

THE DIRECTIONS CONTINUED.

	ARC. D. M.	TIME. YRS. MO.
Sun to the Semiquartile of Venus in Mundo, Direct Direction	17 28	19 5
Sun to the Semiquartile of the Moon in Mundo, Direct Motion	18 14	20 3
Moon to the Sextile of Mercury in the Zodiac, Converse Direction	18 21	20 5
Ascendant to the Biquintile of Venus in Mundo	18 59	21 2
Part of Fortune to the Square of Mercury in Mundo	19 29	21 8
Moon to the Sextile of Mars in Mundo, Converse Motion	19 34	21 9
Moon to the Semiquartile of Mars in the Zodiac	19 41	21 10
Ascendant to the Biquintile of the Moon in Mundo	19 55	22 1
Moon to the Square of Mars in the Zodiac, Converse Direction	20 48	23 2
Part of Fortune to the Square of Saturn in Mundo	21 18	23 8
Sun to the Parallel of Mars in the Zodiac	21 35	23 11
Sun to the Semiquartile of Jupiter in the Zodiac	22 26	24 10
Part of Fortune to the Quintile of Mars in Mundo	22 27	24 10
Moon to the Sextile of Jupiter in the Zodiac, Converse Motion	22 35	25 0
Moon to the Parallel of Venus in the Zodiac	22 50	25 4
Moon to the Body of Jupiter in Mundo, Direct Direction	23 9	25 9
Ascendant to Cor Scorpio	24 41	27 5
Ascendant to the Trine of the Sun in Mundo	24 41	27 5
Sun to the Quintile of Venus in the Zodiac	24 51	27 8
Moon to the Body of Jupiter in the Zodiac	26 25	29 4
Moon to the Quintile of Saturn in the Zodiac, Converse Motion	26 36	29 6
Midheaven to the Sextile of Venus in Mundo	26 52	29 9
Sun to the Semiquartile of Mercury in the Zodiac	27 16	30 3
Sun to the Semiquartile of Mars in the Zodiac, Converse Direction	27 40	30 9
Moon to the Quintile of Mercury in the Zodiac, Converse Motion	27 49	30 11
Moon to the Body of Mercury in Mundo, Direct Direction	28 1	31 2
Midheaven to Spica Virginis	28 11	31 4
Part of Fortune to the Square of the Sun in Mundo	28 37	31 9
Ascendant to the Sesquiquadrate of Jupiter in Mundo	28 39	31 9
Midheaven to the Sextile of the Moon in Mundo	28 50	32 0
Sun to the Semiquartile of Saturn in the Zodiac	29 21	32 7
Moon to the Body of Saturn in Mundo, Direct Motion	29 43	32 11

	ARC.		TIME.	
THE DIRECTIONS CONTINUED.	D.	M.	YRS.	MO.
Moon to the Semiquartile of Saturn in Mundo, Converse Direction.	29	59	33	2
Moon to the Body of Mercury in the Zodiac.	30	5	33	3
Moon to the Parallel of Jupiter in the Zodiac.	30	22	33	7
Moon to Cor Leonis.	30	28	33	8
Moon to the Semiquartile of Venus in the Zodiac, Converse Motion.	31	4	34	5
Part of Fortune to the Trine of Venus in Mundo.	31	29	34	10
Moon to the Body of Saturn in the Zodiac.	31	88	35	0
Moon to the Quintile of Jupiter in the Zodiac, Converse Direction.	32	5	35	6
Moon to the Parallel of Mercury in the Zodiac.	32	8	35	6
Moon to the Semiquartile of Mercury in Mundo, Converse Motion.	32	31	35	11
Sun to the Square of the Moon in the Zodiac.	33	3	36	7
Ascendant to the Sesquiquadrate of Mercury in Mundo.	33	25	37	0
Moon to the Parallel of Saturn in the Zodiac.	33	26	37	0
Part of Fortune to the Trine of the Moon in Mundo.	34	3	37	8
Sun to his own Parallel in the Zodiac.	34	8	37	9
Moon to her own Semiquartile in the Zodiac.	34	14	37	10
Sun to the Semiquartile of Mars in Mundo, Converse Direction.	34	26	38	0

The distance of the Sun from the Meridian, in the preceding Geniture, is eight Degrees, forty-five Minutes, by which he claims the Aphetical Dignity, and consequently the time of the Native's dissolution, must be obtained from his Progressive Motion to the killing Place; but from his *impotent* position, (with the affliction of the other Stars in those stations, which have affinity to Diseases, and Death,) it became apparent to me, that the Native would soon be removed from this state of *Mortality*, as the whole position, properly considered in all its parts, is too feeble to support Life, for any considerable length of time; I therefore judged that lingering Diseases, (during the short period of her existence,) would be produced from so many unfavorable, and conflicting *Causes*, none of which were defeated in producing their *corresponding Effects*. The Hyleg is in Mundane Parallel with Mars, which is a violent affliction, and collects a considerable augmentation of evil from the *Terms* of the enemies, by the Rapt Motion, as they decline from the Zenith, which the use of the Celestial Globe will immediately prove; we may also discover the Sun's additional affliction, by his being conjoined with Saturn, and with Mercury also, who is of the Nature of that Malefic; and as the Hyleg cannot receive any benign applications, when he arrives at the Anaretical Point, in 5° 13' of Libra; where the *second* Zodiacal Parallel of Mars, and his Terms, (with those of Saturn) are nearly united, I judged that her Personal extinction would take place when that Direction shewed its Effects; as it was followed by the Semiquartiles of Mercury, and Saturn in the Zodiac, &c. The Part of Fortune was likewise directed to the Mundane Square of Saturn, and the Moon also applied by Converse Motion, to the Quartile of Mars in the Zodiac, at the same time; hence we may observe, that the Sun, Moon, and Part of Fortune were all afflicted by directional Motion, at the time of the Native's Death.

It may probably be asked by some, why the giver of Life to the Parallel of Mars in the Zodiac, at the Age of thirteen Years, and eleven Months, followed by his Body at fifteen Years and eight

Months, did not produce Death; it is evident that no Sickness, or danger, worthy of notice, could possibly take place from those Directions, because the Sextile of Venus, combined with Jupiter's Terms, and his conjunction, by Converse Direction, interposed at the place, and dissolved the apparent violence; but before I conclude this Nativity, I shall make a few additional observations thereon, which may be of use to the Students, if they think proper to attend to them. The old Tables which contain *certain Numbers* in the signs of the Zodiac, being the *supposed Planetary Terms*, are all *whimsical notions*, and void of Truth; the *true Terms* arise from clear demonstration, they may be discovered by Calculations in every Nativity, and those Calculations fully prove their use and power; the fact is, they are *those places* where the Benefics, and Malefics claim their greatest influence in the *Zodiacal* and *Mundane Circles*, and are found by adjusting the difference, as the Stars approach to, or decline from the preceding Angle at Birth; thus Mars is 6° 27' from the Meridian, and his distance then taken by proportion from the Eastern Horizon, which he beholds by a Mundane Square applying, his Terms fall in 7° 23' of Libra, and those of Saturn, in 9° 41' of the same Sign. Now in this Nativity, when the Sun was directed to the Zodiacal Parallel of Mars, for Death, the *old Terms* of Venus followed, which by the *Ancient Method*, ought to have preserved Life, if they were true, and their Effects of sufficient power. With little difficulty it may be proved, that all the twelve Constellations have changed their Ancient places, so that the Sign Aries has now got into Taurus, and the Constellation Taurus, into that of Gemini, and so of all the other signs of the Zodiac. There are *many errors*, and *deficiences* in Nativities, which I have not disclosed, that have long been received as absolute Facts, though I have never given credit to any of them, because when I demanded *proof*, I soon discovered that it was not to be obtained, and as I have lately observed that it would be *difficult* to turn many from their *old favorite path of Error*, into that of TRUTH, *I shall not attempt to perform that office;* however I shall observe, that if the Students think they have not yet labored long enough in their TRAMMELS,

X

they may still *proceed forward*, until they discover their errors more *visibly*, by proper practice, and experience.

Having stated the Directions which destroyed the Life of this Native, I shall now consider the *quality* of the Disease, which terminated the Native's existence. Jupiter, who is posited in a cadent station, is weak, and afflicted by the Bodies of Mercury, and Saturn, in the fiery sign Leo, near Cor Leonis, so that when the giver of Life, arrived at the first Direction, which produced Death, Jupiter was directed a few Degrees afterwards, in the subsequent train to the Body of Mars, and Venus came also to a conjunction with Mercury, and Saturn; but these Directions have *no power at any time, to give Death, but Diseases only*, from which it is plain, that both those benevolent Planets, being afflicted by furious Directions, produced great injury to the internal parts, governed by those benign Stars, and the Signs in which they are posited at Birth, regard being had to those places, where their hostile Motions are finished. Jupiter, and Venus, govern the *Lungs*, and *Liver*, &c. and being afflicted in the Radix, and by Directional Motion likewise, they always produce incurable Diseases, and a wasting of the Flesh; hence it is obvious, that a Consumption was the *original Cause* of this Native's dissolution.

In her last Revolution, the Sun, the significator of Life, was in Square to Saturn in the Zodiac, and in Mundane Square to Mars; the Moon was also in opposition to her own place in the Nativity; Mars was likewise in zodiacal Quartile to Jupiter, Mercury, and Saturn, in the Geniture, and the Moon applied to the Declination of the three superior Planets in the Revolution; all of which are testimonies of a malignant Nature. At the time she died, the Moon was among violent fixed Stars, in a subterranean station, and applied to the Opposition of Saturn, Mercury, and Mars, and that Luminary at the same time, had nearly the Declination of Saturn, Mercury, and the Sun. Mars, the chief mortal Promittor, was Cadent in the twelfth, in exact Square to his place at Birth, and the Moon was in Quartile to the Prorogator, in the Geniture.

Maria Ferguson was Born on the 28th of October, 1808, 3н. 40м. P. M. and was Drowned in the Fossdyke, near Lincoln Race-ground, on the 12th of July, 1825, about 9 o'clock in the Morning, Aged sixteen Years, eight Months, and thirteen Days.

This young Woman lived in Lincoln when she gave me the above time of her Birth, which she said was true, having been told it was taken with much care. As soon as I beheld the *dreadful appearances* of the Celestial Bodies in the Figure of Birth, I was immediately convinced that a violent Death by *Water*, was plainly visible; for it must appear evident to those, who have but little skill in this noble, and Sublime Study, that a more *alarming position* is seldom seen, than that which follows; particularly when the Directions that destroyed Life, are minutely examined, with those parts of the Heavens in which they complete their courses. It is well known to many respectable persons in this City, that I foretold the *time* of this Native's Death, and its *quality*, which certainly were not difficult to perform, when the proper Precepts in this Work are attended to, by which, not only the length of Life, but also the quality of Death, whether natural, or violent, are soon discovered. According to my usual practice, I first computed the duration of Life, and as the Sun is Hyleg, it appeared obvious to me, that when he arrived on the Western Horizon, followed by several Directions of a Mortal nature, this Native would be no more, that Direction of the Apheta to the West, being the first that made its appearance in the Anaretical train. Now as my previous Calculations, and Judgment have been confirmed, it is impossible for *prejudice*, or any *artful Chicanery*, to oppose those luminous Facts, which admit of no refutation. There are certain characters, who vainly imagine, that they are qualified to discover the limits of a Man's understanding, but when they meet with those difficulties in Science, which they cannot comprehend, (not being willing to acknowledge that others are superior to them in Literature,) they then become offended, and in the most uncandid manner, use every means in their power, to level odious, and gross scurrility against *that*, which throws *their Talents* in the *shade*, and makes them appear *contemptible* in the Eyes of the Public. Those who consider themselves qualified to oppose a Science, ought to understand *all* its principles, otherwise their arguments, and observations, will soon obtain the ignominy they merit, and the Authors, instead of gaining reputation, will establish their own disgrace to succeeding Generations.

Some have, to their shame, asserted, that this is not a commendable Study, and even those who make much *noise* concerning POPISH SUPERSTITION (which is as *dangerous* as the *Tomahawk* in the hand of a *savage*,) display their *learned and dogmatical sentiments*, against this Divine, and sacred Learning; which our forefathers studied with the greatest diligence, and admiration. I have been told by those, whose *Heads are filled with* PRIESTCRAFT, that no person can perform these things, if he had not an *evil Spirit* to assist him, O SHAME! O SHAME! are we to be told in this *enlightened Age*, and in the nineteenth Century, that Astronomical Calculations, the use of the Globe, and the common rules of Arithmetic, are performed by the assistance of BEELZEBUB, who is probably, not a *learned* Astronomer; how degrading must such simple, and delusive notions appear to every impartial observer. With respect to the dissolution of this young Woman, some *learned sciolists*, (with affected Jargon,) say, that she died an *untimely Death*. I never have yet been able to understand the *literal meaning of that*, which appears to be an *Allegorical Theme*, or a jarring, and confused misrepresentation of *something*, which requires plain confirmation; for how can the Death of this Native be considered *untimely*, when it was *visibly* apparent in the *Heavens*, at the moment she came into the World, and which, no human Efforts could alter, or prevent; the word *untimely*, appears to represent, what happens *before* its natural time, or in fact, what Mortal Men are disposed thus to stile *it*; but according to all the researches which have been made in this venerable Study, combined with GOD'S MOST HOLY WORD, *in its purity*, it is manifest that, "*what-*

ever is, is right". The time and quality of every person's Death, are unfolded to us by *Secondary Causes*, according to the ordinance of the MOST HIGH. How imperious and immoral must those persons be, who pronounce the Death of an individual *untimely*, merely because it is of a violent nature in the Eyes of Mortal Men, though it was DECREED in the ETERNAL MIND of the ALMIGHTY, from all Eternity. Many hundreds of such Examples as the above, are continually displaying themselves to us, (if we do not survey them too superficially) as we travel through this Mortal Life, to the glorious Mansions of everlasting felicity, all of which prove, the UNERRING, AND IMMUTABLE DECREE of that ALMIGHTY CREATOR, who is blessed for evermore.

146   CELESTIAL PHILOSOPHY,

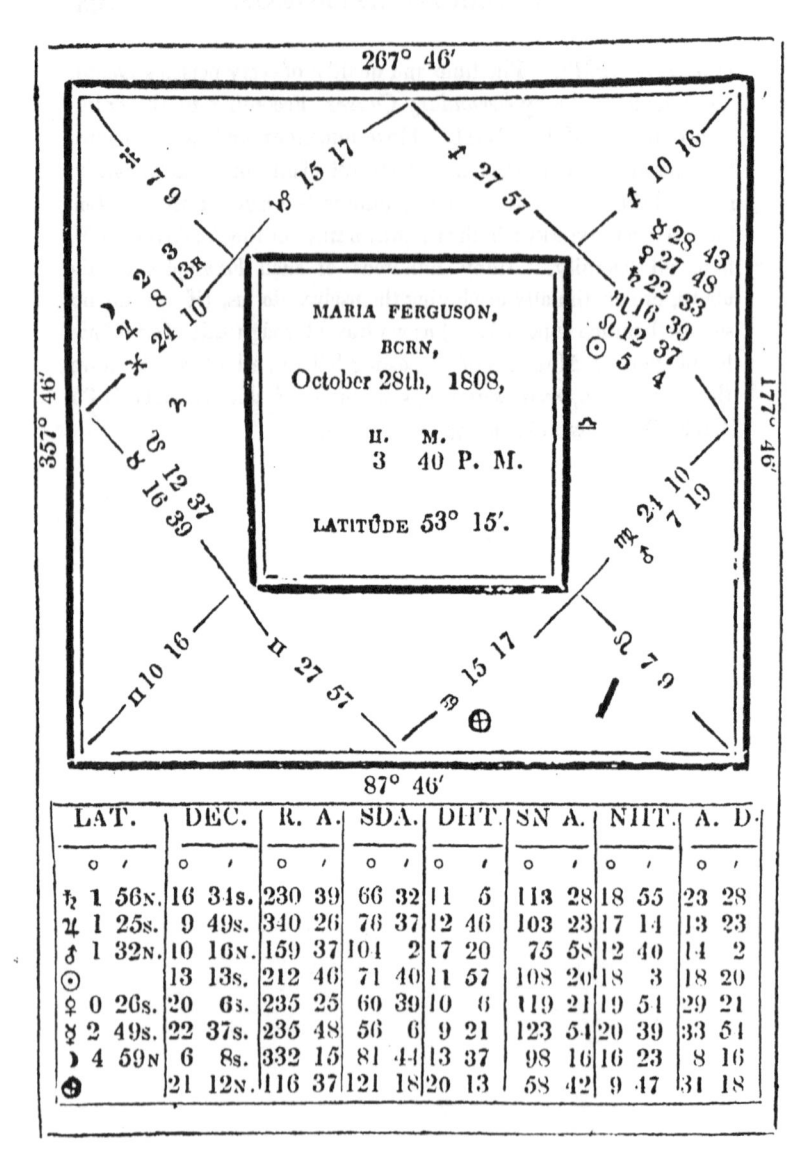

267° 46'

≈ 7 9 | ♑ 15 17 | ♐ 27 57 | ♐ 10 16
♓ 2 3
♈ 2 8 ♓ 13ʀ
♓ 24 10

♉ 28 43
♀ 27 48
♄ 22 33
♏ 16 39
☉ 12 37
5 4

MARIA FERGUSON,
BORN,
October 28th, 1808,
H.   M.
3   40 P. M.

LATITUDE 53° 15'.

357° 46' | 177° 46'

♈
♉ 12 37
16 39

♎ 24 10
♏ 7 19

♊ 10 16 | ♊ 27 57 | ♋ 15 17 | ♌ 7 9
⊕

87° 46'

	LAT.	DEC.	R. A.	SDA.	DHT.	SN A.	NHT.	A. D.
	° '	° '	° '	° '	° '	° '	° '	° '
♄	1 56ɴ	16 34s	230 39	66 32	11 5	113 28	18 55	23 28
♃	1 25s	9 49s	340 26	76 37	12 46	103 23	17 14	13 23
♂	1 32ɴ	10 16ɴ	159 37	104 2	17 20	75 58	12 40	14 2
☉		13 13s	212 46	71 40	11 57	108 20	18 3	18 20
♀	0 26s	20 6s	235 25	60 39	10 6	119 21	19 54	29 21
☿	2 49s	22 37s	235 48	56 6	9 21	123 54	20 39	33 54
☽	4 59ɴ	6 8s	332 15	81 44	13 37	98 16	16 23	8 16
⊕		21 12ɴ	116 37	121 18	20 13	58 42	9 47	31 18

OR GENETHLIACAL ASTRONOMY.

A TABLE OF THE DIRECTIONS.	ARC. D. M.	TIME. YRS. MO.
Moon to the Trine of Venus in Mundo, Direct Direction.	0 40	0 8
Moon to the Trine of Saturn in Mundo, by Converse Motion	1 7	1 1
Sun to the Sextile of Mars in the Zodiac.	1 19	1 3
Ascendant to the Biquintile of Mercury in Mundo.	1 42	1 8
Moon to the Trine of the Sun in the Zodiac.	1 47	1 9
Sun to the Trine of Jupiter in the Zodiac.	1 54	1 10
Moon to the Trine of Mercury in Mundo, Converse Direction.	2 6	2 1
Sun to the Sesquiquadrate of Jupiter in the Zodiac, Converse Motion.	2 45	2 9
Moon to the Square of Mercury in the Zodiac, Converse Direction.	2 48	2 9
Ascendant to the Biquintile of Saturn in Mundo.	2 48	2 9
Sun to the Semiquartile of Mars in the Zodiac, by Converse Motion.	3 2	3 0
Moon to the Opposition of Mars in the Zodiac.	3 7	3 1
Moon to the Square of Venus in the Zodiac, Converse Direction.	3 31	3 6
Moon to the Body of Jupiter in the Zodiac.	3 39	3 8
Ascendant to the Biquintile of Venus in Mundo.	4 2	4 1
Sun to the Sesquiquadrate of the Moon in Mundo, Direct Motion.	4 39	4 8
Part of Fortune to the Sextile of the Sun in Mundo.	4 54	4 11
Midheaven to the Sextile of Mercury in Mundo.	5 26	5 5
Sun to the Biquintile of Jupiter in the Zodiac, Converse Direction.	6 28	6 6
Sun to the Parallel of Mars in Mundo, by the Rapt Motion.	6 35	6 7
Sun to the Parallel of Saturn in the Zodiac.	6 38	6 8
Sun to the Parallel of Jupiter in Mundo, by the Rapt Motion.	6 42	6 9
Midheaven to the Sextile of Saturn in Mundo.	7 15	7 4
Moon to the Parallel of Mercury in Mundo, by the Rapt Motion.	7 18	7 4
Part of Fortune to the Quintile of Mercury in Mundo.	7 26	7 6
Moon to the Square of Saturn in the Zodiac, Converse Direction.	7 54	8 0
Moon to the Sesquiquadrate of Mercury in Mundo, Direct Motion.	7 54	8 0
Midheaven to the Sextile of Venus in Mundo.	8 6	8 3

CELESTIAL PHILOSOPHY,

THE DIRECTIONS CONTINUED.	ARC. D. M.	TIME. YRS. MO.
Moon to the Parallel of Saturn in Mundo, by the Rapt Motion	8 29	8 7
Moon to the Parallel of Venus in Mundo, by the Rapt Motion	8 53	8 11
Sun to the Biquintile of Jupiter in Mundo, Direct Motion.	8 54	8 11
Sun to the Quintile of Mars in the Zodiac	9 2	9 0
Part of Fortune to the Quintile of Saturn in Mundo	9 38	9 8
Midheaven to the Sextile of the Moon in Mundo	10 1	10 2
Moon to the Sesquiquadrate of Saturn in Mundo, Direct Motion	10 11	10 4
Part of Fortune to the Quintile of Venus in Mundo	10 16	10 5
Moon to the Sesquiquadrate of the Sun in the Zodiac	10 33	10 8
Moon to the Sesquiquadrate of Venus in Mundo, by Direct Direction	10 46	10 11
Sun to the Body of Mercury in Mundo, Direct Motion.	11 6	11 3
Sun to the Body of Saturn in the Zodiac	11 16	11 5
Midheaven to the Quintile of Jupiter in Mundo	11 23	11 6
Moon to the Opposition of Mars in Mundo, Direct Direction	11 52	12 0
Moon to the Trine of Saturn in the Zodiac.	11 57	12 1
Moon to the Body of Jupiter in Mundo, Direct Motion.	12 13	12 4
Moon to the Parallel of Mercury in Mundo, Direct Direction	12 17	12 5
Sun to the Parallel of Mars in Mundo, Converse Motion.	12 47	12 11
Midheaven to the Quintile of Mercury in Mundo	12 55	13 1
Sun to the Parallel of Jupiter in Mundo, Converse Direction	12 58	13 1
Moon to the Biquintile of Mercury in Mundo, by Direct Motion	13 31	13 8
Sun to the Parallel of Mars in Mundo, Direct Direction.	13 33	13 8
Moon to the Biquintile of Mars in the Zodiac, Converse Motion	13 44	13 10
Sun to the Parallel of Jupiter in Mundo, Direct Direction.	13 51	13 11
Sun to the Body of Saturn in Mundo, by Direct Motion.	13 58	14 1
Sun to the Body of Venus in Mundo, Direct Direction.	14 13	14 4
Part of Fortune to the Sextile of Mercury in Mundo	14 55	15 0
Moon to the Trine of Venus in the Zodiac	15 4	15 2
Sun to the Body of Venus in the Zodiac	15 7	15 2
Moon to the Parallel of Saturn in Mundo, Direct Motion.	15 23	15 5
Moon to the Parallel of Venus in Mundo, Direct Direction.	15 30	15 6

OR GENETHLIACAL ASTRONOMY. 149

| | ARC. | TIME. |
THE DIRECTIONS CONTINUED.	D. M.	YRS. MO.
Moon to the Trine of Mercury in the Zodiac	15 33	15 7
Moon to the Biquintile of the Sun in the Zodiac	15 47	15 10
Sun to the Body of Mercury in the Zodiac	15 48	15 10
Moon to the Semiquartile of Jupiter in the Zodiac, Converse Motion	15 50	15 10
Midheaven to the Quintile of Saturn in Mundo	16 7	16 1
Midheaven to the Quintile of Venus in Mundo	16 11	16 2
Sun to the Semiquartile of Mars in Mundo, Direct Direction	16 11	16 2
Sun to the Parallel of Venus in the Zodiac	16 33	16 7
Sun to the Sesquiquadrate of Jupiter in Mundo, Direct Motion	16 34	16 7
Ascendant to the Opposition of the Sun in Mundo	16 40	16 8
Midheaven to the Square of the Sun in Mundo	16 40	16 8
Moon to the Biquintile of Venus in Mundo, Direct Motion	16 50	16 10
Moon to the Biquintile of Saturn in Mundo, Direct Direction	16 51	16 10
Part of Fortune to the Semiquartile of the Sun in Mundo	16 51	16 10
Moon to the Parallel of Mercury in Mundo, Converse Motion	17 54	17 11
Moon to the Sesquiquadrate of Mars in the Zodiac, Converse Direction	17 59	18 0
Sun to the Trine of the Moon in Mundo by Direct Motion	18 16	18 3
Part of Fortune to Sextile of Venus in Mundo	18 21	18 4
Sun to the Square of the Moon in the Zodiac	18 22	18 4
Part of Fortune to the Sextile of Saturn in Mundo	18 30	18 6
Moon to the Parallel of Saturn in Mundo, Converse Direction	18 53	18 11
Moon to the Trine of Mars in the Zodiac, by Converse Motion	19 22	19 4
Moon to the Quintile of Venus in the Zodiac, Converse Direction	19 54	19 10
Moon to the Biquintile of Mars in Mundo, by Converse Motion	19 54	19 10
Sun to the Semiquartile of Venus in Mundo, Converse Direction	20 14	20 2
Moon to the Sesquiquadrate of Saturn in the Zodiac	20 44	20 8
Moon to the Parallel of Venus in Mundo, Converse Motion	20 54	20 10
Sun to the Semiquartile of Venus in the Zodiac, Converse Direction	21 6	21 0
Midheaven to the Trine of Mars in Mundo	21 11	21 1

Y

CELESTIAL PHILOSOPHY,

THE DIRECTIONS CONTINUED.	ARC. D. M.	TIME. YRS. MO.
Moon to her own Parallel in the Zodiac.	21 25	21 4
Sun to the Parallel of Mercury in Mundo, by the Rapt Motion.	21 35	21 6
Midheaven to the Sextile of Jupiter in Mundo.	21 36	21 6
Sun to the Opposition of Jupiter in the Zodiac, Converse Direction.	22 14	22 1
Sun to the Opposition of Jupiter in Mundo, Converse Motion.	22 15	22 1
Moon to the Sextile of Jupiter in the Zodiac, by Converse Direction.	22 23	22 3
Sun to the Body of Mars in Mundo, Converse Motion.	22 32	22 5
Sun to the Body of Mars in the Zodiac, Converse Direction.	22 38	22 6
Sun to the Square of Mars in the Zodiac.	22 41	22 7
Sun to the Semiquartile of Saturn in the Zodiac, Converse Motion.	22 41	22 7
Moon to the Quintile of Mercury in the Zodiac, by Converse Direction.	22 47	22 8
Sun to the Semiquartile of Saturn in Mundo, Converse Motion.	22 55	22 10
Sun to the Semiquartile of Mercury in the Zodiac, Converse Direction.	22 56	22 10
Sun to the Square of Jupiter in the Zodiac.	23 27	23 3
Ascendant to the Semiquartile of the Moon in Mundo.	23 38	23 5
Part of Fortune to the Opposition of the Moon in Mundo.	23 50	23 7
Moon to the Sesquiquadrate of Venus in the Zodiac.	23 57	23 9
Moon to the Quintile of Saturn in the Zodiac, Converse Motion.	23 58	23 9
Ascendant to the Opposition of Mercury in Mundo.	24 8	23 11
Midheaven to the Square of Mercury in Mundo.	24 8	23 11
Sun to the Parallel of Venus in Mundo, by the Rapt Motion.	24 8	23 11
Sun to the Semiquartile of Mercury in Mundo, Converse Motion.	24 14	24 0
Moon to the Biquintile of Mars in the Zodiac.	24 16	24 0
Part of Fortune to the Semiquartile of Mercury in Mundo.	24 16	24 0
Moon to the Sesquiquadrate of Mercury in the Zodiac.	24 31	24 4
Sun to the Parallel of Saturn in Mundo, by the Rapt Motion.	24 31	24 4
Ascendant to the Biquintile of Mars in Mundo.	26 15	25 11
Moon to the Biquintile of Saturn in the Zodiac.	26 18	25 11

OR GENETHLIACAL ASTRONOMY. 151

THE DIRECTIONS CONTINUED.	ARC. D. M.	TIME. YRS. MO.
Moon to the Square of Venus in Mundo, Converse Direction.	26 20	26 0
Moon to her own Semiquartile in the Zodiac	26 36	26 3
Moon to the Semiquartile of Jupiter in Mundo, Converse Motion	27 51	27 6
Moon to the Sesquiquadrate of Mars in Mundo, by Converse Direction	28 4	27 9
Ascendant to the Opposition of Venus in Mundo,	28 18	28 0
Midheaven to the Square of Venus in Mundo	28 18	28 0
Moon to the Square of Saturn in Mundo, Converse Motion	28 21	28 0
Part of Fortune to the Semiquartile of Venus in Mundo.	28 27	28 1
Moon to the Parallel of Jupiter in the Zodiac	28 46	28 4
Sun to the Sextile of Mars in Mundo, by Direct Direction.	28 51	28 5
Moon to the Square of Mercury in Mundo, Converse Motion	29 20	28 10
Sun to the Trine of Jupiter in Mundo, Direct Direction.	29 20	28 10
Ascendant to the Opposition of Saturn in Mundo,	29 25	28 11
Midheaven to the Square of Saturn in Mundo	29 25	28 11
Sun to the Parallel of Mercury in the Zodiac	29 30	29 0
Moon to the Biquintile of Venus in the Zodiac	29 33	29 0
Part of Fortune to the Semiquartile of Saturn in Mundo	29 35	29 1
Moon to the Parallel of Mars in the Zodiac	29 48	29 3
Moon to the Sesquiquadrate of Mars in the Zodiac	29 53	29 4

In this Nativity, the alarming testimonies which indicate a violent Death, are many; the Moon is afflicted by the Opposition of Mars, from cadent stations, and is also in Square with Mercury, who is of the nature and power of both the Malefics. The Sun, the giver of Life, is near violent fixed Stars, in the Watery Sign Scorpio, and applying to the Parallel of Saturn's Declination, and also to his Body in the Zodiac, and Mundo; he is likewise afflicted by the Rapt Parallel of Mars, and Mundane Parallel of the Moon, and according to his radical position, as he descends towards the Western Angle, by the Motion of the *Primum Mobile*; he applies to the Mundane Parallel of Mars, both by Direct, and Converse Motion. The Part of Fortune is also posited in the Watery Sign Cancer, in Mundane Square to Saturn, Venus, and Mercury. Jupiter is *afflicted* by the Opposition of Mars, and also by his Parallel of Declination, and Venus is conjoined with Saturn, and Mercury in a violent part of the Heavens; so that both the Luminaries, and the benefics are afflicted at the time of Birth; all these are configurations of a most malignant Nature, and as all the Celestial Bodies, except Mars, are in *Watery Signs*, it is evident that *Drowning* would be the Cause of her Death, which took place at the time I have stated above.

The Sun is the right Prorogator, and the Directions that destroyed Life, were, when he descended on the Cusp of the Seventh House, followed by the Square of the Moon in the Zodiac, and also by the Rapt Parallels of Mercury, Venus, and Saturn; the giver of Life was likewise directed to the Body of Mars in Mundo, by Converse Motion, and by Direct Direction, he arrived at the Quartile of Mars in the Zodiac, and though the rays of Jupiter, and Venus interposed in these Motions, their feeble power was of no avail, as they were afflicted in the Radix, and were also united in the train of Mortal Directions that cut off Life.

There are some who will doubtless ask, why the Sun, when he was directed to the Body of Saturn, at the Age of eleven Years, and five Months, followed by the Conjunction of Venus, and Mercury, did not destroy Life, as the Hyleg passed those baneful Directions, in the Zodiac, and in the World. I know this will prove a mystery to many, as the Native did not experience any Sickness, or danger, at that time; there is no doubt that those Directions would have had sufficient strength to have produced considerable danger to Life, but not Death, if their violent power had not been diminished by the other Motions, through which their Effects were defeated; for when the Sun was directed to the Body of Saturn, that Malefic was received in the Terms of Jupiter, therefore as his baneful power was dissolved, he consequently could not transmit any dangerous qualities to the giver of Life; and moreover, at the time when the Apheta arrived at his Body, he was, by Directional Motion, far removed from his radical station, and constituted in the Rays of Jupiter's Quartile in the Zodiac; all these Motions ought to be properly observed by all Students, as they will find in their practice, that it is not merely computing Directions alone, that will make them proficients in this Sublime Science, without diligent Study, and *intense application*; neither will all the Quadripartites that have yet been *translated* (or *supposed* to have been *translated*,) unveil this, and many other mysteries. It is said these Works were written by PTOLEMY, but in the manner in which they are *now* given to the Public, it is plain to all Students, who think proper to exercise their understanding thereon, that the most they contain, is a *large portion of useless home-manufactured-matter*, to confuse the practitioners without *Examples*, or any *proofs* to *show*, that what has been written is *founded on* TRUTH. I relate these *plain Facts*, which probably may give offence to some, but that I regard not. The genuine Principles of this Science, as they were taught by PTOLEMY, are *short*, and *concise*; his *Original* GREEK QUADRIPARTITE, *in Manuscript*, is yet preserved, and has never been Published, though the time may probably arrive, when it will be given to the Public, including a collection of one hundred Modern Nativities, to *prove* all the *Rules* by true Calculation, and Judgment; but with respect to the Quadripartites *lately* Published, we have no more *proofs* of their having been *originally* written by the *immortal* PTOLEMY, than we have of their been composed by the *Roman Pontiff*.

I have rather made a digression, but shall now return to my subject; In the Secondary Directions, the Sun applied to the Conjunction of Saturn, and Mercury, and Mundane Square of Mars, the Moon was in Parallel with Mars in the World, and also applied to his zodiacal Parallel, the lesser Malefic, having the Declination of the Moon in the Nativity; that Luminary also applied to the hostile stations of the enemies in the Progression; and in the last Revolution, the Moon made application to the Declination of Saturn, and Venus was on her own place, and also on the station of Saturn, and Mercury in the Nativity; Saturn was likewise in Square to the Moon, Jupiter, and Mars in the Radix. At the time she was Drowned, the Moon was applying to the Body of Venus, and Saturn, those Planets being in Quartile to Jupiter, and Mars in the Nativity. The Sun the giver of Life, was in the Watery Sign Cancer, with Castor, and Pollux, separating from the Body of Mars, having the Declination of Saturn, and Mercury; the Moon was also in Square to her own place in the Geniture; hence we may observe all those powerful Motions of the Stars, at those periods, when they were united in obnoxious places, and being joined with the primary Directions, they consequently augmented their power, by various applications, which correctly correspond with the time of Death, and the quality thereof.

The following Geniture is that of a person now living; he was Born in the City of Lincoln, and the estimate time of his Birth was given to me in the Month of October, 1824, which was supposed to be correct; but I will not be positive respecting the accuracy thereof, having no occurrences worthy of notice for rectification, without which no Nativity can be truly corrected; but I have reason to believe that there is not much difference between the Estimate, and the true time of Birth. It is well known to several persons now living, that the Father of this Native, (though unacquainted with this Celestial Study,) was anxious to obtain the times of the Births of all his Children, as near as possible, but what induced him to attend to such observations, I know not, as the true principles of this Science were but little known, or practised at that period. About fifty Years ago, the times of the Births of Children in general, (according to all the information I have been able to obtain,) were seldom ascertained with precision, owing to which, many errors have been committed, for when the Oblique Ascension of the Ascendant, and Right Ascension of the Zenith, are incorrect, (occasioned by a false time of Birth,) they not only alter all the Directions of the two superior Angles to Promittors in Mundo, but likewise cause the greatest errors in all the Mundane Parallels, and in fact, in *every Arc of Direction* in the Nativity, more or less, in the Zodiac, and in the World, both by Direct, and Converse Motion; but I need not trouble the Reader with a reiteration of remarks, which are manifest to the meanest capacity. The imbecile, and hostile appearances of the Celestial Bodies at the time of this Native's Birth, clearly indicate at one view, that he will never rise in the World above his present station in Life. Mercury represents his Person, Profession, &c. because he is ruler of the Ascendant, and Medium Cœli, he is conjoined with the Sun, who is in his fall, under the Earth, and that Luminary, who is the general significator of Promotion, &c. does not receive any assistance from benign applications. The Moon is also in a subterranean Position, in opposition to Jupiter, who is in a cadent station, in his detriment, and in sextile with Saturn, in signs of long Ascensions, and Venus, who governs the *second* House is impotent, being posited in the violent Sign Scorpio, in a subterranean place, where she is afflicted by the Square of Mars in the Zodiac, and Mundo, from obscure parts of the Heavens, that Malefic is also applying to the Conjunction of Jupiter, in an obnoxious position, and the ruler of the Part of Fortune is afflicted in the Radix, and deprived of all his Dignities. I could easily explain what all these *violent* positions, (combined with the Effects of the Directions,) will produce, during the few remaining Years of his Life, but as they exhibit transactions, which every attentive Student in this Science may readily discover, I shall make but few observations thereon, as all the Planets are *weak*, and *none* of them *dignified* at the given time of Birth, neither can those Stars that behold the superior places, produce any benign Effects which will appear in the following Figure of the Heavens.

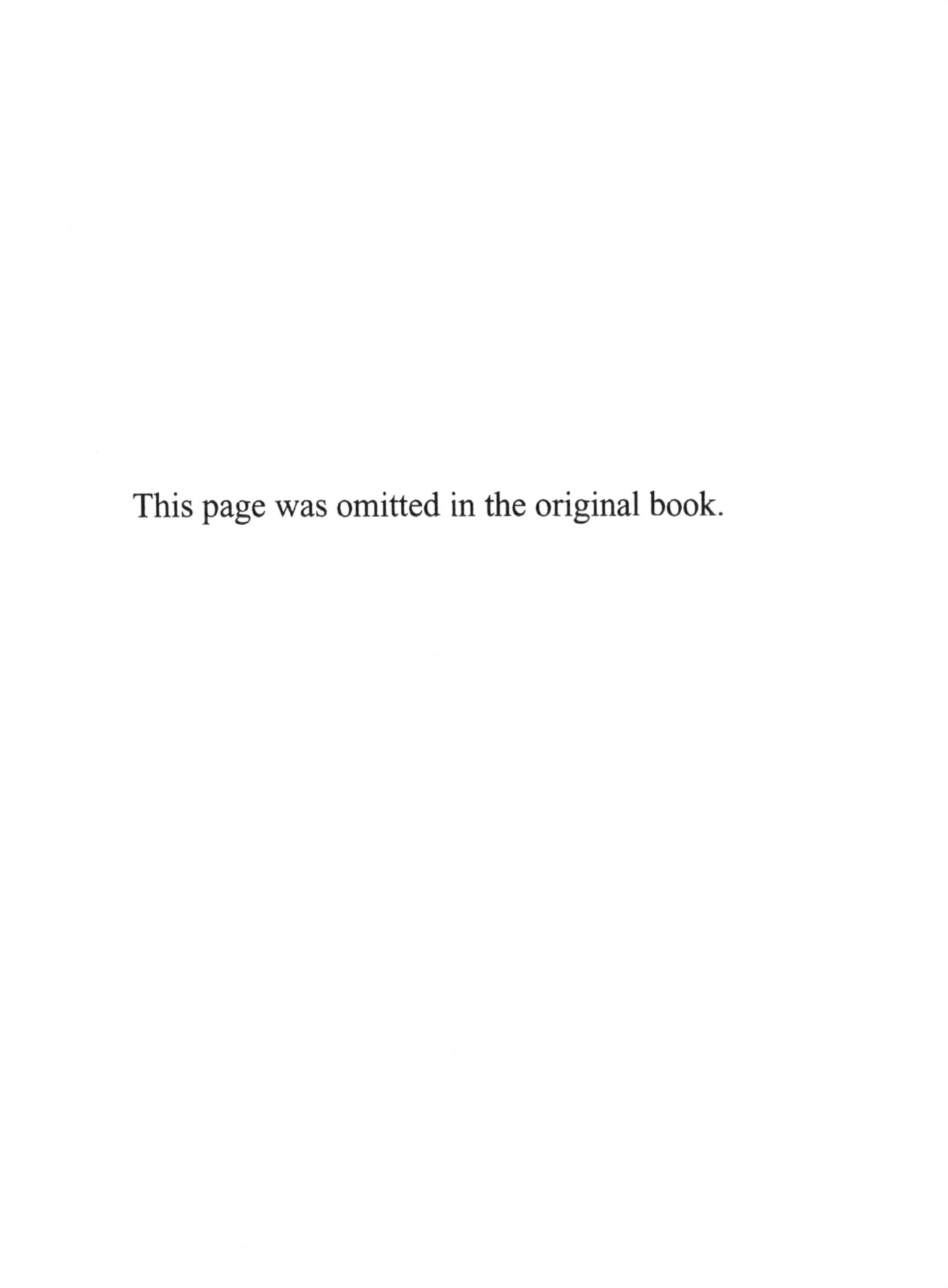

OR GENETHLIACAL ASTRONOMY.

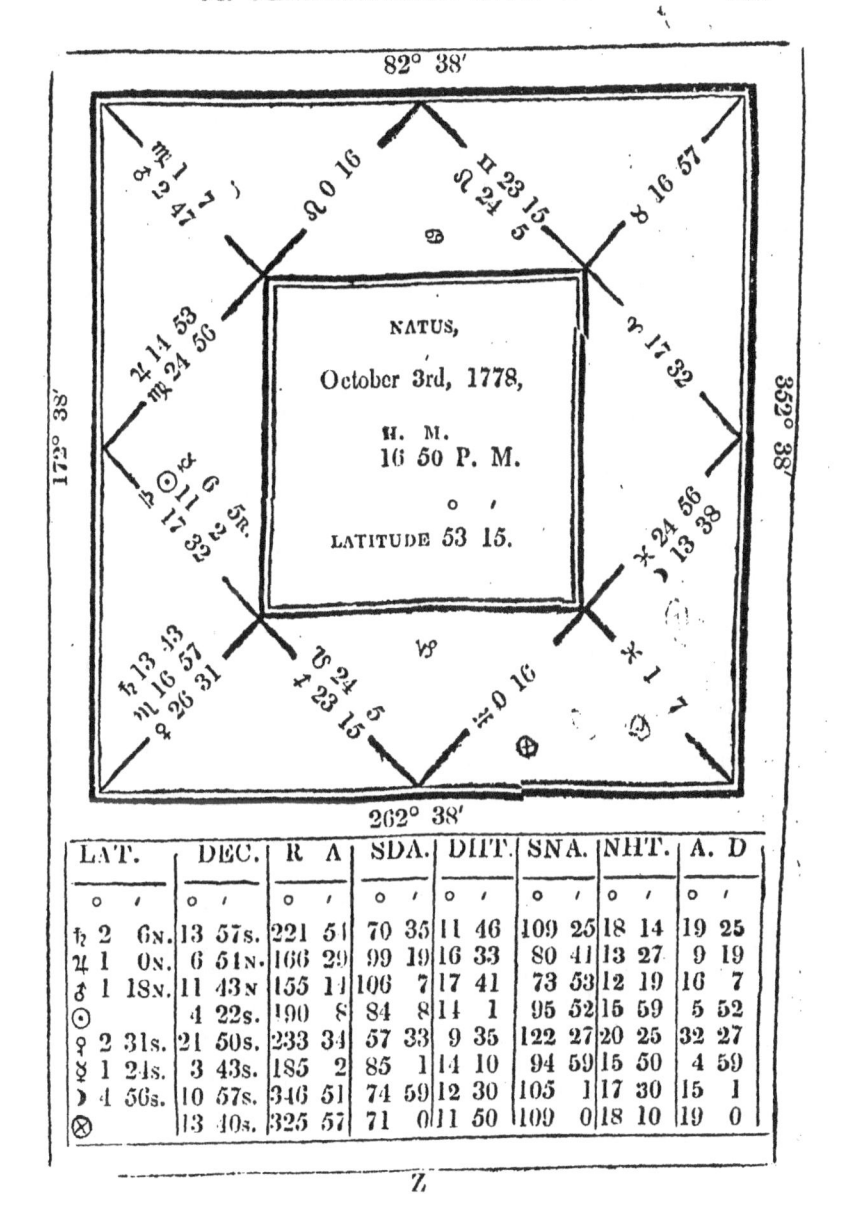

82° 38'

♍ 1
♄ 2 47
0 16
♎
Ⅱ 23 15
♌ 24 5
♉ 16 57

♃ 14 53
♍ 24 56

♈ 17 32

175° 38'

352° 38'

NATUS,

October 3rd, 1778,

H. M.
16 50 P. M.

° ′
LATITUDE 53 15.

♂ 11 ☉
♉ 6 5ʀ
♎ 17 32

♆ 24 56
♓ 13 38

♄ 13 43
♑ 16 57
♏ 26 31
♐

♑ 24 5
♐ 23 15

♒ 0 16

♓ 1 7

262° 38'

	LAT.	DEC.	R A	SDA.	DHT.	SNA.	NHT.	A. D
	° ′	° ′	° ′	° ′	° ′	° ′	° ′	° ′
♄	2 6N.	13 57s.	221 51	70 35	11 46	109 25	18 14	19 25
♃	1 0N.	6 51N.	166 29	99 19	16 33	80 41	13 27	9 19
♂	1 18N.	11 43N	155 14	106 7	17 41	73 53	12 19	16 7
☉		4 22s.	190 8	84 8	14 1	95 52	15 59	5 52
♀	2 31s.	21 50s.	233 34	57 33	9 35	122 27	20 25	32 27
☿	1 24s.	3 43s.	185 2	85 1	14 10	94 59	15 50	4 59
☽	4 56s.	10 57s.	346 51	74 59	12 30	105 1	17 30	15 1
⊗		13 40s.	325 57	71 0	11 50	109 0	18 10	19 0

Z

A TABLE OF THE DIRECTIONS.

	ARC. D. M.	TIME. YRS. MO.
Part of Fortune to the Trine of the Sun in Mundo	0 2	0 1
Moon to the Trine of Saturn in the Zodiac	0 6	0 2
Sun to the Semiquartile of Venus in the Zodiac	0 38	0 9
Moon to the Opposition of Jupiter in the Zodiac	1 40	1 10
Midheaven to the Sextile of Mars in Mundo	1 52	2 0
Moon to the Biquintile of Mercury in Mundo, Converse Motion	2 0	2 2
Sun to the Semiquartile of Venus in Mundo, Direct Direction	2 18	2 6
Sun to the Parallel of the Moon in Mundo, by the Rapt Motion	2 19	2 6
Midheaven to the Biquintile of Saturn in Mundo	3 2	3 4
Moon to the Square of Venus in Mundo, Converse Direction	4 10	4 7
Moon to the Opposition of Jupiter in Mundo, Direct Motion	4 12	4 7
Sun to the Parallel of Jupiter in Mundo, by the Rapt Motion	4 18	4 8
Sun to the Parallel of the Moon in Mundo, Converse Direction	4 21	4 9
Midheaven to the Quintile of Jupiter in Mundo	4 25	4 9
Sun to the Parallel of the Moon in Mundo, Direct Direction	4 50	5 3
Part of Fortune to the Square of Saturn in Mundo	5 35	6 1
Sun to the Semiquartile of Mars in Mundo, Converse Motion	5 42	6 2
Sun to the Body of Mercury in Mundo, Converse Direction	5 49	6 3
Sun to the Sesquiquadrate of the Moon in Mundo, Direct Motion	6 8	6 8
Sun to the Parallel of Jupiter in Mundo, Converse Direction	8 26	9 2
Sun to the Parallel of Jupiter in the Zodiac	8 39	9 5
Sun to the Parallel of Jupiter in Mundo, Direct Motion	8 44	8 6
Sun to the Semiquartile of Mars in the Zodiac	8 59	8 9
Sun to the Semiquartile of Jupiter in Mundo, Direct Direction	10 0	10 10
Part of Fortune to the Sesquiquadrate of Mercury in Mundo	10 6	10 11
Sun to the Semiquartile of Saturn in Mundo, Converse Motion	11 7	12 0

OR GENETHLIACAL ASTRONOMY.

THE DIRECTIONS CONTINUED	ARC. D. M.	TIME. YRS. MO.
Sun to the Sextile of Mars in Mundo, Direct Direction.	11 23	12 3
Part of Fortune to the Opposition of Mars in Mundo....	11 24	12 3
Sun to the Biquintile of the Moon in the Zodiac........	11 26	12 4
Ascendant to the Sextile of Venus in Mundo...........	11 43	12 7
Moon to the Opposition of Mars in Mundo, Converse Motion....	12 22	13 5
Moon to the Sesquiquadrate of Mercury in Mundo, Converse Direction..................................	12 30	13 7
Sun to Spica Virginis..........................	13 42	14 10
Ascendant to the Semiquartile of Saturn in Mundo.....	13 59	15 2
Moon to the Opposition of Mars in the Zodiac, Converse Motion..................................	14 5	15 3
Sun to the Sextile of Venus in Mundo, Converse Direction.	14 12	15 4
Midheaven to the Trine of the Moon in Mundo.......	14 13	15 4
Moon to the Parallel of Jupiter in the Zodiac.........	14 19	15 5
Sun to the Semiquartile of Saturn in the Zodiac, Converse Motion..................................	14 47	15 11
Sun to the Sextile of Venus in the Zodiac, Converse Direction..................................	15 59	17 4
Part of Fortune to the Sesquiquadrate of the Sun in Mundo.	16 1	17 4
Moon to the Biquintile of Mercury in the Zodiac, Converse Motion..................................	16 15	17 7
Ascendant to the Body of Mercury in Mundo.........	17 23	18 8
Midheaven to the Square of Mercury in Mundo.......	17 23	18 8
Moon to the Trine of Saturn in Mundo, Direct Direction.	17 24	18 8
Moon to the Trine of Venus in the Zodiac...........	17 29	18 9
Midheaven to the Sextile of Jupiter in Mundo........	17 39	18 11
Moon to the Square of Saturn in Mundo, Converse Motion.	18 18	19 9
Ascendant to the Semiquartile of Mars in Mundo.....	19 33	21 0
Moon to the Square of Venus in the Zodiac, Converse Direction..................................	19 50	21 3
Midheaven to the Biquintile of Venus in Mundo.......	19 55	21 4
Sun to the Parallel of Mercury in Mundo, by the Rapt Motion..................................	20 12	21 8
Moon to the Sesquiquadrate of Saturn in the Zodiac...	20 28	21 11
Ascendant to the Biquintile of the Moon in Mundo.....	21 13	22 8
Part of Fortune to the Square of Venus in Mundo.....	22 44	24 4
Moon to the Parallel of the Sun in the Zodiac.........	22 55	24 6
Moon to the Parallel of Saturn in Mundo, by the Rapt Motion..................................	23 1	24 7

162 CELESTIAL PHILOSOPHY,

THE DIRECTIONS CONTINUED.	ARC. D. M.	TIME. YRS. MO.
Sun to the Parallel of the Moon in the Zodiac	23 15	24 10
Ascendant to the Body of the Sun in Mundo	23 22	24 11
Midheaven to the Square of the Sun in Mundo	23 22	24 11
Sun to the Sesquiquadrate of the Moon in the Zodiac	23 26	25 0
Sun to the Trine of the Moon in Mundo, Direct Direction	23 38	25 2
Part of Fortune to the Body of the Moon in Mundo	23 39	25 2
Sun to the Semiquartile of Jupiter in the Zodiac	25 6	26 9
Moon to the Parallel of Mercury in the Zodiac	25 8	26 9
Moon to the Quintile of Venus in Mundo, Converse Motion	25 10	26 10
Sun to the Quintile of Mars in Mundo, Direct Direction	25 32	27 2
Sun to the Parallel of Mars in the Zodiac	26 9	27 9
Sun to the Sextile of Jupiter in Mundo, Direct Motion	26 33	28 2
Part of Fortune to the Opposition of Jupiter in Mundo	26 35	28 2
Sun to the Sextile of Saturn in Mundo, Converse Direction	26 38	28 3
Moon to the Sesquiquadrate of Mercury in the Zodiac, Converse motion	28 42	30 5
Sun to the Sextile of Mars in the Zodiac	28 59	30 8
Sun to the Quintile of Venus in the Zodiac, Converse Direction	29 24	31 1
Moon to the Biquintile of Mars in Mundo, Direct Motion	29 56	31 7
Moon to the Trine of Mercury in Mundo, Converse Direction	30 0	31 8
Moon to the Opposition of Mercury in the Zodiac	30 30	32 2
Ascendant to the Sesquiquadrate of the Moon in Mundo	31 43	33 5
Moon to the Parallel of Venus in Mundo, by the Rapt Motion	31 56	33 8
Ascendant to the Semiquartile of Venus in Mundo	32 8	33 10
Sun to the Sextile of Saturn in the Zodiac, Converse Direction	32 12	33 11
Midheaven to the Trine of Saturn in Mundo	32 13	33 11
Moon to the Biquintile of Saturn in the Zodiac	32 42	34 5
Moon to the Biquintile of Mars in the Zodiac	34 9	35 10
Ascendant to the Semiquartile of Jupiter in Mundo	34 12	35 10
Moon to the Opposition of Mercury in Mundo, Direct Motion	34 13	35 11
Midheaven to the Quintile of Mercury in Mundo	34 23	36 1
Sun to the Parallel of Saturn in the Zodiac	34 58	36 6
Moon to the Sesquiquadrate of Saturn in Mundo, Direct Direction	35 38	37 4
Moon to the Trine of Venus in Mundo, Direct Motion	35 58	37 8
Moon to the Square of Saturn in the Zodiac, Converse Direction	36 17	38 0

OR GENETHLIACAL ASTRONOMY.

	ARC.		TIME.	
THE DIRECTIONS CONTINUED.	D.	M.	YRS.	MO.
Sun to the Body of Jupiter in the Zodiac, Converse Motion	36	30	38	3
Moon to the Opposition of the Sun in the Zodiac	37	13	39	0
Ascendant to the Sextile of Mars in Mundo	37	14	39	0
Moon to the Biquintile of Jupiter in Mundo, Converse Direction	37	33	39	3
Moon to the Sesquiquadrate of Venus in the Zodiac	37	52	39	6
Sun to the Parallel of Mercury in Mundo, Direct Motion	38	6	39	9
Sun to the Parallel of Mercury in Mundo, Converse Direction	38	45	40	5
Moon to the Sextile of Venus in Mundo, Converse Motion	39	10	40	10
Sun to the Semiquartile of Mercury in Mundo, Direct Direction	39	10	40	10
Moon to the Quintile of Saturn in Mundo, Converse Motion	39	18	40	11
Sun to the Quintile of Jupiter in Mundo, Direct Direction	39	47	41	5
Moon to the Opposition of the Sun in Mundo, Direct Motion	40	1	41	8
Midheaven to the Quintile of the Sun in Mundo	40	11	41	10
Ascendant to Spica Virginis	40	14	41	10
Moon to the Quintile of Venus in the Zodiac, Converse Direction	40	29	42	1
Moon to the Sesquiquadrate of Mars in Mundo, Direct Motion	40	33	42	2
Sun to the Body of Saturn in Mundo, Direct Direction	42	2	43	7
Part of Fortune to the Trine of Saturn in Mundo	42	3	43	7
Midheaven to the Biquintile of the Moon in Mundo	42	13	43	9
Sun to the Parallel of Saturn in Mundo, by the Rapt Motion	43	4	44	7
Sun to the Square of Venus in Mundo, Converse Direction	43	21	44	10
Sun to the Trine of the Moon in the Zodiac	43	29	45	0
Sun to the Body of Saturn in the Zodiac	43	36	45	1
Moon to the Biquintile of Jupiter in Mundo, Direct Motion	43	55	45	5
Sun to his own Semiquartile in Mundo	44	56	46	5
Sun to the Quintile of Mars in the Zodiac	45	2	46	6
Moon to the Parallel of Saturn in Mundo, Converse Direction	45	8	46	7
Sun to the Sextile of Jupiter in the Zodiac	45	10	46	7
Midheaven to the Sextile of Mercury in Mundo	45	43	47	1
Sun to the Quintile of Saturn in the Zodiac, Converse Motion	45	52	47	3
Moon to the Sesquiquadrate of Mars in the Zodiac	46	20	47	8

THE DIRECTIONS CONTINUED.

	ARC.		TIME.	
	D.	M.	YRS.	MO.
Moon to the Biquintile of Saturn in mundo, Direct Direction	16	34	17	11
Sun to the Square of mars in mundo, Direct motion	16	45	18	1
Moon to the Parallel of Saturn in Mundo, Direct Direction	16	59	18	4
Moon to the Biquintile of Jupiter in the Zodiac by Converse Motion	17	30	18	10
Moon to the Sesquiquadrate of Jupiter in Mundo, Converse Direction	18	3	19	4
Sun to the Square of Venus in the Zodiac, Converse Motion	18	51	50	2
Ascendant to the Trine of the Moon in mundo	19	13	50	5
Moon to the Trine of mercury in the Zodiac, Converse motion	19	14	50	5
Moon to the Parallel of mercury in the Zodiac	19	33	50	9
Sun to the Body of mars in the Zodiac, Converse Direction	19	57	51	2
Moon to the Biquintile of Venus in the Zodiac	50	0	51	2
Sun to the Semiquartile of mercury in mundo, Converse Motion	50	2	51	2
Moon to the Biquintile of Jupiter in the zodiac	50	30	51	7
Ascendant to the Sextile of Jupiter in mundo	50	45	51	10
Ascendant to the Quintile of Mars in mundo	51	23	52	5
Midheaven to the Sextile of the Sun in mundo	51	24	52	5
Moon to the Parallel of the Sun in the zodiac	51	44	52	9
Sun to the Parallel of Venus in mundo, by the Rapt Motion	51	52	52	11
Moon to her own Semiquartile in mundo	52	30	53	6
Midheaven to the Trine of Venus in mundo	52	33	53	7
Moon to the Sextile of Saturn in mundo, Converse motion	53	18	54	4
Sun to the Sextile of mercury in mundo, by Direct Direction	53	20	54	4
Part of Fortune to the Opposition of mercury in mundo	53	22	54	5
Moon to the Sextile of Venus in the zodiac, Converse motion	53	25	54	5
Sun to the Semiquartile of mercury in the zodiac	53	27	54	6
Part of Fortune to the Biquintile of mars in mundo	53	50	54	10
Moon to the Sesquiquadrate of Jupiter in mundo, Direct Direction	53	51	54	10
Moon to the Biquintile of mars in mundo, Converse motion	54	22	55	3
Sun to the Square of Saturn in mundo, by Converse Direction	54	40	55	7
Moon to the Quintile of Saturn in the zodiac, Converse motion	54	51	55	10

OR GENETHLIACAL ASTRONOMY.

THE DIRECTIONS CONTINUED.	ARC. D. M.	TIME. YRS. MO.
Moon to the Sesquiquadrate of Venus in mundo, Direct Direction	56 23	57 3
Moon to the Semiquartile of Venus in mundo, Converse motion	56 40	57 6
Moon to the Trine of mars in mundo, Direct Direction	58 14	58 10
Sun to the Square of the moon in mundo, Direct motion	58 38	59 3
Sun to his own Sextile in mundo	58 57	59 6
Part of Fortune to the Opposition of the Sun in mundo	58 58	59 6
Moon to the Parallel of Venus in mundo, Converse Direction	59 18	59 10
Sun to the Square of Jupiter in mundo, Direct motion	59 39	60 2
Ascendant to the Semiquartile of mercury in mundo	59 53	60 5
Moon to the Sesquiquadrate of Jupiter in the zodiac, Converse Direction	59 58	60 6
Sun to his own Semiquartile in the zodiac	60 0	60 6
Moon to the Parallel of Jupiter in the zodiac	60 13	60 8
Moon to the Biquintile of mars in the zodiac, Converse motion	60 16	60 9
Part of Fortune to the Sesquiquadrate of Saturn in mundo	60 17	60 9
Sun to the Body of Venus in the zodiac	60 39	61 1
Moon to her own Semiquartile in the zodiac	61 4	61 6
Sun to the Quintile of Jupiter in the zodiac	61 7	61 6

The Dignity of Hyleg is claimed by the Sun in this Geniture, and if we examine those Directions of an inimical Power, which that Luminary has passed several Years ago, it will become evident that they could not produce any visible Effects, because their apparent obnoxious qualities were reduced, and counteracted, in proportion as the giver of Life applied to those Mundane places, where the power of the benefics were most prevalent. The Sun was directed to the zodiacal Parallel of Mars, at the Age of twenty-seven Years, and nine Months, but that Direction could not produce any injury to the Native's Health, because the Hyleg was then directed to the Sextile of Jupiter in Mundo, by Direct Motion, he also applied to the Terms of both the benefics, being surrounded by their rays in the mundane Circle, when the Prorogator arrived at the Eastern Horizon. At the Age of thirty-six Years and six months, the Hyleg was directed to the Parallel of Saturn's Declination, but that Direction could not give any Illness, or danger, because the giver of Life applied to the Body of Jupiter, by Converse motion, and was also received in his Terms, where, the rays of Venus, by the Altitude of the Sun's Circle of position, became subsequently conjoined; from which we may observe, that those Directions to mars, and Saturn to the giver of Life, could not produce any indisposition; and when the Sun was directed to the Body of Saturn, many pretenders would judge that the Native would depart this Life at the time limited by that Direction, but it passed over at the Age of forty-five Years, and one month, and left the Native in good Health, and Spirits; therefore from what has been observed, it is plain, that the Sun to the Body of Saturn could neither kill this Native, nor produce any injury to his Life, for the Directions of both the benefics followed, by which the violence of that Direction was impeded; but when the Hyleg is directed to the Body of mars by Converse Direction, united with others which will be in operation at the same time, then this Native will be no more, as the Effects of those Directions will prove mortal, at the Age of fifty-one Years, and two months.

I should not have given this Nativity a place in my Work, if there had not been a *whimsical question* connected therewith, which I conceive may require an answer. The fact is, a Gentleman now living was Born in the Town of Boston, Lincolnshire, October 3rd, 1778, 16H. 30M. P M; by which it will appear that the Native at Boston, was Born twenty minutes in time, earlier than the Native of Lincoln, and therefore the question is, as there are only twenty Minutes difference between the time of each Birth, will both these persons depart this Life at the same time.

I have stated the period of the Demise of the Native of Lincoln, in whose Geniture the Sun is certainly the giver of Life, but in the Nativity of the Native Born at Boston, the Sun's Directions cannot produce Death, because he does not claim the office of Prorogutor, therefore the Ascendant becomes the giver of Life, and at the Age of sixty-nine Years, and eleven Months, that point of the Heavens will be directed to the Semiquartile of the Sun in Mundo, followed by the Body of Saturn, and Mundane Square of Mars, which will certainly produce dissolution; it is therefore not difficult to prove, that these two persons who were Born in the same Hour, and but little more than thirty Miles distant from each other, will not depart this Life at the same time, for by true Astronomical Computation, the difference between the Mortal Directions in each Geniture, will be eighteen Years, and nine Months, so that there will be that space of time between the Demise of each Native, I therefore hope that I have given a satisfactory answer to this *learned Question*, which has occasioned much illiterate disputation.

Mr. G. J. Ping was Born at the time given in the following Figure, and departed this Life, June 27th, 1825, Aged twenty-two Years, nine Months, and five Days.

This Gentleman was by Profession, a Schoolmaster, and resided at Brigg, in the County of Lincoln; at his request I calculated the Directions in his Nativity in the Autumn of 1821, and as both the Luminaries are in Aphetical places, it cannot be difficult to select the proper Moderator, the right of which belongs to the Sun. As soon as I had viewed the different positions and configurations of the Stars in the Radix, I first computed the period of dissolution, which all those who Study this Science, ought always to ascertain, before any Judgment is given; for if that most important, and interesting subject be omitted, the practitioners will frequently wander from one thing to another, and predict impossibilities, and the times of various Events, which were to come to pass when the Native is in his Grave.

I have repeatedly urged the propriety of *first* selecting the *true Hyleg* in every correct Geniture, whether the Native be an Infant, or has advanced to Years of Maturity. The true time of the Birth of a healthy Female Child, named Smalley, (who was Born in the City of Lincoln, February 18th, 1825, 10h. A M.) was given to me for Judgment; it certainly could not be difficult to predict dissolution before the end of the first Year, for both the Luminaries, and Ascendant are afflicted at the time of Birth; the *Sun the giver of Life* was applying to the Square of Saturn in the Zodiac, and also to the Body of the Moon, &c. without any assistance; the fact is, this Child died on the 11th, of August, in the same Year, but there are other Causes that produce Death in Infancy, independent of Directions, which I have explained in this Work; I therefore mention this Example to show, that if I had neglected noticing the proper use of the *true Apheta*, my Judgment would have been erroneous; for some pretenders to this Science declared, that the Child would live to Years of Maturity, and Marry a person of some Property, and remain happy, and comfortable when both the Luminaries were directed to the Sextiles of Saturn, and Mercury, trine of Jupiter in the Zodiac, and Body of Venus, but all this preposterous jargon is totally refuted, by her personal extinction, which took place, according to my previous prediction, before the end of the first Year.

But some will doubtless say, that the Nativity of this Child has nothing to do with the Geniture of Mr. Ping, but as I am writing for Public information, I conceive that nothing ought to be omitted, that will convey genuine Instruction to the Students in this Science; and as the time of the Death of this Child, has puzzled some Practitioners, so also has the period of the dissolution of Mr. Ping on the same principles defeated the Judgment of those Professors, who are ignorant of the true Doctrine of the Sphere, and Rapt Motion of the Earth; for as the time of Birth is correct, I defy any Man to have previously predicted the true time of his Death by any Rules, except those alone that are delivered by the *immortal Ptolemy*, for the Sun is certainly the giver of Life, and does not meet any violent Directions in the Zodiac at the time of his decease, and therefore if there had not been those in Mundo, of equal Malefic power to have destroyed Life at the time he died, the Native would have been now living, and in good Health; therefore I ought not to be reproved in recording such Examples, as may be deemed beneficial to the Students, if they think proper to receive them; by which they may perfectly understand, (in the most perspicuous manner,) how to apply the established Rules, in all primary Directions, and Judgment.

CELESTIAL PHILOSOPHY,

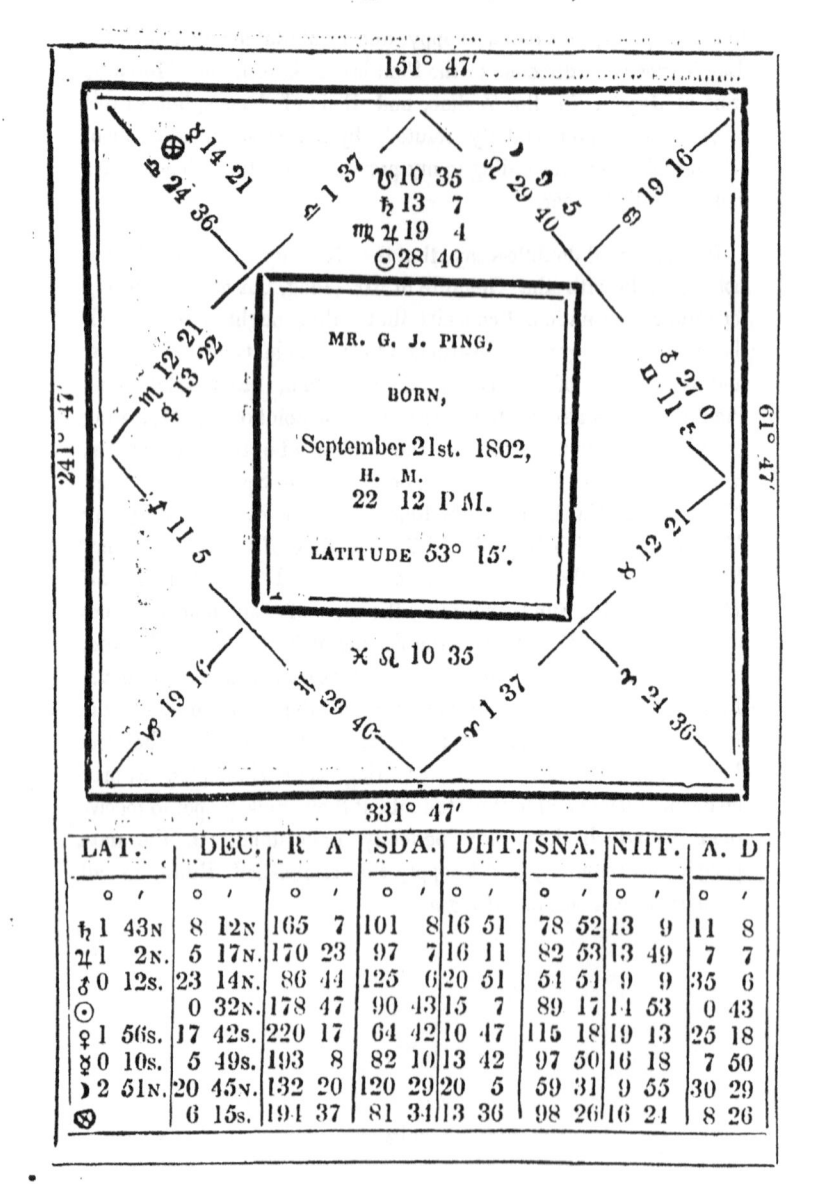

151° 47'

⊕ ♉ 14 21
♎ 24 36

♎ 1 37
♈ 10 35
♄ 13 7
♍ ♃ 19 4
☉ 28 40

☽ ♌ 29 40 5

♋ 19 16

241° 47'

♏ 12 21
♀ 13 22

☿ ♊ 27 0
5 11

♐ 11 5

MR. G. J. PING,

BORN,

September 21st. 1802,
H.   M.
22   12 P M.

LATITUDE 53° 15'.

♂ ♉ 12 21

61° 47'

♑ 19 16

♒ 29 40

♓ ☊ 10 35

♈ 1 37

♐ 24 36

331° 47'

	LAT.	DEC.	R A	SDA.	DHT.	SNA.	NHT.	A. D
	° ′	° ′	° ′	° ′	° ′	° ′	° ′	° ′
♄	1 43N	8 12N	165 7	101 8	16 51	78 52	13 9	11 8
♃	1 2N.	5 17N.	170 23	97 7	16 11	82 53	13 49	7 7
♂	0 12s.	23 14N.	86 44	125 6	20 51	54 54	9 9	35 6
☉		0 32N.	178 47	90 43	15 7	89 17	14 53	0 43
♀	1 56s.	17 42s.	220 17	64 42	10 47	115 18	19 13	25 18
☿	0 10s.	5 49s.	193 8	82 10	13 42	97 50	16 18	7 50
☽	2 51N.	20 45N.	132 20	120 29	20 5	59 31	9 55	30 29
☋		6 15s.	194 37	81 34	13 36	98 26	16 24	8 26

OR GENETHLIACAL ASTRONOMY.

	ARC.	TIME.
A TABLE OF THE DIRECTIONS.	D. M.	YRS. MO.
Ascendant to the Semiquartile of Mercury in Mundo...	0 15	0 3
Moon to the Sextile of Mercury in Mundo, by Converse Motion................	0 15	0 3
Sun to the Quintile of Mars in Mundo, Converse Direction	1 36	1 9
Sun to the Square of Mars in the Zodiac, Converse Motion.	2 2	2 3
Moon to the Semiquartile of Mars in the Zodiac.........	2 39	2 10
Sun to his own Parallel in the Zodiac.................	2 49	3 0
Ascendant to the Body of Venus in Mundo.............	3 48	4 3
Midheaven to the Square of Venus in Mundo..........	3 48	4 3
Moon to the Square of Venus in the Zodiac...........	3 53	4 4
Moon to the Semiquartile of the Sun in the Zodiac.....	4 10	4 8
Moon to the Sextile of Mercury in the Zodiac.........	4 45	5 3
Sun to the Semiquartile of the Moon in Mundo, Direct Motion..................	4 55	5 5
Moon to the Semiquartile of Jupiter in the Zodiac, Converse Direction...............	5 7	5 8
Sun to the Quintile of Venus in Mundo, by Converse Motion..................	5 52	6 6
Sun to the Sextile of Venus in Mundo, Direct Direction...	6 6	6 9
Sun to the Parallel of the Moon in Mundo, by the Rapt Motion.................	7 3	7 10
Moon to the Quintile of Mercury in the Zodiac, Converse Direction...............	8 11	9 1
Ascendant to the Quintile of the Sun in Mundo.........	8 51	9 9
Sun to the Body of Jupiter in the Zodiac, Converse Direction..................	9 38	10 8
Part of Fortune to the Semiquartile of Saturn in Mundo...	10 30	11 7
Moon to the Semiquartile of Saturn in the Zodiac, Converse Motion................	10 58	12 2
Sun to the Sextile of the Moon in the Zodiac...........	11 0	12 2
Sun to the Parallel of the Moon in Mundo, Direct Direction..................	12 22	13 8
Part of Fortune to the Quintile of the Moon in Mundo.	13 19	14 9
Midheaven to the Body of Saturn in Mundo...........	13 20	14 9
Ascendant to the Square of Saturn in Mundo..........	13 20	14 9
Moon to the Semiquartile of Mercury in Mundo, Direct Motion..................	13 32	14 11
Sun to the Sextile of Mars in Mundo, Converse Direction.	13 42	15 1
Ascendant to the Sextile of Mercury in Mundo........	13 57	15 5
Moon to the Square of Venus in Mundo, Direct Direction.	14 14	15 9

172 CELESTIAL PHILOSOPHY,

THE DIRECTIONS CONTINUED.	ARC. D. M.	TIME. YRS. MO.
Sun to the Body of Saturn in the Zodiac, Converse Motion	15 2	16 7
Sun to the Parallel of Jupiter in the Zodiac	15 34	17 2
Moon to the Sextile of Mars in the Zodiac	15 38	17 3
Part of Fortune to the Semiquartile of Jupiter in Mundo.	15 53	17 6
Moon to Cor Leonis	15 55	17 7
Moon to the Quintile of Mercury in Mundo, Converse Motion	16 19	18 0
Sun to the Parallel of the Moon in Mundo, Converse Direction	16 25	18 1
Sun to the Body of Mercury in the Zodiac	16 35	18 3
Moon to the Parallel of Mercury in Mundo, by the Rapt Motion	16 42	18 4
Midheaven to the Quintile of Venus in Mundo	16 44	18 5
Moon to the Trine of Venus in Mundo, Converse Direction	16 44	18 5
Sun to the Body of Mercury in Mundo, Direct Motion	16 53	18 7
Sun to the Semiquartile of Venus in Mundo, Direct Direction	16 53	18 7
Sun to the Parallel of Mercury in the Zodiac	16 59	18 8
Moon to the Semiquartile of Mercury in the Zodiac	17 34	19 5
Moon to the Semiquartile of Mars in Mundo, Direct Motion	17 41	19 6
Moon to the Semiquartile of Jupiter in Mundo, Converse Direction	17 42	19 6
Midheaven to the Sextile of Mars in Mundo	18 21	20 3
Midheaven to the Body of Jupiter in Mundo	18 36	20 6
Ascendant to the Square of Jupiter in Mundo	18 36	20 6
Moon to the Quintile of Venus in the Zodiac	19 14	21 2
Sun to the Sextile of Venus in the Zodiac, Converse Motion	19 40	21 7
Moon to the Sextile of Jupiter in the Zodiac, Converse Direction	20 26	22 6
Sun to the Parallel of Saturn in Mundo, by the Rapt Motion	20 32	22 7
Sun to the Quintile of Mars in the Zodiac, Converse Direction	20 37	22 8
Ascendant to the Trine of the Moon in Mundo	20 42	22 9
Sun to the Square of Mars in Mundo, Direct Motion	22 49	25 0
Sun to the Parallel of Jupiter in Mundo, by the Rapt Motion	22 57	25 2
Sun to the Parallel of Saturn in the Zodiac	23 38	25 11

OR GENETHLIACAL ASTRONOMY. 173

	ARC.		TIME.	
THE DIRECTIONS CONTINUED.	D.	M.	YRS.	MO.
Sun to the Quintile of the Moon in the Zodiac	23	43	26	0
Sun to Spica Virginis	24	0	26	4
Sun to the Square of Venus in Mundo, Converse Direction	24	1	26	4
Part of Fortune to the Semiquartile of the Sun in Mundo	24	28	26	11
Moon to the Semiquartile of Saturn in Mundo, Converse Motion	24	53	27	3
Ascendant to the Quintile of Mercury in Mundo	24	54	27	3
Sun to the Sextile of the Moon in Mundo, Direct Direction	25	0	27	4
Moon to the Quintile of Mars in the Zodiac	25	20	27	8
Midheaven to the Sextile of Venus in Mundo	25	22	27	8
Moon to the Parallel of Saturn in the Zodiac	25	42	28	0
Moon to the Sextile of Saturn in the Zodiac, Converse Motion	25	51	28	2
Sun to the Semiquartile of Mercury in Mundo, Converse Direction	26	43	29	2
Midheaven to the Body of the Sun in Mundo	27	0	29	6
Ascendant to the Square of the Sun in Mundo	27	0	29	6
Moon to the Quintile of Venus in Mundo, Direct Motion	27	10	29	8
Part of Fortune to the Sextile of Saturn in Mundo	27	21	29	10
Moon to the Parallel of Mercury in Mundo, Direct Direction	28	5	30	7
Moon to the Body of Saturn in the Zodiac	28	36	31	2
Moon to the Sextile of Venus in the Zodiac	28	48	31	5
Sun to the Semiquartile of Mars in Mundo, Converse Motion	28	49	31	5
Moon to the Body of Saturn in Mundo, Direct Direction	29	39	32	3
Moon to the Parallel of Mercury in the Zodiac	29	46	32	4
Sun to the Trine of Mars in the Zodiac	30	5	32	8
Moon to the Square of Mercury in the Zodiac, Converse Motion	30	26	33	0
Moon to the Parallel of Jupiter in the Zodiac	30	41	33	4
Sun to the Semiquartile of Saturn in the Zodiac	31	17	34	0
Sun to the Sextile of Mars in the Zodiac, Converse Direction	31	37	34	4
Part of Fortune to the Sextile of Jupiter in Mundo	32	4	34	9
Moon to the Quintile of Jupiter in the Zodiac, Converse Motion	32	45	35	6
Moon to the Body of Jupiter in the Zodiac	33	17	36	1

At the Age of sixteen Years, and nine Months, this Native's Life was exposed to the greatest danger, by a severe Sickness, which continued with unabated violence, for several Weeks. The giver of Life was then directed to the Body of Saturn, by Converse Motion, the Effects of which were of an alarming Nature, and threatened dissolution, but the Hyleg advanced to the Zenith by the Rapt Motion, and entered the Terms of both the benefics, his polar Elevation being constituted in the orbs of Venus, so that the Life of the Native was preserved, and the Effects of that Direction could not produce Death; but as soon as the Apheta was disengaged from those obnoxious Motions he then subsequently applied to other primary Directions of a more furious nature, there being no benign applications sufficient to dissolve any portion of the evil, owing to the *weakness* of the position *in all its parts*. The Sun who is Hyleg, is afflicted by the Square of Mars in the Zodiac, and Jupiter is combust, and in Quartile with that Malefic, being near the Body of Saturn; Venus is also in Square to the Moon, and in Sesquiquadrate with Mars in the Zodiac, and Mundo; so that both the Benefics, as well as the giver of Life, were violently afflicted at the time of Birth, which induced me to judge, that when the Sun was directed to the Parallel of Saturn, by the Rapt Motion, followed by the Mundane Square of Mars, and Parallel of Saturn's Declination, the Life of this Native would be destroyed; he died at the time I had predicted, and though the Directions of Jupiter and Venus were united in the Mortal train to the Prorogator, yet I did not regard their apparent power, which could be of no avail whatsoever, though consequently, by their union, they showed the quality of Death, which must appear plain to every attentive Student in this Science.

By Secondary Motion the Moon was applying to the Squares of Saturn, and Jupiter in the Zodiac, and the Hyleg had nearly the Declination of the superior Malefic; Mars was likewise in Mundane Square to Venus in the Nativity; and from the Progression, the Malefics afflicted both the Lights in the superior places. In his last Revolution the Moon applied to the Body of the Sun from an angular position, and Mars occupied the Ascendant at that time, and was in Mundane quartile to both the Luminaries. At the time of his Death, Saturn had arrived at the Square of his place in the Geniture, and Mars had returned to his *exact station* at the time of Birth, being in Quartile to the place of the giver of Life in the Radix; these stations of the Stars duly considered with the Directions, are of an ominous tendency, as both the Enemies were afflicting all the Vital significators when the Soul took its flight to the immortal abodes of happiness, and Glory.

The next is the Nativity of a young Lady, who was Born at Boston, in the County of Lincoln, on the 4th of May, 1803, at twenty Minutes before eight o'Clock in the Morning; the above time was given by her Friends, who informed me that I might depend on it being exact, as it was taken by a corrected Clock, with the greatest care. This Native died on the 11th of May, 1822, Aged nineteen Years, and seven Days.

Some pretenders to this Sublime Study, made a few observations on the Geniture of this young Lady, when she was living, and took the Ascendant for the giver of Life, though that point of the Heavens cannot be Hyleg, neither can the Sun, Moon, or Part of Fortune claim the Aphetical power; for it is evident, that if the Ascendant had been the true Apheta, the Effects of its Directions to the Semiquartiles of the Sun, and Mercury in Mundo, and Square of Saturn in the World, would certainly have destroyed Life, at the Age of nine Years, and four Months, there being *no benign assistance* at that period to preserve Life; but the unexpected demise of this Native, has caused those pretenders to witness the full extent of their Error, which has impeached, and invalidated every portion of their sterling Skill, (if they ever possessed any,) in this Science.

There are some who always take the Ascendant for Hyleg, in every Nativity they pretend to Calculate, and by their absurd notions, and ignorance, they endeavor to make the *untaught Vulgar* believe, that they possess *all* the sterling Wisdom of the Eastern Sages; they generally inform those who apply to them that they are Born under such, and such a Planet, and that they are able to discover all the Moles, Marks, or Scars on the person of the Native, and also, that the configurations of various Stars at the time of Birth, give black, dark, grey, or blue Eyes, &c. &c. Now I do affirm that all this is complete nonsense, and absurdity, and cannot be too much exposed, being performed for the purpose of *deceiving* those who apply to such *learned Sages* for Judgment; for you must observe that most of those *talkative Gentlemen* are very *soon puzzled*; therefore from what I have stated, it is evident, that when a person applies to a Professor of this Science, and delivers to him the true time, and place of his Birth, the Native does not require such *paltry Themes* to be sounded in his Ears, which are irrelevant to the Questions proposed to be resolved from the true time of Birth; for the form and stature, Moles, Marks, and colour of the Eyes, Hair, &c. &c. are wholly unconnected with these Astronomical Calculations, though they are doubtless *a refuge for ignorance* to which most of those Professors, (who know but little of Directional Motion,) generally resort. All the Questions required to be answered from a correct Geniture, are, the true periods when all important Events, (during the Native's Life,) will come to pass, including their respective qualities, and whether they are good, or evil.

The Dignity of Hyleg in this Geniture is claimed by Venus, who is not only in an Aphetical Place, but receives the proper Prorogatory power from every part of the Heavens, &c. which entitle her to possess that Dominion. I have computed the Anaretical Directions in full to the true giver of Life, not only to assist the genuine Student in his labors, but also to explain to him the vanity, and absurdity of selecting a *false* Prorogator, which is done in numberless cases, by which the fallacious Judgment of the Practitioners is justly held in derision, and the invalidity of their Skill rendered contemptible to every Scientific observer in this department of Celestial Philosophy.

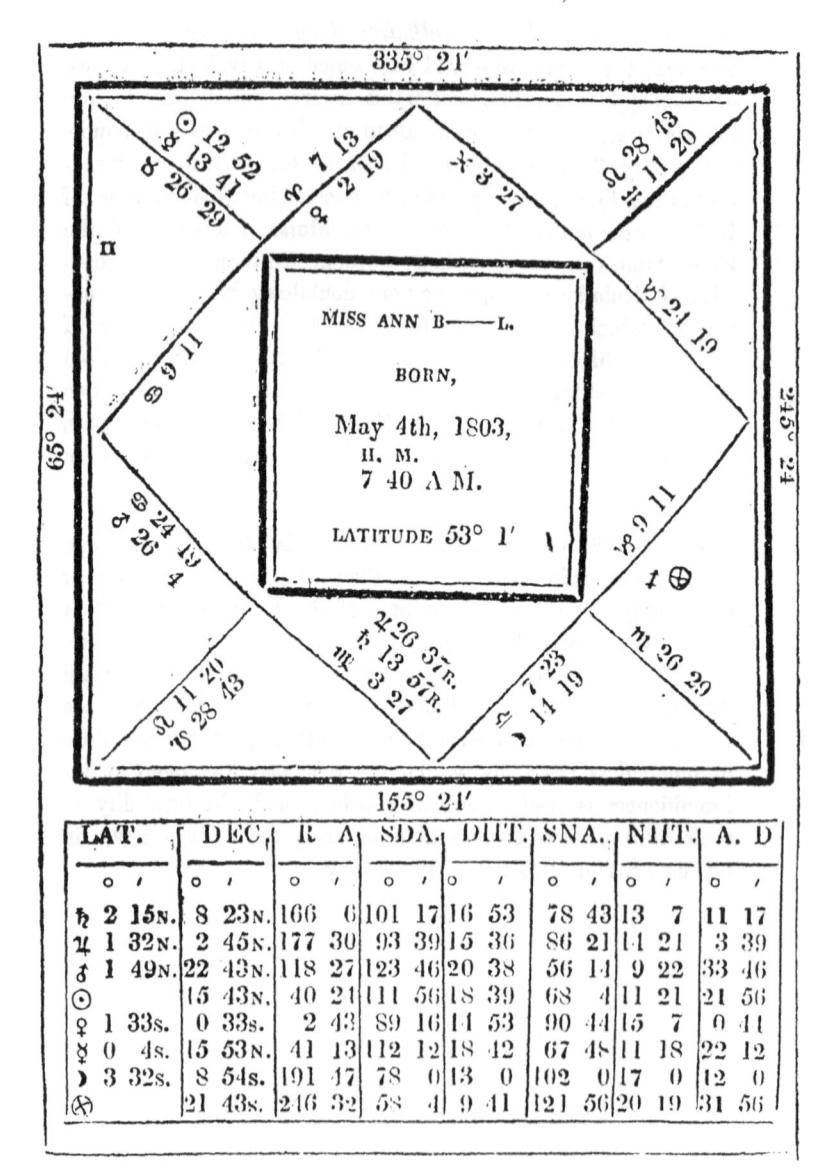

178   CELESTIAL PHILOSOPHY.

335° 21'

♂ ☉ 12 52
♂ 13 41
♀ 26 29

♈ 7 13
♀ 2 19

♓ 3 27

♌ 28 43
♒ 11 20

Ⅱ

♋ 6 9 11

65° 24'

MISS ANN B——L.

BORN,

May 4th, 1803,
H. M.
7 40 A M.

LATITUDE 53° 1'

♑ 21 19

245° 24'

♋ 24 19
♂ 26 4

♐ 11 9

⊕ 11 6 ♌

♐ 7 23
☋ 11 19

♏ 26 29

♑ 11 20
♑ 28 43

♃ 26 37ʀ
♄ 13 57ʀ
♏ 3 27

155° 24'

LAT.	DEC.	R. A.	SDA.	DHT.	SNA.	NHT.	A. D
° '	° '	° '	° '	° '	° '	° '	° '
♄ 2 15ɴ.	8 23ɴ.	166 6	101 17	16 53	78 43	13 7	11 17
♃ 1 32ɴ.	2 45ɴ.	177 30	93 39	15 36	86 21	14 21	3 39
♂ 1 49ɴ.	22 43ɴ.	118 27	123 46	20 38	56 14	9 22	33 46
☉	15 43ɴ.	40 21	111 56	18 39	68 4	11 21	21 56
♀ 1 33s.	0 33s.	2 43	89 16	14 53	90 44	15 7	0 44
☿ 0 4s.	15 53ɴ.	41 13	112 12	18 42	67 48	11 18	22 12
☽ 3 32s.	8 54s.	191 47	78 0	13 0	102 0	17 0	12 0
⊕	21 43s.	246 32	58 4	9 41	121 56	20 19	31 56

OR GENETHLIACAL ASTRONOMY.

	ARC.	TIME.
A TABLE OF THE DIRECTIONS.	D. M.	YRS. MO.
Sun to the Parallel of Mercury in the Zodiac	0 25	0 5
Midheaven to the Trine of Mars in Mundo	0 33	0 7
Sun to the Body of Mercury in the Zodiac	0 35	0 7
Sun to the Body of Mercury in Mundo, Direct Direction	0 39	0 8
Part of Fortune to the Semiquartile of Jupiter in Mundo	0 45	0 9
Sun to the Trine of Saturn in the Zodiac	0 47	0 9
Moon to the Square of Mars in Mundo, Converse Motion	1 23	1 5
Venus to the Square of Mars in Mundo, Direct Direction	2 5	2 1
Ascendant to the Trine of the Moon in Mundo	2 23	2 5
Sun to the Semiquartile of Venus in the Zodiac	3 18	3 4
Sun to the Quintile of Mars in Mundo, Converse Motion	4 13	4 4
Moon to the Biquintile of Mercury in the Zodiac Converse Direction	4 16	4 4
Sun to the Sesquiquadrate of Saturn in Mundo, Direct Motion	4 20	4 5
Part of Fortune to the Sextile of Saturn in Mundo	4 22	4 5
Venus to the Opposition of Jupiter in Mundo, Converse Direction	4 29	4 6
Moon to Spica Virginis	4 54	5 0
Sun to the Biquintile of Saturn in Mundo, Converse Motion	5 1	5 2
Venus to the Opposition of the Moon in Mundo, Direct Direction	5 11	5 4
Part of Fortune to the Sesquiquadrate of Venus in Mundo	5 15	5 5
Sun to the Sextile of Mars in Mundo, Direct Motion	5 22	5 6
Part of Fortune to the Sesquiquadrate of Mars in Mundo	5 24	5 7
Sun to the Biquintile of the Moon in the Zodiac	5 35	5 9
Sun to the Biquintile of Jupiter in Mundo, Direct Direction	6 29	6 8
Sun to the Biquintile of Jupiter in the Zodiac, Converse Motion	6 58	7 2
Moon to the Quintile of Mars in the Zodiac, by Converse Direction	8 10	8 5
Moon to the Square of Mars in the Zodiac	8 18	8 7
Ascendant to the Semiquartile of the Sun in Mundo	9 3	9 4
Venus to the Opposition of the Moon in the Zodiac	9 20	9 7
Ascendant to the Quintile of Venus in Mundo	9 27	9 8
Ascendant to the Semiquartile of Mercury in Mundo	9 43	9 11
Sun to the Sextile of Mars in the Zodiac	10 9	10 5
Moon to the Body of Jupiter in Mundo, Converse Motion	10 18	10 7
Moon to the Semiquartile of Saturn in the Zodiac	10 21	10 8

	ARC.	TIME
THE DIRECTIONS CONTINUED.	D. M.	YRS. MO.
Sun to the Sesquiquadrate of Saturn in the Zodiac, Converse Direction............	10 35	10 10
Sun to the Trine of Jupiter in the Zodiac............	10 37	10 10
Sun to the Pleiades............	10 41	10 11
Ascendant to the Square of Saturn in Mundo.........	10 42	10 11
Midheaven to the Opposition of Saturn in Mundo.......	10 42	10 11
Moon to the Sesquiquadrate of Mercury in the Zodiac, Converse Motion............	10 44	11 0
Part of Fortune to the Biquintile of Mars in Mundo.....	11 1	11 4
Part of Fortune to the Semiquartile of the Moon in Mundo.	11 11	11 6
Moon to the Parallel of the Sun in the Zodiac.........	11 32	11 10
Moon to the Parallel of Mercury in the Zodiac.......	11 53	12 2
Sun to the Sesquiquadrate of the Moon in the Zodiac. .	12 52	13 2
Venus to the Biquintile of Saturn in the Zodiac........	13 33	13 10
Moon to the Body of Jupiter in the Zodiac, Converse Direction............	13 40	13 11
Part of Fortune to the Quintile of Saturn in Mundo.....	14 52	15 3
Sun to the Sesquiquadrate of Jupiter in Mundo, Direct Direction............	15 7	15 6
Part of Fortune to the Sextile of Jupiter in Mundo. ...	15 9	15 6
Venus to the Opposition of Saturn in Mundo, Converse Motion............	15 11	15 7
Sun to the Sextile of Venus in the Zodiac............	15 23	15 9
Moon to the Biquintile of Mercury in Mundo, Converse Direction............	17 21	17 8
Sun to the Trine of Saturn in Mundo, Direct Motion...	17 27	17 9
Moon to the Biquintile of Venus in the Zodiac.........	17 33	17 10
Sun to the Biquintile of the Moon in Mundo, Direct Direction,............	17 56	18 3
Moon to the Trine of Mars in Mundo, Direct Motion	17 58	18 3
Venus to the Biquintile of Saturn in Mundo, Direct Direction............	18 6	18 5
Sun to the Biquintile of Saturn in the Zodiac, Converse Motion............	18 10	18 6
Venus to the Parallel of Saturn in Mundo, by the Rapt Motion............	18 29	18 11
Venus to the Square of Mars in the Zodiac,..........	18 38	19 1
Venus to the Parallel of Saturn in the Zodiac........	18 46	19 2
Ascendant to the Body of Mars in Mundo............	19 17	19 8
Midheaven to the Square of Mars in Mundo	19 17	19 8

	ARC.	TIME.
THE DIRECTIONS CONTINUED	D. M.	YRS. MO.
Sun to Aldebaran..................................	19 48	20 2
Venus to the Parallel of the Moon in the Zodiac.......	20 1	20 4
Sun to Semiquartile of Venus in Mundo, Direct Direction.	20 6	20 5
Part of Fortune to the Trine of Venus in Mundo,....	20 8	20 5
Moon to the Semiquartile of Jupiter in the Zodiac.....	20 11	20 6
Venus to the Sesquiquadrate of Saturn in the Zodiac,..	20 58	21 4
Moon to the Opposition of the Sun in the Zodiac.......	21 13	21 7
Moon to the Quintile of Mars in Mundo, Converse Direction	21 47	22 2
Moon to the Parallel of Saturn in Mundo, by the Rapt Motion.	21 53	22 3
Moon to the Opposition of Mercury in the Zodiac.....	21 55	22 3
Moon to the Semiquartile of Saturn in Mundo, Direct Direction..............	21 59	22 4
Ascendant to the Square of Jupiter in Mundo..........	22 6	22 5
Midheaven to the Opposition of Jupiter in Mundo.....	22 6	22 5
Moon to the Sextile of Saturn in the Zodiac..	22 7	22 5
Moon to the Body of Saturn in Mundo, Converse Motion.	22 31	22 10
Venus to the Sextile of Mars in Mundo, Direct Direction.	22 41	23 0
Sun to the Square of Mars in the Zodiac, Converse Motion.	23 7	23 5
Moon to the Trine of Mercury in the Zodiac, Converse Direction..............	23 13	23 6
Sun to the Semiquartile of Mars in the Zodiac.......	23 16	23 7
Venus to the Biquintile of Jupiter in the Zodiac.......	23 56	24 3
Moon to the Sextile of Mars in the Zodiac, Converse Motion.	24 2	24 4
Venus to the Parallel of Jupiter in Mundo, by the Rapt Motion.............	24 40	24 11
Moon to the Sesquiquadrate of Venus in the Zodiac.....	24 55	25 2
Moon to the Opposition of the Sun in Mundo, Direct Direction.............	25 5	25 4
Moon to the Opposition of Mercury in Mundo, Direct Motion	25 48	26 1
Moon to the Body of Saturn in the Zodiac, Converse Direction.............	25 49	26 1
Venus to the Sesquiquadrate of Saturn in Mundo, Direct Motion.............	25 58	26 3
Sun to the Square of Saturn in the Zodiac,............	26 0	26 3
Part of Fortune to the Biquintile of the Sun in Mundo.	26 10	26 5
Sun to the Trine of the Moon in the Zodiac.........	26 21	26 7
Sun to the Quintile of Venus in the Zodiac...........	26 21	26 7
Ascendant to the Quintile of Saturn in Mundo.........	26 27	26 8
Sun to the Square of Mars in Mundo, Converse Direction.	26 36	26 10
Part of Fortune to the Quintile of Jupiter in Mundo...	26 40	26 11

THE DIRECTIONS CONTINUED.

	ARC.		TIME.	
	D.	M.	YRS.	MO.
Part of Fortune to the Biquintile of Mercury in Mundo.	26	53	27	2
Midheaven to the Body of Venus in Mundo.	27	19	37	7
Ascendant to the Square of Venus in Mundo.	27	19	27	7
Moon to the Sesquiquadrate of Mercury in Mundo, Converse Motion.	27	33	27	10
Ascendant to the Sextile of the Sun in Mundo.	27	42	28	0
Moon to the Parallel of Mars in the zodiac.	27	50	28	2
Sun to the Parallel of Mars in the zodiac.	27	50	28	2
Sun to the Sesquiquadrate of the Moon in Mundo Direct Direction.	28	8	28	5
Part of Fortune to the Sextile of the Moon in Mundo.	28	11	28	5
Ascendant to the Sextile of Mercury in Mundo.	28	25	28	8
Moon to the Parallel of Jupiter in Mundo, by the Rapt Motion.	28	39	28	11
Sun to the Trine of Jupiter in Mundo, Direct Direction.	29	31	29	9
Part of Fortune to the Square of Saturn in Mundo.	30	36	30	9
Venus to the Body of the Sun in the zodiac.	31	6	31	3

OR GENETHLIACAL ASTRONOMY.

The Student may observe, that as Venus is the giver of Life, no violent Directions could produce Death, but those alone to which that Planet was directed, for she beholds the Moon by an opposition, and the Horoscope by a Mundane Sextile, and disposes of both the Luminaries at the time of Birth, and also of the preceding Conjunction; these were the *chief* reasons which induced me to select that Star for the true Prorogator; I computed the following Directions in full for the Native's Death, which correctly corresponded with the period of that solemn Event.

THE POLAR ALTITUDE OF VENUS, IS THUS CALCULATED.

	°	′
As her duplicate diurnal horary times	29	46
Is to her distance from the Zenith	27	19
So are thirty Degrees	30	0
To the proportional part	27	32
Right Ascension of the Meridian, add	335	24
And the sum is	362	56
From which subtract the Circle	360	0
Remains the Oblique Ascension of Venus	2	56
Subtract the Right Ascension	2	43
Ascensional Difference under her Pole	0	13

	° ′	
Then from Sine, with Radius	0 13=	17,57766
Subtract Tangent of her Declination	0 33=	7,98225
Tangent of the Pole of Venus	21 30=	9,59541

Venus to the Parallel of Saturn in Mundo, by the Rapt Motion.

	°	′
Diurnal horary times of Venus	14	53
Nocturnal horary times of Saturn	13	7
Sum of the horary times	28	0

2C

	°	′
As the sum of the horary times....................	28	0
Is to the Nocturnal horary times of Saturn............	13	7
So is the distance in Right Ascension between Saturn, and Venus in Opposition....................	16	37
To the proportional part.........................	7	47
Add the primary distance of Saturn from the Nadir.....	10	42
And the sum is the Arc of Direction.................	18	29

Venus to the Square of Mars in the Zodiac.

The Quartile of Mars falls in 26° 4′ of Aries, with 1° 51′ South Latitude.

	°	′
Then from the Oblique Ascension of the Square of Mars, taken under the Polar Elevation of Venus.........	21	34
Subtract the Oblique Ascension of Venus.............	2	56
Remains the Arc of Direction......................	18	38

Venus to the Parallel of Saturn in the Zodiac.

She meets the Declination of Saturn in 26° 15′ of Aries, with 1° 54′ South Latitude.

	°	′
From the Oblique Ascension of the Parallel of Saturn's Declination...............................	21	42
Subtract the Oblique Ascension of Venus.............	2	56
Arc of Direction................................	18	46

Venus to the Parallel of the Moon in the Zodiac.

She obtains the Declination of the Moon in 27° 45′ of Aries, with 1° 56′ South Latitude.

	°	′
Then from the Oblique Ascension of the Moon's Zodiacal Parallel.....................................	22	57

		°	′
Subtract the Oblique Ascension of Venus........		2	56
And the Arc of Direction will be................		20	1

Venus to the Sesquiquadrate of Saturn in the Zodiac.
This Direction falls in 28° 57′ of Aries, with 1° 57′ South Latitude.

	°	′
From the Oblique Ascension.....................	23	54
Subtract the Oblique Ascension of Venus............	2	56
Arc of Direction................................	20	58

Venus to the Sesquiquadrate of Saturn in Mundo, Direct Direction.
I first direct to the Trine in the World.

	°	′
As the diurnal horary times of Venus...............	14	53
Are to her distance from the Eleventh.............	2	27
So are the nocturnal horary times of Saturn.........	13	7
To his secondary distance from the third...........	2	9
Primary distance from the third, add..............	36	56
Arc of Direction to the Trine in Mundo............	39	5
Subtract the nocturnal horary times of Saturn........	13	7
Remains the Arc of Direction.....................	25	58

Question.—It appears that you have taken much trouble in computing the Mortal Directions to Venus, as Hyleg in this Nativity, but why should not the Effects of the Ascendant to the Body of Mars have been sufficient to have destroyed Life at the time she died, with a very *small* alteration in time, as it came up so near the other Directions, which you have allowed to be the *only cause* of the Native's Death?

Answer.—If the Ascendant had been the giver of Life, this Native would have died in her Infant state, but the Horoscope has nothing to do with Diseases, and Death, in this Nativity, and therefore it is a most *pitiful,* and *absurd* notion to mention the Ascendant to the Body of Mars for the Native's demise, as that Direction could not produce any Illness, neither could any visible Accident appear from its *supposed* Malefic power; now I could wish that those who take the Horoscope as the giver of Life in other Genitures, (when it has no right to exercise that Dominion;) to notice, what Effects the Ascendant to the Body of Mars will produce, when the Directions of both the Benefics immediately follow in regular succession to that point in the Mundane Circle. In this Example, when the Ascendant was directed to the Body of that Malefic, it was succeeded by the Mundane Squares of Jupiter, and Venus, with their Terms, so that the violent power of Mars was dissolved, by which he could not give the least Sickness, or danger. But the only *true Anaretical Directions,* were, Venus Hyleg, to the Parallel of Saturn in Mundo, by the Rapt Motion, and also to the Square of Mars in the Zodiac, with the Parallel of Saturn's Declination, Zodiacal Parallel of the Moon, and Sesquiquadrate of Saturn in the Zodiac, and in Mundo; these were the Directions that destroyed Life, which may be seen progressively arranged in the foregoing Table.

By Secondary Motion the giver of Life was in a violent station, in Quartile to the place of Mars in the Geniture; the Sun and Mars were in Mundane Square, and the Declination of both were nearly the same; the Moon was on the Mundane place of Mars in the Nativity, and in Zodiacal Square to the Apheta in the Geniture. In the Revolutional Figure for the nineteenth Year, the Moon was applying to the Opposition of Saturn, and Mercury, and also to the Declination of Jupiter, Mars, and the Sun; she also applied to the Square of Mars in the Nativity, and had separated from her Radical place. At the time she died, the Hyleg was near her place in the Geniture, and the Moon was likewise in Square to her own radical station, and was also in Quartile to the place of Mars in the Nativity.

Several respectable Gentlemen who reside in Paris, have requested me to publish the Nativity of the Duke of Bordeaux: I have complied with their requests, and have given his Geniture a place in this publication. The time of Birth communicated to me, is that which I have inserted in the following Figure. Those Scientific persons who are acquainted with the primitive principles of Stellar power, will acknowledge, that this Nativity is a very *remarkable one*, when considered in all its parts, which may be proved by the illustration of the Precepts given in this Work.

At the Baptism of this illustrious Native, who is now living, the late Louis the eighteenth, spoke to the Assemblage as follows. 'Let us invoke for him the protection of the Mother of God, the Queen of the Angels, let us implore her to watch over his Days, to remove far from his Cradle the misfortunes with which it has pleased Providence to afflict his Relatives, and to conduct him by a less rugged path, than I have trod to Eternal felicity.'

It will probably appear singular to some, that I have omitted the Computations of all the various Arcs of Directions in this Geniture, and given them in others in a copious manner, throughout the whole of this Work; my *particular reasons* for so doing must remain in *obscurity*, as I do not wish to give the least offence to any party, and as I am not disposed to create discord, or multiply disputations among those Characters, who are, or may be interested in subjects that are yet in Oblivion, I therefore trust that I have not acted improperly in omitting the primary Directions, and Judgment, having given all the correct numbers that are required to complete the various Calculations, the sublimity of which cannot fail to elevate the mind of those who are inclined to contemplate the infinite Wisdom, and power of the OMNIPOTENT CREATOR, in his wondrous Works.

CELESTIAL PHILOSOPHY,

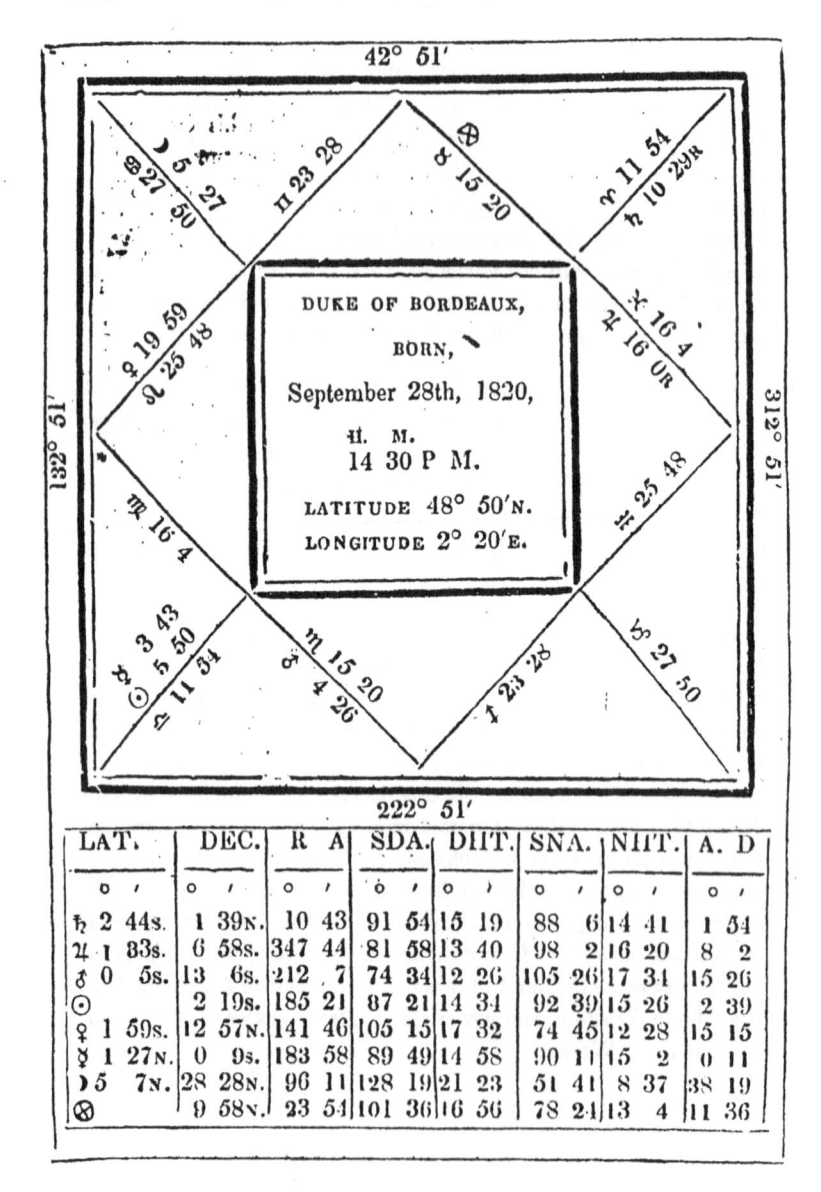

DUKE OF BORDEAUX,

BORN,

September 28th, 1820,

H. M.
14 30 P M.

LATITUDE 48° 50′ N.
LONGITUDE 2° 20′ E.

	LAT.	DEC.	R A	SDA.	DHT.	SNA.	NHT.	A. D
	° ′	° ′	° ′	° ′	° ′	° ′	° ′	° ′
♄	2 44s.	1 39N.	10 43	91 54	15 19	88 6	14 41	1 54
♃	1 33s.	6 58s.	347 44	81 58	13 40	98 2	16 20	8 2
♂	0 5s.	13 6s.	212 7	74 34	12 26	105 26	17 34	15 26
☉		2 19s.	185 21	87 21	14 34	92 39	15 26	2 39
♀	1 59s.	12 57N.	141 46	105 15	17 32	74 45	12 28	15 15
☿	1 27N.	0 9s.	183 58	89 49	14 58	90 11	15 2	0 11
☽	5 7N.	28 28N.	96 11	128 19	21 23	51 41	8 37	38 19
⊕		9 58N.	23 54	101 36	16 56	78 24	13 4	11 36

As several persons will doubtless be disposed to compute the Directions in this Nativity, I have given the true Circles of Positions of the Planets, with their Oblique Ascensions, and Descensions, under their own Poles, which immediately follow; they are accurately Calculated, so that the Practitioners, may, without much difficulty, or trouble, calculate the true Arcs in an accurate, and explanatory manner, which will amply recompense them for their labors, and give sufficient satisfaction.

The primary distance of the Sun from the Horoscope, is 55° 9', and his Seminocturnal Arc 92° 39'; his duplicate horary times below the Earth, are 30° 52', and his Pole of Position 24° 22', under which his Oblique Ascenion is 186° 24'.

The distance of the Moon by her Latitude from the Zenith, is 53° 20', and her double diurnal horary times, 42° 46'; her Semidiurnal Arc is 128° 19'; these numbers produce her Pole 26° 51', and her true Oblique Ascension 80° 15'.

The distance of Saturn from the Western Horizon, is 59° 46', and his double horary times above the Earth, are 30° 38', his Circle of Position will then become 22°, and his Oblique Descension, 11° 23'.

Jupiter's distance from the West, is 26° 51', and his duplicate horary times above the Earth, 27° 20'; his Semidiurnal Arc is 81° 58', and his Pole 37° 26', consequently his Oblique Descension will be 342° 22'.

The distance of Mars from the Northern Angle, is 10° 44', therefore his Seminocturnal Arc is 105° 26', and his double horary times 35° 8'; his Pole of Position will then be 6° 42', and his Oblique Ascension 213° 41'.

The primary distance of Venus from the Horoscope, is 6° 20', and her duplicate horary times above the Earth 35° 4'; her Circle of Position will then be 47° 3', and her Oblique Ascension 127° 28'.

By Right Ascension, the distance of Mercury from the Imum Cœli, is 38° 53′, and his double horary times 30° 4′; consequently his Seminocturnal Arc is 90° 11′, which will produce his Circle of Position 29° 3′, and his Oblique Ascension 184° 3′.

The next is the Geniture of a Gentleman, who was Born near Boston, October 7th, 1789, 13H. 0M. P.M; and died on the 15th of August, 1814, aged twenty-four Years, ten Months, and seven Days.

This Native had acquired considerable knowledge in this department of Astronomy, which the Astral significators of Science, &c. exhibit in the following Figure of his Birth. His noble and excellent qualifications, and pious demeanour were such, that all those who had the pleasure of his acquaintance, soon became convinced of his superior Talents in Literature, which, combined with a dignified Mind, free from Pride, and ostentation, truly adorn the character of the Scholar, and the Gentleman. He was not much attached to the sports of the Field, yet he sometimes accompanied my Father in Shooting, and Coursing, in the Lordships of Helpringham, Hale, Heckington, Swaton, Seredington, Spanby, and Donington, &c. &c. He computed the Moon's Direction to the quartile of Saturn in the Zodiac, in his own Geniture, (that Luminary being the giver of Life,) and observed, that he believed it was a baneful Direction, as Saturn was in the *eighth House*, and posited in the *Watery sign* Pisces, he therefore told my Father that he anticipated considerable danger to his Life by *Water*, when the Effects of that Direction were in operation, but his Judgment in this case was founded on the false principles of the old School, for it is not the lord of the *Eighth*, nor Planets posited in the *Eighth*, that can produce Death, but the *true Anareta* only, which will always be found to perform that office; hence it is of no consequence where the destroying Star is stationed at the time of Birth, neither is it of any importance what Mansion of Heaven it governs in the Radix, for it will always retain its own destructive power, except its influence becomes defeated by other Motions, which may be visibly discovered by its Progressive movements, at the period when the giver of Life comes in contact with its Malefic Directions, joined with others of a similar nature in the Zodiac, and Mundo; for if the Hyleg be not *then* assisted by benefic Rays, and if the power of the *Anareta* be not counteracted at the same time by Directions, or Terms of a reverse denomination, then consequently dissolution will take place, in defiance of all human exertions; but the Examples I have given in this Work, will doubtless be deemed sufficient to establish the verity of these observations.

OR GENETHLIACAL ASTRONOMY.

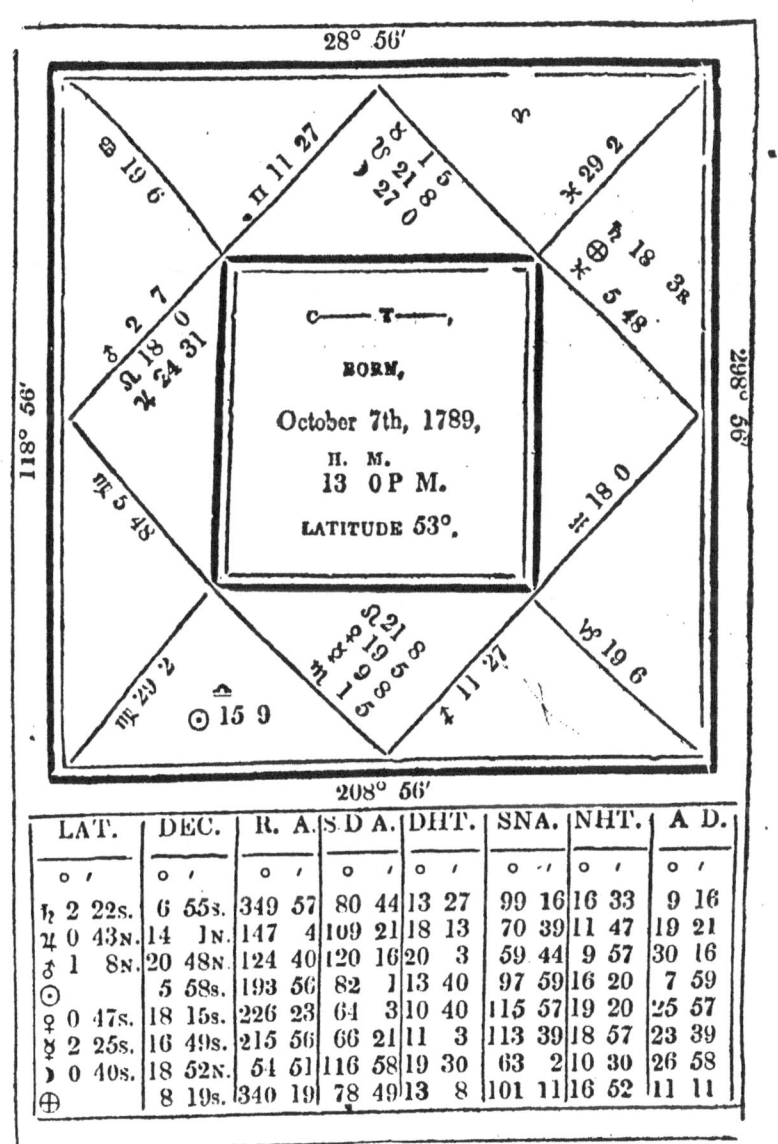

Chart:

- Top: 28° 56′
- Right: 298° 56′
- Bottom: 208° 56′
- Left: 118° 56′

Houses (clockwise from ascendant):
- ♋ 19 6
- ♊ 11 27
- ☊ 21 8, ♂ 15, 27 0
- ♓ 29 2
- ♄ 18 3 ℞, ♆ 5 48
- ♐ 18 0, ♃ 24 31, ♌ 2 7
- ♎ 18 0
- ♍ 5 48
- ♑ 19 6
- ♐ 11 27
- ♍ 21 8, ☿ 19 5, ♀ 8 15
- ♏ 29 2, ☉ 15 9

Center:
C — T —
BORN,
October 7th, 1789,
H. M.
13 0 P M.
LATITUDE 53°.

	LAT.	DEC.	R. A.	S D A.	D H T.	S N A.	N H T.	A D.
	° ′	° ′	° ′	° ′	° ′	° ″	° ′	° ′
♄	2 22s.	6 55s.	349 57	80 44	13 27	99 16	16 33	9 16
♃	0 43n.	14 1n.	147 4	109 21	18 13	70 39	11 47	19 21
♂	1 8n.	20 48n.	124 40	120 16	20 3	59 44	9 57	30 16
☉		5 58s.	193 56	82 1	13 40	97 59	16 20	7 59
♀	0 47s.	18 15s.	226 23	64 3	10 40	115 57	19 20	25 57
☿	2 25s.	16 49s.	215 56	66 21	11 3	113 39	18 57	23 39
☽	0 40s.	18 52n.	54 51	116 58	19 30	63 2	10 30	26 58
⊕		8 19s.	340 19	78 49	13 8	101 11	16 52	11 11

CELESTIAL PHILOSOPHY,

A TABLE OF THE DIRECTIONS.	ARC. D. M.	TIME. YRS. MO.
Ascendant to the Sesquiquadrate of Saturn in Mundo	1 24	1 8
Part of Fortune to the Trine of Mercury in Mundo	1 40	1 11
Sun to the Parallel of Saturn in the Zodiac	2 28	2 8
Moon to the Biquintile of the Sun in Mundo, Direct Direction	2 29	2 8
Sun to the Quintile of Mars in the Zodiac, Converse Motion	2 32	2 9
Moon to the Quintile of Saturn in the Zodiac	3 5	3 4
Moon to the Sesquiquadrate of the Sun in the Zodiac	3 11	3 5
Moon to the Square of Jupiter in the Zodiac, Converse Direction	3 26	3 8
Sun to the Parallel of the Moon in Mundo, by the Rapt Motion	3 39	3 11
Moon to the Sextile of Saturn in Mundo, Converse Direction	4 23	4 9
Ascendant to the Quintile of the Sun in Mundo	4 35	4 11
Part of Fortune to the Quintile of the Moon in Mundo	4 49	5 2
Sun to the Square of Mars in Mundo, Converse Motion	5 0	5 5
Moon to the Sextile of Mars in the Zodiac	5 12	5 7
Sun to the Sextile of Jupiter in Mundo, Converse Direction	5 29	5 11
Sun to the Biquintile of Saturn in Mundo, Direct Motion	5 41	6 1
Sun to the Biquintile of the Moon in the Zodiac	5 55	6 4
Sun to Spica Virginis	6 16	6 9
Part of Fortune to the Biquintile of the Sun in Mundo	6 31	7 0
Sun to the Parallel of the Moon in Mundo, Converse Direction	6 42	7 2
Ascendant to the Square of Mercury in Mundo	7 0	7 7
Midheaven to the Opposition of Mercury in Mundo	7 0	7 7
Moon to the Opposition of Venus in the Zodiac, Converse Motion	7 29	8 1
Moon to the Quintile of Saturn in Mundo, Direct Direction	7 44	8 4
Sun to the Parallel of the Moon in Mundo, Direct Motion	8 1	8 8
Moon to the Opposition of Venus in Mundo, Converse Direction	8 19	9 0
Sun to the Semiquartile of Jupiter in the Zodiac, Converse Motion	8 27	9 2
Ascendant to the Body of Jupiter in Mundo	8 47	9 6
Midheaven to the Square of Jupiter in Mundo	8 47	9 6
Moon to the Semiquartile of Mars in Mundo, Direct Direction	8 58	9 8
Sun to the Biquintile of Saturn in the Zodiac	9 2	9 9

OR GENETHLIACAL ASTRONOMY.

THE DIRECTIONS CONTINUED.	ARC. D. M.	TIME. YRS. MO.
Moon to the Quintile of Mars in the Zodiac, Converse Motion	9 6	9 10
Ascendant to the Biquintile of Saturn in Mundo	9 27	10 2
Sun to the Sextile of Jupiter in the Zodiac	9 30	10 2
Part of Fortune to the Trine of Mars in Mundo	9 53	10 7
Moon to Aldebaran	10 30	11 3
Moon to the Sextile of Saturn in the Zodiac, by Converse Direction	10 35	11 4
Moon to the Sextile of Mars in Mundo, Converse Motion	10 48	11 7
Part of Fortune to the Biquintile of Jupiter in Mundo	10 56	11 8
Part of Fortune to the Body of Saturn in Mundo	11 4	11 10
Sun to the Semiquartile of Venus in the Zodiac, Converse Direction	11 7	11 11
Moon to the Square of Jupiter in Mundo, Converse Motion	11 23	12 2
Part of Fortune to the Trine of Venus in Mundo	12 0	12 10
Moon to the Sesquiquadrate of the Sun in Mundo, Direct Direction	12 17	13 1
Ascendant to Cor Leonis	13 11	14 1
Sun to the Sesquiquadrate of Saturn in Mundo, Direct Motion	13 45	14 8
Midheaven to the Sextile of Saturn in Mundo	14 51	15 10
Midheaven to the Sextile of Mars in Mundo	15 32	16 7
Moon to the Quintile of Jupiter in the Zodiac	15 57	17 0
Moon to the Parallel of Mercury in Mundo, by the Rapt Motion	16 19	17 5
Sun to the Square of Mars in the Zodiac	17 10	18 4
Ascendant to the Square of Venus in Mundo	17 27	18 7
Midheaven to the Opposition of Venus in Mundo	17 27	18 7
Ascendant to the Sextile of the Sun in Mundo	17 39	18 9
Sun to the Sesquiquadrate of Saturn in the Zodiac	18 17	19 5
Moon to the Opposition of Mercury in Mundo, Converse Direction	18 43	19 10
Sun to the Sextile of Mars in the Zodiac, Converse Motion	18 45	19 10
Moon to the Biquintile of Mercury in the Zodiac	18 46	19 11
Moon to the Trine of the Sun in the Zodiac	18 47	19 11
Moon to the Opposition of Mercury in the Zodiac, Converse Motion	18 55	20 1
Sun to the Semiquartile of Venus in Mundo, Converse Direction	19 14	20 5
Part of Fortune to the Sextile of the Moon in Mundo	20 25	21 8

CELESTIAL PHILOSOPHY,

THE DIRECTIONS CONTINUED.	ARC. D. M.	TIME. YRS. MO.
Part of Fortune to the Sesquiquadrate of Mercury in Mundo.	20 37	21 10
Moon to the Semiquartile of Mars in the Zodiac.......	20 50	22 1
Moon to the Sextile of Jupiter in Mundo, Direct Motion.	21 0	22 3
Moon to the Parallel of Venus in Mundo, by the Rapt Motion............................	21 40	22 11
Sun to the Semiquartile of Mercury in the Zodiac, Converse Direction........................	21 42	22 11
Sun to the Semiquartile of Jupiter in Mundo, by Converse Motion........................	21 49	23 1
Moon to the Square of Saturn in the Zodiac..........	21 51	23 1
Part of Fortune to the Sesquiquadrate of Jupiter in Mundo	21 52	23 1
Sun to the Quintile of Jupiter in the Zodiac..........	21 53	23 1
Sun to the Parallel of Jupiter in the Zodiac..........	22 54	24 2
Moon to the Parallel of Mars in the Zodiac..........	23 36	24 11
Moon to the Semiquartile of Saturn in Mundo, Converse Motion............................	23 52	25 2
Moon to the Square of Saturn in Mundo, Direct Direction.	23 53	25 2
Midheaven to the Biquintile of the Sun in Mundo......	24 11	25 6
Midheaven to the Pleiades........................	24 19	25 7
Sun to the Body of Mercury in Mundo, Direct Motion...	24 24	25 8
Sun to the Quintile of Mars in Mundo, Converse Direction	24 36	25 10
Sun to the Body of Mercury in the Zodiac............	24 39	25 11
Sun to the Square of Jupiter in Mundo, Direct Motion.	25 31	26 10
Midheaven to the Quintile of Saturn in Mundo........	25 37	26 11
Midheaven to the Body of the Moon in Mundo........	25 55	27 3
Ascendant to the Square of the Moon in Mundo.......	25 55	27 3
Moon to the Quintile of Mars in Mundo, Converse Motion.	26 24	27 9
Sun to the Sextile of Venus in the Zodiac, Converse Direction.	26 28	27 10
Sun to the Trine of Saturn in Mundo, Direct Motion...	27 12	28 7
Moon to the Biquintile of Mercury in Mundo, Direct Direction...........................	27 18	28 8
Sun to the Semiquartile of Mercury in Mundo, Converse Motion.............................	27 57	29 3
Moon to the Semiquartile of Saturn in the Zodiac, Converse Direction........................	28 11	29 6
Moon to the Sesquiquadrate of Mercury in the Zodiac...	28 22	29 8
Moon to the Trine of the Sun in Mundo, Direct Motion.	28 37	29 11
Moon to the Sextile of Jupiter in the Zodiac..........	28 47	30 1
Moon to the Biquintile of Venus in the Zodiac.......	29 23	30 9
Ascendant to the Quintile of Mercury in Mundo.......	29 44	31 1

OR GENETHLIACAL ASTRONOMY. 197

	ARC.		TIME.	
THE DIRECTIONS CONTINUED.	D.	M.	YRS.	MO.
Midheaven to the Quintile of Jupiter in Mundo	30	39	32	0
Part of Fortune to the Sesquiquadrate of Venus in Mundo.	31	20	32	9
Part of Fortune to the Biquintile of Mercury in Mundo	31	59	33	4
Moon to the Parallel of Mercury in Mundo, Direct Motion.	32	11	33	6
Sun to the Opposition of Saturn in the Zodiac, Converse Direction	32	20	33	8
Sun to the Parallel of Mercury in the Zodiac.	32	31	33	10
Moon to the Parallel of Mercury in Mundo, Converse Motion.	33	7	34	5
Sun to the Trine of Mars in Mundo, Direct Direction.	33	57	35	3
Ascendant to the Semiquartile of the Sun in Mundo.	33	59	35	3
Sun to the Trine of Saturn in the Zodiac.	34	4	35	4
Sun to the Body of Venus in the Zodiac.	35	11	36	5
Sun to the Sextile of Venus in Mundo, Converse Direction	35	34	36	10
Ascendant to the Semiquartile of Mars in Mundo.	35	35	36	10

This Native was Married twice, the first Matrimonial Union took place under the Effects of the Direction of the Moon to the Trine of the Sun in the Zodiac; and his Marriage to his second Wife was solemnized, when the Moon was directed to the Sextile of Jupiter in Mundo, by Direct Motion. At the Age of twenty-three Years and one Month, the Hyleg was directed to the Square of Saturn in the Zodiac, at which time, according to the Native's Judgment, he expected his Life would be exposed to the greatest danger by *Water*, but no dangerous Accident of any kind took place, for the Moon was then directed to the Rapt Parallel of Venus, and her Terms, which destroyed the apparent dangerous Effects of that *single* Direction; but though it had not power to destroy Life, yet it produced a lingering disease, which continued until the time of his Death. The Mortal Directions which I previously computed, were, the Apheta to the Parallel of Mars in the Zodiac, the Semiquartile of Saturn in the World, by Converse Motion, and Square of that Malefic in Mundo, by Direct Direction, succeeded by the Hyleg to the Semiquartile of Saturn in the Zodiac, by Converse Motion, and Sesquiquadrate of Mercury in the Zodiac, and Parallel of that promittor in Mundo, by Direct, and Converse Motion; these were the Directions which I allowed for his Death, and though the Moon the giver of Life, was directed to the Sextile of Jupiter in the Zodiac, which appeared to dissolve a large portion of the violence of the above train of Directions, yet his benign qualities were wholly destroyed, for he was directed at the same time to the Rapt Parallel of Saturn, he also ascended to the Body of Mars, and applied to the opposition of Saturn, so that he could produce no assistance, for being thus overcome by the power of the Enemies, he specified the nature of the disease that destroyed Life, which was a Consumption, and though every human effort was used for the recovery of the Native, yet all exertions proved ineffectual, as it was not in the power of the most learned Physician, to subdue the progress of that *dreadful disease*, which terminated the Mortal existence of this valuable member of society

In the Secondary Directions, the Sun was applying to the Square of Mars, and the Moon had nearly obtained the Declination of the Sun; the applications from the Progression, were of an inimical power. In his last Revolution, the Hyleg was posited on the place of Saturn in the Nativity, the Sun, and Mercury were also in Quartile to that Malefic from Cardinal Signs, and at the time he died, Saturn was posited in the Oriental Horizon, in Opposition to Venus, there was likewise a new Moon a few Hours before his Death, which was celebrated in a violent part of the Heavens, and both the Luminaries were at the same time conjoined with Mars in the Radical Ascendant, and in Quartile to the place of the Hyleg in the Geniture.

As a further confirmation of the power, and important use of the true Prorogator, and that the Angles cannot be computed to Directions in the Zodiac, I have inserted the following Nativity, which is that of a young Man, who was Born in the City of Lincoln, March 11th, 1802, 20h. 12m. P. M. and died on the 2nd. of June, 1823, Aged twenty-one Years, two Months, and twenty-one Days.

When this Native was eighteen Years of Age, he gave me the above time of his Birth, which he said was carefully taken by his Grandfather, who remained confident that the estimate time could not possibly differ three Minutes from the true Radix. As soon as I had viewed the Figure of the Heavens, I told the Native I had rather not make any observations thereon; he asked me why I took so little notice of it, and further observed, that he did not wish to give me trouble, without remuneration; I told him that the whole Position, (when properly considered in all its parts,) was of a *violent* nature, and indicated severe afflictions, and *short Life*, but when I delivered this impartial Judgment, and that the twenty-first Year of his Age would prove fatal, he appeared not to place confidence in what I related, being at that time in a good state of Health; he said there were many learned Men in this Nation who did not sanction this Study, and if the art of Calculating Nativities was to be depended on without error, it appeared extraordinary that the Truth of the Science was not publicly developed before the nineteenth Century. I told him I had no doubt that there were many persons of high respectability, who, having received a liberal Education, studied this Science in a private manner, being perfectly satisfied with its truth, and utility, and I was also *well convinced*, that there were others that appeared to be *rich* and *pious*, who traduced, and condemned these Astronomical enquiries, and at the same time applied themselves *closely* to the *Study* and *Practice* of *other Arts of a detestable nature*, which are too *abominable* for description; the *sanguine actions* of *some* of those BEINGS, who are frequently *bedecked* in the *Robes* of *innocence*, will never be forgotten, as by their command, the *notorious* CANNIBALS, (on the verge of the Sepulchre,) received directions to *finish* their *last unmerciful* REPAST, on the *withered limbs of dying individuals*. The Native asked me what my opinion was, respecting *Deaf*, and *Dumb* People, as some of both Sexes frequently visit the City of Lincoln, and appear to relate *strange things*, concerning the Fortune of those who apply to them for advice; I told him they were all KNAVES, and VAGABONDS, and that I was sorry to observe many respectable Persons became the dupes of such notorious impostors, as some of them could *hear*, and *speak* as occasion requires; but I always observed, that those who Possess superior Talents in Learning, never notice such Beings, but view their *vile*, and *artful pretensions* with the contempt they merit. But the *Deaf*, and *Dumb*, are not the only characters who impose on the credulous, for there are others, who, being destitute of *shame*, are now Publishing the *refuse* of several *disgraceful Arts*, which ought to be treated with universal contempt, in this enlightened Age.

THE MAGICIAN OF THE NINETEENTH CENTURY, DISSECTED.

Reader behold! the *Sage Magician* tries,
To show *his Arts*, with wonder, and surprise;
His *skill* is us'd, with all his *knavish* THEMES,
To *dupe* his Readers, with romantic DREAMS;
He aims at Cash, and if his Works will *sell*,
The *Pirate is conceal'd*, and all is well;
The learned Writer, *hides his proper Name*,
Which proves he's not *quite* destitute of *Shame*;
He lays his *Bait*, with *invocating Arts*,
To show what GHOSTLY SECRETS he imparts;
Falsehood for TRUTH, he's not asham'd to tell,
Because we know not where the SAGE does *dwell*;
From all the DEEP RESEARCHES he has made,
He's in the *dark*, and carries on his *Trade*;
Arm'd by deception, he, with sapient care,
Brings *Anecdotes* to make the *vulgar stare*.

Romances oft, the thoughtless mind engage,
More than the Truth, in this our learned Age;
Deceit and *Guile* are mask'd,—Mark well the Man,
Then you'll discover the IMPOSTORS plan;
By *Rites* he'll teach you, without fear, or dread,
To hold *Nocturnal converse* with the dead;
Thus through his *Visions*, he's dispos'd to *stain*,
His *learned Pages*, for the sake of *Gain*;
By TRICKS like these, his *knavish* efforts show,
What *wit*, and *learned Parts* can sometimes do;
His TALISMANS, (those wondrous things of note,)
With all their force, were never worth a Groat;
There's *Geomancy*, which some say, excel
All other Wonders, if its manag'd well;
His *puny schemes*, to every Man of sense,
Declare at once, the *Pirates* impudence;
All those *alluring Arts*, to puzzle Youth,
He has reviv'd, *without a word of Truth*;
Come candid Readers, now behold the *Snare*
Is laid to take your *Cash*, therefore beware;
For all these things are nothing more, or less,
Than *vile deceit*, in its polluted dress;
PROOFS I DEMAND, but nothing can obtain,
Except OLD STORIES, insolent, and Vain;
Some Students may, (without much care,) imbibe
The GHOSTLY VISIONS of this *learned Tribe*;
When HONEST PARTRIDGE wrote, he took a view,
And gave Examples of this *learned Crew*;
He stiles their Practice, 'cheating tricks', and then,
Proclaims them *villains*, and *dishonest Men*;
Now *Straggling Members*, spread those forged Lies,
Which in their *tender conscience*, they despise;
I therefore trust, the Students will disdain,
Those *groundless Arts*, which I've exposed plain;
Alarm'd at TRUTH, the *Pious Jugglers fly*,
Which soon discover *all their* VILLANY.

OR GENETHLIACAL ASTRONOMY.

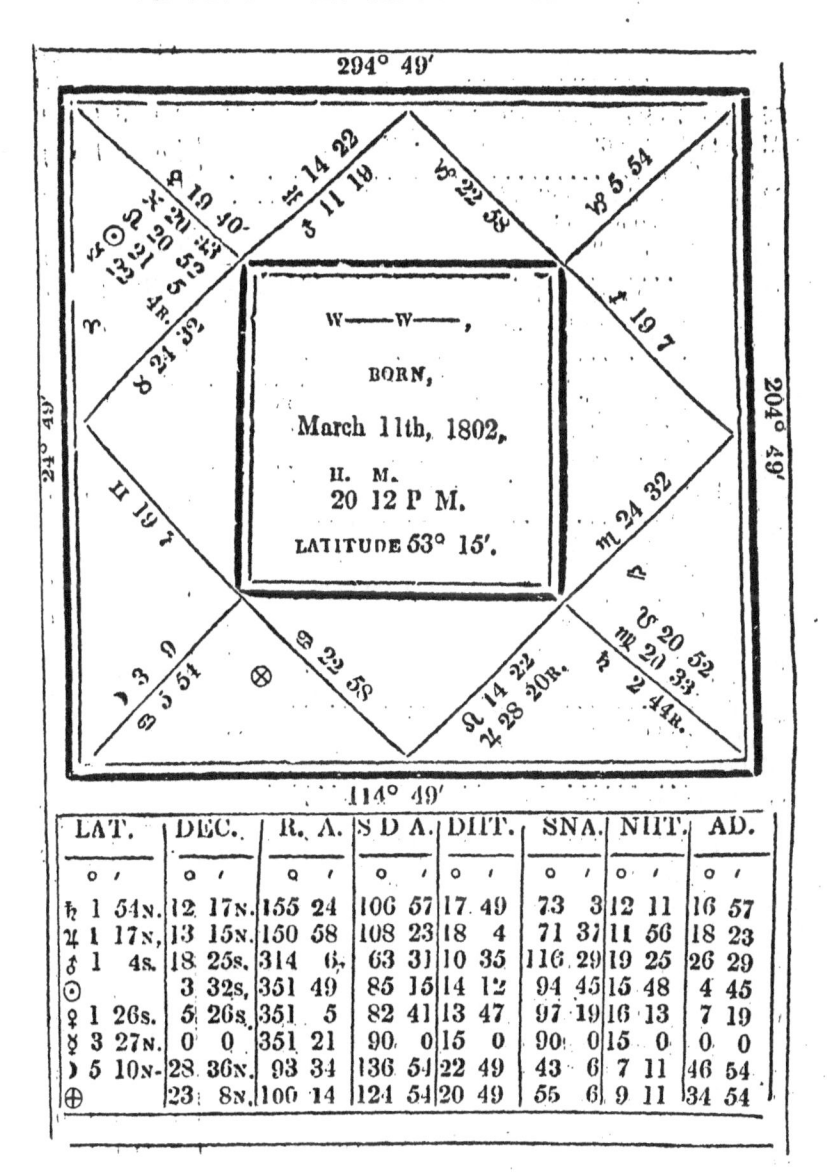

Chart:
- Top: 294° 49'
- Right: 204° 49'
- Bottom: 114° 49'
- Left: 24° 49'

Cusps and placements:
- ♈ ♃ ♄ 19 40, ♓ ⊙ ♀ 20 53, ♓ 13 20, ♓ 12 ☿, ≈ 14 22, ♒ ♂ 8 12, ♐ 11 19, ♑ 22 58, ♑ 5 54
- ♏ 24 32, ♎ 20 52, ♍ 20 33, ♌ 19 7, ♌ 14 22, 2½ 28 20 R, ♏ 20 44 R
- ♋ 22 58, ⊕, ♋ 5 54, ☽ 3 9, ♊ 19 7

Center:
W—— W——,
BORN,
March 11th, 1802,
H. M.
20 12 P M.
LATITUDE 53° 15'.

	LAT.	DEC.	R. A.	S D A	DIFF.	SNA.	NHT.	AD.
	° ′	° ′	° ′	° ′	° ′	° ′	° ′	° ′
♄	1 54N.	12 17N.	155 24	106 57	17 49	73 3	12 11	16 57
♃	1 17N.	13 15N.	150 58	108 23	18 4	71 37	11 56	18 23
♂	1 4S.	18 25S.	314 6	63 31	10 35	116 29	19 25	26 29
⊙		3 32S.	351 49	85 15	14 12	94 45	15 48	4 45
♀	1 26S.	5 26S.	351 5	82 41	13 47	97 19	16 13	7 19
☿	3 27N.	0 0	351 21	90 0	15 0	90 0	15 0	0 0
☽	5 10N.	28 36N.	93 34	136 54	22 49	43 6	7 11	46 54
⊕		23 8N.	100 14	124 54	20 49	55 6	9 11	34 54

CELESTIAL PHILOSOPHY,

A TABLE OF THE DIRECTIONS.	ARC. D. M.	TIME. YRS. MO.
Moon to the Square of Jupiter in Mundo, Converse Motion.	0 5	0 1
Moon to the Sextile of Saturn in the Zodiac, Converse Direction	0 6	0 1
Midheaven to the Sextile of the Sun in Mundo	0 12	0 2
Ascendant to the Semiquartile of the Moon in Mundo,	0 18	0 3
Moon to the Parallel of Jupiter in Mundo, by the Rapt Motion	0 19	0 3
Ascendant to the Sesquiquadrate of Jupiter in Mundo	0 21	0 4
Moon to the Parallel of Jupiter in Mundo, Converse Motion	0 31	0 7
Sun to the Body of Mercury in the Zodiac	0 34	0 8
Moon to the Parallel of Jupiter in Mundo, Direct Direction.	0 51	0 11
Sun to the Body of Venus in Mundo, by Direct Motion.	0 56	1 0
Midheaven to the Sextile of Venus in Mundo	1 8	1 3
Moon to the Quintile of Venus in Mundo, Converse Direction	1 9	1 3
Sun to the Quintile of the Moon in Mundo, Direct Motion	1 38	1 9
Moon to the Parallel of Saturn in Mundo, by the Rapt Motion	1 41	1 10
Part of Fortune to the Parallel of Mars in Mundo	2 29	2 9
Moon to the Biquintile of Mars in the Zodiac	2 36	2 10
Moon to the Parallel of Saturn in Mundo, Converse Direction	2 41	2 11
Sun to the Semiquartile of Mars in the Zodiac	2 56	3 2
Moon to the Sextile of Jupiter in the Zodiac, Converse Motion	3 8	3 5
Moon to the Quintile of Mercury in Mundo, Converse Direction	3 24	3 8
Moon to the Square of Saturn in Mundo, Direct Direction	3 32	3 10
Ascendant to the Sesquiquadrate of Saturn in Mundo	4 2	4 5
Part of Fortune to the Sesquiquadrate of Mars in Mundo	4 20	4 9
Moon to the Parallel of Saturn in Mundo, Direct Motion	4 33	5 0
Moon to the Sesquiquadrate of Mars in the Zodiac, Converse Direction	5 58	6 6
Ascendant to the Quintile of Mars in Mundo	6 35	7 2
Sun to the Square of the Moon in the Zodiac	6 42	7 3
Moon to the Sextile of Venus in Mundo, Converse Motion.	6 54	7 6
Moon to the Square of Venus in the Zodiac, Converse Direction	7 19	8 0
Sun to the Biquintile of Jupiter in the Zodiac	7 21	8 0

OR GENETHLIACAL ASTRONOMY. 205

THE DIRECTIONS CONTINUED.	ARC. D. M.	TIME. YRS. MO.
Part of Fortune to the Sextile of Jupiter in Mundo....	7 22	8 0
Sun to the Sextile of the Moon in Mundo, Direct Motion.	7 23	8 1
Midheaven to the Trine of the Moon in Mundo.......	7 29	8 2
Midheaven to the Biquintile of Jupiter in Mundo.......	7 30	8 2
Moon to the Quintile of Saturn in the Zodiac, Converse Direction...	7 53	8 8
Moon to the Trine of Mars in Mundo, by Direct Motion.	8 15	9 1
Sun to the Semiquartile of Mars in Mundo, Direct Direction...	8 33	9 5
Moon to the Square of Mars in Mundo, Converse Motion.	8 45	9 7
Moon to the Sextile of Mercury in Mundo, Converse Direction...	9 9	10 0
Sun to the Opposition of Saturn in the Zodiac, Converse Motion...	9 42	10 8
Sun to the Biquintile of Saturn in the Zodiac.........	9 49	10 9
Sun to his own Parallel in the Zodiac.................	9 55	10 10
Part of Fortune to the Biquintile of Mars in Mundo...	10 41	11 9
Moon to the Square of Mercury in Mundo, Direct Direction...	10 54	12 0
Moon to the Quintile of Jupiter in the Zodiac, Converse Motion...	11 10	12 3
Part of Fortune to the Sextile of Saturn in Mundo.....	11 14	12 4
Sun to the Sextile of Mars in the Zodiac.............	11 16	12 4
Midheaven to the Biquintile of Saturn in Mundo.......	11 22	12 5
Ascendant to the Semiquartile of Mercury in Mundo.....	11 32	12 7
Part of Fortune to the Semiquartile of the Moon in Mundo	11 43	12 9
Ascendant to the Trine of Jupiter in Mundo..........	12 17	13 6
Moon to the Trine of Saturn in Mundo, Converse Motion.	12 17	13 6
Sun to the Sesquiquadrate of Jupiter in the Zodiac.....	12 23	13 7
Moon to the Semiquartile of Jupiter in the Zodiac.......	12 24	13 7
Sun to the Parallel of Venus in the Zodiac............	12 37	13 10
Moon to the Square of Mercury in the Zodiac, Converse Direction...	13 37	14 11
Moon to the Square of the Sun in Mundo, Direct Motion	13 48	15 1
Sun to the Opposition of Jupiter in the Zodiac, Converse Direction...	14 0	15 4
Moon to the Semiquartile of Venus in Mundo, Converse Motion...	14 5	15 5
Moon to the Quintile of Jupiter in Mundo, Direct Direction...	14 10	15 6

206 CELESTIAL PHILOSOPHY,

	ARC.	TIME.
THE DIRECTIONS CONTINUED.	D. M.	YRS. MO.
Moon to the Square of Venus in Mundo, Direct Motion.	14 20	15 8
Ascendant to the Semiquartile of the Sun in Mundo......	14 24	15 9
Moon to the Trine of Jupiter in Mundo, Converse Motion.	14 27	15 9
Sun to the Semiquartile of the Moon in Mundo, Direct Direction.	14 34	15 10
Sun to the Sesquiquadrate of Saturn in the Zodiac........	14 53	16 2
Ascendant to the Semiquartile of Venus in Mundo......	14 55	16 2
Ascendant to the Trine of Saturn in Mundo............	16 13	17 10
Moon to the Semiquartile of Mercury in Mundo, Converse Motion.	16 20	17 11
Sun to the Biquintile of Jupiter in Mundo, Direct Direction.	16 53	18 6
Sun to the Quintile of the Moon in the Zodiac.........	16 53	18 6
Part of Fortune to the Parallel of Jupiter in Mundo...	17 12	18 11
Moon to the Quintile of Venus in the Zodiac, Converse Motion.	17 12	18 11
Moon to the Quintile of Mars in Mundo, Converse Direction.	17 22	19 1
Moon to the Semiquartile of Saturn in the Zodiac......	17 59	19 9
Sun to the Quintile of Mars in the Zodiac...........	18 8	19 11
Moon to the Quintile of Saturn in Mundo, Direct Motion.	18 9	19 11
Moon to the Trine of Mars in the Zodiac, Converse Direction.	18 24	20 2
Ascendant to Aldebaran............................	18 49	20 7
Moon to the Sesquiquadrate of Mars in Mundo, Direct Motion.	18 50	20 7
Part of Fortune to the Sextile of the Moon in Mundo...	18 54	20 8
Sun to the Sextile of Mars in Mundo, Direct Direction.	19 8	21 0
Ascendant to the Square of Mars in Mundo...........	19 17	21 2
Midheaven to the Body of Mars in Mundo...........	19 17	21 2
Part of Fortune to the Semiquartile of Jupiter in Mundo.	19 18	21 2
Moon to the Sesquiquadrate of Saturn in Mundo, Converse Motion.	19 28	21 4
Moon to the Square of Saturn in the Zodiac, Converse Direction.	19 36	21 6
Part of Fortune to the Trine of Mercury in Mundo...	20 21	22 4
Moon to the Trine of Venus in the Zodiac..........	20 28	22 5
Sun to the Biquintile of Saturn in Mundo, Direct Motion.	20 55	22 11
Sun to the Trine of Jupiter in the Zodiac...........	21 9	23 3
Part of Fortune to the Parallel of Saturn in Mundo...	21 14	23 4
Moon to her own Semiquartile in Mundo............	21 33	23 8
Ascendant to the Body of the Moon in Mundo........	21 51	24 0

THE DIRECTIONS CONTINUED.	ARC. D. M.	TIME. YRS. MO.
Midheaven to the Square of the Moon in Mundo.......	21 51	24 0
Moon to the Trine of the Sun in the Zodiac............	22 19	24 6
Part of Fortune to the Trine of the Sun in Mundo.....	22 45	24 11
Moon to the Square of Jupiter in the Zodiac, Converse Motion..	22 59	25 3
Part of Fortune to the Trine of Venus in Mundo.......	23 1	25 4
Part of Fortune to the Semiquartile of Saturn in Mundo.	23 25	25 9
Sun to the Parallel of Saturn in the Zodiac............	23 34	25 11
Moon to the Trine of Mercury in the Zodiac..........	23 34	25 11
Moon to the Sextile of Jupiter in Mundo, Direct Motion.	23 43	26 1
Sun to the Trine of Saturn in the Zodiac..............	23 51	26 3
Moon to the Quintile of Mercury in the Zodiac, Converse Motion...	24 2	26 5
Sun to the Sesquiquadrate of Jupiter in Mundo, Direct Direction..	24 3	26 5
Moon to the Sextile of Venus in the Zodiac, Converse Motion..	24 4	26 5
Sun to the Sextile of the Moon in the Zodiac.........	24 7	26 6
Sun to the Semiquartile of Venus in the Zodiac, Converse Direction.......................................	25 1	27 6
Sun to the Semiquartile of Venus in the Zodiac	25 4	27 6
Moon to the Biquintile of Mars in Mundo, Direct Motion..	25 11	27 7
Sun to the Parallel of Jupiter in the Zodiac...........	25 23	27 9
Moon to the Sextile of Mars in Mundo, Converse Motion..	25 54	28 4
Sun to his own Semiquartile in the Zodiac............	25 58	28 5
Ascendant to the Sextile of Mercury in Mundo........	26 32	29 2
Sun to the Semiquartile of Mercury in the Zodiac......	26 37	29 3
Sun to the Quintile of Mars in Mundo, Direct Direction..	27 36	30 4
Moon to the Sextile of Saturn in Mundo, Direct Motion..	27 54	30 8
Sun to the Sesquiquadrate of Saturn in Mundo, Direct Direction..	28 14	31 0
Ascendant to the Sextile of the Sun in Mundo.......	28 36	31 4
Ascendant to the Sextile of Venus in Mundo..........	28 42	31 5
Sun to the Square of Mars in the Zodiac..............	29 26	32 3
Moon to the Sextile of Mercury in the Zodiac, Converse Motion...	30 51	33 10

2F

	ARC.	TIME.
THE DIRECTIONS CONTINUED.	D. M.	YRS. MO.
Sun to the Semiquartile of Mercury in the Zodiac, Converse Direction..............................	30 59	33 11
Sun to the Body of Mars in the Zodiac, by Converse Motion......................................	31 10	34 2

As there are several Pretenders to this Science, who consider themselves *able* to direct the Angles to the Aspects of the Stars in the Zodiac, contrary to the true Motions of the Heavens, I could wish to be informed, how they would proceed to make the Square of Mars, by their Method, correspond with the time of this Native's decease; though I believe it would not be difficult to anticipate what they would bring forth, as a plausible *Cause* of this Native's Sickness, and Death; they certainly must be convinced, (if they know any thing relative to the true Doctrine of the Sphere,) that such Motions as they consider to be right, are certainly wholly *undemonstrable*, which the use of the Celestial Globe will evidently Prove, for it must appear obvious to those who are acquainted with the true Method of Directional Motion, that in the preceding Geniture, there is but one *true* Method, by which the Ascendant can be directed to the Square of Mars, and that is, by directing the Zenith to the Body of that Planet; for when that Direction is finished, which is when Mars ascends exactly on the Meridian, then, and then only, the Ascendant will come to the true Quartile of that Star, in the World; not by any *vain*, and *imaginary Movements*, but by those unerring, and demonstrable Motions of the Heavens, which become visibly apparent to those observers, who, by diligence, and delight, contemplate the regular harmony, and Effects of the Celestial Bodies, in their different stations, in all parts of the Heavens.

In the Geniture of this unfortunate young Man, the Ascendant is the giver of Life, and the Directions which I computed for his Death, were, the Horoscope to the Square of Mars in Mundo, followed by the Body of the Moon, which will destroy Life in any Geniture, when the Hyleg is not supported by benevolent Directions, which is the case in this Example. At the time of his Death, the Moon was directed to the Sesquiquadrate of Saturn in Mundo, by Converse Motion, and also to the Square of that Malefic in the Zodiac, by Converse Direction, followed by her own Semiquartile in the World, and the Sun to the Parallel of

Saturn's Declination; and though these violent Directions have no power to destroy Life, yet, being joined with those which were the true Cause of dissolution, they increased their Mortal power. It would be unnecessary were I to point out the nature of the conflicting diseases, which terminated his Mortal career, as that must appear plain to all those, who are but superficially conversant in this Sublime speculation.

In computing the Secondary Directions, the Luminaries were in Conjunction, and both the Malefics afflicted the Eastern, and Western Angles, by an Opposition; Jupiter was in the Ascendant, in conjunction with Saturn, and in Opposition to Mars, where the Lights, at the time of the Progression, became afflicted by the subsequent inimical Motions, below the Earth; the Moon was in Quartile to her own place in the Nativity, and was likewise in the same violent Aspect with the Sun in the Mundane Circle; the three superior Planets, having nearly the same Declination. In the Revolutional Figure for his twenty-first Year, the Moon, and Mars, the Mortal Promittors, were in Conjunction with the Sun, and Saturn was near the Ascendant; the Moon was likewise in a Mundane Square to her radical place. At the time he died, that Luminary was near the Zodiacal, and Mundane Square of the Sun, and applied to the obnoxious Rays of Saturn, and Mars, from malignant stations, and Terms; the Moon also applied to the place of the Sun in the Radix, and Saturn was in Square to the place of Mars in the Geniture, and that Mortal Promittor (by primary Direction,) was in Quartile to the Zodiacal position of Saturn, and Jupiter, in the Nativity.

OR GENETHLIACAL ASTRONOMY. 211

This is the Geniture of a young Man, who was Born in Hull, on the 30th of September, 1797, at eight o'Clock in the Morning, and was Drowned in returning from a Voyage, on the fifth of January, 1814, Aged sixteen Years, three Months, and six Days.

In this Nativity, it may seem doubtful to some, what Star ought to be selected as the proper Moderator; but according to my Judgment, no doubts on that subject can possibly appear, for the Geniture is Diurnal, and therefore the Sun, by being posited in the twelfth House, cannot possess the Hylegiacal power, because he does not occupy an Aphetical place, neither can the Moon claim that Dominion, as she is under the Earth, in the Imum Cœli. Now as Mercury is posited in the Ascendant, he may appear to claim the Aphetical influence, and more particularly, because he seems to dispose of the preceding new Moon, which happened in the twenty-eighth Degree of Virgo, in the Dignities of Mercury; therefore there is no doubt, that some would select that Star, to represent the Aphetical Office, but the Horoscope advocates would take the Ascendant for Hyleg, and thus, by directing that point of the Heavens to the Body of Mercury, for the Native's Death, with a *little* alteration in Time, they would become culpable in adhering to those inconsistencies, which cannot be adjusted without confusion; and thus by adopting this absurd practice, they would then direct their *supposed* Prorogators to each other, (without the power of a proper Anareta,) as the apparent cause of the Native's Death.

The above Method of selecting the significator of Life, is nothing more than presisting in errors, and rejecting Truth, which will show the Practitioners, as they advance in this Study, that they will never be able to perform any Computation worthy of notice, so long as they adhere to such *groundless notions*; for in this Nativity, it is impossible for the Ascendant to be Hyleg, neither can Mercury, or Venus, possess any portion of Vital influence; but the true Aphetical power, belongs to Saturn alone, he having the proper Dignities, to qualify him to receive, and support that office; for if the *Latitude of the Moon* be properly considered, at the time of the preceding Conjunction of the Luminaries, it will then appear evident, that she was in Square to Saturn, and disposed of him at that time; and in the Nativity, was also in reception with that Planet, as the true giver of Life, having each of them nearly the same Parallel of Declination; the Hyleg was also in Quartile with the Sun in the Geniture, and occupied the proper Aphetical place in the Heavens; so that I did not discover any difficulty in selecting the proper Apheta, which I positively affirm, belongs to Saturn in this Nativity, which is proved by the quality of the Native's Death, and the Directions that were the true *Causes* thereof.

OR GENETHLIACAL ASTRONOMY.

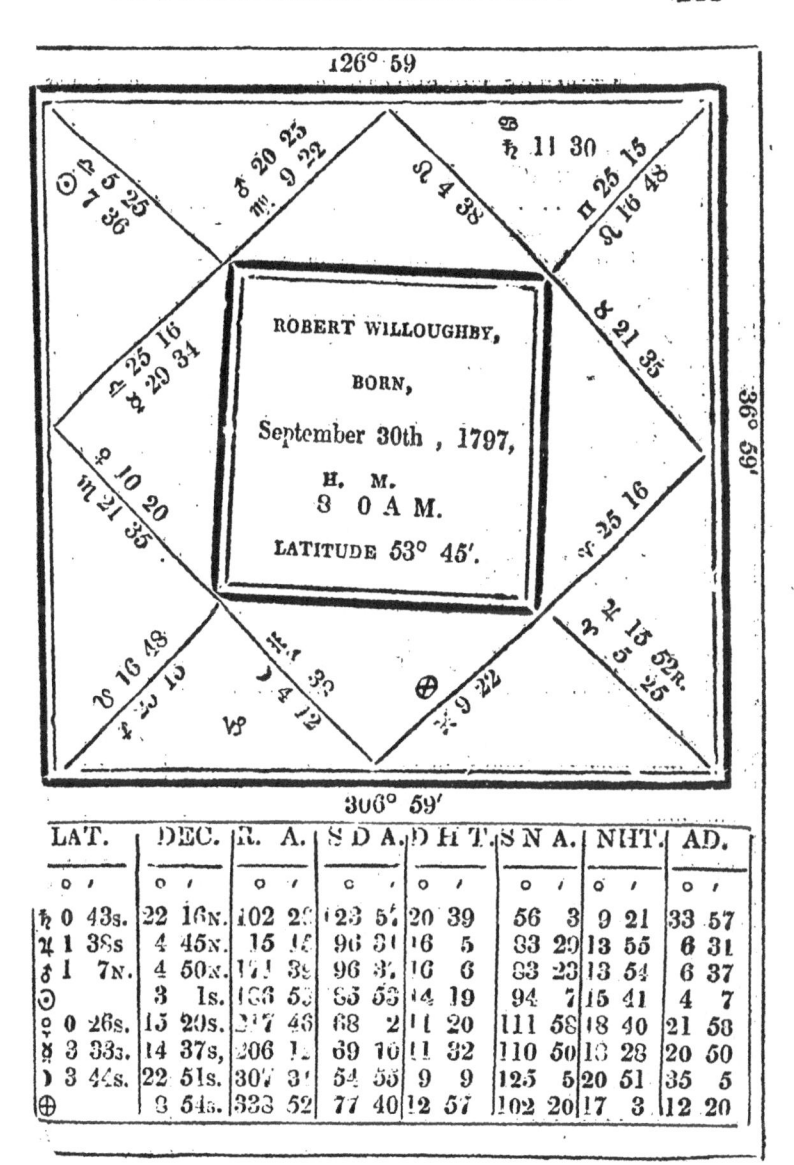

126° 59'

☉ ♎ 5 25
 7 36
♂ 20 25
♍ 9 22
♄ 11 30
♊ 25 15
♌ 16 48
♌ 4 38
♎ 25 16
♉ 20 34
♉ 21 35

ROBERT WILLOUGHBY,
BORN,
September 30th, 1797,
H.   M.
8 0 A M.
LATITUDE 53° 45'.

♏ 10 20
♏ 21 35
♈ 25 16
♃ 13 52R
 5 25
♂ 16 48
♐ 7 28
☽ 4 12
♒ 4 36
♑
⊕ 9 22

306° 59'

36° 59'

	LAT.	DEC.	R. A.	S D A	D H T	S N A	N H T	A D
	° '	° '	° '	° '	° '	° '	° '	° '
♄	0 43s.	22 16N.	102 29	23 54	20 39	56 3	9 21	33 57
♃	1 38s.	4 45N.	15 15	96 30	16 5	83 29	13 55	6 31
♂	1 7N.	4 50s.	171 39	96 31	16 6	83 23	13 54	6 37
☉		3 1s.	186 53	85 53	14 19	94 7	15 41	4 7
♀	0 26s.	15 20s.	217 46	68 2	11 20	111 58	18 40	21 58
☿	3 33s.	14 37s.	206 12	69 10	11 32	110 50	18 28	20 50
☽	3 44s.	22 51s.	307 31	54 55	9 9	125 5	20 51	35 5
⊕		8 54s.	333 52	77 40	12 57	102 20	17 3	12 20

CELESTIAL PHILOSOPHY,

A TABLE OF THE DIRECTIONS.	ARC. D. M.	TIME. YRS. MO.
Moon to the Quintile of Venus in Mundo, Converse Direction	0 8	0 2
Sun to the Semiquartile of Venus in Mundo, Direct Motion	0 31	0 7
Ascendant to the Square of the Moon in Mundo	0 32	0 7
Midheaven to the Opposition of the Moon in Mundo	0 32	0 7
Moon to the Quintile of Jupiter in the Zodiac, Converse Direction	0 44	0 10
Saturn to the Sextile of Mars in Mundo, by Converse Motion	0 49	0 11
Moon to the Quintile of Jupiter in Mundo, Direct Direction	1 7	1 3
Saturn to the Square of Jupiter in Mundo, Direct Motion	1 17	1 5
Moon to the Sesquiquadrate of Mars in the Zodiac	1 18	1 5
Saturn to the Trine of Venus in the Zodiac, Converse Direction	1 39	1 9
Moon to the Square of Mercury in the Zodiac, Converse Motion	1 53	2 0
Moon to the Trine of the Sun in Mundo, Direct Direction	2 22	2 7
Midheaven to the Sextile of the Sun in Mundo	2 44	2 11
Moon to the Parallel of Saturn in the Zodiac	3 7	3 5
Saturn to the Quintile of Mars in the Zodiac, Converse Motion	3 34	3 11
Moon to the Trine of the Sun in the Zodiac	3 36	3 11
Saturn to the Square of Jupiter in the Zodiac	4 45	5 3
Sun to the Square of Saturn in the Zodiac	5 3	5 7
Moon to the Sesquiquadrate of Mars in Mundo, Converse Direction	5 15	5 9
Saturn to the Trine of Mercury in Mundo, Converse Motion	5 34	6 1
Moon to the Biquintile of Mars in Mundo, Direct Direction	5 36	6 1
Sun to the Parallel of Jupiter in the Zodiac	5 42	6 3
Sun to the Parallel of Mars in the Zodiac	5 59	6 7
Moon to the Square of Venus in the Zodiac	6 29	7 2
Saturn to the Trine of Venus in Mundo, Direct Direction	7 34	8 4
Saturn to the Quintile of the Sun in Mundo, Direct Motion	8 18	9 1
Sun to the Semiquartile of Mercury in Mundo, Converse Direction	9 15	10 2
Saturn to the Sextile of Mars in the Zodiac	9 26	10 4
Moon to the Square of Mercury in Mundo, Direct Motion	9 35	10 6

OR GENETHLIACAL ASTRONOMY.   215

	ARC.	TIME.
THE DIRECTIONS CONTINUED.	D. M.	YRS. MO.
Sun to the Opposition of Jupiter in Mundo, Direct Direction.	9 57	10 11
Ascendant to the Body of Mercury in Mundo.	10 3	11 0
Midheaven to the Square of Mercury in Mundo.	10 3	11 0
Moon to the Biquintile of Mars in the Zodiac.	10 42	11 8
Sun to the Opposition of Jupiter in the Zodiac.	10 44	11 8
Part of Fortune to the Trine of Mercury in Mundo.	11 44	12 10
Moon to the Sextile of Jupiter in the Zodiac.	12 12	13 4
Moon to the Sextile of Jupiter in Mundo, Direct Motion.	12 15	13 5
Saturn to the Sesquiquadrate of Venus in Mundo, Converse Direction.	12 16	13 5
Ascendant to the Sextile of Mars in Mundo.	12 28	13 7
Saturn to the Trine of Mercury in the Zodiac, Converse Motion.	12 34	13 8
Midheaven to the Trine of Jupiter in Mundo.	12 36	13 8
Sun to the Square of Saturn in Mundo, Direct Direction.	12 52	13 11
Moon to the Biquintile of Saturn in the Zodiac.	13 53	15 2
Sun to the Sextile of Venus in Mundo, Converse Motion.	13 55	15 3
Moon to the Quintile of Mercury in Mundo, Converse Direction.	14 12	15 7
Saturn to the Parallel of Mars in Mundo, by the Rapt Motion	14 21	15 9
Saturn to the Quintile of the Sun in the Zodiac.	14 44	16 2
Part of Fortune to the Opposition of Mars in Mundo.	14 49	16 3
Saturn to the Semiquartile of Mars in Mundo, Direct Motion.	15 31	16 11
Moon to the Trine of Mars in the Zodiac, Converse Direction.	16 9	17 7
Sun to the Semiquartile of Venus in the Zodiac, Converse Motion.	16 23	17 10
Moon to the Sesquiquadrate of the Sun in Mundo, Direct Direction.	16 41	18 2
Ascendant to the Trine of Saturn in Mundo.	16 48	18 3
Moon to the Sextile of Venus in Mundo, Converse Motion.	16 49	18 3
Moon to the Quintile of Venus in the Zodiac, Converse Direction.	16 59	18 5
Ascendant to the Semiquartile of the Sun in Mundo.	17 3	18 6
Saturn to the Quintile of Mars in Mundo, Converse Motion.	17 20	18 10
Sun to Spica Virginis.	17 51	19 4

2G

CELESTIAL PHILOSOPHY,

	ARC.		TIME.	
THE DIRECTIONS CONTINUED.	D.	M.	YRS.	MO.
Ascendant to the Biquintile of Jupiter in Mundo.	18	10	19	8
Saturn to the Square of Mercury in the Zodiac.	18	49	20	4
Saturn to the Quintile of Jupiter in the Zodiac, Converse Direction.	18	57	20	6
Moon to the Sesquiquadrate of the Sun in the Zodiac.	19	3	20	8
Saturn to the Sextile of the Sun in Mundo, Direct Motion.	19	45	21	5
Part of Fortune to the Trine of Saturn in Mundo.	19	48	21	5
Sun to the Body of Mars in the Zodiac, Converse Direction.	20	19	21	11
Moon to the Square of Venus in Mundo, Direct Motion	22	16	24	0
Midheaven to Cor Leonis.	22	43	24	5
Ascendant to the Body of Venus in Mundo.	22	45	24	5
Midheaven to the Square of Venus in Mundo.	22	45	24	5
Saturn to the Sesquiquadrate of Venus in the Zodiac, Converse Direction.	22	49	24	6
Saturn to the Quintile of Jupiter in Mundo, Converse Motion.	22	54	24	7
Saturn to the Sesquiquadrate of the Moon in the Zodiac, Converse Direction.	22	56	24	8
Part of Fortune to the Sesquiquadrate of Mercury in Mundo.	23	16	25	1
Saturn to the Opposition of the Moon in the Zodiac.	23	18	25	1
Moon to the Square of Jupiter in Mundo, Converse Motion.	23	22	25	2
Sun to the Sextile of Mercury in Mundo, Converse Direction.	23	34	25	4
Saturn to the Square of Mercury in Mundo, Direct Motion.	23	46	25	7
Midheaven to the Quintile of Mercury in Mundo.	23	53	25	8
Sun to the Biquintile of Jupiter in Mundo, Converse Direction.	24	8	26	0
Part of Fortune to the Trine of Venus in Mundo.	24	24	26	3
Part of Fortune to the Semiquartile of the Moon in Mundo.	24	25	26	3
Saturn to the Semiquartile of Mars in the Zodiac.	24	30	26	4
Saturn to the Biquintile of the Moon in Mundo, Converse Direction.	24	32	26	4
Saturn to the Biquintile of Venus in Mundo, Converse Motion.	24	39	26	5
Saturn to the Square of Mars in the Zodiac, Converse Direction.	24	41	26	6

OR GENETHLIACAL ASTRONOMY.

THE DIRECTIONS CONTINUED.	ARC. D. M.	TIME. YRS. MO.
Moon to the Biquintile of the Sun in Mundo, Direct Motion.	25 16	27 2
Saturn to the Opposition of the Moon in Mundo, Direct Direction.	25 19	27 3
Sun to the Quintile of Venus in Mundo, Converse Direction.	25 22	27 3
Ascendant to the Quintile of Mars in Mundo.	25 22	27 3
Saturn to the Parallel of the Sun in Mundo, by the Rapt Motion.	25 23	27 3
Moon to the Square of Jupiter in the Zodiac, Converse Direction.	25 24	27 4
Moon to the Parallel of Mars in Mundo, by the Rapt Motion.	25 26	27 4
Sun to the Semiquartile of Mars in Mundo, Direct Direction.	25 30	27 5
Saturn to the Parallel of Mars in Mundo, Direct Motion.	25 31	27 5
Ascendant to the Quintile of the Moon in Mundo.	25 33	27 5
Moon to the Trine of Mercury in the Zodiac.	25 58	27 10
Moon to the Trine of Mars in Mundo, Converse Direction.	26 6	28 0
Moon to the Semiquartile of Jupiter in Mundo, Direct Motion.	26 10	28 1
Saturn to the Sesquiquadrate of Mercury in Mundo, Converse Direction.	26 13	28 2
Saturn to the Sextile of the Sun in the Zodiac.	26 20	28 3
Ascendant to the Sesquiquadrate of Jupiter in Mundo.	26 31	28 5

There can be no difficulty in defining the quality of this Native' Death, for all the Celestial Bodies afflict each other by alarming configurations; the Sun is of the nature of the enemies, being in Square to Saturn, from Cardinal Signs, and cadent places; he is in opposition to Jupiter, and that Planet is afflicted by the Quartile of Saturn in the Zodiac, and Mundo, and likewise by the Parallel of Mars' Declination; the Moon is in a Mundane Square to the Ascendant, and is afflicted by the Quartile of Mercury, and Zodiacal Parallel of Saturn, and that Planet, being the Prorogator, is posited in the watery Sign Cancer, in the Ninth House, which with other additional, and malignant testimonies, prove in the clearest manner, that *Drowning* would be the cause of the Native's Death.

Hence we have sufficient arguments to confirm the violence of the Native's dissolution, and the Anaretical Directions, demonstrate the time thereof, in the plainest manner; for at the period of his Death, Saturn, the giver of Life, was directed to the Parallel of Mars, by the Motion of the *Primum Mobile*, and also to the Semiquartile of that Malefic in Mundo, by Direct Direction, with the Square of Mercury in the Zodiac, which is of the nature of the Malefics, followed by eight others, without any benevolent assistance, to diminish their destructive power; it is also worthy of observation, that the Sun, Moon, Ascendant, and Part of Fortune, were all afflicted by violent Directions, united with the Mortal train to the Hyleg: the first Direction for Death, was six Months deficient in shewing its Effects, but the Figure I have given, is computed according to the estimate time, so that if it was two Minutes earlier, that Direction to the Apheta, (at the head of the Mortal train,) would correctly correspond with the time when he departed this Life; all the others follow in regular order, which may be seen in the Table of Directions.

In computing the other Motions, it will be found, that Saturn, the giver of Life, had descended below the Western Horizon by

Secondary Direction, and was in Square to Mercury in the Zodiac; the two Luminaries were in obnoxious places, and Terms; the Moon also applied to the radical place of Mars; and in Mundo, was configurated with Saturn, Mars, and Mercury in the Progression from the superior Angles. In the Revolutional Figure for the sixteenth Year of the Native's Age, both the Malefics had nearly the same Declination; Saturn was in Opposition to his place in the Geniture, and received the hostile rays of the Sun from a violent part of the Heavens, and Mercury was on the place of Mars in the Nativity. At the time he was Drowned, (which was January 5th, 1814, at seven o'Clock in the Morning,) the Moon was near the Cusp of the Western Angle, applying to the Square of Mars, and opposition of the Sun; the Apheta was conjoined with the Sun in the East, united with the Parallel of Mercury's Declination, he being in Zodiacal Quartile to Mars in the Geniture; the Moon was in Mundane Square to her place in the Nativity, and applied to the Zodiacal position of the Apheta at the time of Birth,

Miss Amelia Farrow, was Born in Lincoln, on the 2nd of March, 1799, at 6H, 45M. A. M; and departed this Life, on the 4th of October, 1824; Aged twenty-five Years, seven Months, and two Days.

The above time was given to me by the Native, a few Years before her Death, which she said was taken with the greatest care, by her Parents. I first observed, that the Sun was the giver of Life, and at the Age of seventeen, eighteen, and nineteen, he was directed to the Squares of Saturn, and the Moon in the Zodiac, from violent Cardinal Signs, the Effects of which, I judged, produced considerable danger to her Life, by Sickness, &c; she said in the Years I mentioned, she was violently indisposed, and was not expected to live; but those Directions, though they certainly were of a dangerous nature, could not destroy Life. I will therefore prove to the Students, (in as plain a manner as possible, and in few words,) the *true Causes* which defeated those apparent Mortal Directions, from executing the work of Mortality.

It is evident that nothing worthy of notice can be performed in this noble Science, without such Directions as are accurately computed, by which, the time, and quality of all important Events, are previously known; but though these Facts admit of no refutation, yet there are other subjects of considerable importance, which the Students ought to know, if they are not *too learned* to receive instruction. The Sun (to whom the Dignity of Hyleg belongs,) is strong, and free from affliction in this Geniture, he is in conjunction, and Mundane Parallel with Venus, and near her Parallel of Declination; he is also applying to the Sextile of Jupiter in the Zodiac, and is received in the Terms of that benefic, as he ascends the Eastern Horizon, by which his powerful influence (as Prorogator,) is considerably augmented; now as Saturn, and the Moon, are in Opposition to each other, from Cardinal Signs, it clearly shows the apparent fury of their Quartiles, when the Hyleg was directed to them in the Eastern Angle; for when the Sun came to the Squares of Saturn, and the Moon, he was then directed to the Sextile of Jupiter in Mundo, by Converse Motion, and also to the Quartile of that benefic in the Zodiac, by Converse Direction; and it must be further observed, that when those two Malefic Directions were in operation, Saturn was directed to the Sextile of Jupiter in the World, by Converse Motion, and also to the trine of that benefic, by Direct Direction; the Moon was also directed to the Mundane Trine of Jupiter, by Converse Motion, near the same period. Hence it is plain, that the places of all the violent *Promittors*, and their Directions, must always be strictly regarded, as well as those of the *Significators*; for when the *Promittors* are unable to execute their Mortal Effects, owing to benign Directions, and Terms, to which they are joined, they then only produce diseases, &c; so that when the giver of Life, in this Geniture, was directed to the Quartiles of Saturn, and the Moon, in the Zodiac, those *two Promittors*, then received the power of both the benefics, by Directional Motion, to which they were united in the Mundane Circle. From these remarks, the Students may observe, that the time of Death ought not to be pronounced, when the Hyleg meets with Malefic Directions, until they have properly examined the intervention of all the benefic rays, and those places in the Heavens, where the Promittors arrive at that time; for if their violent power be defeated, by other Motions, so that their influence becomes of a reverse quality, Life will be preserved; but when they retain their own destructive power, without alteration, or diminution, the Native will then be removed from the land of the Living.

CELESTIAL PHILOSOPHY,

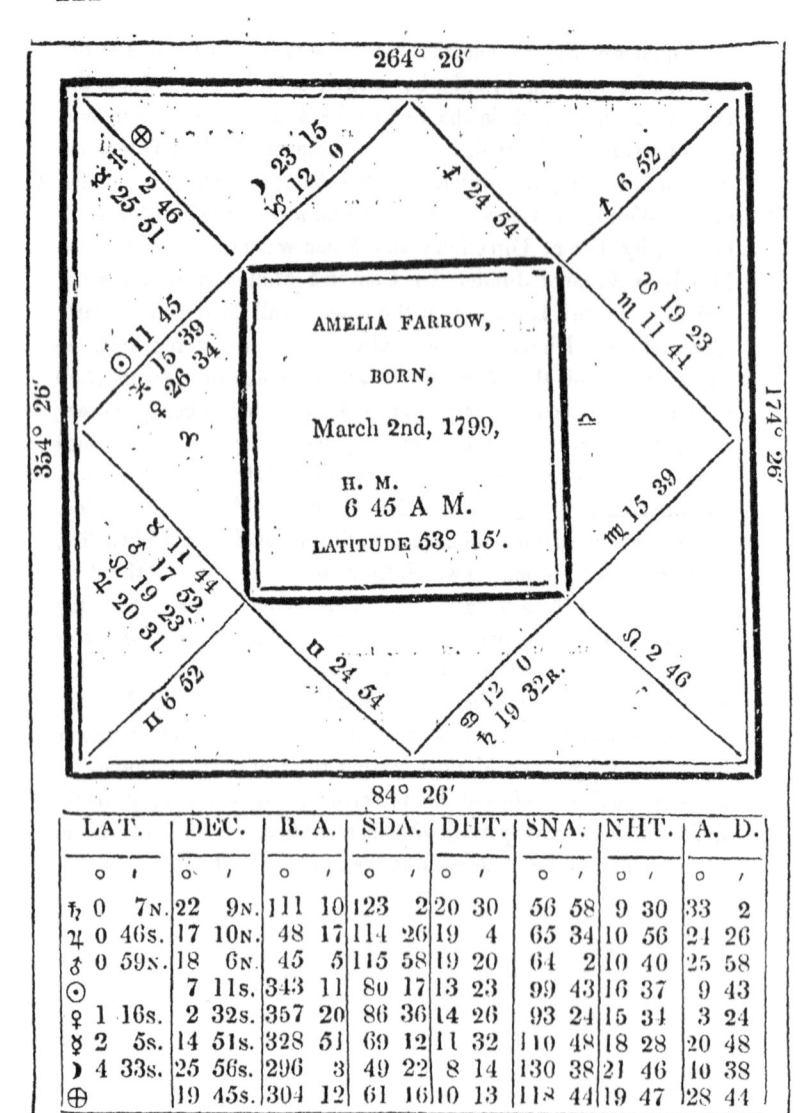

264° 26'

354° 26'   174° 26'

84° 26'

♉ 2 46
♅ 25 51
☊ 11
⊕ 11 45
☽ 23 15
♇ 12 0
♐ 24 54
♏ 6 52
♌ 19 23
♍ 11 41
☉ 11 45
♓ 15 39
♀ 26 34
♎
♏ 15 39
♉ 11 44
♂ 17 52
♃ 19 23
♆ 20 31
♊ 6 52
♊ 24 54
♋ 12 0
♄ 19 32 R.
♌ 2 46

AMELIA FARROW,
BORN,
March 2nd, 1799,
H. M.
6 45 A M.
LATITUDE 53° 15'.

	LAT.	DEC.	R. A.	SDA.	DHT.	SNA.	NHT.	A. D.
	° '	° '	° '	° '	° '	° '	° '	° '
♄	0 7n.	22 9n.	111 10	123 2	20 30	56 58	9 30	33 2
♃	0 46s.	17 10n.	48 17	114 26	19 4	65 34	10 56	21 26
♂	0 59n.	18 6n.	45 5	115 58	19 20	64 2	10 40	25 58
☉		7 11s.	343 11	80 17	13 23	99 43	16 37	9 43
♀	1 16s.	2 32s.	357 20	86 36	14 26	93 24	15 34	3 24
☿	2 5s.	14 51s.	328 51	69 12	11 32	110 48	18 28	20 48
☽	4 33s.	25 56s.	296 3	49 22	8 14	130 38	21 46	10 38
⊕		19 45s.	304 12	61 16	10 13	118 44	19 47	28 44

OR GENETHLIACAL ASTRONOMY.

A TABLE OF THE DIRECTIONS.	ARC. D. M.	TIME. YRS. MO.
Moon to the Quintile of Jupiter in Mundo, Direct Motion.	0 33	0 7
Sun to the Sesquiquadrate of Saturn in Mundo, Converse Direction..........	0 57	1 0
Sun to the Quintile of Jupiter in the Zodiac, Converse Motion..........	1 43	1 10
Sun to the Parallel of Venus in Mundo, by the Rapt Motion..........	2 5	2 3
Moon to the Trine of Jupiter in the Zodiac, Converse Direction..........	2 5	2 3
Sun to the Sextile of Mars in the Zodiac..........	2 28	2 8
Sun to the Semiquartile of Jupiter in Mundo, Converse Motion..........	2 36	2 10
Moon to the Sextile of Venus in the Zodiac..........	2 56	3 2
Moon to the Semiquartile of the Sun in the Zodiac.....	3 6	3 4
Sun to the Trine of Saturn in the Zodiac..........	3 9	3 4
Moon to the Quintile of Venus in the Zodiac, Converse Direction..........	3 20	3 7
Midheaven to the Trine of Mars in Mundo..........	3 21	3 7
Sun to the Sextile of Jupiter in the Zodiac..........	3 32	3 9
Moon to the Semiquartile of Venus in Mundo, Converse Motion..........	3 35	3 10
Moon to the Opposition of Saturn in the Zodiac, Converse Direction..........	3 38	3 10
Sun to the Parallel of Venus in Mundo, Converse Motion.	3 53	4 2
Midheaven to the Biquintile of Saturn in Mundo.......	3 57	4 3
Moon to the Trine of Mars in the Zodiac, Converse Direction..........	3 58	4 3
Part of Fortune to the Sextile of Mars in Mundo.......	4 3	4 4
Sun to the Body of Mercury in the Zodiac, Converse Motion..........	4 4	4 4
Sun to the Parallel of Venus in Mundo, Direct Direction..........	4 32	4 10
Sun to the Sextile of the Moon in the Zodiac..........	4 38	4 11
Sun to the Parallel of Venus in the Zodiac..........	4 48	5 1
Moon to the Sextile of Mars in Mundo, Direct Motion.	5 3	5 5
Sun to the Quintile of Mars in the Zodiac, Converse Direction..........	5 39	6 0
Moon to the Semiquartile of Mercury in the Zodiac, Converse Motion..........	5 53	6 ?
Sun to the Body of Venus in the Zodiac..........	5 57	6 .

	ARC.		TIME.	
THE DIRECTIONS CONTINUED.	D.	M.	YRS.	MO.
Ascendant to the Body of Venus in Mundo	6	18	6	9
Midheaven to the Square of Venus in Mundo	6	18	6	9
Sun to the Sesquiquadrate of Saturn in the Zodiac, Converse Motion	6	36	7	2
Ascendant to the Semiquartile of the Moon in Mundo	6	55	7	6
Midheaven to the Trine of Jupiter in Mundo	7	33	8	2
Sun to the Semiquartile of Mars in Mundo, Converse Motion	7	38	8	3
Ascendant to the Trine of Saturn in Mundo	7	44	8	4
Sun to the Semiquartile of the Moon in Mundo, Direct Direction	7	51	8	5
Sun to the Body of Venus in Mundo, Direct Motion	7	56	8	6
Part of Fortune to the Sextile of Jupiter in Mundo	8	16	8	11
Sun to the Semiquartile of Mars in the Zodiac	8	25	9	1
Moon to the Opposition of Saturn in Mundo, Converse Motion	8	27	9	1
Sun to the Trine of Saturn in Mundo, Direct Direction	8	49	9	6
Sun to the Biquintile of Saturn in Mundo, Converse Motion	8	58	9	8
Midheaven to the Quintile of Mercury in Mundo	9	3	9	10
Sun to the Quintile of the Moon in the Zodiac	9	3	9	10
Moon to the Sextile of Jupiter in Mundo, Direct Direction	9	18	10	1
Moon to the Square of Jupiter in Mundo, Converse Motion	9	28	10	3
Sun to the Semiquartile of Jupiter in the Zodiac	9	28	10	3
Sun to the Parallel of Venus in the Zodiac	9	47	10	8
Moon to the Semiquartile of Mercury in Mundo, Converse Direction	10	20	11	2
Moon to the Square of Venus in the Zodiac, Converse Motion	10	24	11	3
Sun to the Semiquartile of Venus in the Zodiac, Converse Direction	10	59	11	10
Moon to the Sextile of Mercury in the Zodiac, Converse Motion	11	36	12	7
Sun to the Semiquartile of Mercury in the Zodiac	11	37	12	7
Moon to the Sextile of Venus in Mundo, Converse Direction	11	49	12	10
Part of Fortune to the Biquintile of Saturn in Mundo	12	9	13	2
Moon to the Square of Mars in Mundo, Converse Motion	12	34	13	7
Sun to the Parallel of Mars in Mundo, by the Rapt Motion	13	3	14	2

THE DIRECTIONS CONTINUED.	ARC D. M.	TIME YRS. MO.
Moon to the Biquintile of Saturn in Mundo, Direct Direction.................................	13 4	14 2
Sun to the Biquintile of Saturn in the Zodiac, Converse Motion.....................................	14 28	15 8
Midheaven to the Quintile of the Sun in Mundo........	14 31	15 9
Sun to his own Parallel in the Zodiac.................	14 36	15 10
Moon to the Parallel of Saturn in the Zodiac.........	14 39	15 11
Part of Fortune to the Semiquartile of Mars in Mundo.	14 43	16 0
Moon to the Sesquiquadrate of Jupiter in the Zodiac, Converse Direction...........................	14 49	16 2
Moon to the Semiquartile of Venus in the Zodiac......	14 59	16 4
Ascendant to the Sextile of the Moon in Mundo........	15 9	16 7
Sun to the Square of Saturn in the Zodiac.............	15 11	16 7
Sun to the Parallel of Jupiter in Mundo, by the Rapt Motion..	15 30	17 0
Moon to the Quintile of Mercury in the Zodiac, Converse Direction.................................	15 31	17 0
Moon to the Semiquartile of Mars in Mundo, Direct Motion.	15 43	17 2
Sun to the Sextile of Jupiter in Mundo, Converse Direction.	15 59	17 5
Sun to the Sextile of the Moon in Mundo, Direct Motion.	16 5	17 6
Moon to the Sesquiquadrate of Mars in the Zodiac, Converse Direction...........................	16 22	17 10
Sun to the Square of the Moon in the Zodiac..........	16 46	18 4
Sun to the Square of Jupiter in the Zodiac, Converse Motion..	17 28	19 1
Part of Fortune to the Sesquiquadrate of Saturn in Mundo.	17 51	19 4
Sun to the Sextile of Mercury in the Zodiac...........	17 53	19 5
Sun to his own Semiquartile in the Zodiac.............	18 17	19 11
Midheaven to the Sextile of Mercury in Mundo........	18 17	19 11
Moon to the Quintile of Venus in Mundo, Converse Direction...................................	18 24	20 0
Sun to the Sextile of Venus in the Zodiac, Converse motion.	18 27	20 1
Moon to the sextile of mercury in mundo, Converse Direction.	18 34	20 2
Moon to the sesquiquadrate of saturn in mundo, Direct motion.......................................	18 45	20 4
Part of Fortune to the Body of mercury in mundo......	19 2	20 8
Part of Fortune to the Semiquartile of Jupiter in mundo...	19 12	20 10
Moon to the square of mars in the zodiac.............	19 20	21 0
Moon to the Body of mercury in mundo, Direct motion...	20 8	21 10
Moon to the semiquartile of Jupiter in mundo, Direct Direction..................................	20 14	22 0

226 CELESTIAL PHILOSOPHY,

	ARC.		TIME.	
THE DIRECTIONS CONTINUED.	D.	M.	YRS.	MO.
Moon to the square of mercury in the zodiac, Converse Motion	20	56	22	10
Sun to the square of mars in the zodiac, Converse Direction	20	59	22	11
Sun to the sextile of mars in mundo, Converse motion	21	1	22	11
Moon to the square of Jupiter in the zodiac	21	6	23	0
Ascendant to the Quintile of the moon in mundo	21	44	23	9
Ascendant to the Pleiades	22	35	24	8
Sun to the Quintile of the moon in mundo, Direct motion	22	40	24	9
Sun to the Quintile of saturn in the zodiac	23	19	25	6
Moon to the Biquintile of Jupiter in the zodiac, Converse Direction	23	20	25	6
Moon to the Parallel of mars in the zodiac	23	26	25	7
Sun to the Parallel of mars in mundo, Direct motion	23	28	25	7
Sun to the Quintile of mercury in the zodiac	23	29	25	7
Midheaven to the Quintile of Venus in mundo	23	37	25	9
Part of Fortune to the semiquartile of the moon in mundo	23	55	26	1
Moon to the Biquintile of saturn in the zodiac	24	11	26	5
Moon to the Trine of Venus in the zodiac, Converse Motion	24	19	26	7
Moon to the Body of mercury in the zodiac	24	33	26	10
Sun to the Parallel of mercury in the zodiac	24	35	26	10
Ascendant to the Body of mars in mundo	24	41	27	0
Midheaven to the Square of mars in mundo	24	41	27	0
Moon to her own semiquartile in mundo	24	41	27	0
Moon to the Biquintile of mars in the zodiac, Converse Direction	24	50	27	2
Moon to the Parallel of Jupiter in the zodiac	24	58	27	4
Moon to the Quintile of mercury in mundo, Converse Motion	25	9	27	6
Midheaven to the sextile of the sun in mundo	25	13	27	7
Sun to the semiquartile of Venus in the zodiac	25	22	27	9
Sun to the Quintile of Venus in the zodiac, Converse Direction	25	29	27	10
Sun to his own sextile in the zodiac	25	29	27	10
Moon to the Trine of Jupiter in mundo, Converse motion	25	56	28	4
Part of Fortune to the Body of the sun in mundo	26	5	28	6
Sun to the Quintile of Jupiter in mundo, Converse motion	26	42	29	2
Ascendant to the Square of saturn in mundo	26	44	29	2
Midheaven to the Opposition of saturn in mundo	26	44	29	2
Sun to the Body of mars in mundo, Direct Direction	26	52	29	4
Sun to the Body of the moon in mundo, Converse motion	27	21	29	11

OR GENETHLIACAL ASTRONOMY.

THE DIRECTIONS CONTINUED.	ARC. D. M.	TIME. YRS. MO.
Part of Fortune to the Trine of saturn in mundo......	27 21	29 11
Sun to the square of saturn in mundo, Direct Direction..	27 49	30 5
Sun to the Parallel of Jupiter in mundo, Direct Direction.	28 11	30 10
Moon to the Trine of saturn in mundo, Direct motion...	28 15	30 11
Moon to the square of Venus in mundo, Converse Direction.	28 17	30 11
Sun to the Parallel of Jupiter in the zodiac............	28 46	31 5
Sun to the Body of mars in the zodiac.................	28 47	31 5
Moon to the Parallel of mercury in the zodiac..........	28 47	31 5
Moon to the Trine of mars in mundo, Converse motion....	29 2	31 9
Ascendant to the Body of Jupiter in mundo............	29 25	32 2
Midheaven to the Square of Jupiter in mundo..........	29 25	32 2
Sun to the Parallel of mars in mundo, Converse Direction.	29 26	32 2
Moon to the sesquiquadrate of saturn in the zodiac......	29 32	32 3
Sun to the sextile of saturn in the zodiac.............	29 44	32 5
Ascendant to the semiquartile of mercury in mundo......	29 49	32 6
Moon to the Quintile of mars in the zodiac............	30 14	33 1
Sun to the Body of Jupiter in the zodiac..............	30 19	33 2
Sun to the Parallel of mars in the zodiac..............	30 44	33 7
Sun to the semiquartile of mercury in mundo, Direct motion.	31 7	34 0
Moon to her own semiquartile in the zodiac............	31 31	34 5
Sun to the Body of Jupiter in mundo, Direct Direction..	31 34	34 6
Ascendant to the square of the moon in mundo.........	31 37	34 7
Midheaven to the Body of the moon in mundo..........	31 37	34 7
Moon to the Quintile of Jupiter in the zodiac..........	31 41	34 8
Sun to the Quintile of mars in mundo, Converse motion..	31 43	34 8
Sun to the Trine of the moon in the zodiac............	31 55	34 11
Part of Fortune to the sextile of the moon in mundo......	32 9	35 2
Sun to his own Quintile in the zodiac................	32 16	35 4
Sun to the square of the moon in mundo, Direct Direction.	32 33	35 8
Moon to her own sextile in mundo...................	32 55	36 1
Sun to the semiquartile of Venus in mundo, Converse motion.	33 11	36 4
Moon to the Body of the sun in the zodiac............	33 24	36 7
Sun to the square of mercury in the zodiac............	33 34	36 9
Moon to the Biquintile of saturn in the zodiac, Converse Direction..............................	33 54	37 1
Moon to the sesquiquadrate of Venus in the zodiac, Converse motion..............................	33 56	37 1
Sun to the sextile of Venus in the zodiac.............	34 1	37 3
Sun to the Pleiades................................	34 6	37 4

The Directions that destroyed the Life of this Native, were, the Sun Hyleg, to the Parallels of Mars in Mundo, by Direct, and Converse Motion, and also to the Zodiacal Parallel of Mercury, and Bodies of the Moon, and Mars, with the Parallel of Mars' Declination, the Mundane Square of Saturn, and Quartile of the Moon in the World, by Direct Direction; and though the rays of Jupiter interposed in the Mortal train, he was unable to abate the influence thereof, being afflicted by the furious Directions of the Malefics at the time of Death, by which his benevolent qualities were destroyed, both in strength, and operation, so that he could not render any assistance to preserve Life, though he properly specified the quality of Death, of which I need not make any comments, having (in preceding Examples,) stated the nature of the Mortal diseases, produced by that Star, when his power was overcome by obnoxious rays.

By secondary Direction, the Hyleg applied to the Square of Saturn, and the Moon was nearly in Quartile with the Sun from Cardinal Signs, and subterranean positions. In her last Revolution, the Moon separated from the Body of the Sun, and applied to the Opposition of Mars, who afflicted the Horoscope by his opposite rays; Saturn was then in Square to Mercury, being posited on the place of Jupiter, and Mars in the Nativity. At the time she died, the Moon was applying to the Quartiles of Saturn, and Mars, both of which were in Square to the true significator of Life, in the Geniture.

My observations are founded on Truth, and will ever remain irrefutable; but there are many *noisy pretenders* to this Science, who believe themselves able to perform WONDERS, and in fact, if WONDERS are to be executed by *long Epistles*, with a host of *whimsical chimeras*, and SENTENCES without meaning, I have no doubt that such characters may be esteemed superior to their contemporaries; I will therefore give the following *true time* of a Female's Birth, that they may erect a Figure, and pronounce Judgment thereon. The Native was Born near Lincoln, on the 29th of May, 1797, at 7H. 20M, P M; and at the time of my writing this, (which is, November 3rd, 1825,) she is in a good state of Health. The Sun is the giver of Life, and has passed the Bodies of Saturn, Mercury, and Mars, with their *old Terms,* and the Moon at the same time was directed to those Promittors by Converse Direction; now if those *learned* Gentlemen in this Science, are able to prove by true Astronomical demonstration, why those Directions did not destroy Life, and when the Native's dissolution will take place, I shall then acknowledge that they are acquainted with some of the true principles of this Sublime, and incomparable Study.

The next is the Nativity of a Child, that was Born near Donington, in the County of Lincoln, on the 6th of September, 1814, at 7H. 10M. P M; and died July 4th, 1825, Aged ten Years, and ten Months, nearly.

The stations of the Stars in this Geniture, plainly show the short duration of the Native's Life; for their qualities in the different parts of the Heavens, are malignant, and impotent, which, with the Radical affliction of the Prorogator, produced an ill state of Health, during the time she lived; and though the most judicious means were used for her recovery, I judged, that in a few Years, she would exchange this transitory Life, for a glorious immortality, as all the vital significators are afflicted in the Zodiac, and in the World, without assistance, which show the rapid approach of Death, in the early part of Life.

This Native died by Directions to the Hyleg, and not by the *violence* of the position; and in selecting the true Aphetical significator, I have no doubt that some would take their favorite point, the Ascendant; but I shall endeavor to undeceive such persons by this Example; for as neither of the Luminaries are in an Aphetical position, the true significator of Life, is Jupiter, who has the proper Dignities to claim that power, according to the true principles of the IMMORTAL PTOLEMY: for that Star is in an Aphetical place, and disposed of the preceding full Moon, and at the time of Birth, was ruler of the Part of Fortune, being conjoined with the Sun, and in exact Trine to the Moon in Mundo, and also in Opposition to the Ascendant. The following is the Figure of Birth, with the Directions, which produced the *Terminus Vitæ*.

———'She fell,
Like some fair Lilly, or a Poppy green,
Which from its Parent Root, the Blast hath rent.'

OR GENETHLIACAL ASTRONOMY.

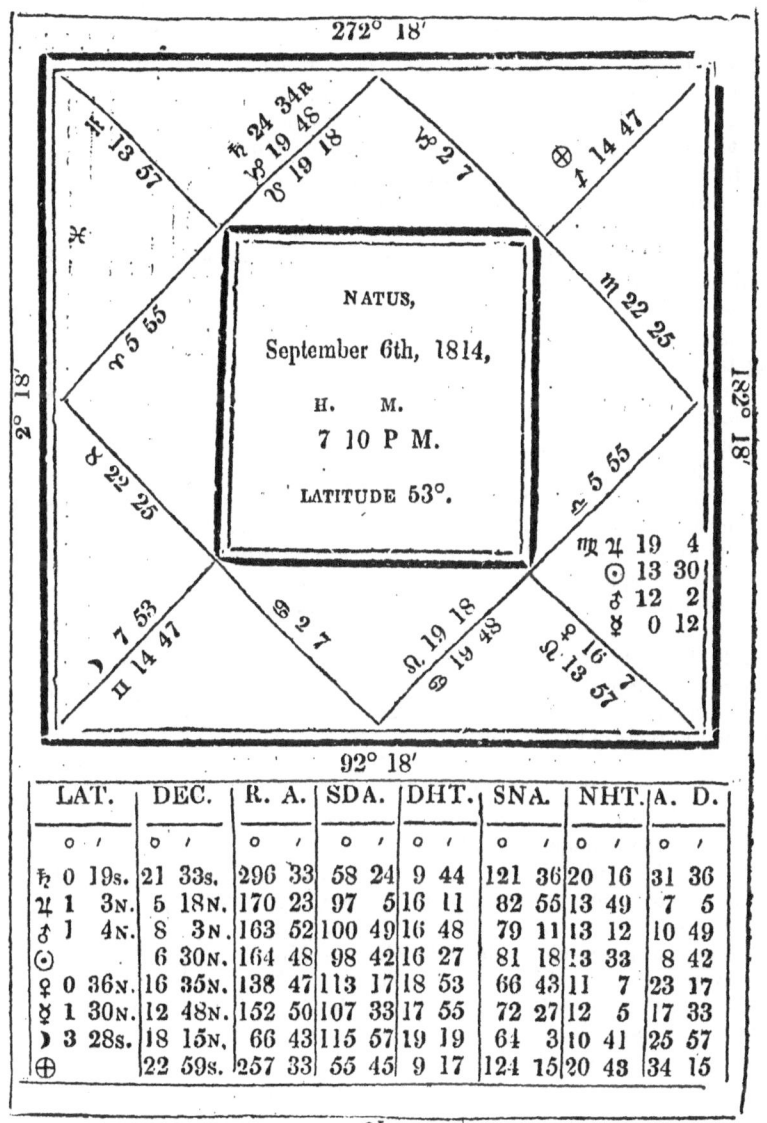

272° 18'

♅ 13 57
♆ 24 34ʀ ♄ 19 48 ♋ 19 18
♑ 2 7
⊕ ♐ 14 47
♓
♈ 5 55
♏ 22 25

NATUS,
September 6th, 1814,
H.   M.
7 10 P.M.
LATITUDE 53°.

♉ 22 25
♎ 5 55
2° 18'
182° 18'

☽ 7 53
♊ 14 47
♋ 2 7
♌ 19 18 ♍ 19 48
♃ 16 7 ♌ 13 57

♍ ♃ 19 4
☉ 13 30
♂ 12 2
☿ 0 12

92° 18'

	LAT.	DEC.	R. A.	SDA.	DHT.	SNA.	NHT.	A. D.
	° ′	° ′	° ′	° ′	° ′	° ′	° ′	° ′
♄	0 19s.	21 33s.	296 33	58 24	9 44	121 36	20 16	31 36
♃	1 3ɴ.	5 18ɴ.	170 23	97 5	16 11	82 55	13 49	7 5
♂	1 4ɴ.	8 3ɴ.	163 52	100 49	16 48	79 11	13 12	10 49
☉		6 30ɴ.	164 48	98 42	16 27	81 18	13 33	8 42
♀	0 36ɴ.	16 35ɴ.	138 47	113 17	18 53	66 43	11 7	23 17
☿	1 30ɴ.	12 48ɴ.	152 50	107 33	17 55	72 27	12 5	17 33
☽	3 28s.	18 15ɴ.	66 43	115 57	19 19	64 3	10 41	25 57
⊕		22 59s.	257 33	55 45	9 17	124 15	20 43	34 15

A TABLE OF THE DIRECTIONS.

	ARC. D. M.	TIME. YRS. MO.
Part of Fortune to the Quintile of Jupiter in Mundo....	0 32	0 7
Moon to the Trine of Jupiter in Mundo, Direct Direction.	0 42	0 9
Part of Fortune to the Sextile of Saturn in Mundo......	0 46	0 10
Sun to the Sesquiquadrate of Saturn in Mundo, Direct Motion.....	1 22	1 6
Sun to the Parallel of Jupiter in the Zodiac............	1 25	1 7
Moon to the Sesquiquadrate of Saturn in the Zodiac....	1 30	1 8
Moon to the Trine of Mars in Mundo, Converse Direction	1 55	2 2
Midheaven to the Trine of Venus in Mundo..........	2 1	2 3
Jupiter to the Sesquiquadrate of Saturn in Mundo, Converse Motion..........	2 13	2 6
Jupiter to the Trine of Saturn in the Zodiac...........	2 20	2 8
Sun to the Body of Jupiter in the Zodiac.............	2 32	2 11
Moon to the Quintile of Venus in the Zodiac, Converse Direction..........	2 39	3 0
Sun to the Trine of the Moon in Mundo, Direct Motion...	2 10	3 0
Jupiter to the Body of Mars in the Zodiac, Converse Direction..........	3 5	3 5
Jupiter to the Body of Mars in Mundo, Converse Motion.	3 11	3 6
Sun to the Sesquiquadrate of Saturn in the Zodiac, Converse Direction..........	3 21	3 8
Moon to the Square of Mars in the Zodiac............	3 43	4 1
Sun to the Body of Jupiter in Mundo, Direct Motion....	4 10	4 7
Moon to the Square of Mercury in the Zodiac, Converse Direction..........	4 20	4 9
Sun to the Body of Mercury in the Zodiac, Converse Motion.	4 38	5 1
Ascendant to the Sextile of Saturn in Mundo..........	4 47	5 3
Sun to the Trine of Saturn in the Zodiac.............	5 2	5 7
Moon to the Square of the Sun in the Zodiac..........	5 6	5 8
Jupiter to the Semiquartile of Venus in the Zodiac......	5 8	5 8
Sun to the Biquintile of Saturn in Mundo, Converse Motion.	6 13	6 10
Moon to the Trine of Mercury in Mundo, Converse Direction..........	6 19	6 11
Ascendant to the Semiquartile of the Moon in Mundo....	6 25	7 1
Moon to the Square of Venus in Mundo, Direct Motion..	6 27	7 1
Ascendant to the Biquintile of Venus in Mundo........	6 28	7 2
Moon to the Sextile of Venus in the Zodiac...........	6 51	7 8
Part of Fortune to the Square of Mercury in Mundo....	7 12	8 0
Sun to the Semiquartile of Venus in the Zodiac.........	7 56	8 9
Jupiter to the Trine of the Moon in the Zodiac........	8 13	9 1

	ARC	TIME
THE DIRECTIONS CONTINUED.	D. M.	YRS. MO.
Jupiter to the Trine of Saturn in Mundo, Direct Direction.	8 14	9 1
Moon to the Trine of Saturn in Mundo, Direct Motion..	8 40	9 6
Jupiter to the Sesquiquadrate of Saturn in the Zodiac, Converse Direction............................	8 43	9 7
Part of Fortune to the Parallel of Saturn in Mundo....	8 47	9 8
Jupiter to the Body of Mercury in Mundo, Converse Motion.	8 52	9 9
Moon to the Quintile of Mercury in the Zodiac.........	9 31	10 6
Moon to the Parallel of Venus in Mundo, by the Rapt Motion................................	9 44	10 9
Jupiter to the Body of Mercury in the Zodiac, Converse Direction...........................	9 48	10 10
Moon to the Biquintile of Saturn in the Zodiac........	9 52	10 11
Jupiter to the Sesquiquadrate of the Moon in Mundo, Direct Motion............................	10 9	11 2
Jupiter to the Square of the Moon in the Zodiac, Converse Direction...........................	10 20	11 4
Jupiter to the Biquintile of Saturn in Mundo, Converse Motion.................................	10 30	11 6
Part of Fortune to the Semiquartile of Saturn in Mundo..	10 30	11 6
Sun to the Trine of the Moon to the Zodiac...........	10 58	12 1
Jupiter to the Semiquartile of Mercury in the Zodiac....	11 5	12 3
Sun to the Trine of Saturn in Mundo, Direct Motion......	11 6	12 3
Sun to the Biquintile of Saturn in the Zodiac, Converse Direction...........................	11 17	12 5
Jupiter to his own Parallel in the Zodiac.............	11 25	12 7
Jupiter to the Sextile of Venus in the Zodiac..........	11 29	12 8
Moon to the Trine of Mars in the Zodiac, Converse Motion.	11 34	12 9
Moon to the Square of Saturn in Mundo, Converse Direction................................	11 51	13 1
Moon to the Trine of Saturn in the Zodiac, Converse Motion.................................	12 4	13 5
Midheaven to the Trine of Mercury in Mundo..........	12 12	13 7
Ascendant to the Quintile of Saturn in Mundo.........	12 34	13 11
Moon to the Sesquiquadrate of Mars in Mundo, Converse Direction............................	12 36	13 11
Part of Fortune to the Square of the Sun in Mundo.....	12 42	14 1
Jupiter to the Parallel of the Sun in the Zodiac........	12 50	14 3
Ascendant to the Sesquiquadrate of Venus in Mundo....	13 8	14 7
Sun to the Sesquiquadrate of the Moon in Mundo, Direct Motion.................................	13 21	14 10

THE DIRECTIONS CONTINUED.

	ARC.		TIME.	
	D.	M.	YRS.	MO.
Sun to the Parallel of Jupiter in the Zodiac	13	29	15	0
Part of Fortune to the Square of Mars in Mundo	13	49	15	4
Sun to the Semiquartile of Mercury in the Zodiac	14	18	15	11
Moon to the Square of Venus in the Zodiac, Converse Direction	14	19	15	11
Jupiter to the Sesquiquadrate of the Moon in the Zodiac	14	31	16	2
Jupiter to the Parallel of Mars in the Zodiac	14	45	16	5
Sun to the Sextile of Venus in the Zodiac	14	46	16	5
Moon to the Parallel of Mercury in Mundo, by the Rapt Motion	14	50	16	6
Sun to his own Parallel in the Zodiac	14	51	16	7
Ascendant to the Pleiades	15	6	16	9
Moon to the Trine of Venus in Mundo, Converse Direction	15	10	16	10
Jupiter to the Square of Saturn in the Zodiac	15	19	17	0
Sun to the Body of Venus in the Zodiac, Converse Motion	15	56	17	8
Jupiter to the Semiquartile of Mars in the Zodiac	16	27	18	3
Jupiter to the Biquintile of the Moon in Mundo, Direct Direction	16	34	18	5
Jupiter to the Biquintile of Saturn in the Zodiac, Converse Motion	16	44	18	7
Sun to the Parallel of Mars in the Zodiac	16	50	18	8
Part of Fortune to the Biquintile of the Moon in Mundo	16	57	18	10
Jupiter to the Quintile of Venus in the zodiac	16	59	18	11
Moon to the Sesquiquadrate of Mercury in Mundo, Converse Direction	17	0	18	11
Moon to the Square of Mercury in Mundo, Direct Motion	17	1	18	11
Ascendant to the Biquintile of Mercury in Mundo	17	2	18	11
Midheaven to the Trine of the Moon in Mundo	17	6	19	0
Part of Fortune to the Square of Jupiter in Mundo	17	7	19	0
Jupiter to the Semiquartile of the Sun in the zodiac	17	9	19	0
Sun to Spica Virginis	17	11	19	1
Moon to the Trine of Mercury in the zodiac, Converse Direction	17	38	19	7
Moon to the Parallel of the Sun in Mundo, by the Rapt Motion	17	39	19	7
Moon to the Sesquiquadrate of Mars in the zodiac, Converse Direction	17	52	19	10
Moon to the Parallel of Mars in Mundo, by the Rapt Motion	17	53	19	10
Sun to the Sesquiquadrate of the Moon in the zodiac	17	56	19	11

OR GENETHLIACAL ASTRONOMY. 235

	ARC.		TIME.	
THE DIRECTIONS CONTINUED.	D.	M.	YRS.	MO.
Jupiter to the Sextile of Mercury in the zodiac......	18	0	20	0
Midheaven to the Trine of the Sun in Mundo..........	18	18	20	4
Moon to the Sesquiquadrate of Saturn in Mundo, Direct Direction.................................	18	24	20	5
Sun to the Square of Saturn in the zodiac............	18	45	20	10
Midheaven to the Trine of Mars in Mundo............	18	46	20	10
Jupiter to the Biquintile of the Moon in the zodiac......	18	50	20	11
Moon to the Biquintile of Mars in Mundo, Converse Motion.	19	1	21	2
Moon to the Parallel of Venus in Mundo, Converse Direction.................................	19	5	21	3
Moon to the Parallel of Jupiter in Mundo, by the Rapt Motion..................................	19	37	21	10
Part of Fortune to the Trine of Venus in Mundo	19	40	21	11
Sun to the Biquintile of the Moon in Mundo, Direct Direction.................................	19	45	22	0
Midheaven to the Biquintile of Venus in Mundo........	19	48	22	1
Moon to the Quintile of Venus in Mundo, Direct Motion.	19	49	22	1
Moon to the Parallel of Venus in Mundo, Direct Direction.	19	52	22	2
Sun to the Semiquartile of Mars in the zodiac..........	19	57	22	3
Jupiter to his own Semiquartile in the zodiac..........	19	59	22	3
Jupiter to the Body of Venus in Mundo, Converse Motion.	20	19	22	7
Sun to his own Semiquartile in the zodiac............	20	42	23	0
Jupiter to the Body of Venus in the zodiac, Converse Direction.................................	20	49	23	2
Moon to the Parallel of Saturn in the zodiac..........	21	3	23	5
Moon to the Quintile of Mars in the zodiac............	21	11	23	7
Moon to the Sextile of Mercury in the zodiac..........	21	22	23	9
Sun to the Sextile of Mercury in the zodiac..........	21	33	23	11

I calculated this Nativity in the Month of November, 1821, and foretold the time of her Death, which is well known to many. It is probable that some may object to my selecting Jupiter, as the true significator of Life, because he is under the Earth, and under the rays of the Sun also, which, (to those who consider themselves *learned* in this Science,) may appear contrary to my rules, and practice. I do affirm that the Luminaries, &c. when in a subterranean location, cannot exercise the Hylegiacal power, except when they are within the proper limits of the Eastern, and Western Horizon. Now if the Latitude, and Declination of Jupiter, are taken into consideration, his distance from the Western Angle, will be found to qualify him to become the true Apheta; the authenticity of which, may be proved by those who think proper to compute the true Motions, and distances, according to the Examples I have given in this Work.

In the preceding Table, the Reader will observe, that there are twelve Directions to the Hyleg, which formed the Mortal train, in regular succession; the Body of Mercury, and the Terms of Saturn, were first encountered by the Apheta, which shewed the time of Death; and as Mercury is in Zodiacal, and Mundane Sesquiquadrate with Saturn, and also in Quartile to the Moon, and near the Body of Mars, and his Terms, he consequently became of the nature of both the Enemies. The Hyleg was directed to the Sextile of Venus in the Zodiac, which were united with the Directions for dissolution, but her rays could not render the least assistance, though their union shewed the quality of the lingering disease, by which the Native's Life was destroyed.

The Sun was conjoined with Jupiter, Mars, and Mercury, by Secondary Direction, and Saturn afflicted the Horoscope, in which position he communicated his violent power to the Luminaries, and Benefics in the Progression. In the Revolutional Figure for the tenth Year, the Moon was in a violent Sign, and in a cadent station, having separated from the Quartile of Mars, she then applied to the

Square of Saturn in the Zodiac; Mercury was in Opposition to the Ascendant, and the three superiors had nearly the same Parallel of Declination; Saturn was also on the place of the Moon in the Nativity, in which position he was in Quartile with the Sun, and in Square to the Radical place of that Luminary. At the time she died, the Sun, Mars, and Mercury, were in Conjunction; the Moon was also afflicted, and the Hyleg received the malignant power of Saturn, and Mars, in the Mundane Circle, all which confirm the verity of these important Calculations, and the baneful Effects of the primary Motions, particularly when their rays are projected in an uniform manner, from Nocturnal applications, to the true significator of Life.

The next is the Geniture of Eliza Ingraham, who lived at Billingborough, near Folkingham, Lincolnshire; she was Born on the 2nd of August, 1771, at 21h. 55m. P. M.

The time of this Birth was lately given to me, by one of the Native's Female Relatives, now living, who requested me to state the period, when any particular Event would take place; I was also desired to ascertain, whether the Native was likely to Travel, or take long Voyages, and, if she would be fortunate, or unfortunate, in general, during Life. As soon as I had examined the *violent* positions of the Celestial Bodies, and the *Mortal Directions* in Infancy, I immediately told her, I was confident, that her relation *was dead*, and that she died before the end of the sixth Year; the answer which I received, was, that my Judgment was true, and, that she departed this Life, at the time I mentioned. I then asked, what induced her to try to deceive me, by *false questions*, as I was not disposed to waste my time, to satisfy her curiosity; she said, her chief motive was, because she wished to be convinced of the truth of the Science, and, that she had now sufficiently proved the accuracy of my Judgment; she said she had always been an unbeliever, and considered the Science to be a false, and groundless Study; but was now of a different opinion, and firmly believed in its truth, when practised by skilful Professors. I asked her, if she could put me in possession of the time of her own Geniture, she answered in the affirmative, and produced the true time thereof, written by her late Father. I then computed the Directions of the Hyleg, to all the mortal Promittors, (which were seven in number,) and, that she might not any longer consider these Astronomical Computations, as imaginary whims, and vain delusions, I informed her, that before the end of the Month of June, 1832, she would then, no longer remain an inhabitant of this Earthly World.

OR GENETHLIACAL ASTRONOMY.

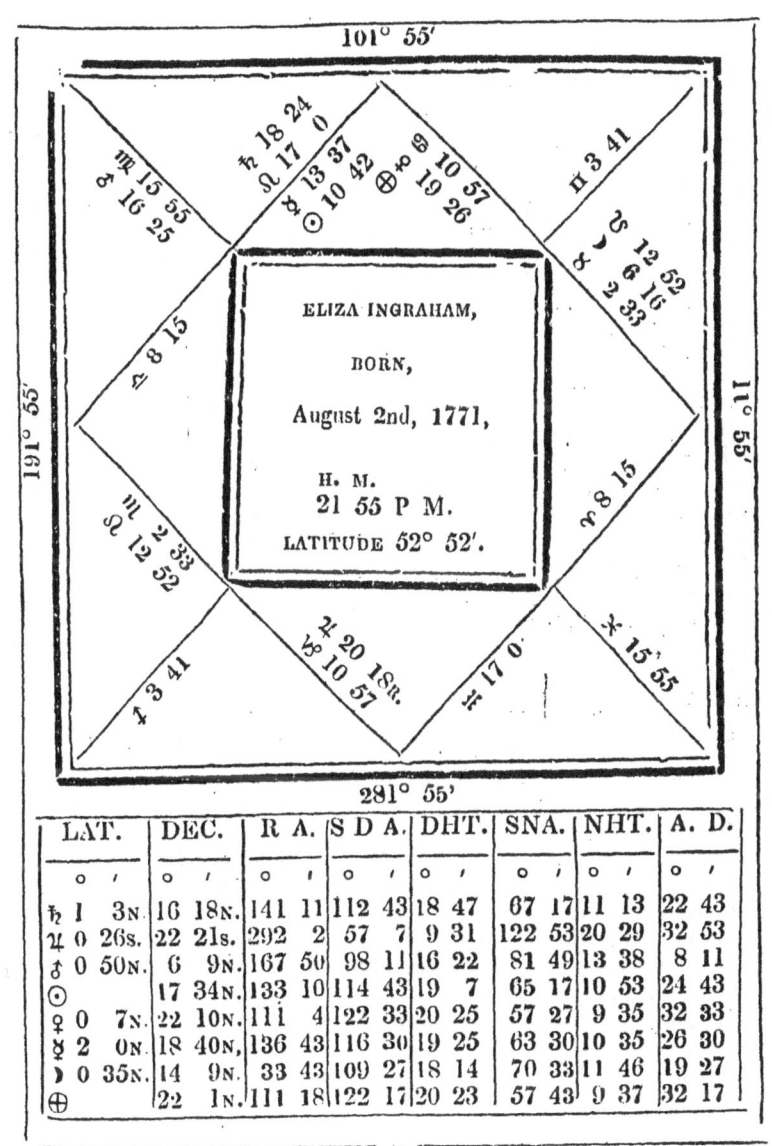

101° 55'

♍ 15 55
♂ 16 25

♄ 18 24
☊ 17 0

☿ 13 37
☉ 10 42

⊕ 10 57
☌ 19 26

♊ 3 41

♋ 12 52
☽ 2 33

♎ 8 15

ELIZA INGRAHAM,
BORN,
August 2nd, 1771,
H. M.
21 55 P M.
LATITUDE 52° 52'.

♏ 2 33
♌ 12 52

♐ 3 41

♃ 20 18R.
♑ 10 57

♒ 17 0

♓ 15 55

♈ 8 15

191° 55'

11° 55'

281° 55'

	LAT.	DEC.	R A.	S D A.	DHT.	SNA.	NHT.	A. D.
	° '	° '	° '	° '	° '	° '	° '	° '
♄	1 3N.	16 18N.	141 11	112 43	18 47	67 17	11 13	22 43
♃	0 26s.	22 21s.	292 2	57 7	9 31	122 53	20 29	32 53
♂	0 50N.	6 9N.	167 50	98 11	16 22	81 49	13 38	8 11
☉		17 34N.	133 10	114 43	19 7	65 17	10 53	24 43
♀	0 7N.	22 10N.	111 4	122 33	20 25	57 27	9 35	32 33
☿	2 0N.	18 40N.	136 43	116 30	19 25	63 30	10 35	26 30
☽	0 35N.	14 9N.	33 43	109 27	18 14	70 33	11 46	19 27
⊕		22 1N.	111 18	122 17	20 23	57 43	9 37	32 17

2K

A TABLE OF THE DIRECTIONS.	ARC. D. M.	TIME. YRS. MO.
Midheaven to the Sextile of Mars in Mundo............	0 27	0 5
Part of Fortune to the Opposition of Jupiter in Mundo..	0 41	0 8
Moon to the Quintile of Venus in the Zodiac..........	1 28	1 6
Ascendant to the Sextile of Saturn in Mundo..........	1 42	1 9
Sun to the Body of Mercury in Mundo, Direct Direction..	3 4	3 2
Moon to the Square of Saturn in Mundo, Converse Motion..	3 8	3 3
Sun to the Body of Mercury in the Zodiac..........	3 15	3 5
Moon to the Sextile of Venus in Mundo, Direct Direction..	3 48	3 11
Moon to the Trine of Mars in Mundo, Converse Motion.	4 17	4 5
Moon to the Trine of Jupiter in Mundo, Direct Direction..	4 45	4 11
Midheaven to the Sextile of the Moon in Mundo.......	4 47	4 11
Sun to the Parallel of Saturn in the Zodiac..........	5 1	5 3
Moon to the Square of the Sun in the Zodiac........	5 28	5 8
Moon to the Sesquiquadrate of Mars in the Zodiac, Converse Motion......................................	6 14	6 6
Ascendant to the Quintile of the Sun in Mundo......	8 18	8 7
Sun to the Body of Saturn in Mundo, Direct Direction.	8 34	8 10
Moon to the Square of Mercury in Mundo, Converse Motion..	8 37	8 11
Sun to the Body of Saturn in the Zodiac............	8 37	8 11
Moon to the Square of Mercury in the Zodiac........	9 1	9 5
Midheaven to the Body of Venus in Mundo..........	9 9	9 7
Ascendant to the Square of Venus in Mundo........	9 9	9 7
Part of Fortune to the Semiquartile of Mars in Mundo.	9 18	9 9
Ascendant to the Square of Jupiter in Mundo........	10 7	10 7
Midheaven to the Opposition of Jupiter in Mundo....	10 7	10 7
Moon to the Quintile of the Sun in Mundo, Direct Motion..	10 56	11 5
Part of Fortune to the Quintile of the Moon in Mundo.	10 58	11 5
Moon to the Quintile of Venus in Mundo, Converse Direction...	11 12	11 9
Sun to the Square of the Moon in Mundo, Direct Motion..	11 26	12 0
Ascendant to the Quintile of Mercury in Mundo......	11 30	12 1
Sun to the Semiquartile of Mars in Mundo, Converse Direction...	11 37	12 3

OR GENETHLIACAL ASTRONOMY.

THE DIRECTIONS CONTINUED.	ARC D. M.	TIME. YRS. MO.
Moon to the Parallel of Saturn in the Zodiac	11 54	12 6
Sun to the Semiquartile of Mars in the Zodiac, Converse Motion	12 13	12 10
Moon to the Trine of Mars in the Zodiac	12 29	13 1
Sun to the Parallel of the Moon in the Zodiac	12 41	13 4
Moon to the Quintile of Mercury in Mundo, Direct Direction	14 10	14 10
Moon to the Square of Saturn in the Zodiac	14 52	15 7
Moon to the Sextile of Venus in the Zodiac	16 7	17 0
Ascendant to the Quintile of Saturn in Mundo	16 44	17 8
Ascendant to the Semiquartile of Mars in Mundo	16 49	17 9
Moon to the Trine of Jupiter in the Zodiac	17 8	18 1
Moon to the Square of Jupiter in the Zodiac, Converse Motion	17 12	18 2
Sun to the Biquintile of Jupiter in the Zodiac	17 18	18 3

In this Nativity the Sun is the giver of Life, and as he was surrounded by the formidable irradiations of Saturn, Mars, and the Moon, without any assistance from Jupiter, or Venus, I peremptorily affirmed, that the Child died, when the giver of Life was directed to the Zodiacal Parallel of Saturn, followed by six others that were joined in the deadly train, which I have inserted in the preceding Table. The position of Mercury, could not produce any injury to Life, because the Terms of Jupiter, immediately succeeded his Radical station, but the rapidity of the subsequent Directions of the Moon, and Mars in the Zodiac, and Mundo, shewed, that the quality of Death was a putrid Fever, which soon destroyed the Native's Life. If the Students think proper to attend to these Examples, and first select the Hyleg in their Calculations, they will be able to discover all premeditated deception, which may be artfully brought in action to traduce, and dishonor this Celestial Science. This Nativity was given to me, after the Native had been forty-six Years in her Grave.

In computing the other Motions of the Stars which have superior dominion in those places, where the interjacent rays of the Promittors form their union with the true significator of Life, it will plainly appear, that their Effects were powerfully increased in the ascending part of the Heavens, by which their violence was collected from both the superior Angles, according to their progressive Movements above the Earth. In the Native's last Revolution, Saturn was in the Ascendant, in Square to Jupiter, and Mars, from Cardinal Signs, and Angular stations; Venus was combust of the Sun, and the Moon applied to her own Radical place; and likewise to the Quartile of the Sun, the true Prorogator. All these violent applications, when compared with the Primary Motions, plainly prove their Effects, in conveying additional power to those Directions, which produced the Native's Death.

The following Nativity is that of Mr. John Ward, who was Born at Scotter, near Wragby, in the County of Lincoln, October 23rd, 1791, at 6H. 48M. P. M, and died on the 7th of May, 1809, Aged seventeen Years, six Months, and fourteen Days.

The Celestial Bodies in this Geniture, exhibit a remarkable appearance of violence, for they are all under the Earth, except Saturn, who is in the twelfth House, by his Latitude, Retrograde, and in Opposition to Mercury, Jupiter, Venus, and the Sun, from violent Constellations, and places: the Moon is applying by a Converse Motion, to the Body of Mars, who is in the Nadir, near the Heart of the Lion, that Malefic being one of the Mortal Promittors in the Directions for dissolution.

The Death of this Native was occasioned by his drinking cold stagnated Water from a Ditch, which I have reasons to judge, (from the whole position,) was considerably impregnated with Animal matter of a poisonous quality, from the Effects of which, he languished a considerable time in severe affliction, before his personal extinction took place.

244 CELESTIAL PHILOSOPHY,

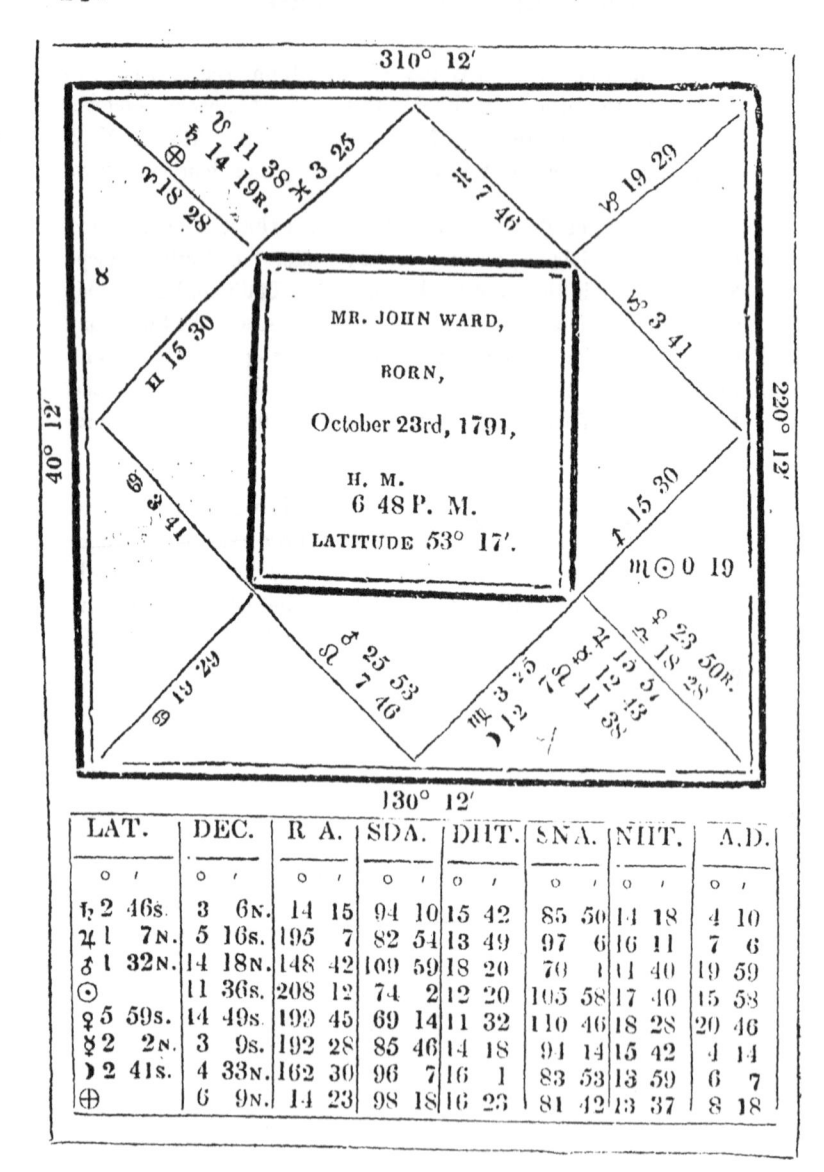

MR. JOHN WARD,
BORN,
October 23rd, 1791,
H. M.
6 48 P. M.
LATITUDE 53° 17'.

LAT.	DEC.	R A.	SDA.	DHT.	SNA.	NHT.	A.D.
° '	° '	° '	° '	° '	° '	° '	° '
♄ 2 46s.	3 6n.	14 15	94 10	15 42	85 50	14 18	4 10
♃ 1 7n.	5 16s.	195 7	82 54	13 49	97 6	16 11	7 6
♂ 1 32n.	14 18n.	148 42	109 59	18 20	70 1	11 40	19 59
☉	11 36s.	208 12	74 2	12 20	105 58	17 40	15 58
♀ 5 59s.	14 49s.	199 45	69 14	11 32	110 46	18 28	20 46
☿ 2 2n.	3 9s.	192 28	85 46	14 18	94 14	15 42	4 14
☽ 2 41s.	4 33n.	162 30	96 7	16 1	83 53	13 59	6 7
⊕	6 9n.	14 23	98 18	16 23	81 42	13 37	8 18

OR GENETHLIACAL ASTRONOMY.

A TABLE OF THE DIRECTIONS.	ARC. D. M.	TIME. YRS. MO.
Midheaven to the Trine of Jupiter in Mundo	0 11	0 2
Part of Fortune to the Biquintile of Mars in Mundo	0 58	1 0
Midheaven to the Sextile of Saturn in Mundo	1 15	1 3
Moon to the Biquintile of Saturn in the Zodiac, Converse Direction	1 32	1 7
Part of Fortune to the Opposition of Jupiter in Mundo	1 45	1 10
Sun to the Semiquartile of Mars in Mundo, Direct Motion	1 59	2 1
Moon to the Semiquartile of the Sun in the Zodiac	2 33	2 8
Sun to the Sextile of Mars in the Zodiac, Converse Direction	2 35	2 8
Part of Fortune to the Body of Saturn in Mundo	2 46	2 10
Ascendant to the Biquintile of Venus in Mundo	3 4	3 2
Moon to the Parallel of Mercury in the Zodiac	3 27	3 7
Moon to the Parallel of Saturn in the Zodiac	3 35	3 9
Ascendant to the Trine of the Moon in Mundo	4 20	4 6
Sun to the Quintile of Mars in the Zodiac	4 34	4 9
Sun to the Parallel of Mars in the Zodiac	4 52	5 1
Ascendant to the Biquintile of Mercury in Mundo	5 45	6 0
Sun to the Parallel of Venus in the Zodiac	5 51	6 1
Sun to the Opposition of Saturn in Mundo, Converse Motion	5 56	6 2
Ascendant to the Biquintile of Jupiter in Mundo	6 39	6 11
Moon to the Semiquartile of Jupiter in the Zodiac, Converse Direction	6 45	7 0
Moon to the Sesquiquadrate of Saturn in the Zodiac, Converse Motion	6 49	7 1
Sun to the Body of Jupiter in the Zodiac, Converse Direction	7 13	7 6
Sun to the Sextile of the Moon in the Zodiac	7 15	7 6
Midheaven to the Trine of the Sun in Mundo	7 20	7 7
Part of Fortune to the Sesquiquadrate of Mars in Mundo	7 58	8 2
Sun to the Body of Mercury in the Zodiac, Converse Motion	8 5	8 4
Moon to the Semiquartile of Mercury in the Zodiac, Converse Direction	8 8	8 5
Part of Fortune to the Biquintile of the Moon in Mundo	8 35	8 10
Moon to the Biquintile of Saturn in Mundo, Converse Motion	8 49	9 1
Part of Fortune to the Opposition of the Sun in Mundo	9 3	9 4

246 CELESTIAL PHILOSOPHY,

THE DIRECTIONS CONTINUED.	ARC. D. M.	TIME. YRS. MO.
Moon to the Body of Mars in Mundo, Converse Direction	10 8	10 5
Sun to the Body of Venus in Mundo, Converse Motion.	11 28	11 9
Moon to the Semiquartile of Venus in the Zodiac, Converse Direction	11 38	11 11
Sun to the Semiquartile of the Moon in Mundo, Direct Motion	12 31	12 10
Sun to the Biquintile of Saturn in the Zodiac	12 45	13 1
Moon to the Body of Mars in the Zodiac, Converse Direction	13 31	13 10
Sun to the Sextile of Mars in Mundo, Direct Motion	13 39	14 0
Ascendant to the Sesquiquadrate of Venus in Mundo	14 9	14 6
Ascendant to the Biquintile of the Sun in Mundo	14 24	14 9
Sun to the Semiquartile of Mars in the Zodiac, Converse Direction	14 36	15 0
Ascendant to the Sesquiquadrate of Mercury in Mundo	15 10	15 6
Moon to the Sextile of Mercury in the Zodiac, Converse Motion	15 26	15 9
Sun to the Quintile of the Moon in the Zodiac	15 28	15 9
Moon to the Sextile of Jupiter in the Zodiac, Converse Direction	16 4	16 5
Moon to the Trine of Saturn in the Zodiac, Converse Motion	16 17	16 8
Ascendant to the Sesquiquadrate of Jupiter in Mundo	16 22	16 9
Sun to the Square of Mars in the Zodiac	16 48	17 2
Ascendant to the Semiquartile of Saturn in Mundo	16 57	17 4
Part of Fortune to the Sesquiquadrate of the Moon in Mundo	16 58	17 4
Moon to the Sesquiquadrate of Saturn in Mundo, Converse Direction	17 12	17 7
Moon to the Semiquartile of Jupiter in Mundo, Converse Motion	18 9	18 6
Sun to the Semiquartile of Mercury in the Zodiac	18 12	18 7
Ascendant to the Square of Mars in Mundo	18 30	18 11
Midheaven to the Opposition of Mars in Mundo	18 30	18 11
Moon to the Opposition of Mercury in Mundo, Converse Direction	18 48	19 2
Moon to the Parallel of Saturn in the Zodiac	19 18	19 7
Sun to the Sesquiquadrate of Saturn in the Zodiac	19 26	19 9
Moon to the Parallel of Mercury in the Zodiac	19 27	19 9
Part of Fortune to the Trine of Mars in Mundo	19 38	19 11

	ARC.	TIME.
THE DIRECTIONS CONTINUED.	D. M.	YRS. MO.
Sun to the Semiquartile of Jupiter in the Zodiac	20 43	21 0
Moon to the Semiquartile of Venus in Mundo, Converse Motion	21 35	21 10
Moon to the Semiquartile of Mars in the Zodiac........	22 51	23 1
Moon to the Sextile of Venus in the Zodiac, Converse Direction	23 4	23 4
Moon to her own Parallel in the Zodiac	23 8	23 5
Moon to the Quintile of Mercury in the Zodiac, Converse Motion	24 17	24 6
Moon to the Body of Mercury in the Zodiac	24 21	24 7
Midheaven to the Biquintile of Mercury in Mundo	24 35	24 9
Moon to the Quintile of Jupiter in the Zodiac, Converse Direction	24 42	24 10
Moon to the Parallel of Mars in Mundo, by the Rapt Motion	24 47	24 11
Ascendant to the Sesquiquadrate of the Sun in Mundo ..	25 0	25 2
Moon to the Parallel of Jupiter in the Zodiac..........	25 2	25 2
Midheaven to the Biquintile of Venus in Mundo........	25 14	25 4
Moon to the Opposition of Saturn in the Zodiac	25 35	25 8
Moon to the Body of Mercury in Mundo, Direct Direction	25 59	25 11
Midheaven to the Biquintile of Jupiter, in Mundo	26 5	26 1
Sun to the Sextile of the Moon in Mundo, Direct Motion.	26 30	26 6
Moon to the Semiquartile of Mars in Mundo, Direct Direction	26 33	26 7
Moon to the Body of Jupiter in the Zodiac	26 50	26 11
Moon to the Body of Venus in Mundo, Direct Motion ..	26 54	27 0
Sun to the Semiquartile of Venus in the Zodiac	27 15	27 4
Moon to the Body of Jupiter in Mundo, Direct Direction.	27 32	27 7
Moon to the Opposition of Saturn in Mundo, Direct Motion	27 47	27 10

The Horoscope is the Apheta in this Nativity, and the Directions that destroyed Life, were, the Semiquartile of Saturn in the World, the Mundane Square of Mars, and Sesquiquadrate of the Sun, their true Astronomical Computations, are performed as follow.

The Right Ascension of the Medium Cœli, is, 310° 12', which subtracted from the Right Ascension of Saturn, with the Circle, 374° 15', his distance from the Zenith will be, 64° 3', from which subtracting his triplicate diurnal horary times, 47° 6', the Arc of Direction, of the Ascendant to the Semiquartile of Saturn in Mundo, will be 16° 57'.

The Horoscope's Direction to the Mundane Square of Mars, is ascertained, by subtracting the Right Ascension of the Nadir, 130° 12', from the Right Ascension of Mars, with his Latitude, 148° 42', and the Direction's Arc then becomes, 18° 30'.

The Right Ascension of the Imum Cœli, is, 130° 12', and that of the Sun, 208° 12', by subtraction, the distance of the Sun from the Northern Angle, is, 78° 0', from which his treble nocturnal horary times, 53° 0', being subtracted, the Arc of Direction of the Ascendant to the Mundane Sesquiquadrate of the Sun, will be, 25° 0'.

The Effects of these Directions to the giver of Life, were the true Cause of the Native's Death, and in consequence of the violence of the position, the Directions of the Benefics could not give any support to the Aphetical point; the Sun's Direction to the Quartile of Mars in the Zodiac, was united with those to the Hyleg, that produced his demise; but their combined power was retarded for a time, owing to the stations of the Promittors, as they slowly approached the Anaretical places, in those subterranean parts of the Heavens, where their mortal rays became in contact with the true significator of Life.

In adjusting the Secondary Directions, and comparing them with the other motions of the Stars in their Genethliacal stations, we find the Moon posited in the Western Angle, in opposition to Mercury, and the Sun, and applying to the Quartile of Mars, in the Radix, who was separating from his own place at the time of Birth, and near the Moon's place in the Nativity. In the Revolutional Figure for the seventeenth year of his age, the Moon was in Opposition to the Radical Ascendant, and Mars was near the Moon's place in the Geniture; these configurations of the Stars, when their Declinations are considered, with the Progression, &c. evidently show their violence, as they assume the most formidable appearance, in uniting their power with the mortal primary Directions. At the time the Native died, the Moon was in Square to the superior Malefic, and Jupiter was in Opposition to Mars; Venus was likewise in opposition with Saturn, by which the Benefics were afflicted by both the Malefics, at the time of Death.

The next is the Nativity of Mr. George Golding, of North Hyckham, near Lincoln; he was born on the 10th of August, 1753, at 3h. 45m. P. M.; and died June 26th, 1822, aged sixty-eight years, ten months, and sixteen days.

I was personally acquainted with this Native, a few years before his death; his honesty, and integrity, combined with every inestimable virtue, which constitute the human character, are far beyond the limits of my feeble power to describe. In the early part of his life, he moved in a respectable station, but before his dissolution, he was placed in adverse circumstances, yet his firmness of mind, probity, and fidelity, remained the same; and though he was insulted by the vulgar, and treated with unbecoming insolence, by ignoble persons, yet he was always unmoved, and in the midst of all his difficulties, and WRONGS, he possessed that christian fortitude, which enabled him calmly to view those storms of affliction, (the effects of which, he was unable to mitigate,) with a serene, and smiling countenance.

TESTATORS should, by WILLS, or DEEDS, employ,
HONEST TRUSTEES, who never will annoy
THE ORPHAN's RIGHTS; but then, if they *too late*,
Those *Reptiles* in *Sheeps clothing*, nominate,
The die is cast, they'll oft *embezzle all*,
Whether the sums in CASH, are great or small.
With HOUSE, and LAND, (the vulgar often say,)
Knavish Trustees, can never run away;
I'll grant the fact, but what the Lands *produce*,
They very *oft convert*, to their *own use*;
Stealing the RENTS, and PROFITS of the same,
Thereby possessing a most ROGUISH NAME.
All public courts, the GUILTY ROBBERS fear,
And with reluctance, in the same appear;
The injur'd HEIRS, THERE, all their *Rights obtain*,
And leave the *Robbers* in remorse, and pain;

Excuses then, will be of no avail,
When SPLENDID FACTS, their *tender ears* assail;
The Law declares this TRUTH, which none deny,
There is no WRONG, without a REMEDY.

252 CELESTIAL PHILOSOPHY,

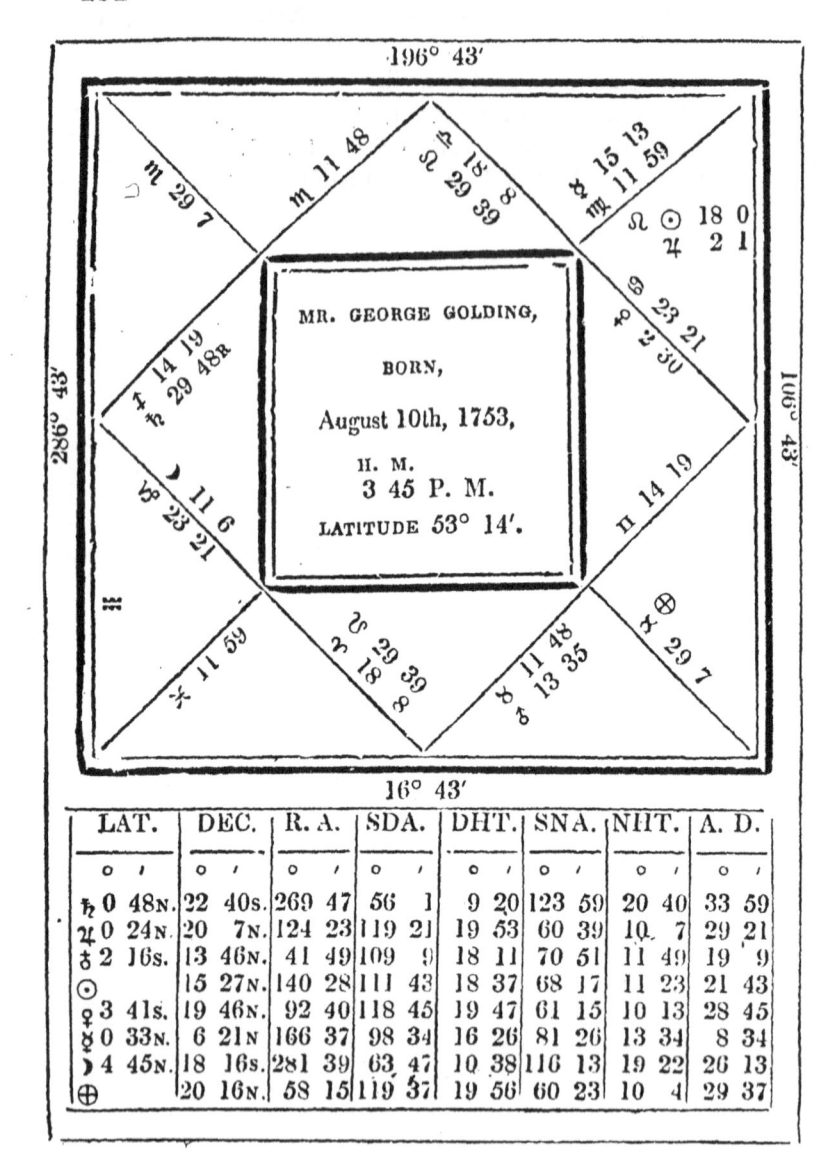

MR. GEORGE GOLDING,

BORN,

August 10th, 1753,

H. M.
3 45 P. M.

LATITUDE 53° 14'.

	LAT.	DEC.	R. A.	SDA.	DHT.	SNA.	NHT.	A. D.
	° ′	° ′	° ′	° ′	° ′	° ′	° ′	° ′
♄	0 48N.	22 40s.	269 47	56 1	9 20	123 59	20 40	33 59
♃	0 24N.	20 7N.	124 23	119 21	19 53	60 39	10 7	29 21
♂	2 16s.	13 46N.	41 49	109 9	18 11	70 51	11 49	19 9
☉		15 27N.	140 28	111 43	18 37	68 17	11 23	21 43
♀	3 41s.	19 46N.	92 40	118 45	19 47	61 15	10 13	28 45
☿	0 33N.	6 21N.	166 37	98 34	16 26	81 26	13 34	8 34
☽	4 45N.	18 16s.	281 39	63 47	10 38	116 13	19 22	26 13
⊕		20 16N.	58 15	119 37	19 56	60 23	10 4	29 37

OR GENETHLIACAL ASTRONOMY.

	ARC.	TIME.
A TABLE OF THE DIRECTIONS.	D. M.	YRS. MO.
Part of Fortune to the Sesquiquadrate of Saturn in Mundo.	0 10	0 2
Part of Fortune to the Quintile of the Sun in Mundo	0 15	0 3
Moon to the Biquintile of the Sun in the Zodiac	0 49	0 10
Moon to the Sesquiquadrate of Mercury in Mundo, Direct Motion	1 14	1 3
Ascendant to the Trine of Mars in Mundo	1 28	1 6
Midheaven to Spica Virginis	2 12	2 4
Moon to the Trine of Mars in the Zodiac	2 14	2 4
Ascendant to the Trine of Mercury in Mundo	2 44	2 10
Moon to the Trine of Mercury in the Zodiac	3 40	3 10
Part of Fortune to the Sextile of Jupiter in Mundo	3 55	4 1
Sun to the Parallel of Mars in the Zodiac	3 56	4 1
Sun to the Sesquiquadrate of Saturn in the Zodiac, Converse Motion	4 42	5 0
Part of Fortune to the Sesquiquadrate of the Moon in Mundo	5 1	5 4
Moon to the Body of Saturn in Mundo, Converse Motion.	5 10	5 6
Sun to the Square of Mars in the Zodiac, Converse Direction	5 30	5 10
Sun to the Sesquiquadrate of the Moon in the Zodiac	5 58	6 4
Moon to the Opposition of Venus in Mundo, Converse Motion	6 46	7 2
Sun to Cor Leonis	6 51	7 3
Midheaven to the Sextile of Jupiter in Mundo	7 15	7 8
Sun to the Trine of Saturn in the Zodiac	8 35	9 2
Moon to the Opposition of Venus in the Zodiac, Converse Direction	9 27	10 1
Part of Fortune to the Parallel of Jupiter in Mundo	9 48	10 5
Sun to the Sextile of Venus in the Zodiac	10 28	11 2
Ascendant to the Biquintile of the Sun in Mundo	10 47	11 6
Moon to the Biquintile of Mercury in Mundo, Direct Motion	11 6	11 10
Part of Fortune to the Semiquartile of Mars in Mundo	11 16	12 0
Sun to the Body of Jupiter in the Zodiac, Converse Direction	11 38	12 5
Moon to the Biquintile of Jupiter in the Zodiac, Converse Motion	11 44	12 6
Moon to the Body of Saturn in the Zodiac, Converse Direction	12 2	12 10
Moon to the Square of Mars in Mundo, Direct Motion	12 12	13 0

CELESTIAL PHILOSOPHY,

THE DIRECTIONS CONTINUED.	ARC D. M.	TIME. YRS. MO.
Part of Fortune to the Biquintile of Saturn in Mundo....	12 34	13 5
Sun to the Semiquartile of Mercury in the Zodiac, Converse Direction	12 59	13 11
Sun to the Trine of Mars in Mundo, Direct Motion	13 31	14 6
Sun to the Biquintile of Saturn in the Zodiac, Converse Direction	13 41	14 8
Moon to the Sesquiquadrate of Mars in the Zodiac, Converse Motion	14 18	15 4
Moon to the Parallel of the Sun in the Zodiac..........	14 31	15 7
Ascendant to the Opposition of Venus in Mundo........	14 42	15 9
Midheaven to the Square of Venus in Mundo..........	14 42	15 9
Sun to the Semiquartile of Venus in Mundo, Direct Direction	14 55	16 0
Part of Fortune to the Sextile of the Sun in Mundo......	15 7	16 3
Moon to the Sesquiquadrate of Mercury in the Zodiac ..	15 44	16 11
Sun to the Square of Mars in Mundo, Converse Motion ..	15 55	17 2
Sun to the Trine of the Moon in the Zodiac............	16 19	17 7
Part of Fortune to the Biquintile of the Moon in Mundo..	16 38	17 11
Moon to the Parallel of Venus in Mundo, by the Rapt Motion	16 56	18 2
Ascendant to the Body of Saturn in Mundo............	17 3	18 4
Midheaven to the Square of Saturn in Mundo..........	17 3	18 4
Moon to the Opposition of Jupiter in the Zodiac	17 6	18 5
Sun to the Sesquiquadrate of Saturn in Mundo, Direct Direction	17 14	18 7
Moon to the Sesquiquadrate of Jupiter in the Zodiac, Converse Motion	17 34	18 11
Moon to the Trine of Mercury in Mundo, Converse Direction	17 56	19 3
Sun to the Trine of Mars in the Zodiac	17 57	19 3
Sun to the Parallel of Mercury in the Zodiac	18 8	19 6
Midheaven to the Sextile of the Sun in Mundo	18 14	19 8
Moon to the Parallel of Saturn in Mundo, by the Rapt Motion	18 23	19 10
Sun to the Quintile of Venus in the Zodiac	18 33	20 0
Moon to the Trine of Mars in Mundo, Converse Direction	18 45	20 3
Sun to the Body of Mercury in the Zodiac............	19 1	20 6
Ascendant to the Sesquiquadrate of Mercury in Mundo ..	19 10	20 8
Sun to the Body of Mercury in Mundo, Direct Motion ..	19 30	21 0
Part of Fortune to the Quintile of Mercury in Mundo	19 43	21 3

	ARC.	TIME.
THE DIRECTIONS CONTINUED.	D. M.	YRS. MO.
Sun to the Semiquartile of Jupiter in the Zodiac	20 13	21 10
Moon to the Parallel of Mars in the Zodiac	20 21	22 0
Moon to the Square of Mercury in the Zodiac, Converse Direction	20 25	22 1
Part of Fortune to the Parallel of the Sun in Mundo	20 37	22 4
Ascendant to the Body of the Moon in Mundo	21 9	22 10
Midheaven to the Square of the Moon in Mundo	21 9	22 10
Moon to the Biquintile of Venus in the Zodiac	21 47	23 6
Moon to the Biquintile of Mercury in the Zodiac	22 18	24 2
Part of Fortune to the Sextile of Mars in Mundo	23 7	25 0
Midheaven to the Quintile of Jupiter in Mundo	23 9	25 0
Part of Fortune to the Semiquartile of Jupiter in Mundo	23 48	25 8
Sun to the Sextile of Mercury in the Zodiac, Converse Motion	24 24	26 5
Ascendant to the Square of Mars in Mundo	25 6	27 3
Midheaven to the Opposition of Mars in Mundo	25 6	27 3
Sun to the Sextile of Venus in Mundo, Direct Direction	25 8	27 3
Moon to the Square of Mars in the Zodiac	25 16	27 5
Moon to the Opposition of Jupiter in Mundo, Direct Direction	25 18	27 6
Sun to the Sesquiquadrate of Mars in Mundo, Direct Motion	25 20	27 6
Moon to the Parallel of Venus in Mundo, Direct Direction	25 51	28 0
Moon to the Biquintile of Mars in the Zodiac, Converse Motion	26 1	28 3
Moon to the Semiquartile of Saturn in the Zodiac	26 3	28 3
Sun to the Quintile of Mars in the Zodiac, Converse Motion	26 20	28 7
Moon to the Quintile of Mars in Mundo, Direct Direction	26 22	28 7
Sun to the Trine of Saturn in Mundo, Direct Motion	26 34	28 10
Moon to the Parallel of Saturn in Mundo, Direct Direction	27 15	29 7
Sun to the Sesquiquadrate of Mars in the Zodiac	27 42	30 1
Moon to the Trine of Jupiter in the Zodiac, Converse Motion	27 47	30 2
Moon to the Sesquiquadrate of Venus in the Zodiac	27 53	30 4
Moon to the Sesquiquadrate of Jupiter in Mundo, Converse Direction	27 54	30 4
Moon to the Biquintile of Venus in Mundo, Direct Motion	28 4	30 6
Moon to the Opposition of the Sun in the Zodiac	28 14	30 9
Midheaven to the Quintile of Saturn in Mundo	28 15	30 9
Sun to the Square of Saturn in the Zodiac	28 29	31 0

256 CELESTIAL PHILOSOPHY,

THE DIRECTIONS CONTINUED.

	ARC. D. M.	TIME. YRS. MO.
Ascendant to the Biquintile of Mercury in Mundo	29 2	31 7
Moon to the Parallel of Venus in Mundo, Converse Direction	29 3	31 7
Sun to the Parallel of Venus in Mundo, by the Rapt Motion	29 9	31 9
Sun to the Parallel of Saturn in Mundo, by the Rapt Motion	29 52	32 6
Sun to the Sextile of Jupiter in the Zodiac	29 54	32 6
Moon to the Parallel of Saturn in Mundo, Converse Direction	29 55	32 7
Moon to the Parallel of Jupiter in Mundo, by the Rapt Motion	30 10	32 10
Sun to the Square of Venus in the Zodiac	30 12	32 10
Moon to the Sesquiquadrate of Mars in Mundo, Converse Direction	30 29	33 2
Sun to his own Semiquartile in the Zodiac	30 31	33 2
Sun to the Trine of the Moon in Mundo, Direct Motion	32 0	34 11
Sun to the Biquintile of Mars in Mundo, Direct Direction	32 25	35 4
Part of Fortune to the Quintile of Mars in Mundo	32 34	35 6
Part of Fortune to the Sextile of Mercury in Mundo	32 51	35 10
Moon to her own Semiquartile in the Zodiac	33 8	36 2
Midheaven to the Quintile of the Sun in Mundo	33 8	36 2
Sun to the Quintile of Venus in Mundo, Direct Motion	33 18	36 4
Part of Fortune to the Body of Venus in Mundo	33 25	36 6
Sun to the Biquintile of Mars in the Zodiac	33 30	36 7
Moon to the Parallel of the Sun in Mundo, by the Rapt Motion	33 37	36 8
Moon to the Quintile of Mercury in the Zodiac, Converse Direction	33 38	36 8
Part of Fortune to the Semiquartile of the Sun in Mundo	33 44	36 10
Sun to the Semiquartile of Mercury in Mundo, Converse Motion	33 45	36 10
Sun to the Quintile of Mercury in the Zodiac, Converse Direction	33 50	36 11
Midheaven to the Quintile of the Moon in Mundo	33 54	37 0
Part of Fortune to the Opposition of Saturn in Mundo	34 9	37 3
Moon to the Sesquiquadrate of Venus in Mundo, Direct Motion	34 12	37 4
Moon to the Semiquartile of Saturn in Mundo, Direct Direction	34 51	38 1
Midheaven to the Trine of Venus in Mundo	35 8	38 5
Moon to the Opposition of the Sun in Mundo, Direct Motion	35 8	38 5

OR GENETHLIACAL ASTRONOMY.

	ARC.		TIME.	
THE DIRECTIONS CONTINUED.	D.	M.	YRS.	MO.
Midheaven to the Sextile of Mercury in Mundo	35	36	38	11
Moon to the Sextile of Saturn in the Zodiac	35	43	39	1
Midheaven to the Sextile of Saturn in Mundo	35	43	39	1
Sun to the Square of the Moon in the Zodiac	35	47	39	2
Moon to the Sextile of Mars in Mundo, Direct Direction	35	50	39	3
Moon to the Quintile of Mars in the Zodiac	36	49	40	3
Moon to the Biquintile of Mars in Mundo, Converse Motion	36	51	40	3
Moon to the Trine of Venus in the Zodiac	37	23	40	11
Sun to the Quintile of Jupiter in the Zodiac	37	41	41	3
Part of Fortune to the Parallel of Mercury in Mundo	37	42	41	3
Moon to the Parallel of Mercury in the Zodiac	37	48	41	5
Sun to the Quintile of Mars in Mundo, Converse Direction	38	16	41	10
Moon to the Trine of Jupiter in Mundo, Converse Motion	38	32	42	2
Moon to the Biquintile of Venus in Mundo, Converse Direction	38	46	42	5
Sun to the Parallel of Mercury in the Zodiac	39	4	42	9
Ascendant to the Biquintile of Venus in Mundo	39	13	42	11
Ascendant to the Quintile of Mars in Mundo	39	16	43	0
Sun to the Semiquartile of Jupiter in the Zodiac, Converse Motion	39	36	43	4
Moon to the Parallel of Mercury in Mundo, by the Rapt Motion	39	46	43	6
Sun to the Sextile of Mars in the Zodiac, Converse Direction	40	6	43	11
Sun to the Quintile of Saturn in the Zodiac	40	10	44	0
Sun to the Opposition of Saturn in the Zodiac, Converse Motion	40	16	44	2
Sun to his own Sextile in the Zodiac	40	17	44	2
Moon to the Biquintile of Venus in the Zodiac, Converse Direction	40	36	44	6
Moon to the Biquintile of Jupiter in the Zodiac	40	36	44	6
Part of Fortune to the Opposition of the Moon in Mundo	40	38	44	7
Moon to the Square of Mercury in Mundo, Converse Motion	40	39	44	7
Moon to her own Semiquartile in Mundo	41	26	45	5
Sun to the Body of Venus in the Zodiac, Converse Direction	41	43	45	9
Midheaven to the Sextile of the Moon in Mundo	42	25	46	6
Moon to her own Sextile in the Zodiac	42	29	46	7
Sun to Spica Virginis	42	32	46	8

THE DIRECTIONS CONTINUED.	ARC. D. M.	TIME. YRS. MO.
Moon to the Sextile of Mercury in the Zodiac, Converse Motion	42 43	46 11
Moon to the Quintile of Saturn in the Zodiac	42 54	47 1
Moon to the Sextile of Mars in the Zodiac	43 56	48 2
Moon to the Sextile of Saturn in Mundo, Direct Direction	44 11	48 6
Moon to the Semiquartile of Saturn in Mundo, Converse Motion	44 17	48 8
Moon to the Trine of Venus in Mundo, Direct Motion	44 25	48 10
Moon to the Opposition of Mercury in the Zodiac	44 42	49 1
Sun to the Parallel of Saturn in Mundo, Direct Direction	44 52	49 3
Ascendant to the Semiquartile of Saturn in Mundo	45 3	49 5
Sun to the Parallel of Venus in Mundo, Direct Motion	45 8	49 6
Moon to the Sesquiquadrate of Venus in Mundo, Converse Direction	45 9	49 6
Sun to the Square of Saturn in Mundo, Direct Motion	45 14	49 7
Ascendant to the Sesquiquadrate of Venus in Mundo	45 21	49 9
Sun to the Square of Venus in Mundo, Direct Direction	45 34	50 0
Moon to the Square of Jupiter in the Zodiac, Converse Motion	45 45	50 2
Moon to the Sesquiquadrate of Jupiter in the Zodiac	45 56	50 4
Moon to the Parallel of Jupiter in Mundo, Converse Direction	46 16	50 9
Moon to the Sesquiquadrate of Venus in the Zodiac, Converse Motion	46 31	51 0
Moon to the Semiquartile of Saturn in the zodiac, Converse Direction	46 40	51 2
Part of Fortune to the Square of Mars in Mundo	46 45	51 3
Ascendant to the Opposition of Jupiter in Mundo	47 1	51 7
Midheaven to the Square of Jupiter in Mundo	47 1	51 7
Sun to the Semiquartile of Jupiter in Mundo, Direct Motion	47 13	51 10
Moon to the Semiquartile of Mars in Mundo, Direct Direction	47 39	52 3
Sun to the Quintile of the Moon in the zodiac	47 52	52 6
Sun to the Sextile of Saturn in the zodiac	48 21	53 1
Sun to the Sextile of Jupiter in the zodiac, Converse Motion	48 29	53 3
Sun to his own Quintile in the zodiac	48 29	53 3
Sun to the Semiquartile of Mercury in the zodiac	48 38	53 5
Ascendant to the Sextile of Mars in Mundo	48 44	53 6
Midheaven to the Quintile of Mercury in Mundo	48 45	53 6

OR GENETHLIACAL ASTRONOMY.

	ARC.	TIME.
A TABLE OF THE DIRECTIONS.	D. M.	YRS. MO.
Sun to the Square of Mercury in the Zodiac, Converse Motion	48 55	53 8
Part of Fortune to the Semiquartile of Mercury in Mundo.	49 17	54 1
Moon to her own Quintile in the Zodiac	49 28	54 3
Sun to the Square of Jupiter in the Zodiac	49 55	54 9
Moon to the Biquintile of the Sun in the Zodiac	49 58	54 10
Sun to the Parallel of Jupiter in Mundo, by the Rapt Motion	49 59	54 10
Sun to the Trine of Venus in the Zodiac	50 15	55 2
Moon to the Opposition of Mercury in Mundo, Direct Direction	50 31	55 5
Midheaven to the Biquintile of Venus in Mundo	51 29	56 6
Moon to the Quintile of Saturn in Mundo, Direct Motion.	51 39	56 8
Moon to her own Sextile in Mundo	52 4	57 1
Sun to the Sextile of Mercury in Mundo, Converse Direction	52 22	57 5
Moon to the Semiquartile of Mars in the Zodiac	52 39	57 9
Moon to the Parallel of the Sun in Mundo, Converse Motion	52 49	57 11
Ascendant to the Semiquartile of the Moon in Mundo.	53 3	58 2
Sun to the Sextile of Mars in Mundo, Converse Direction.	53 9	58 4
Sun to the Square of the Moon in Mundo, Direct Motion.	53 16	58 6
Sun to the Parallel of Mars in the Zodiac	53 16	58 6
Moon to the Square of Saturn in the Zodiac	53 22	58 8
Moon to the Quintile of Mercury in Mundo, Converse Direction	53 24	58 8
Midheaven to the Biquintile of Mars in Mundo	53 28	58 9
Ascendant to the Sextile of Saturn in Mundo	54 23	59 8
Moon to the Trine of Jupiter in the Zodiac	54 36	59 11
Moon to the Square of Venus in the Zodiac	54 53	60 3
Moon to the Sextile of Saturn in Mundo, Converse Motion.	54 55	60 4
Moon to the Sextile of Saturn in the Zodiac, Converse Direction	54 56	60 4
Moon to the Trine of Venus in the Zodiac, Converse Motion	55 0	60 5
Moon to the Sesquiquadrate of the Sun in the Zodiac	55 11	60 7
Moon to the Semiquartile of Mercury in the Zodiac, Converse Direction	55 23	60 9
Ascendant to the Opposition of the Sun in Mundo	55 23	60 10
Midheaven to the Square of the Sun in Mundo	55 28	60 10

20

260 CELESTIAL PHILOSOPHY,

THE DIRECTIONS CONTINUED.	ARC D. M.	TIME. YRS. MO.
Ascendant to the Trine of Venus in Mundo	55 34	61 0
Sun to his own Semiquartile in Mundo	55 42	61 2
Moon to the Trine of Venus in Mundo, Converse Motion	55 47	61 3
Sun to the Quintile of Jupiter in the Zodiac, Converse Direction	56 0	61 5
Sun to the Quintile of Saturn in Mundo, Direct Motion	56 26	61 10
Sun to the Sextile of the Moon in the Zodiac	56 31	61 11
Part of Fortune to the Biquintile of Saturn in Mundo	56 33	61 11
Moon to the Parallel of Mars in Mundo, by the Rapt Motion	56 37	62 0
Moon to the Quintile of Jupiter in the Zodiac, Converse Direction	56 40	62 1
Sun to the Semiquartile of Mars in the Zodiac, Converse Motion	56 42	62 1
Sun to his own Parallel in the Zodiac	57 13	62 9
Sun to the Sextile of Jupiter in Mundo, Direct Direction	57 20	62 11
Moon to the Parallel of Jupiter in Mundo, Direct Motion	58 4	63 8
Sun to the Biquintile of Saturn in the Zodiac, Converse Direction	58 11	63 10
Sun to the Opposition of Mars in the Zodiac	58 25	64 1
Sun to the Semiquartile of Saturn in the Zodiac	59 21	65 0
Sun to the Sextile of Mercury in the Zodiac	59 40	65 4
Moon to the Square of Jupiter in Mundo, Converse Motion	59 48	65 6
Moon to her own Square in the Zodiac	60 1	65 9
Moon to the Biquintile of Jupiter in Mundo, Direct Direction	60 15	66 0
Ascendant to the Semiquartile of Mars in Mundo	60 33	66 4
Moon to her own Quintile in Mundo	60 34	66 4
Sun to the Opposition of Mars in Mundo, Direct Motion	60 47	66 7
Sun to the Parallel of Mercury in Mundo, by the Rapt Motion	60 47	66 7
Moon to the Parallel of Mercury in the Zodiac	60 59	66 9
Moon to the Quintile of Saturn in the Zodiac, Converse Direction	61 7	66 11
Sun to the Sesquiquadrate of Venus in the Zodiac	61 27	67 3
Sun to his own Square in the Zodiac	61 50	67 8
Ascendant to the Quintile of Saturn in Mundo	61 51	67 8
Moon to the Sextile of Mercury in Mundo, Converse Motion	61 55	67 9
Part of Fortune to the Sesquiquadrate of Saturn in Mundo	62 9	68 0
Sun to the Sesquiquadrate of Saturn in the Zodiac, Converse Direction	62 13	68 1

OR GENETHLIACAL ASTRONOMY.

	ARC.	TIME.
THE DIRECTIONS CONTINUED.	D. M.	YRS. MO.
Moon to the Opposition of Mars in Mundo, Converse Motion	62 22	68 3
Sun to the Semiquartile of Jupiter in Mundo, Converse Direction	62 42	68 7
Sun to the Quintile of Mercury in Mundo, Converse Motion	62 42	68 7
Moon to the Square of Saturn in Mundo, Direct Direction	62 51	68 9
Moon to the Quintile of Saturn in Mundo, Converse Motion	63 25	69 4
Sun to the Semiquartile of Venus in the Zodiac, Converse Direction	63 30	69 5
Ascendant to the Sextile of the Moon in Mundo	63 41	69 7
Sun to the Sextile of Saturn in Mundo, Direct Motion	63 54	69 10
Sun to the Parallel of Venus in Mundo, Converse Direction	63 55	69 10
Part of Fortune to the Semiquartile of Venus in Mundo	64 4	70 1
Moon to the Trine of the Sun in the Zodiac	64 12	70 3
Moon to the Sextile of Jupiter in the Zodiac, Converse Motion	64 45	70 10
Moon to the Square of Venus in Mundo, Direct Direction	64 51	71 0
Sun to the Parallel of Saturn in Mundo, Converse Motion	64 52	71 0
Sun to the Parallel of the Moon in the Zodiac	64 59	71 1
Sun to the Quintile of Jupiter in Mundo, Direct Direction	65 26	71 6
Sun to the Semiquartile of Mars in Mundo, Converse Motion	65 27	71 6
Moon to the Parallel of Mercury in Mundo, Converse Direction	65 29	71 7
Part of Fortune to the Body of Jupiter in Mundo	65 34	71 8
Moon to the Quintile of Venus in the Zodiac	65 47	71 11
Sun to the Trine of Venus in Mundo, Direct Motion	66 0	72 2
Sun to the Quintile of the Moon in Mundo, Direct Direction	66 1	72 2
Part of Fortune to the Biquintile of the Moon in Mundo	66 9	72 4
Moon to the Biquintile of Mercury in the Zodiac	66 13	72 5
Moon to the Sesquiquadrate of Jupiter in Mundo, Direct Motion	66 19	72 7
Moon to the Opposition of Mars in the Zodiac, Converse Direction	66 22	72 8
Sun to his own Sextile in Mundo	67 5	73 3
Midheaven to the Trine of Jupiter in Mundo	67 15	73 5
Moon to the Parallel of the Sun in Mundo, Direct Motion	67 54	74 1
Sun to the Square of Jupiter in the Zodiac, Converse Direction	68 24	74 8
Sun to the Semiquartile of the Moon in the Zodiac	68 27	74 9

	ARC.	TIME.
THE DIRECTIONS CONTINUED.	D. M.	YRS. MO.
Ascendant to the Opposition of Mercury in Mundo......	68 28	74 9
Midheaven to the Square of Mercury in Mundo	68 28	74 9
Sun to the Biquintile of Venus in the Zodiac	68 48	75 1
Sun to the Trine of Saturn in the Zodiac, Converse Motion	69 5	75 4
Sun to the Quintile of Mercury in the Zodiac	69 24	75 8
Moon to the Square of Saturn in the Zodiac, Converse Direction	69 33	75 10
Moon to the Square of Venus in the Zodiac, Converse Motion	69 45	76 0
Sun to the Parallel of Venus in the Zodiac	70 12	76 6
Sun to the Sextile of Venus in the Zodiac, Converse Direction	70 18	76 8
Moon to the Biquintile of the Sun in Mundo, Direct Motion	70 21	76 9
Part of Fortune to the Trine of Mars in Mundo	70 23	76 9
Ascendant to the Biquintile of Jupiter in Mundo........	71 18	77 8
Part of Fortune to the Trine of Saturn in Mundo........	71 29	77 10
Sun to the Parallel of Jupiter in the zodiac.............	71 37	78 0
Moon to the Trine of Saturn in the zodiac	71 43	78 2
Moon to the Sesquiquadrate of Mercury in the zodiac....	72 1	78 5
Ascendant to the Quintile of the Moon in Mundo	72 12	78 8
Midheaven to the Trine of Mars in Mundo	72 22	78 10
Part of Fortune to the Sesquiquadrate of the Moon in Mundo...	72 32	79 0
Moon to the Semiquartile of Mercury in Mundo, Converse Direction	72 33	79 0
Moon to the Quintile of Jupiter in Mundo, Converse Motion	72 34	79 0
Ascendant to the Square of Saturn in Mundo	73 3	79 6
Midheaven to the Body of Saturn in Mundo	73 3	79 6
Sun to the Semiquartile of Saturn in Mundo, Direct Direction	73 14	79 8
Moon to the Square of Jupiter in the zodiac............	73 15	79 8
Moon to her own Square in Mundo...................	73 20	79 9
Sun to the Biquintile of Saturn in Mundo, Converse Motion	73 23	79 10
Moon to the Sextile of Venus in the zodiac	73 30	80 0
Sun to the Trine of Jupiter in the zodiac	73 34	80 1
Sun to the Sextile of Jupiter in Mundo, Converse Direction.	74 5	80 6
Part of Fortune to the Sextile of Venus in Mundo	74 17	80 9
Sun to the Sextile of the Moon in Mundo, Direct Motion..	74 32	81 0
Sun to the Parallel of Mars in Mundo, by the Rapt Motion.	75 21	81 10

The preceding Directions are computed according to Astronomical principles, and those three Arcs to the Angles, which I have here selected, prove the correctness of the time of Birth; as they accurately correspond with those Events of the Native's Life, which they produced at those periods, when their Effects were in operation.

At the Age of eighteen Years, and four Months, the Ascendant was directed to the Body of Saturn; at that time he suffered severely from the Effects of a dangerous fall; he was also much afflicted with a violent cough, and pleurisy, which continued several Months before his health was re-established.

The Horoscope was directed to the Square of Mars in Mundo, at the Age of twenty-seven Years, and three Months, which was the cause of a sudden, and alarming sickness; and as the power of the Promittor was increased by the rays of the Sun, and Mercury, the baneful Effects of that Direction produced the greatest danger in Life, by a violent Fever, with pains in the Head, and Breast, and difficulty in breathing, &c.; but after he had remained in that afflicted state, during twelve Days, he perfectly recovered, to the astonishment of his Medical Attendants.

The Ascendant arrived by Direction, at the Opposition of the Sun, (or the Medium Cœli to the Mundane Square of that Luminary,) at the age of sixty Years, and ten Months; the Effects of which, produced great difficulties, and troubles; he was then afflicted by an intermitting Fever, with injury to the Eyes, and also with acute pains in the Breast and Abdomen; those who attended him, believed that his recovery was impossible, but though this Direction was armed with direful fury, owing to many existing causes, which must appear plain to every attentive Student, its Effects could not destroy Life, because the Ascendant is not Hyleg, and therefore, though it was unable to produce Death, yet, after he recovered from its malevolent power, he never enjoyed a good state of Health any more, during the remaining Years of his Life.

The Moon is the Apheta, or giver of Life, and the time of Death must be discovered by her directional Motion to those Promittors, which have power to produce dissolution. At the Age of fifty-eight Years, and eight Months, the Prorogator was directed to the Square of Saturn in the Zodiac, but that Direction could not produce any Sickness, or danger to the Native's Health, even though it was joined with the Sun's Parallel in the World, by Converse Direction; for the Trine of Jupiter, and Quartile of Venus in the Zodiac, immediately followed, united with the Trine of Venus in the Zodiac, and Mundo, by Converse Motion; but when the Moon was directed to the Opposition of Mars in Mundo, by Converse Direction, and also to the Square of Saturn in the World, by Direct Motion, succeeded by the Trine of the Sun in the Zodiac, and Parallel of Mercury in Mundo, by Converse Direction, (those two Promittors being of the nature of the Enemies in this Geniture,) I judged, that he could not survive the Effects of those Directions, particularly, because the Hyleg was subsequently directed to the Opposition of Mars in the Zodiac, by Converse Motion, and to the Parallel of the Sun in Mundo, by Direct Direction, with the Quartile of Saturn in the Zodiac, by Converse Motion. These Directions formed the mortal train to the giver of Life, and though the rays of the Benefics interposed. yet they could not save, being weak, and surrounded by the obnoxious Directions, and stations of the Malefics. The Native died of an inflamation of the Bowels, at the time I had previously predicted, from which it is evident, that the Effects of the above Directions to the true Hyleg, were the original cause of his Death.

By Secondary Direction, the Moon was in Opposition to Saturn, from the Eastern, and Western Angles, both being in Cardinal Signs, and that Luminary was in Opposition to her own place in the Nativity. In his last Revolution, the Moon was applying to the Square of Saturn, and Opposition of Mars, by Converse Direction, Mars being in the West, in Opposition to the place of Saturn in the Geniture; the Moon had returned to her own station at the time of Birth, and Saturn was in an Angular position, in Conjunction with Jupiter. At the time he died, the Moon was in Quartile to the Sun, and applied to the Square of her own Radical place; Saturn was near the station of Mars in the Radix, and the latter Malefic was applying to the Quartile of Saturn's place at the time of Birth; all these Motions, and applications of the Stars, shew their powerful, and baneful influence, in giving assistance to those Primary Directions to the Hyleg, which destroyed the Life of the Native.

The primitive Principles of this Science, are regularly taught by the Author of this Work, by whom, any Person may have any Nativity calculated with expedition, on immediate application.

John Davison was Born near Hull, on the 21st of July, 1808, at 6h. 48m. P. M. and was drowned, September 26th, 1825; Aged seventeen Years, two Months, and four Days.

I have observed that those persons, in whose Genitures, the Stars are unfortunately posited, generally disregard, and treat with levity, and contempt, all human admonition; and instead of receiving the warnings displayed by the Celestial Messengers, with fortitude, and composure, they impiously condemn them in the most insulting, and ignominious terms of disapprobation. It is out of my power to relate the abuse, levelled against the HEAVENLY HOSTS, as Secondary Causes by those, who are unbelievers; though the most notorious Infidels *feel* their powerful influence, at those periods, appointed by the MOST HIGH, during the time they inhabit this Terrestrial Globe.

This Native in company with five others, attended a Marriage, in the Church of Bardney, near Lincoln; and in attempting to cross the River Witham, in a small Boat, one of them, regardless of danger, shaked the Boat with considerable violence, which occasioned Water to flow over the sides; in this situation, as the Boat was fast filling, they all went to the stern, by which it instantly upset, and they were all precipitated into the Water; two others of the Names of Dent, and Kennington, (each about twenty years of age,) were drowned with this Native; the other three were saved with the greatest difficulty. The time of this Native's Birth was given to me by his Parents, who are now living. The following Figure of the Heavens, and Directions, exemplify the *Terminus Vitæ*, with the quality of Death.

OR GENETHLIACAL ASTRONOMY. 267

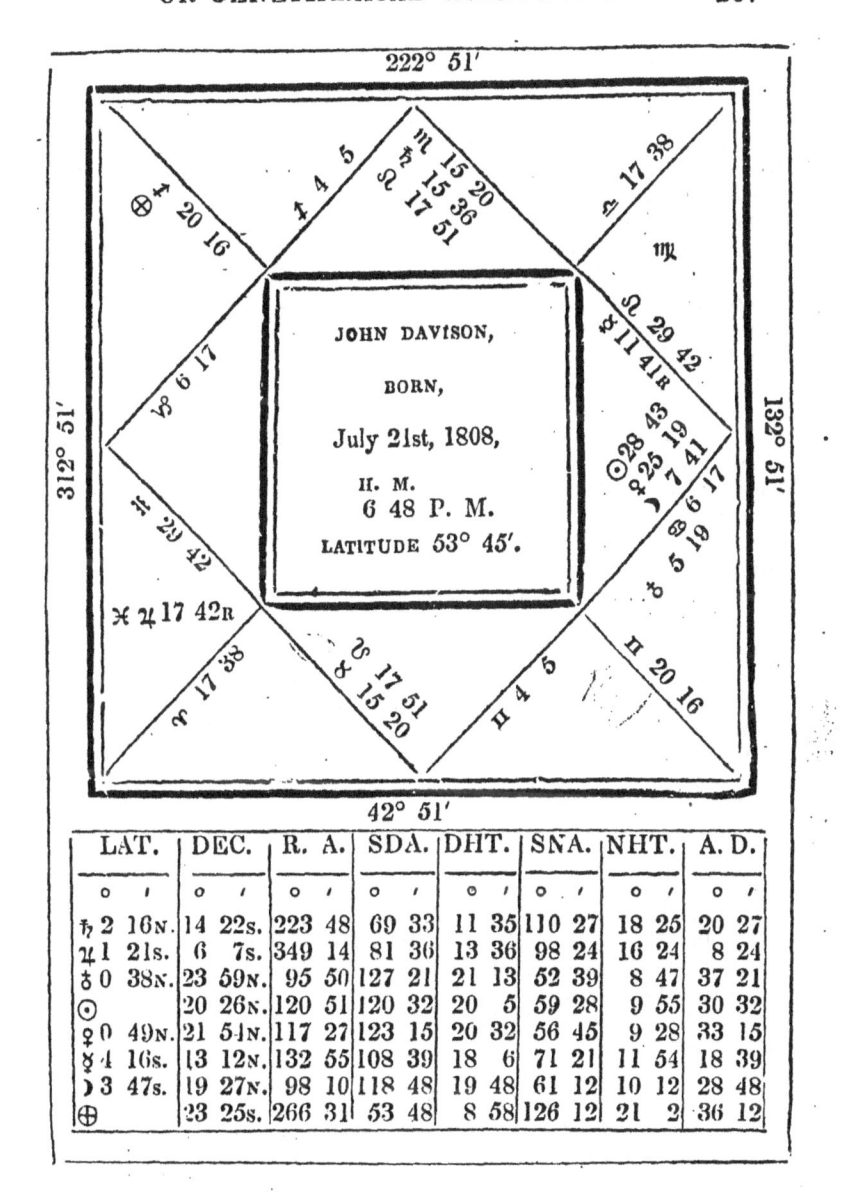

222° 51'

♐ 4 5
♏ 15 20
♄ 15 36
☊ 17 51
⚎ 17 38
♎

⊕ ♐ 20 16
♏

♋ 6 17

♌ 29 42
♉ 11 41 ʀ

⊙ 28 43
♀ 25 19
☽ 7 41
♋ 6 17
♐ 5 19

JOHN DAVISON,
BORN,
July 21st, 1808,
H. M.
6 48 P. M.
LATITUDE 53° 45'.

312° 51'

132° 51'

♒ 29 42

♓ ♃ 17 42ʀ

♈ 17 38
♉ 15 20
♉ 17 51
♊ 4 5
♊ 20 16

42° 51'

	LAT.	DEC.	R. A.	SDA.	DHT.	SNA.	NHT.	A. D.
	° '	° '	° '	° '	° '	° '	° '	° '
♄	2 16ɴ.	14 22s.	223 48	69 33	11 35	110 27	18 25	20 27
♃	1 21s.	6 7s.	349 14	81 36	13 36	98 24	16 24	8 24
♂	0 38ɴ.	23 59ɴ.	95 50	127 21	21 13	52 39	8 47	37 21
⊙		20 26ɴ.	120 51	120 32	20 5	59 28	9 55	30 32
♀	0 49ɴ.	21 5ɴ.	117 27	123 15	20 32	56 45	9 28	33 15
☿	1 16s.	13 12ɴ.	132 55	108 39	18 6	71 21	11 54	18 39
☽	3 47s.	19 27ɴ.	98 10	118 48	19 48	61 12	10 12	28 48
⊕		23 25s.	266 31	53 48	8 58	126 12	21 2	36 12

CELESTIAL PHILOSOPHY,

	ARC.		TIME.	
A TABLE OF THE DIRECTIONS.	D.	M.	YRS.	MO.
Ascendant to the Opposition of Mars in Mundo	0	20	0	4
Midheaven to the Square of Mars in Mundo	0	20	0	4
Part of Fortune to the Quintile of Saturn in Mundo	0	31	0	6
Midheaven to the Body of Saturn in Mundo	0	57	0	11
Ascendant to the Square of Saturn in Mundo	0	57	0	11
Sun to the Body of Venus in Mundo, Converse Motion	1	4	1	1
Sun to the Body of Venus in the Zodiac, Converse Direction	1	10	1	2
Moon to the Parallel of Venus in Mundo, by the Rapt Motion	1	59	2	0
Sun to the Body of Mercury in Mundo, Direct Direction	2	1	2	0
Moon to the Parallel of the Sun in Mundo, by the Rapt Motion	2	20	2	4
Sun to the Sesquiquadrate of Jupiter in the Zodiac	2	53	2	10
Moon to the Parallel of Mercury in Mundo, by the Rapt Motion	2	59	3	0
Moon to the Parallel of Venus in Mundo, Converse Direction	2	59	3	0
Moon to the Parallel of the Sun in Mundo, Converse Motion	3	32	3	7
Sun to the Quintile of Saturn in Mundo, Direct Direction	4	10	4	2
Moon to the Parallel of Mercury in Mundo, Converse Motion	4	40	4	8
Moon to the Sesquiquadrate of Jupiter in Mundo, Direct Direction	5	3	5	1
Sun to the Trine of Jupiter in the Zodiac, Converse Motion	5	23	5	5
Moon to the Body of Mars in Mundo, Direct Direction	5	24	5	5
Sun to the Parallel of Mars in Mundo, by the Rapt Motion	5	52	5	11
Part of Fortune to the Opposition of the Moon in Mundo	5	59	6	1
Moon to the Parallel of Venus in Mundo, Direct Direction	6	0	6	1
Moon to the Trine of Saturn in the Zodiac	6	35	6	8
Moon to the Parallel of the Sun in Mundo, Direct Motion	6	57	7	0
Moon to the Sesquiquadrate of Saturn in the Zodiac, Converse Motion	7	2	7	1
Moon to the Trine of Jupiter in Mundo, Converse Direction	7	4	7	1
Moon to the Square of Saturn in Mundo, Direct Motion	7	38	7	8
Moon to the Trine of Jupiter in the Zodiac	8	15	8	4
Moon to the Parallel of Mercury in Mundo, Direct Direction	8	17	8	4

OR GENETHLIACAL ASTRONOMY.

	ARC.	TIME.
THE DIRECTIONS CONTINUED.	D. M.	YRS. MO.
Sun to the Parallel of Mars in Mundo, Direct Motion	8 26	8 6
Sun to the Body of Mercury in the Zodiac	8 51	8 11
Sun to the Biquintile of Jupiter in the Zodiac	8 52	8 11
Part of Fortune to the Opposition of Mars in Mundo	10 33	10 8
Sun to the Square of Saturn in the Zodiac	11 13	11 4
Midheaven to the Trine of Jupiter in Mundo	11 59	12 2
Moon to the Square of Jupiter in the Zodiac, Converse Direction	12 8	12 4
Sun to the Trine of Saturn in the Zodiac, Converse Motion	12 47	13 0
Sun to the Sextile of Saturn in Mundo, Direct Direction	13 26	13 8
Moon to the Trine of Saturn in Mundo, Converse Motion	13 41	13 11
Moon to the Body of Venus in the Zodiac	13 55	14 2
Sun to the Semiquartile of Mars in the Zodiac	13 59	14 3
Moon to the Semiquartile of Mercury in Mundo, Converse Direction	14 10	14 5
Part of Fortune to the Square of Saturn in Mundo	14 26	14 8
Midheaven to the Trine of the Moon in Mundo	14 31	14 9
Sun to the Parallel of Saturn in the Zodiac	14 36	14 10
Part of Fortune to the Semiquartile of Jupiter in Mundo	14 40	14 11
Moon to the Biquintile of Jupiter in Mundo, Direct Motion	14 53	15 2
Moon to the Semiquartile of Mercury in the Zodiac, Converse Direction	15 6	15 5
Sun to the Semiquartile of the Moon in the Zodiac	15 17	15 7
Sun to the Semiquartile of the Moon in Mundo, Direct Motion	15 18	15 7
Moon to the Semiquartile of Venus in Mundo, Converse Direction	15 51	16 2
Moon to the Biquintile of Saturn in the Zodiac, Converse Motion	16 15	16 7
Moon to the Body of the Sun in the Zodiac	16 26	16 9
Sun to the Parallel of Mercury in the Zodiac	16 32	16 10
Sun to the Square of Saturn in Mundo, Converse Direction	16 53	17 3
Sun to Cor Leonis	17 47	18 2
Ascendant to the Opposition of Venus in Mundo	17 51	18 3
Midheaven to the Square of Venus in Mundo	17 51	18 3
Midheaven to the Trine of Mars in Mundo	17 54	18 4
Sun to the Parallel of Venus in Mundo, by the Rapt Motion	18 4	18 6
Sun to the Body of Mars in the Zodiac, Converse Direction	18 14	18 8

	ARC	TIME
THE DIRECTIONS CONTINUED.	D. M.	YRS. MO.
Moon to the Semiquartile of Venus in the Zodiac, Converse Motion	18 24	18 10
Ascendant to the Opposition of the Sun in Mundo	18 32	19 0
Midheaven to the Square of the Sun in Mundo	18 32	19 0
Sun to the Semiquartile of Mars in Mundo, Direct Direction	18 35	19 1
Ascendant to the Biquintile of the Moon in Mundo	18 36	19 1
Sun to the Parallel of Mercury in Mundo, by the Rapt Motion	18 36	19 1
Sun to the Parallel of Mars in Mundo, Converse Direction	18 41	19 2
Ascendant to the Opposition of Mercury in Mundo	18 43	19 2
Midheaven to the Square of Mercury in Mundo	18 43	19 2
Moon to the Sesquiquadrate of Jupiter in the Zodiac	18 57	19 5
Moon to the Parallel of Saturn in the Zodiac	19 51	20 5
Sun to the Quintile of Saturn in the Zodiac	21 0	21 7
Sun to the Sesquiquadrate of Jupiter in Mundo, Converse Motion	21 12	21 10
Ascendant to the Biquintile of Mars in Mundo	21 25	22 1
Moon to the Quintile of Saturn in Mundo, Direct Direction	21 33	22 3
Sun to the Sextile of Mars in the Zodiac	21 50	22 6
Moon to the Parallel of Mercury in the Zodiac	22 38	23 4
Sun to the Sextile of the Moon in the Zodiac	22 59	23 9
Moon to the Body of Venus in Mundo, Direct Motion	23 19	24 1
Moon to the Quintile of Jupiter in the Zodiac, Converse Direction	23 38	24 5
Moon to the Sextile of Mercury in the Zodiac, Converse Motion	23 39	24 5
Moon to the Sesquiquadrate of Saturn in Mundo, Converse Motion	23 53	24 8
Sun to the Semiquartile of Mercury in the Zodiac, Converse Direction	23 59	24 9
Ascendant to the Trine of Saturn in Mundo	24 7	24 11
Moon to the Body of the Sun in Mundo, Direct Motion	24 15	25 1
Sun to the Semiquartile of Venus in the Zodiac	24 17	25 1
Moon to the Sextile of Mercury in Mundo, Converse Direction	24 22	25 2
Sun to the Square of Jupiter in the Zodiac, Converse Motion	24 31	25 4
Moon to the Body of Mercury in the Zodiac	24 31	25 4

OR GENETHLIACAL ASTRONOMY.

	ARC.		TIME.	
THE DIRECTIONS CONTINUED.	D.	M.	YRS.	MO.
Moon to the Biquintile of Jupiter in the Zodiac	24	32	25	4
Moon to the Semiquartile of Mars in Mundo, Converse Direction	24	33	25	4
Ascendant to the Sesquiquadrate of the Moon in Mundo..	24	43	25	6
Sun to the Semiquartile of Saturn in Mundo, Direct Motion	25	1	25	10
Sun to the Sextile of the Moon in Mundo, Direct Direction	25	30	26	4
Moon to the Body of Mercury in Mundo, Direct Motion	25	35	26	5
Sun to his own Semiquartile in the Zodiac	25	53	26	9
Moon to the Sextile of Venus in Mundo, Converse Direction	26	3	27	0
Sun to the Parallel of Jupiter in the Zodiac............	26	14	27	3
Sun to the Parallel of Venus in Mundo, Direct Motion ..	26	35	27	7
Ascendant to the Sesquiquadrate of Mars in Mundo	26	41	27	8
Sun to the Sextile of Saturn in the Zodiac	26	45	27	9
Sun to the Semiquartile of Venus in the Zodiac, Converse Direction	26	48	27	9
Moon to the Square of Saturn in the Zodiac	26	51	27	10
Sun to the Parallel of Venus in Mundo, Converse Motion..	27	9	28	2
Sun to the Sextile of Mars in Mundo, Direct Direction ..	27	22	28	5
Moon to the Square of Jupiter in Mundo, Converse Motion	27	28	28	6
Sun to the Quintile of Mars in the Zodiac	27	33	28	7
Sun to the Opposition of Jupiter in the Zodiac	27	43	28	10
Sun to the Quintile of the Moon in the Zodiac	28	38	29	9
Sun to the Sesquiquadrate of Saturn in the Zodiac, Converse Direction	28	43	29	10
Sun to the Parallel of Mercury in Mundo, Converse Motion	28	47	29	11
Part of Fortune to the Opposition of Venus in Mundo ..	28	52	30	0

There cannot be stronger testimonies of a violent Death, in any Geniture, than in this under consideration. The learned and immortal Ptolemy, has, in his precepts, *clearly defined* the *cause*, and *quality* of *Death* in all cases, whether *violent*, or *natural*; and, he *plainly informs us* how to select the rulers of Death, in any Nativity, which are chiefly to be regarded; for, if the Luminaries are in the superior Angles, and afflicted by the Malefics in violent Signs, and Terms without assistance; and at the same time, if the *Benefics* are found in obnoxious places, and *afflicted by Position*, and are also inimically joined in the Directions for dissolution, then, when such testimonies prevail, *a violent Death is evidently foreboded*, which is always pointed out by the Effects of the Mortal Directions, when they are in operation to the giver of Life; the *first* of which ascertains the true period of dissolution, (when benevolent rays do not precede,) *and those that follow*, indicate the quality thereof; thus when remarkable, and violent Deaths happen, *we always find* both the Malefics ruling the Anaretic places, *and assuming power, and superior dominion* over the Luminaries, and afflicting them at the same time in the Radix, as well as in the *subsequent train* of the Mortal Directions, which was the case in this Nativity.

Those who adhere to the infallible precepts, (contained in this Work,) for defining the Apheta, will find, that in the Geniture of this unfortunate young Man, the Sun claims the dominion of Prorogator, and, at the time of Death, that Luminary was directed to the Quartile of Saturn, in the World, Converse Motion; succeeded by the Hyleg to the Body of Mars, in the Zodiac, Converse Direction; the giver of Life, also subsequently arrived at the West; Semiquartile of Mars, in Mundo, by a right Motion; Rapt Parallel of Mercury; and Parallel of Mars, in the World, Converse Direction; followed by many other direful Motions to the significator of Life. Some may probably say, that the two foremost Directions, in the Mortal train, *are only Converse*, and have not sufficient power to produce dissolution; to this I answer, that both those Malevolent Motions, were formed *from Angles, and Signs of the Watery Trigon*, and, under those circumstances, they became equal to the formidable efficacy *of any direct Aspect*, and, were qualified with others, to portend Death by Drowning. The foregoing Motions of the Celestial Bodies, were preceded by the giver of Life, to the Zodiacal Parallel of Mercury, *who is of the nature of Saturn, in the Radix;* and, when this Direction *was completed*, that Star was received in the *Orbs, and Terms of Mars;* but, as the Promittor *was retrograde, and declining to the Occidental Horizon*, it was retarded in shewing its Effects, until the other Motions of the Stars displayed their ominous, and inimical power to the Sun, the legal Prorogator of Life.

In computing the Secondary Motion, we find, the Apheta was Angular, and applying to the Zodiacal Quartile of Saturn; and, that Luminary was in Mundane Square to his position, in the Geniture. In the Revolutional Figure, the Moon had just separated from the Square of Mars, in the Zodiac, and was exactly in the same Aspect with Saturn, in the World. At the time he was Drowned, the Moon was posited in a Watery Sign, beholding the greater Malefic, by hostile applications; she likewise *applied to the Mundane Parallel of Mercury*, who was of the nature of the Malevolents; and both the Benefics were extremely afflicted by the Conjunction of Mars, which correspond with the Directions, and gave additional violence to the other stations, and configurations of the Planets in the Geniture.

274   CELESTIAL PHILOSOPHY,

The following is the Nativity of Charlotte, Daughter of the late Mr. William Booth, Schoolmaster, at Brant Broughton, near Grantham, Lincolnshire. This Gentleman was an eminent Mathematician, and a good Astronomer. The time of Birth, taken, and given by himself, was April 29th 1780, 7h. 12m. P. M. She died on the 2nd of August, 1818, aged thirty-eight years, three months, and three days, (according to my previous Calculation,) which will appear evident from the following Figure of the Heavens, at the time of Birth, and the Anaretical Directions, which are correctly computed, according to the unerring principles of Astronomy.

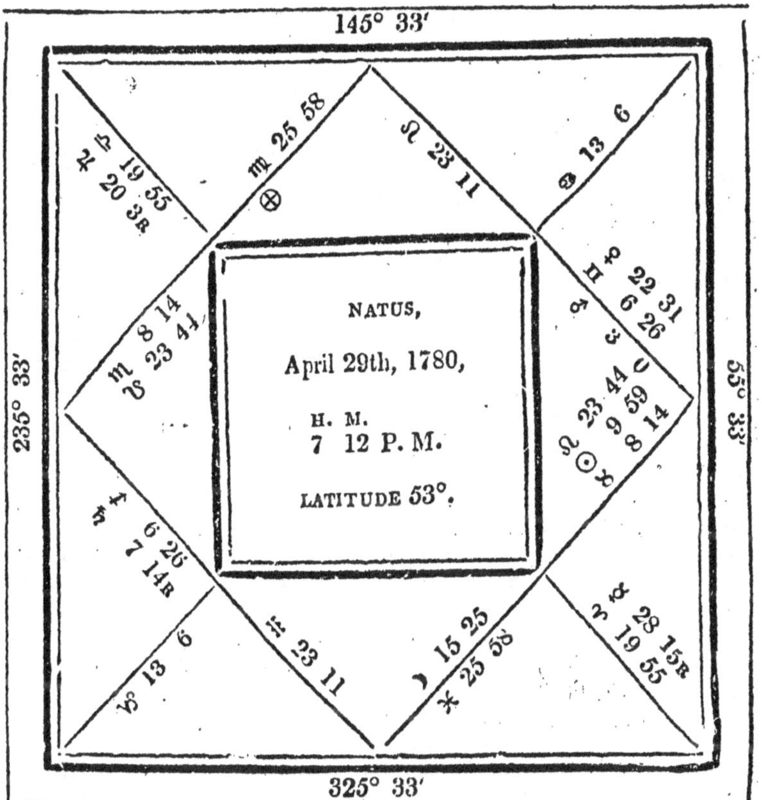
145° 33'
235° 33'
55° 33'
325° 33'
NATUS,
April 29th, 1780,
H. M.
7 12 P. M.
LATITUDE 53°.

	LAT.	DEC.	R. A.	S D A.	DHT.	SNA.	NHT.	A D.
	° '	° '	° '	° '	° '	° '	° '	° '
♄	2 1N.	19 33S.	245 46	61 53	10 19	118 7	19 41	28 7
♃	1 34N.	6 23S.	199 6	81 28	13 35	98 32	16 25	8 32
♂	0 35N.	21 20N.	60 49	121 13	20 12	58 47	9 48	31 13
☉		14 49N.	37 33	110 33	18 25	69 27	11 35	20 33
♀	2 28N.	25 42N.	81 41	129 42	21 37	50 18	8 23	39 42
☿	1 2S.	9 54N.	26 37	103 24	17 14	76 36	12 46	13 24
☾	4 51S.	10 13S.	348 29	76 10	12 42	103 50	17 18	13 50
⊕		5 56N	166 9	97 56	16 19	82 4	13 41	7 56

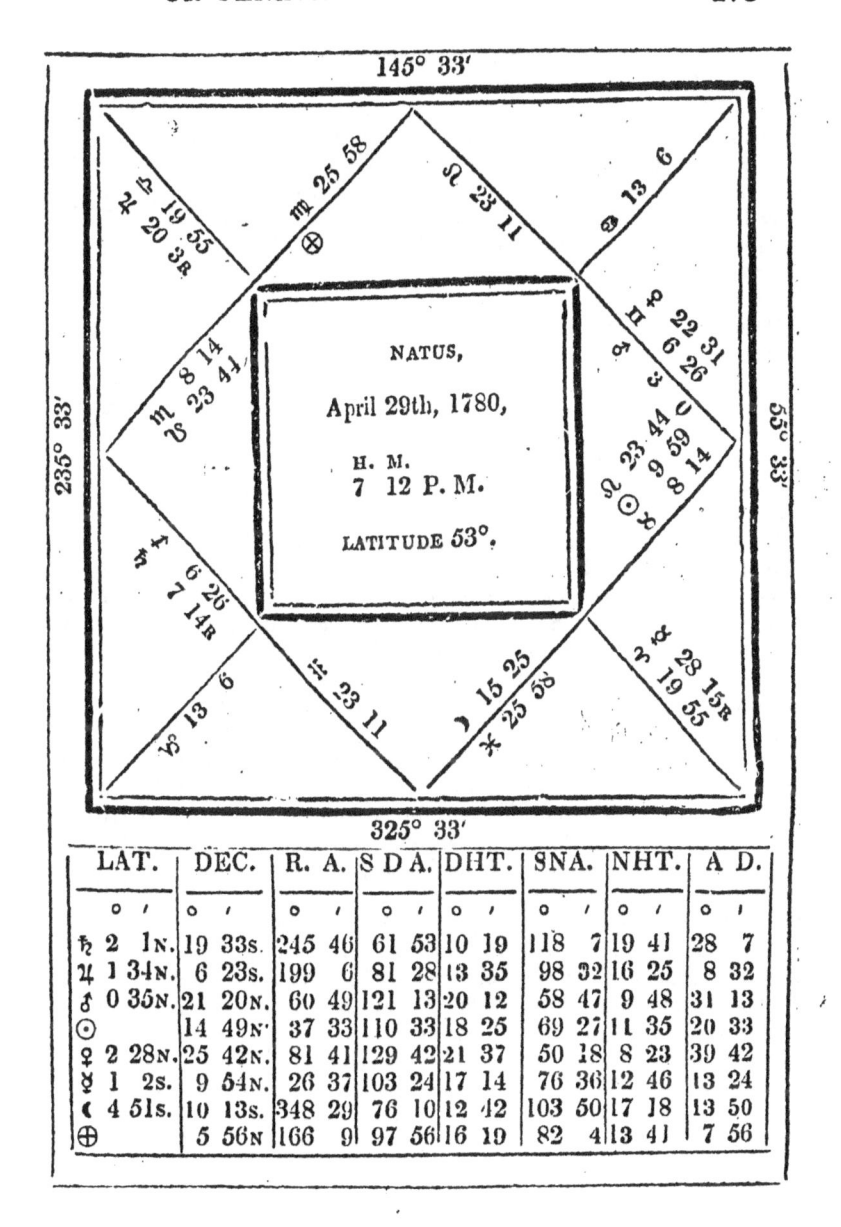

A TABLE OF THE DIRECTIONS.

Direction	Arc D. M.	Time Yrs. Mo.
Sun to the Semiquartile of Venus in the Zodiac, Converse Direction	0 47	0 9
Ascendant to the Sesquiquadrate of Venus in Mundo	0 59	0 11
Part of Fortune to the Opposition of the Moon in Mundo	1 14	1 2
Moon to the Semiquartile of Mercury in the Zodiac, by Converse Direction	1 19	1 3
Moon to the Biquintile of Jupiter in the Zodiac, Converse Motion	1 55	2 0
Sun to the Semiquartile of Venus in Mundo, Converse Direction	2 2	2 2
Ascendant to the Opposition of the Sun in Mundo	2 33	2 8
Midheaven to the Square of the Sun in Mundo	2 33	2 8
Sun to the Biquintile of Jupiter in Mundo, Direct Direction	2 47	2 11
Midheaven to the Lion's Heart	4 9	4 4
Moon to the Trine of Venus in Mundo, Converse Direction	4 51	5 0
Moon to the Quintile of Mars in the Zodiac	5 49	6 1
Moon to the Sesquiquadrate of Jupiter in Mundo, by Converse Direction	6 38	6 11
Part of Fortune to the Sesquiquadrate of Mercury, in Mundo	6 46	7 1
Moon to the Square of Venus in the Zodiac	7 23	7 8
Sun to the Biquintile of Saturn in Mundo, Converse Motion	7 49	8 1
Sun to the Sextile of the Moon in the Zodiac	7 51	8 1
Moon to the Parallel of Jupiter in the Zodiac	9 5	9 5
Moon to the Sextile of Mercury in Mundo, Converse Direction	9 23	9 9
Moon to the Square of Mars in Mundo, by Direct Motion	9 42	10 1
Moon to the Semiquartile of the Sun in the Zodiac	9 55	10 4
Midheaven to the Trine of Mercury in Mundo	10 0	10 5
Moon to the Sextile of the Sun in Mundo, Direct Direction	10 22	10 9
Moon to the Square of Saturn in the Zodiac, by Converse Motion	10 24	10 9
Sun to the Sesquiquadrate of Jupiter in Mundo, Direct Direction	10 56	11 4
Part of Fortune to the Square of Mars in Mundo	11 10	11 7
Part of Fortune to the Trine of the Sun in Mundo	11 12	11 7
Midheaven to the Quintile of Mars in Mundo	12 15	12 8
Moon to the Square of Saturn in Mundo, Direct Direction	12 15	12 8
Sun to the Biquintile of Saturn in the Zodiac, by Converse Motion	12 35	13 0
Ascendant to the Semiquartile of Jupiter in Mundo	12 48	13 3

OR GENETHLIACAL ASTRONOMY. 277

	ARC.	TIME.
THE DIRECTIONS CONTINUED.	D. M.	YRS. MO.
Part of Fortune to the Quintile of Venus in Mundo	12 48	13 3
Moon to the Sesquiquadrate of Jupiter in the Zodiac, Converse Direction	13 27	13 10
Sun to the Sextile of Venus in Mundo, by Converse Motion	13 36	14 0
Part of Fortune to the Square of Saturn in Mundo	13 41	14 1
Part of Fortune to the Biquintile of Mercury in Mundo	14 26	14 10
Sun to the Sesquiquadrate of Saturn in Mundo, Converse Direction	14 45	15 2
Sun to the Parallel of Mars in Mundo, by the Rapt Motion	14 55	15 4
Ascendant to the Biquintile of Mercury in Mundo	15 6	15 16
Moon to the Square of Mars in the Zodiac, by Converse Direction	15 45	16 1
Sun to the Parallel of Saturn in Mundo, by the Rapt Motion	15 48	16 2
Sun to the Semiquartile of Mars in Mundo, Converse Direction	16 24	16 10
Sun to the Body of Mercury in the Zodiac, Converse Motion	16 32	17 0
Sun to the Body of Mercury in the World, by Converse Direction	16 39	17 2
Sun to the Sextile of Venus in the Zodiac, Converse Motion	16 52	17 4
Moon to the Sextile of Mars in the Zodiac	18 17	18 9
Sun to the Square of the Moon in Mundo, Direct Direction	20 32	21 0
Sun to the Semiquartile of Mercury in Mundo, by Direct Motion	21 0	21 6
Moon to the Sextile of Mercury in the Zodiac, Converse Direction	21 39	22 2
Moon to the Semiquartile of the Sun in Mundo, Direct Motion	21 58	22 5
Moon to the Sesquiquadrate of Venus in Mundo, by Converse Direction	22 9	22 7
Moon to the Trine of Saturn in the Zodiac	22 32	23 0
Midheaven to the Sextile of Venus in Mundo	22 36	23 1
Part of Fortune to the Sesquiquadrate of the Sun in Mundo	22 46	23 3
Ascendant to the Sesquiquadrate of Mercury in Mundo	22 46	23 3
Sun to the Quintile of Venus in Mundo, by Converse Motion	22 53	23 5
Midheaven to the Opposition of the Moon in Mundo	22 56	23 6

278 CELESTIAL PHILOSOPHY,

	ARC.	TIME.
THE DIRECTIONS CONTINUED.	D. M.	YRS. MO.
Ascendant to the Square of the Moon in Mundo	22 56	23 6
Sun to the Sesquiquadrate of Saturn in the Zodiac, Converse Direction	23 6	23 8
Sun to the Biquintile of Jupiter in the Zodiac	23 7	23 8
Moon to the Sextile of Mercury in Mundo, Converse Motion	23 13	23 10
Sun to the Parallel of Mars in Mundo, by Converse Direction	23 28	24 0
Moon to the Sextile of Saturn in Mundo, Converse Motion	23 51	24 4
Moon to the Trine of Jupiter in Mundo, by Converse Direction	23 56	24 5
Sun to the Pleiades in the Zodiac	24 2	24 6
Sun to the Trine of Jupiter in Mundo, Direct Direction	24 30	24 11
Sun to the Parallel of Venus in Mundo, by the Rapt Motion	24 38	25 1
Sun to the Parallel of Saturn in the Zodiac	24 38	25 1
Sun to the Quintile of the Moon in the Zodiac	25 0	25 5
Moon to the Trine of Venus in the Zodiac, Converse Direction	25 7	25 7
Sun to the Parallel of Saturn in Mundo, by Converse Motion	25 7	25 7
Midheaven to the Trine of the Sun in Mundo	25 43	26 2
Moon to the Quintile of Venus in the Zodiac	25 57	26 5
Sun to the Semiquartile of Mars in the Zodiac, Converse Direction	26 10	26 8
Sun to the Opposition of Jupiter in the Zodiac, by Converse Motion	26 13	26 9
Moon to the Trine of Mars in Mundo, Converse Direction	26 17	26 10
Sun to the Trine of Saturn in Mundo, by Converse Motion	26 19	26 10
Ascendant to the Sextile of Jupiter in Mundo	26 23	26 11
Sun to the Opposition of Jupiter in Mundo, Converse Direction	26 23	26 11
Sun to the Sextile of Mars in Mundo, Converse Motion	27 58	28 5
Sun to the Quintile of Venus in the Zodiac, by Converse Direction	28 33	29 0
Part of Fortune to the Biquintile of the Sun in Mundo	29 44	30 2
Ascendant to the Biquintile of the Sun in Mundo	30 21	30 9
Midheaven to the Biquintile of Mercury in Mundo	30 26	30 10
Moon to the Quintile of Saturn in the Zodiac, by Converse Motion	31 30	31 11
Moon to the Biquintile of Venus in Mundo, Converse Direction	32 32	32 11

OR GENETHLIACAL ASTRONOMY. 279

	ARC.		TIME.	
THE DIRECTIONS CONTINUED.	D.	M.	YRS.	MO.
Moon to the Trine of Jupiter in the Zodiac, Converse Motion	32	35	33	0
Sun to the Body of Mars in the Zodiac	32	48	33	3
Moon to the Semiquartile of Mars in the Zodiac	33	35	34	0
Sun to the Body of Mars in the World, by Direct Direction	33	41	34	1
Sun to the Sextile of Mercury in Mundo, Direct Motion	33	46	34	2
Moon to the Quintile of Mars in Mundo, Direct Direction	33	57	34	4
Ascendant to the Trine of Mercury in Mundo	35	32	35	9
Moon to the Opposition of Jupiter in Mundo, by Direct Motion	35	33	35	9
Sun to the Opposition of Saturn in Mundo, Direct Direction	35	36	35	10
Sun to the Sesquiquadrate of Jupiter in the Zodiac	35	38	35	10
Moon to the Opposition of Jupiter in the Zodiac	35	42	36	0
Sun to his own Semiquartile in Mundo	35	43	36	0
Moon to the Sesquiquadrate of Venus in the Zodiac, by Converse Motion	36	29	36	8
Ascendant to the Opposition of Mars in Mundo	36	29	36	8
Midheaven to the Square of Mars in Mundo	36	29	36	8
Part of Fortune to the Body of Jupiter, in Mundo	36	31	36	8
Sun to the Square of Venus in Mundo, by Converse Motion	36	46	36	11
Sun to the Parallel of Mars in the Zodiac	36	55	37	1
Moon to the Square of Venus in Mundo, Direct Direction	37	11	37	4
Sun to the Quintile of Mars in the World, Converse Direction	37	15	37	5
Ascendant to the Quintile of Jupiter in Mundo	37	15	37	5
Part of Fortune to the Quintile of Saturn in Mundo	37	17	37	5
Ascendant to the Sesquiquadrate of the Sun in Mundo	37	18	37	6
Sun to the Parallel of Venus in Mundo, by Converse Motion	37	50	38	2
Sun to the Parallel of Mars in Mundo, Direct Direction	37	51	38	2
Moon to the Sesquiquadrate of Saturn in the Zodiac	38	1	38	4
Moon to the Sextile of Venus in the Zodiac	38	15	38	6
Ascendant to the Body of Saturn in Mundo	38	20	38	7
Midheaven to the Square of Saturn in Mundo	38	20	38	7
Moon to the Quintile of Mercury in the Zodiac, Converse Direction	38	21	38	7
Moon to the Parallel of Jupiter in the Zodiac	38	30	38	9
Sun to the Opposition of Saturn in the Zodiac	38	33	38	10

2R

CELESTIAL PHILOSOPHY,

	ARC.		TIME.	
THE DIRECTIONS CONTINUED.	D.	M.	YRS.	MO.
Sun to Aldebaran in the Zodiac	38	39	39	0
Part of Fortune to the Square of Venus, in the World	38	44	39	1
Sun to the Trine of Saturn in the Zodiac, by Converse Motion	39	6	39	4
Sun to the Parallel of Saturn in Mundo, Direct Direction	39	45	39	10
Midheaven to the Quintile of Venus in Mundo	39	54	40	0
Moon to the Semiquartile of Saturn in Mundo, by Converse Motion	41	9	41	2
Sun to the Sextile of Mars in the Zodiac, Converse Motion	42	9	42	2
Part of Fortune to the Biquintile of the Moon, in Mundo	42	46	42	9
Moon to the Sextile of Mars in Mundo, Direct Direction	43	5	43	1
Moon to the Sesquiquadrate of Mars in the World, Converse Motion	43	35	43	6
Ascendant to the Quintile of the Moon in Mundo	43	42	43	8
Part of Fortune to the Trine of Mars in Mundo	43	48	43	10
Moon to the Square of Mercury in the World, by Converse Motion	43	59	44	0
Sun to the Quintile of Mercury in Mundo, Direct Direction	43	59	44	0
Sun to the Square of Venus in the Zodiac, Converse Direction	44	5	44	1
Moon to the Body of Mercury in Mundo, Direct Motion	44	8	44	1
Moon to the Body of Mercury in the Zodiac	44	11	44	2
Midheaven to the Biquintile of the Sun in Mundo	44	15	44	3
Moon to the Sextile of Saturn in the Zodiac, Converse Direction	44	43	44	8
Moon to the Parallel of Mercury in Mundo, by the Rapt Motion	44	52	44	10
Part of Fortune to the Opposition of Mercury in Mundo	45	4	45	0
Moon to the Trine of Saturn in Mundo, Direct Direction	45	17	45	3
Moon to the Biquintile of Venus in the Zodiac, Converse Motion	45	25	45	5
Part of Fortune to the Sextile of Saturn in Mundo	46	2	45	11
Moon to her own Semiquartile in the Zodiac	46	30	46	5
Sun to the Semiquartile of Mercury in the Zodiac	46	33	46	5
Moon to the Parallel of Mercury in the Zodiac	46	49	46	9
Sun to his own Semiquartile in the Zodiac	47	17	47	2
Moon to the Biquintile of Saturn in the Zodiac	47	21	47	2
Moon to her own Parallel in the Zodiac	47	42	47	6
Moon to the Trine of Mars in the Zodiac, Converse Direction	48	43	48	6
Ascendant to the Trine of the Sun in Mundo	48	53	48	8

OR GENETHLIACAL ASTRONOMY.

This Native was Married to a Gentleman *far* above her station in Life, which is plainly visible in the Heavens. An honorable connexion was formed at the Age of twenty-six Years, and two Months, under the Effects of the Direction of the Midheaven to the Trine of the Sun, in the World, he being ruler of the Tenth, and posited in the Western Angle, which is the Husband's Ascendant. At the Age of twenty-six Years, and eleven Months, the Horoscope came by Direction to the Sextile of Jupiter, in Mundo, which may be proved by the use of the Celestial Globe; and as Jupiter was in a Cardinal Sign, disposed of by Venus, lady of the Husband's Ascendant, and was also in the Radix, in a Mundane Sextile to the Medium Cæli, the supreme Angle of Dignity, and Promotion; and was likewise in Trine to Venus in the Eighth, which is the Husband's second, with Mercury lord of the Eighth, in Sextile to Venus, lady of the seventh; these Radical positions, united with the efficacy of the primary Directions in operation, from the Age of twenty-six Years, and two Months, until twenty-six Years, and eleven Months, were proper to produce a respectable, and Wealthy Marriage. She was Married to a Gentleman of considerable Property, on the sixth of May, 1807, Aged twenty-seven Years, and six Days.

The Sun, in this Geniture, is the undoubted Apheta, or giver of Life; and, at the Age of thirty-eight Years, and two Months, that Luminary came to the Parallel of Mars, in Mundo, by Direct Direction, followed by the Opposition of Saturn, in the Zodiac, with Aldebaran, and also to the Parallel of Saturn, in the World, by a right Motion; these were the Directions which I judged would produce Dissolution, the truth of which was verified, though she lived one Month, and three Days, beyond the period pointed out by the first Direction in the train for Death.

But some will ask, why I have not noticed the Direction of the Ascendant to the Body of Saturn, it being in operation with those of the Sun, which I have allowed for Death? to such inquiries,

I shall only say, that the *true Hyleg alone, in every Geniture, must be directed for Death, its time, and quality*; the Direction of the Horoscope to the Body of Saturn, might augment the fury of the other Directions to the Prorogator, yet, it was of its own nature, *wholly unqualified* to produce Death, or any serious or alarming Indisposition; but being united with those that compose the Anaretic train, it doubtless gave some additional assistance to the Effects of the Mortal Directions to the Hyleg before mentioned, when they were in operation. The *Horoscope Advocates* may believe this if they please, for it is an established fact, that the most violent, and malignant Directions to the Ascendant, can never destroy Life, when the Luminaries, &c; are in the proper Aphetical places, and claim the Prorogatory power; though evil Directions to the Horoscope may, (without others of a violent nature,) produce Sickness, and Accidents, with various troubles, &c. These things are manifestly apparent to every Practitioner; but before I proceed further, I shall make some observations on the Directions of the Sun to the Body of Mars in the Zodiac, and in the World, which were followed by the Opposition of Saturn, in Mundo, as I shall probably be asked why they did not destroy Life, before the Age of thirty-eight Years, and two Months. The Sun certainly passed those Directions without causing the Death of the Native; and I am convinced, that *many pretenders to this Science*, would judge inevitable Dissolution, in similar instances, from such apparent violence; but in this case, those Directions *were not Anaretic*, and therefore were not armed with a sufficient portion of inimical power to destroy Life; neither were they able to produce any dangerous Sickness, or Accidents, so as to put Life in jeopardy; because when the same Directions were finished, those Malefic Promittors were received in the *Orbs, Terms*, and *Directions* of the Benevolents, which deprived them of part of their *own natural*, and *violent influence, and power*. The preceding Directions were followed by the Sun to the Parallel of Mars, in the Zodiac, the Effects of which, assisted by the Direction of the Horoscope to the

Opposition of that Malefic, could not prove Mortal, because the Hyleg was succeeded by the Square of Venus, in Mundo, Converse Direction, and Parallel of that Star in the World, by Converse Motion; and Saturn, and Mars, were likewise conjoined with benign Directions, by the Motion of the *Primum Mobile*, by which a *large portion* of the *evil* was *dissolved, which must be constantly, and particularly attended to, in all similar Calculations, and Judgment.*

But though the Directions before quoted, had not sufficient power to destroy Life, owing to the causes above assigned; yet, when they shewed their Effects, the Native experienced a lingering Illness, with which she was afflicted for more than a Year previous to her dissolution; the rays of Venus falling in by Direction at the time of Death, were unable to save, against the evil train then in operation that succeeded, though they described the nature of the affliction, or quality of the Mortal disease, which was a disorder of the Stomach, and Liver. The use of Medical skill was of no avail, neither was human assistance able to alleviate her lingering afflictions; but Death put a final period to her Earthly sufferings, at the Age before recorded.

There may probably be some difficulties arise among practitioners, concerning the nature, and power of those Directions that are Anaretic, and those that are not; for *in all cases, the Rules of the immortal Ptolemy, are substantial*; he tells us in plain language, that Directions of the *Hyleg* to the Bodies, and other destructive rays of Saturn, and Mars, &c; *do not always destroy Life*; he also informs us, that when the Apheta is at any time directed to the Malefics, or their furious beams, the evil though apparently great, is much abated, if the enemies at the same time, do not *possess their own natural, and violent power;* for if they are then in the Terms of the benevolent Stars, and are directed to the Benefics, either in the *Zodiac*, or *Mundo*, they *cannot destroy Life;* though they may be qualified to produce long, and lingering diseases, which may be considered as the *fore-runners of Death*; so that when the practitioners have (as they suppose,) computed a violent train of Directions to the Prorogator, they then absurdly judge Death from their Effects, without consulting other sideral causes of the *greatest importance*, previous to giving final Judgment; for if the Benefic Directions intervene to break the train, or if the Malefics, &c, as I have before observed be directed at the same time in *peculiar parts of the Heavens*, to the Bodies, or rays of Jupiter, or Venus, or their Terms, life will be *preserved*, notwithstanding the apparent fury, and violence of the Directions.

The Revolutional Figure for the Native's thirty-eighth Year, contained the greatest testimonies of violence; for Saturn was posited exactly on the Radical place of the Moon, and Jupiter had nearly returned to the Square of his own place in the Nativity, where he was afflicted by the hostile beams of Mars, from Cardinal Signs. Mars was likewise in Quartile to the Radical place of Jupiter at Birth, and the Moon, in the Revolution, was applying to the Body of Saturn. Mercury was also near the Conjunction of Mars in the Geniture, and likewise near the Square of the Moon in the Revolution. By Secondary Motion, the Moon was in Square to the Sun, in the World, and the Hyleg was also afflicted by both the Malefics, having then the Declination of the Moon. Saturn had also returned to his opposite place at Birth, and Mercury was likewise applying to the Opposition of Saturn, and had his Declination also; the Sun had passed the Opposition of Saturn, and applied to the Body of Mars; and in the Progression, that Malefic was posited on the place of the Moon in the Revolution, who was afflicted by the violent rays of Saturn; the Sun having at the same time gained the Declination of Saturn, was likewise in Square to the Moon in the Nativity. On the Morning of Death, there was a New Moon in nine Degrees, thirteen Minutes of Leo, in Square to the place of the Sun at Birth; and what is most remarkable, Venus, (whose primary Directions interposed in the train of Death, but could not save,) was in Conjunction with Mars, and in Opposition of Saturn at the time of Dissolution; these things duly considered, not only prove the Verity of the Computations, but also the great, and important use of Revolutions, and Secondary Directions. &c, when properly attended to at those periods, and in all cases, when Anaretical Directions are in operation to the true Prorogator, or giver of Life.

The following Nativity is that of a Female Child, who was Born on the 20th. of September 1803, at half past eleven o'Clock at Night; and was Drowned at the Age of six Years, five Months, and sixteen days. The Figure of the Heavens, with the Mortal Directions, prove, that the true Hyleg alone, must, (in all cases,) be directed for Death, its time, and quality.

In this Geniture, both the Luminaries are under the Earth, and all the other Planets are likewise posited in a Subterranean position, so that the Horoscope claims the Aphetical power. Now as the time of Birth was correctly taken by an adjusted Clock, I think all those who absurdly suppose that the Angles may be directed to *Aspects in the Zodiac*, will doubtless be convinced of their Error, for it is evident that there can be no such Directions, according to the true Doctrine of the Sphere, which has been before observed. I have in numerous Examples, proved the absurdity of such whimsical notions; and if any advocates are now to be found, who are disposed to rely on the Effects of Directions *in the Zodiac, to the Angles,* I must inform them from the highest Authority, and the most substantial proof, that no such Directions have been in Existence, according to the true Motions of the Heavens, since the beginning of the World.

OR GENETHLIACAL ASTRONOMY. 267

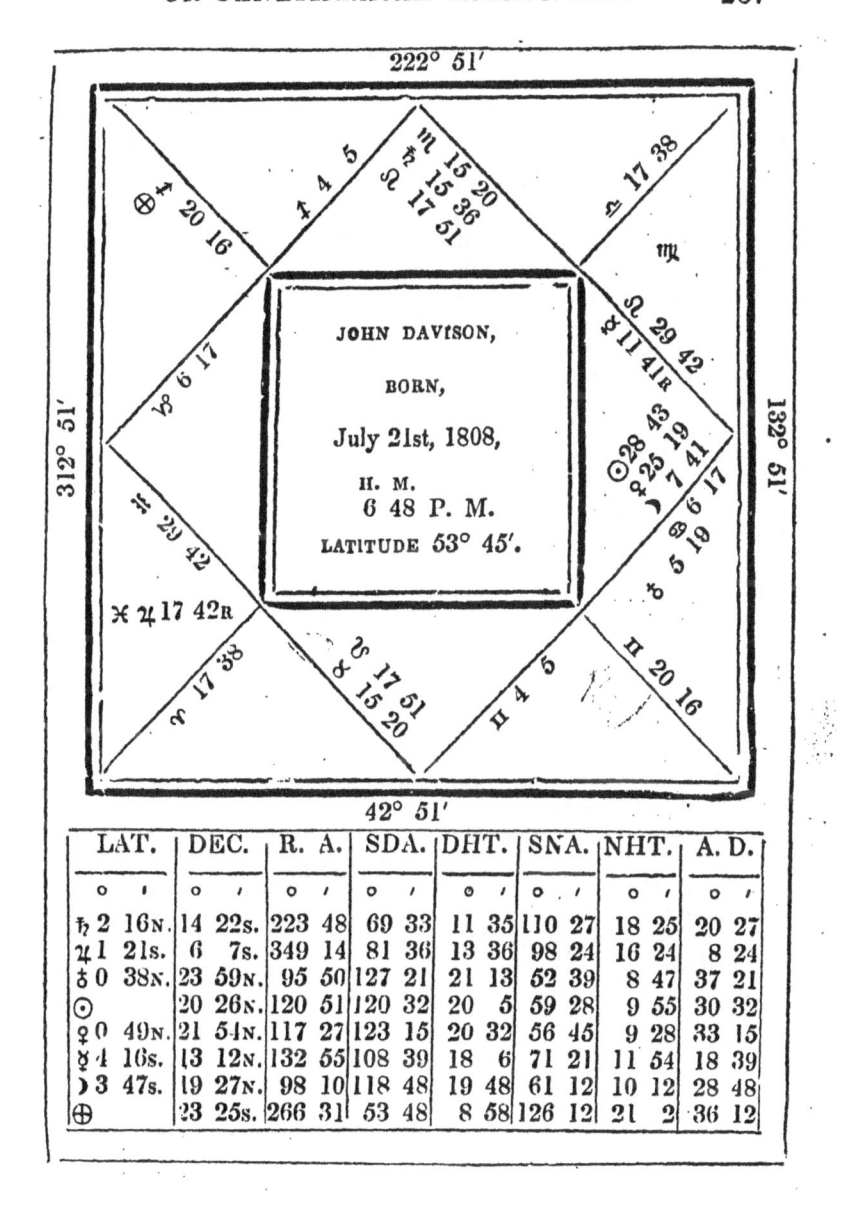

222° 51'

⊕ ♐ 20 16
♐ 4 5
♏ ♄ 15 20
♌ 15 36
♌ 17 51
♎ 17 38
♏
♌ 29 42
♉ 11 41 ʀ
☉ 28 43
☿ 25 19
☽ 7 41
♋ 6 17
♐ ☌ 5 19
♐ 20 16
♊ 20 16
♊ 4 5
♉ 17 51
♉ 15 20
♈ 17 38
♓ ♃ 17 42 ʀ
♒ 29 42
♑ 6 17

312° 51'   132° 51'

JOHN DAVISON,

BORN,

July 21st, 1808,

H. M.
6 48 P. M.

LATITUDE 53° 45'.

42° 51'

	LAT.	DEC.	R. A.	SDA.	DHT.	SNA.	NHT.	A. D.
	° ′	° ′	° ′	° ′	° ′	° ′	° ′	° ′
♄	2 16ɴ.	14 22s.	223 48	69 33	11 35	110 27	18 25	20 27
♃	1 21s.	6 7s.	349 14	81 36	13 36	98 24	16 24	8 24
♂	0 38ɴ.	23 59ɴ.	95 50	127 21	21 13	52 39	8 47	37 21
☉		20 26ɴ.	120 51	120 32	20 5	59 28	9 55	30 32
♀	0 49ɴ.	21 54ɴ.	117 27	123 15	20 32	56 45	9 28	33 15
☿	4 16s.	13 12ɴ.	132 55	108 39	18 6	71 21	11 54	18 39
☽	3 47s.	19 27ɴ.	98 10	118 48	19 48	61 12	10 12	28 48
⊕		23 25s.	266 31	53 48	8 58	126 12	21 2	36 12

CELESTIAL PHILOSOPHY,

A TABLE OF THE DIRECTIONS	ARC. D. M.	TIME. YRS. MO.
Moon to the Sextile of Venus in the Zodiac, Converse Motion	0 28	0 7
Part of Fortune to the Sextile of Saturn in Mundo	1 4	1 2
Sun to the Body of Saturn in Mundo, Converse Direction	1 23	1 6
Midheaven to the Opposition of Venus in Mundo	2 20	2 8
Ascendant to the Square of Venus in Mundo	2 20	2 8
Part of Fortune to the Sextile of the Sun in Mundo	2 31	2 10
Moon to the Sextile of Saturn in the Zodiac	2 32	2 10
Part of Fortune to the Quintile of Jupiter in Mundo	3 41	4 1
Moon to the Sextile of the Sun in the Zodiac	4 49	5 4
Sun to the Parallel of Venus in Mundo, by the Rapt Motion	4 50	5 4
Moon to the Semiquartile of Jupiter in the Zodiac	4 53	5 5
Sun to the Body of Venus in the Zodiac, Converse Direction	5 0	5 7
Sun to his own Parallel in the Zodiac	5 14	5 10
Ascendant to the Square of Saturn in Mundo	5 50	6 6
Midheaven to the Opposition of Saturn in Mundo	5 50	6 6
Moon to the Semiquartile of Venus in Mundo, Direct Motion	5 50	6 6
Sun to the Parallel of Saturn in Mundo, by the Rapt Motion	6 39	7 4
Midheaven to the Biquintile of the Moon in Mundo	7 18	8 2
Ascendant to the Square of the Sun in Mundo	7 30	8 4
Midheaven to the Opposition of the Sun in Mundo	7 30	8 4
Sun to the Semiquartile of the Moon in the Zodiac	8 5	8 11
Part of Fortune to the Square of the Moon in Mundo	8 34	9 6
Moon to the Semiquartile of Saturn in Mundo, Direct Direction	9 23	10 4
Sun to the Parallel of Venus in Mundo, Direct Motion	9 23	10 4
Part of Fortune to the Quintile of Mercury in Mundo	9 24	10 4
Part of Fortune to the Quintile of Mars in Mundo	9 56	11 0
Sun to the Parallel of Venus in Mundo, Converse Direction	9 59	11 1
Moon to the Quintile of Venus in the Zodiac	10 3	11 2
Moon to the Semiquartile of Saturn in the Zodiac, Converse Motion	10 38	11 9
Sun to the Parallel of Jupiter in the Zodiac	10 55	12 1
Moon to the Semiquartile of the Sun in Mundo, Direct Direction	11 14	12 5
Part of Fortune to the Semiquartile of Venus in Mundo	11 29	12 8
Sun to the Parallel of Saturn in the Zodiac	11 39	12 10
Moon to the Semiquartile of Mars in the Zodiac	12 20	13 7

OR GENETHLIACAL ASTRONOMY.

	ARC.		TIME.	
THE DIRECTIONS CONTINUED.	D.	M.	YRS.	MO.
Sun to the Parallel of Saturn in Mundo, Direct Motion	13	0	14	4
Sun to the Body of Jupiter in the Zodiac	13	12	14	7
Moon to the Semiquartile of Mercury in the Zodiac	13	12	14	7
Moon to the Quintile of Saturn in the Zodiac	13	24	14	10
Sun to the Parallel of Saturn in Mundo, Converse Direction	13	37	15	1
Sun to the Parallel of Venus in the Zodiac	13	40	15	2
Sun to the Body of Jupiter in Mundo, Direct Motion	13	43	15	3
Moon to the Semiquartile of Venus in the Zodiac, Converse Direction	13	57	15	6
Sun to the Parallel of Jupiter in Mundo, by the Rapt Motion	14	23	15	11
Part of Fortune to the Semiquartile of Saturn in Mundo	15	8	16	9
Ascendant to the Trine of the Moon in Mundo	15	40	17	4
Moon to the Quintile of the Sun in the Zodiac	15	59	17	8
Part of Fortune to the Sextile of Jupiter in Mundo	16	26	18	2
Part of Fortune to the Semiquartile of the Sun in Mundo	17	15	19	0
Sun to the Parallel of Mercury in Mundo, by the Rapt Motion	17	26	19	3
Sun to the Semiquartile of Mars in the Zodiac, Converse Direction	17	31	19	4
Sun to the Parallel of Mars in Mundo, by the Rapt Motion	17	34	19	5

In every Nativity, all the true Arcs of Directions to the vital significators, whether of a benevolent nature, or of a Malefic power, ought to be computed, which fall within the Orbs, and Terms of the Erratics, after the arrival of the true Prorogator, at the foremost in the Mortal train, (as in this case,) according to the Doctrine of the *immortal Ptolemy*, which he has clearly demonstrated in his Original Greek Quadripartite; for if *all* the Mortal Directions are not truly wrought, which *precede*, as well as those that *follow*, or unite in the Anaretic train, the Student will not be able to distinguish those that destroy Life, from others, which shew the *nature*, and *quality* of Death; for it is not *always* the first Malefic Direction to the Hyleg which destroys Life, though it is *generally* the case; for it sometimes happens, that when the giver of Life has arrived at the *first Direction* in the beginning of those hostile primary Motions, which threaten dissolution, Life is preserved by other benign Rays, Orbs, and Terms, in which the Prorogator, assuming the powerful Aphetical Dignity, is surrounded in the Zodiac, and in Mundo. Those benevolent Directions, (whether Converse, or Direct,) formed from the superior places, and Angles, &c. will dissolve a considerable portion of the evil; so that *no material injury to Life* is experienced; but when the giver of Life arrives at the *next* Malefic Direction in the train, then Death will ensue, because the power of those preceding Directions, (though of a benevolent nature,) is destroyed, and can afford no assistance to the true Prorogator, and particularly when other vital significators are afflicted by violent primary Directions, at, or near the same period.

There are many testimonies in this Geniture, which clearly portend a violent Death. The Sun is conjoined with Saturn, in the Imum Cæli, and Venus is united with them in that Angle. The Moon is in the Watery Sign Scorpio, in Sextile with the Sun, Saturn, and Venus; and as those rays are formed from Signs of *long Ascension*, they are of the nature, and power of a Square in this case. Mercury is in Conjunction with Mars, in the Nativity, and both are transmitting violent, and obnoxious qualities to Jupiter, who is also afflicted by the Parallel of Saturn's Declination; and the prevailing evil testimonies are considerably increased, in consequence of all the Planet's being Angular, the Moon excepted, and under the Earth at the time of Birth, and in those *violent Signs*, and places, which give Death by *Drowning;* for *Ptolemy* informs us, that when the Moon is in moist Signs, and evilly configurated with the Sun, and Saturn in obnoxious places, (the benevolent Stars being afflicted at the same time;) then Death will occur by *Suffocation*, and *Drowning;* and thus it happened in the present instance.

The Directions that destroyed this Native's Life, were the Ascendant Hyleg, to the Squares of Saturn, and the Sun in Mundo, according to *true, and natural* Motion; and it is evident, that no other Directions could destroy Life. The Horoscope was *separating* from the Sesquiquadrate of the Moon, in Mundo, but was not free from the Effects of that *inimical*, and *previous* application at the time of Birth. Some will say, that the Ascendant is afflicted by the Squares of Saturn, and Mercury, *in the Zodiac,* and ought not their rays to be esteemed of sufficient power to destroy Life? To this I answer, the Native lived past the expiration of the fifth Year, and therefore she died by Directions. In the course of all my practice, I have never seen any Zodiacal Squares of the Malefics to the Ascendant, destroy Life, when that point of the Heavens was the TRUE PROROGATOR.

But as I do not wish to sanction any project, nor rely on any Rules, and Precepts, which cannot be proved by *Reason,* and demonstrated by *Truth;* I will now prove to the Reader, (if he is not wilfully blind,) that when Mars, and Mercury arrive at the Cusp of the Northern Angle, then is the Ascendant directed to their *true Squares in Mundo;* this Motion may be instantly proved by the Celestial Globe, to the satisfaction of all those who wish to inquire after Truth, and adhere to Reason in all their operations; for it must be impossible for the Ascendant in this case, to be directed to the Squares of Mars, and Mercury, by two *distinct*, and separate Motions; indeed if that was the case, we should have very *small* Arcs of Directions in one operation, and in the other, very *large* ones; but I do positively say, that the true Arc of Direction, of the Ascendant to the Square of Mars, in Mundo, in this Geniture, is 29° 2′; and that of Mercury 29° 5′; and if we subtract the correct distance of Mars from the Northern Angle, 29° 2′ from his duplicate nocturnal horary times 33° 32′, we shall find, the true distance of Mars from the Cusp of the fifth to be 4° 30′; by which it appears plain, that both Mars and Mercury, were nearly in a Mundane Trine to the Oriental Horizon, at the time of Birth.

In the Native's last Revolution, Saturn was nearly on the place of the Moon in the Geniture; and that Luminary was likewise in Square to her place in the Nativity, and applying to the Quartile of Saturn, in the Revolution; and as her Declination was then decreasing, she consequently applied to the Zodiacal Parallels of all the Planets, in the Radix; the union of such violent testimonies, whenever they are found to correspond with the nature of the Progressions, Lunations, and Secondary Motion, &c.; always increase the violent, and dangerous Effects of the hostile primary Directions, to the Aphetical place. By Secondary Motion, Saturn was found in the Midheaven, conjoined with Venus, in Mundane Opposition to his position, in the Radix; he was also on the Solar place, in the Revolution. At the time of Death, the Sun was found in Opposition to Venus, and Saturn, at Birth; the latter Star was in Zodiacal Quartile with Venus at the time of expiration, and on the place of the lesser Malefic, in the Revolution, in Opposition to his own Mundane station in the Geniture; the Moon was unpropitiously irradiated by Mercury, and Mars in the Nativity, and the latter Star was in direct Opposition with Jupiter, in the Geniture; and Jupiter was in an hostile Aspect with Mars, and Mercury, in the Radical Constitution. Such evil, and violent Motions of the Stars, when agreeing with the Effects of the malignant primary Directions in operation to the Hyleg, always increase their fury, and produce sudden Dissolution.

The next Geniture which I shall give to the Public, is that of Elizabeth Thompson, who was Born near Hull, on the 11th of November, 1810, 7H. 5M. P M; and departed this Life, on the 3rd of December, 1824, Aged fourteen Years, and twenty-one Days.

This Native's Father, who is now living, gave me the above time of Birth, which he informed me, was taken by himself, by a well regulated Clock, so that the Nativity is not skeptical, but strictly correct.

The Immortal Ptolemy, that illustrious Master of Genethliacal Astronomy, &c.; informs us in *plain terms, without the least ambiguity,* that the *most important subject,* which ought *first* to engage our *serious attention, in all Genitures,* is THE DOCTRINE OF THE SPACE OF LIFE; for it would be *vain,* and *inconsistent* to give Judgment, concerning the time of *Prosperity, Adversity, Sickness,* &c.; with other occurrences at distant periods in the Life of an Individual, when malevolent Directions to the proper Apheta, are qualified to produce dissolution, in the early part of Life. In the following Nativity, I believe many pretenders to this Sublime Study, would *absurdly take the Ascendant as the Prorogator, or giver of Life;* but according to the Precepts given in this Work, for selecting the Hyleg, which will *always be found certain, and infallible,* it may *easily* be discovered, that the *Part of Fortune claims the Aphetical power,* as a full Moon preceded the Nocturnal Birth, and none of the Planets are in the Prorogatory places, which will appear evident, from the following Figure of the Heavens; and the Mortal Directions, to that *powerful* Mundane configuration, correspond with the period of personal extinction.

CELESTIAL PHILOSOPHY,

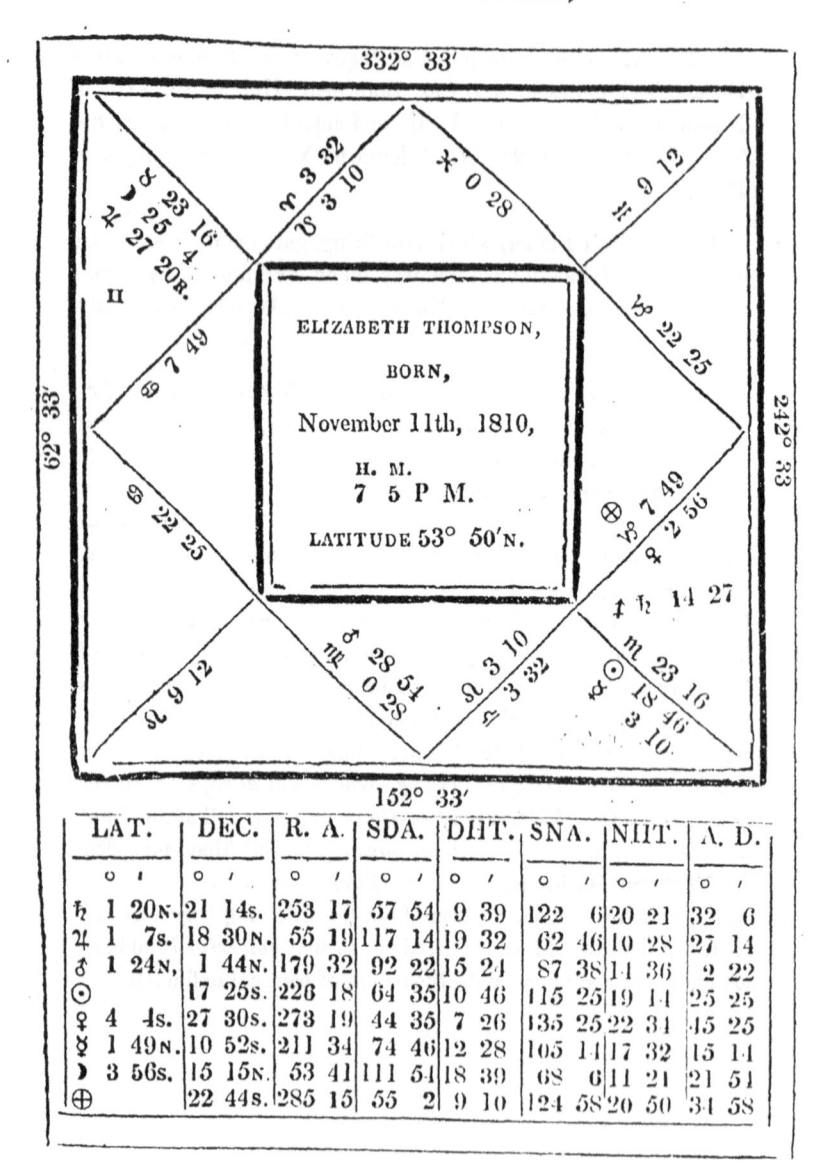

ELIZABETH THOMPSON,

BORN,

November 11th, 1810,

H. M.
7 5 P M.

LATITUDE 53° 50′ N.

	LAT.	DEC.	R. A.	SDA.	DHT.	SNA.	NHT.	A. D.
	° ′	° ′	° ′	° ′	° ′	° ′	° ′	° ′
♄	1 20 N.	21 14 s.	253 17	57 54	9 39	122 6	20 21	32 6
♃	1 7 s.	18 30 N.	55 19	117 14	19 32	62 46	10 28	27 14
♂	1 24 N.	1 44 N.	179 32	92 22	15 24	87 38	14 36	2 22
☉		17 25 s.	226 18	64 35	10 46	115 25	19 14	25 25
♀	4 4 s.	27 30 s.	273 19	44 35	7 26	135 25	22 34	45 25
☿	1 49 N.	10 52 s.	211 34	74 46	12 28	105 14	17 32	15 14
☽	3 56 s.	15 15 N.	53 41	111 54	18 39	68 6	11 21	21 51
⊕		22 44 s.	285 15	55 2	9 10	124 58	20 50	34 58

OR GENETHLIACAL ASTRONOMY.

	ARC.	TIME.
A TABLE OF THE DIRECTIONS	D. M.	YRS. MO.
Moon to the Pleiades	1 21	1 4
Moon to the Biquintile of Venus, in the Zodiac	1 32	1 6
Moon to the Body of Jupiter, in the Zodiac	1 53	1 10
Moon to the Biquintile of Mars in Mundo, Converse Motion	1 54	1 10
Moon to the Body of Jupiter in Mundo, Converse Direction	2 7	2 1
Sun to the Semiquartile of Mars in the Zodiac, Converse Motion	2 33	2 6
Sun to the Parallel of Jupiter, in the Zodiac	2 59	2 11
Moon to the Trine of Mars, in the Zodiac	3 13	3 2
Ascendant to the Biquintile of the Sun, in Mundo	4 31	4 5
Midheaven to the Sextile of Jupiter, in Mundo	4 38	4 6
Sun to the Opposition of the Moon, in the Zodiac	4 43	4 7
Ascendant to the Sesquiquadrate of Mercury in Mundo	6 25	6 3
Sun to the Opposition of Jupiter, in the Zodiac	6 29	6 4
Midheaven to the Sextile of the Moon, in Mundo	6 32	6 5
Moon to the Sesquiquadrate of Mars in Mundo, Direct Direction	7 16	7 1
Part of Fortune to the Sesquiquadrate of Jupiter in Mundo	7 41	7 6
Sun to the Sextile of Mars, in the Zodiac	7 45	7 7
Sun to the Opposition of Jupiter in Mundo, Direct Motion	7 52	7 8
Moon to the Sesquiquadrate of Mars in the Zodiac, Converse Motion	8 24	8 2
Sun to the Semiquartile of Venus in the Zodiac, Converse Direction	8 38	8 5
Sun to the Body of Mercury in Mundo, Converse Motion	9 1	8 9
Part of Fortune to the Sextile of Mercury, in Mundo	9 9	8 11
Sun to the Body of Mercury in the Zodiac, Converse Direction	9 14	9 0
Part of Fortune to the Sesquiquadrate of the Moon in Mundo	9 27	9 3
Sun to the Opposition of the Moon in Mundo, Direct Direction	9 37	9 5
Moon to the Sesquiquadrate of Venus in the Zodiac, Converse Motion	9 43	9 6
Moon to Aldebaran	10 31	10 2
Moon to the Biquintile of Mercury, in the Zodiac	12 12	11 10
Moon to the Opposition of Saturn in Mundo, Direct Direction	12 12	11 10
Moon to the Parallel of the Sun, in the Zodiac	13 9	12 8
Sun to the Parallel of Saturn, in the Zodiac	13 13	12 9
Moon to the Opposition of Mercury in the Zodiac, Converse Motion	14 33	14 0

2U

THE DIRECTIONS CONTINUED.

	ARC.		TIME.	
	D.	M.	YRS.	MO.
Part of Fortune to the Square of Mars, in Mundo	14	40	14	1
Sun to the Semiquartile of Mars in Mundo, Direct Direction	14	48	14	3
Moon to the Biquintile of Mars in the Zodiac, Converse Motion	15	17	14	9
Moon to the Biquintile of Saturn in the Zodiac, Converse Direction	15	49	15	3
Ascendant to the Sesquiquadrate of the Sun, in Mundo	16	3	15	6
Midheaven to the Biquintile of Mercury, in Mundo	16	55	16	3
Moon to the Opposition of Saturn, in the Zodiac	17	6	16	5
Sun to the Semiquartile of Saturn in the Zodiac, Converse Motion	17	32	16	10
Sun to the Quintile of Mars, in the Zodiac	18	2	17	4
Moon to the Opposition of Mercury in Mundo, Converse Direction	18	22	17	7
Part of Fortune to the Sextile of the Sun, in Mundo	19	3	18	3
Midheaven to the Trine of Saturn, in Mundo	19	20	18	6
Moon to the Sesquiquadrate of Mercury, in the Zodiac	20	40	19	9
Sun to the Body of Saturn, in the Zodiac	21	20	20	4
Moon to the Trine of Mars in Mundo, Direct Motion	21	52	20	10
Part of Fortune to the Semiquartile of Saturn, in Mundo	22	31	21	5
Moon to the Opposition of Venus in Mundo, Direct Direction	22	36	21	6
Sun to the Body of Saturn in Mundo, Direct Motion	22	40	21	7
Sun to the Biquintile of Jupiter in the Zodiac, Converse Direction	23	3	21	11
Part of Fortune to the Quintile of Mercury, in Mundo	23	10	22	0
Ascendant to the Trine Mercury in Mundo	23	57	22	9
Ascendant to the Semiquartile of Jupiter, in Mundo	24	10	23	0
Moon to the Biquintile of Mercury in Mundo, Direct Motion	24	49	23	6
Sun to the Semiquartile of Mercury, in the Zodiac	24	54	23	7
Ascendant to the Semiquartile of the Moon, in Mundo	25	11	23	10
Moon to the Sesquiquadrate of Saturn in the Zodiac, Converse Direction	25	35	24	2
Moon to the Biquintile of Venus in Mundo, Converse Motion	26	6	24	8
Ascendant to the Square of Mars, in Mundo	26	59	25	6
Midheaven to the Opposition of Mars, in Mundo	26	59	25	6

In the foregoing Nativity, the Lunar Horoscope is in exact *Semiquartile with the Sun*, which *forcible*, and *inimical Aspect*, combined with the impotent stations, and configurations of other vital significators, were evident testimonies of short Life: and that the Native would experience *lingering diseases*, during the transitory period of her existence, is clearly foreboded by the cadent positions, and afflictions of the superior Stars, in the Geniture.

In this ORIGINAL WORK, I have inserted the *correct Computation of the Part of Fortune*, with the arrangement of some of its Directions, which are precisely wrought *in full*, in page 128, 129, and 130; and without the least deviation from these precepts, which must be constantly attended to in every Geniture: the distance of the Part of Fortune from the Occidental Horizon, in this Nativity, is 7° 44', by which position, that Mundane point, claims the Prorogatory power; and the Directions that destroyed the Life of this Native, were, the Part of Fortune to the Square of Mars, in the World, and Mundane Semiquartile of Saturn, *without the least portion of benevolent assistance;* the latter Anaretical Direction was *several* degrees distant from the first, which produced Death; but I wish every Student in this *incomparable Science*, to notice, that when similar Nativities are observed, *two* destructive Directions to the Apheta, (even when they are far remote,) *without sufficient benign aid*, will never fail to cause dissolution.

It is worthy of remark, that both the benevolents were afflicted by Direction, at the time of Death; Jupiter was directed to the Opposition of Saturn, and Venus arrived on the place of that Malefic; the *hostile prevalence* of those Stars, at the time of expiration, united with the *violent nature, and power of the Anaretical Directions*, apparently point out the Mortal disease, to be a Consumption.

In the Native's last Revolution, the Prorogator was in Quartile with Saturn, in the World, and the Moon applied to the Declinations of the Sun, and Saturn, and Zodiacal Semiquartile of the greater Malefic. Mars, the chief Mortal Promittor, in the primary Directions, who was Angular in the Geniture, was then *descending below the Western Horizon*, in Opposition to the Horoscope, and communicated *deadly qualities to the Moon*; while Venus occupied the place of Saturn, in the Radix. By Secondary Direction, the Part of Fortune, the significator of Life, was in *Square with Mars*, in the Mundane Circle; and the Moon applied to the obnoxious rays of that Malevolent, in a subterranean position: but in the Progression, *the affliction of the Lunar Horoscope, was still more striking*. She departed this Life, when the diurnal Luminary made Oriental appearance, and consequently the Hyleg was then conjoined with the Moon; it also approached the Mundane Quartile of Mars. The proximity of these direful configurations, to the Moderator, produced the greatest degree of inauspicious influence.

The subsequent Geniture is that of Sabina Dayles, who was Born near Boston, Lincolnshire, on the 19th of February, 1816, 23H. 11M. P M; and died at Lincoln, June 2nd 1826, Aged ten Years, three Months, and twelve Days.

The Sun is certainly the true Hyleg, or giver of Life, and it would be preposterous to foretel the time of Death from Directions to any other significator; though I am convinced, there are some who would in this, and similar Nativities, neglect the austral position of that Luminary, and *improperly* allow the Horoscope to claim that momentous Dominion, and attempt to ascertain the period of the Native's dissolution from inimical Aspects to that Angle.

It is extraordinary to observe the *contradictory, and unintelligible* information given by various Authors, both Ancient, and Modern, who have written on the Doctrine of Nativities; but in one *essential point*, the *vague assertions,* and *exorbitant Tenacity,* with which the generality of writers agree, *is still more notoriously confused,* and that *essential point*, is in selecting the Moderator. Those who have written on this subject, vainly endeavor to *dilucidate,* and even *alter,* and *oppose the incontrovertible precepts of that luminous character,* the IMMORTAL PTOLEMY, by which, they have absurdly invented the most *sophistical,* and *injudicious Examples*; which *Examples* are adhered to by many to this time, and are considered preferable to the *primitive* Method of ascertaining the Prorogator, which the Author above quoted, has faithfully, and clearly elucidated in his *Original Greek Quadripartite.*

300   CELESTIAL PHILOSOPHY,

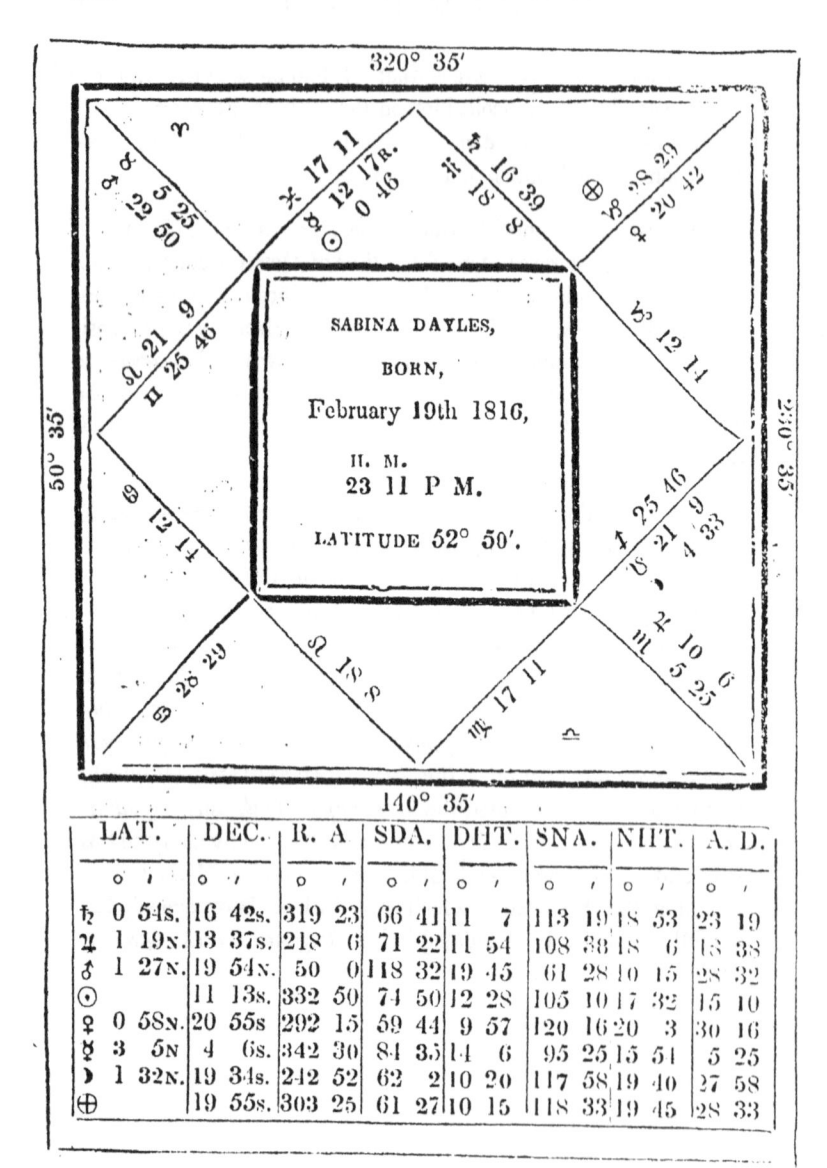

320° 35'

♈
♉ 5 25
  29 50
♊ 21 9
  25 46
♓ 17 11
☿ 12 17R.
   0 46
☉
♄ 16 39
   18 8
⊕ 28 29
♀ 20 42
♑ 12 11

50° 35'   230° 35'

♋ 12 11
♌ 28 29
♌ 18 8
♍ 17 11
♎
♐ 25 46
  21 9
  4 33
♏ 10 6
   5 25

SABINA DAYLES,
BORN,
February 19th 1816,
H. M.
23 11 P M.
LATITUDE 52° 50'.

140° 35'

	LAT.	DEC.	R. A	SDA.	DHT.	SNA.	NHT.	A. D.
	° '	° '	° '	° '	° '	° '	° '	° '
♄	0 54s.	16 42s.	319 23	66 41	11 7	113 19	18 53	23 19
♃	1 19n.	13 37s.	218 6	71 22	11 54	108 38	18 6	13 38
♂	1 27n.	19 54n.	50 0	118 32	19 45	61 28	10 15	28 32
☉		11 13s.	332 50	74 50	12 28	105 10	17 32	15 10
♀	0 58n.	20 55s.	292 15	59 44	9 57	120 16	20 3	30 16
☿	3 5n	4 6s.	342 30	84 35	14 6	95 25	15 51	5 25
☽	1 32n.	19 34s.	242 52	62 2	10 20	117 58	19 40	27 58
⊕		19 55s.	303 25	61 27	10 15	118 33	19 45	28 33

OR GENETHLIACAL ASTRONOMY.

	ARC.		TIME.	
A TABLE OF THE DIRECTIONS.	D.	M.	YRS.	MO.
Moon to the Quintile of Saturn in the Zodiac	0	4	0	1
Moon to the Semiquartile of Venus in the Zodiac	0	45	0	9
Moon to the Sextile of Venus in Mundo, Converse Motion.	0	53	0	11
Moon to the Parallel of Mars in the Zodiac	1	0	1	0
Ascendant to the Sesquiquadrate of Venus in Mundo	1	33	1	7
Sun to the Sextile of Venus in Mundo, Direct Direction	1	43	1	9
Sun to the Square of the Moon in the Zodiac	3	18	3	5
Part of Fortune to the Semiquartile of Mercury in Mundo.	3	20	3	5
Part of Fortune to the Square of Mars in Mundo	4	7	4	4
Sun to the Trine of the Moon in Mundo, Direct Motion	4	17	4	6
Moon to the Parallel of Venus in the Zodiac	4	17	4	6
Sun to the Semiquartile of Venus in the Zodiac	4	17	4	6
Moon to the Trine of Mercury in Mundo, Direct Direction.	4	58	5	2
Ascendant to the Quintile of Mercury in Mundo	5	0	5	2
Midheaven to the Trine of Jupiter in Mundo	5	7	5	4
Sun to the Parallel of Saturn in Mundo, by the Rapt Motion.	5	8	5	4
Moon to the Square of Mercury in the Zodiac	5	19	5	7
Sun to the Sesquiquadrate of Jupiter in Mundo, Direct Direction	5	25	5	9
Sun to the Sextile of Mars in Mundo, Converse Motion	5	40	6	0
Ascendant to the Biquintile of Venus in Mundo	7	30	7	11
Moon to the Square of Saturn in Mundo, Direct Direction	7	39	8	1
Sun to the Square of Mars in the Zodiac, Converse Motion	7	57	8	5
Sun to the Trine of Jupiter in the Zodiac	8	3	8	6
Sun to the Body of Mercury in Mundo, Direct Direction.	8	4	8	6
Moon to the Sextile of Saturn in the Zodiac	8	37	9	1
Sun to the Quintile of Mars in the Zodiac	8	41	9	2
Sun to the Trine of Jupiter in Mundo, Converse Motion	8	44	9	3
Moon to the Opposition of Mars in the Zodiac, Converse Direction	8	59	9	6
Moon to the Semiquartile of Venus in Mundo, Direct Motion	9	30	10	0
Sun to the Quintile of Venus in Mundo, Direct Direction	9	40	10	2
Sun to the Parallel of Saturn in Mundo, Direct Motion	9	43	10	3
Sun to the Body of Mercury in the Zodiac	9	54	10	5
Sun to the Semiquartile of Venus in Mundo, Converse Direction	10	18	10	10
Moon to the Quintile of the Sun in the Zodiac	10	19	10	10
Midheaven to the Sextile of Mars in Mundo	10	25	11	0
Sun to the Semiquartile of Mars in Mundo, Direct Motion	10	45	11	4

302   CELESTIAL PHILOSOPHY.

	ARC.		TIME.	
THE DIRECTIONS CONTINUED.	D.	M.	YRS.	MO.
Sun to the Parallel of Saturn in mundo, Converse Direction.	10	54	11	6
Midheaven to the Sextile of Venus in mundo	11	30	12	2
Midheaven to the Body of the Sun in mundo	12	15	12	11
Ascendant to the Square of the Sun in mundo	12	15	12	11
Ascendant to the Biquintile of Jupiter in mundo	12	21	13	1
Moon to the Sesquiquadrate of Mercury in mundo, Converse motion	12	44	13	6
Sun to the Square of Jupiter in the Zodiac, Converse Direction	13	12	14	0
Moon to the Opposition of mars in Mundo, Converse motion.	13	15	14	1
Sun to the Body of Saturn in mundo, Converse Direction.	13	36	14	5
Moon to the Semiquartile of Jupiter in the Zodiac	15	31	16	6
Moon to the Parallel of Venus in mundo, by the Rapt motion.	15	35	16	7
Sun to the Quintile of Mars in mundo, Converse Direction.	15	38	16	8
Sun to the Parallel of mercury in the zodiac	16	5	17	2
Moon to the Sextile of Venus in the zodiac, Converse motion.	16	7	17	2
Sun to the Biquintile of Jupiter in mundo, Direct Direction	16	18	17	4
Moon to the Quintile of Venus in mundo, Converse motion.	16	37	17	8
Sun to the Parallel of mercury in mundo, by the Rapt motion	16	47	17	10
Sun to the Sextile of Venus in the zodiac	16	56	18	0
Part of Fortune to the Square of the moon in mundo	17	21	18	5
Moon to the Body of Jupiter in the zodiac, Converse Direction	17	25	18	6
Part of Fortune to the Body of Saturn in mundo	17	28	18	7
Moon to the Square of Saturn in the zodiac, Converse motion	17	42	18	10
Moon to the Body of Jupiter in mundo, Converse Direction.	18	3	19	2
Part of Fortune to the Semiquartile of Venus in mundo	18	17	19	6
Sun to the Sextile of mars in the zodiac	18	44	20	0
Moon to the Biquintile of mars in the zodiac	19	12	20	7
Midheaven to the Quintile of Venus in mundo	19	28	20	10
Moon to the Quintile of mercury in the zodiac	20	25	21	10
Sun to the Sesquiquadrate of Jupiter in the zodiac	20	38	22	1
Moon to the Sextile of the Sun in the zodiac	20	53	22	4
Moon to the Quintile of Saturn in mundo, Direct motion.	20	59	22	6
Ascendant to the Trine of Saturn in mundo	21	1	22	6
Sun to the Semiquartile of Saturn in mundo, Direct Direction	21	13	22	8
Moon to the Trine of mercury in the zodiac, Converse motion	21	26	22	11
Sun to the Square of Venus in mundo, Direct Direction	21	37	23	1
Moon to the Semiquartile of Saturn in the zodiac	21	46	23	3

From the positions, and Directions in the preceding Geniture, there are several subjects worthy of observation, particularly the shortness of her Life, and the nature of the disease which terminated her existence. At the Age of three Years, and five Months, the Sun, the Prorogator, or giver of Life, arrived at the Quartile of the Moon, in the Zodiac; (succeeded by the Apheta to the Rapt Parallel of Saturn,) at that time she experienced a *dangerous Illness*, which remained with considerable Vehemence *for several Weeks*, and no hopes were entertained of her recovery; but as the Hyleg was in Mundane Sextile with Venus, and subsequently applied to the Zodiacal Trine of Jupiter, those malevolent Directions had not sufficient power to produce dissolution.

At the time of Death, the Aphetical point was directed to the Parallel of Saturn in Mundo, by a right Motion, followed by the Body of Mercury in the Zodiac, Semiquartile of Mars in the World, Direct Direction, Parallel of Saturn in Mundo, Converse Motion, and Conjunction of that Malefic, by Converse Direction; these Mortal Directions produced personal Expiration at the Age before mentioned; and though the Zodiacal Sextile of Venus succeeded, that Aspect was *unable to yield any assistance*, because it was *more* than seven Degrees distant from the *killing place*: and the Promittor was *violently afflicted* when this Direction was completed. The Sun to the Body of Mercury, being the *second* Direction in the *Mortal* train, most WONDERFULLY points out the quality of Death; for notwithstanding the Trine of that Star with Jupiter, he beholds the Moon by a *violent Square*, and is also in the *Terms of Saturn;* he therefore is of a *mischievous nature*, and *power*: Mercury thus afflicted in the Geniture, and also near the obnoxious Aspects of the Enemies at the time of dissolution, and in Pisces a Sign of the *Watery Trigon*, evidently describes the Mortal disease; which was occasioned by *Water in the Brain*.

The Revolutional Figure for the tenth Year, was very inimical, and violent, for the giver of Life was applying to the Square of

Saturn in the Zodiac, and Mars was on the radical place of Jupiter, and in Zodiacal Quartile with Saturn, in the Nativity. At the time of Death, the Apheta was applying to the Conjunction of Saturn, *in a violent part of the Heavens;* and the Moon was in *direct Opposition with Mars.* The Progression was also as dangerous as the other Motions, and stations of the Stars; for Saturn, and Mars were *unpropitiously configurated* with the Sun, in the Mundane Circle. By Secondary Motion, the Prorogator was near the Occidental Horizon, in Square to Mars in the World, and in Parallel with Mercury in Mundo; and Mars was on the Mundane place of Saturn in the Geniture: all these obnoxious irradiations, being combined with the Anaretical primary Directions to the Hyleg, greatly augmented the sudden, and furious union of their violent Beams, which not being counteracted by benign applications, always produce in similar cases, certain, and inevitable dissolution.

Elizabeth Gilliatt was Born at Lincoln, October 18th 1798, 12h. 28m. P M; and departed this Life, August 5th 1819, Aged twenty Years, nine Months, and seventeen Days.

This Celestial Science is founded on *Reason*, and *Truth*, and may be proved by *all;* but those who are disposed to deny its Utility, and Authenticity, soon disgrace their Arguments by their *vague, and contradictory observations.* All their *wire drawn Texts*, and disreputable Exclamations, when displayed in hostile array against the primitive principles of this prophetic Science, become instantly vanquished by the narration of one established Fact. In attempting to state the Fallacy of this Celestial Study, those who wantonly abuse the Works of the Creator, ought to produce public, and substantial Truths to support their assertions, without which, their bigoted Ideas will ever become disreputable, and comtemptible. Such characters vainly believe, that they possess universal Wisdom, and will by no means allow, that any Man can possibly excel them in Literature; but when they are finally defeated, they then attempt to proclaim a VISIONARY VICTORY by IMMODE- RATE PASSION, AND ABUSIVE LANGUAGE, &c. How unmanly, base, and wretched, must the mind of those Men be, who attempt to traduce a Science, the *true* principles of which, they are *wholly* unable to *define, or comprehend.* A man may deliver his opinion on any subject, either in the negative, or affirmative, but that will by no means establish the validity of his Judgment, except he is able (by the aid of Truth, and Reason,) to confirm his remarks, and support his Animadversions, *without fraud, or deception.*

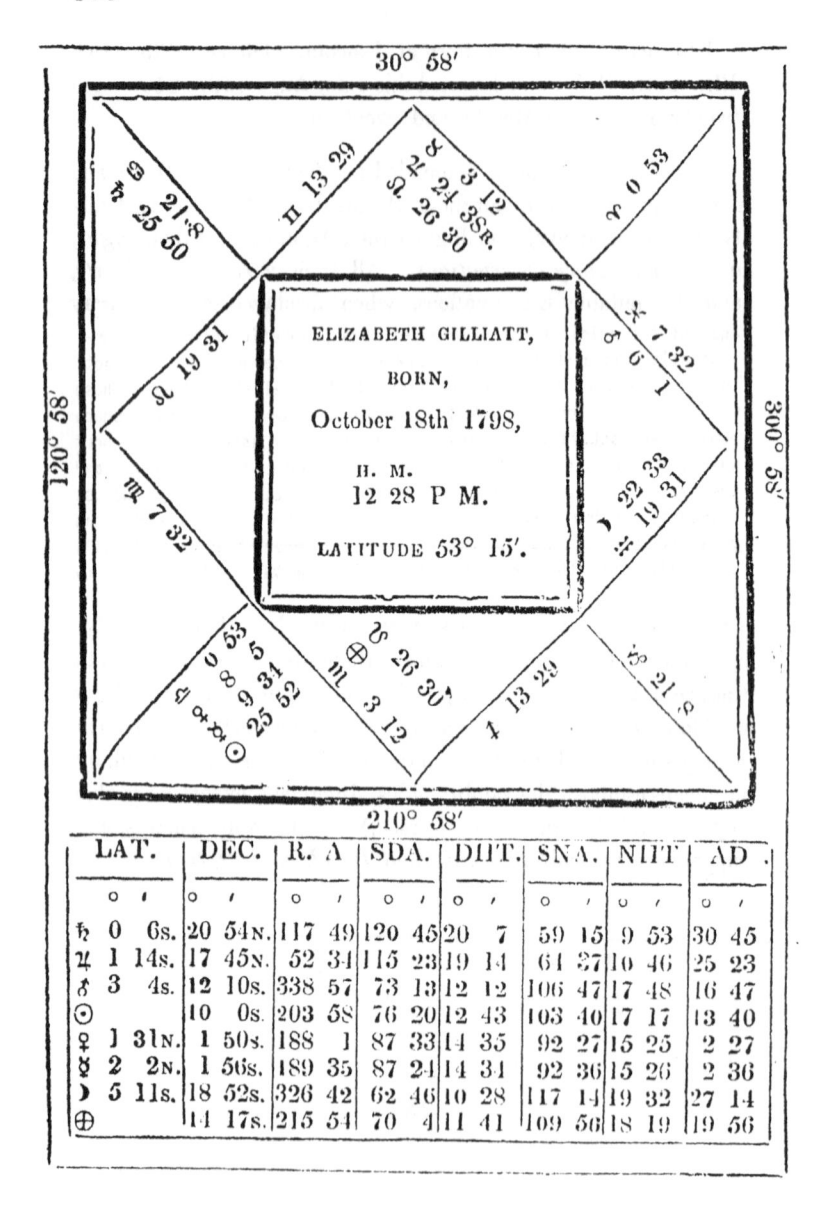

CELESTIAL PHILOSOPHY

30° 58'

♋ 21 ♌ 25 50

♊ 13 29

♃ ☌ 3 12
☊ 24 3 S R.
26 30

♈ 0 53

♌ 19 31

ELIZABETH GILLIATT,

BORN,

October 18th 1798,

H. M.
12 28 P M.

LATITUDE 53° 15'.

♓ 7 32
6 1

♒ 22 33
☽ 19 31

♍ 7 32

♎ 0 53
8 5
♀ 9 31
♄ 25 52
☉

♏ 26 30
3 12

♐ 13 29

♑ 21 8

120° 58' **300° 58'**

210° 58'

	LAT.	DEC.	R. A	SDA.	DHT.	SNA.	NHT	AD
	° '	° '	° '	° '	° '	° '	° '	° '
♄	0 6s.	20 54N.	117 49	120 45	20 7	59 15	9 53	30 45
♃	1 14s.	17 45N.	52 34	115 23	19 14	61 27	10 46	25 23
♂	3 4s.	12 10s.	338 57	73 13	12 12	106 47	17 48	16 47
☉		10 0s.	203 58	76 20	12 43	103 40	17 17	13 40
♀	1 31N.	1 50s.	188 1	87 33	14 35	92 27	15 25	2 27
☿	2 2N.	1 56s.	189 35	87 24	14 34	92 36	15 26	2 36
☽	5 11s.	18 52s.	326 42	62 46	10 28	117 14	19 32	27 14
⊕		14 17s.	215 54	70 4	11 41	109 56	18 19	19 56

	ARC.	TIME.
A TABLE OF THE DIRECTIONS.	D. M.	YRS. MO.
Moon to the Sesquiquadrate of Venus in the Zodiac ...	0 50	0 11
Part of Fortune to the Trine of Saturn in Mundo........	0 58	1 1
Sun to the Trine of Mars in Mundo, Direct Direction....	1 46	1 10
Moon to the Sesquiquadrate of Mercury in the Zodiac....	3 7	3 4
Moon to the Square of Jupiter in the Zodiac	3 12	3 5
Sun to the Biquintile of Mars in Mundo, Converse Motion.	4 26	4 8
Moon to the Trine of the Sun in the Zodiac.............	5 6	5 6
Moon to the Parallel of Jupiter in the Zodiac	5 6	5 6
Sun to the Parallel of Mars in the Zodiac	6 1	6 5
Sun to the Biquintile of Jupiter in the Zodiac, Converse Direction..................................	6 22	6 9
Midheaven to the Sextile of Saturn in Mundo..........	6 23	6 9
Sun to the Square of the Moon in Mundo, Direct Motion.	6 29	6 10
Sun to the Parallel of Jupiter in Mundo, by the Rapt Motion.	6 32	6 11
Midheaven to the Quintile of Mars in Mundo	6 33	6 11
Ascendant to the Sextile of Venus in Mundo	7 50	8 3
Sun to the Sesquiquadrate of Mars in the Zodiac, Converse Direction	8 6	8 6
Moon to the Trine of Venus in Mundo, Direct Motion....	9 1	9 5
Ascendant to the Sextile of Mercury in Mundo	9 29	9 11
Sun to the Trine of Mars in the Zodiac	10 4	10 6
Moon to the Trine of Mercury in Mundo, Direct Direction.	10 40	11 1
Ascendant to Cor Leonis	10 58	11 5
Sun to the Parallel of Jupiter in Mundo, Converse Motion.	12 25	13 0
Moon to the Parallel of Mars in Mundo, by the Rapt Motion	12 28	13 0
Moon to the Trine of Mercury in the Zodiac, Converse Direction..................................	13 33	14 1
Ascendant to the Quintile of the Sun in Mundo	13 44	14 3
Sun to the Parallel of Jupiter in Mundo, Direct Motion ..	13 49	14 4
Midheaven to the Biquintile of Venus in Mundo	14 2	14 7
Moon to the Biquintile of Saturn in the Zodiac	14 12	14 9
Sun to the Trine of Saturn in Mundo, Direct Direction....	14 32	15 1
Moon to the Biquintile of Venus in the Zodiac.........	14 37	15 2
Sun to the Sesquiquadrate of Mars in Mundo, Converse Motion...................................	14 48	15 4
Sun to the Biquintile of Jupiter in Mundo, Converse Direction	15 2	15 7
Moon to the Trine of Venus in the Zodiac, Converse Motion.	15 17	15 10
Sun to the Sesquiquadrate of Jupiter in the Zodiac, Converse Direction..................................	15 25	16 0
Moon to the Trine of Jupiter in Mundo, Converse Motion.	15 38	16 3

308 CELESTIAL PHILOSOPHY,

THE DIRECTIONS CONTINUED.	ARC. D. M.	TIME. YRS. MO.
Midheaven to the Biquintile of Mercury in Mundo......	15 39	16 3
Moon to the Biquintile of Saturn in Mundo, Direct Direction.	15 59	16 7
Part of Fortune to the Opposition of Jupiter in Mundo ..	16 25	17 0
Part of Fortune to the Quintile of the Moon in Mundo....	16 42	17 3
Moon to the Biquintile of Mercury in the Zodiac.........	16 51	17 5
Sun to the Body of Mercury in Mundo, Converse Motion.	16 55	17 6
Part of Fortune to the Square of Mars in Mundo........	17 55	18 6
Sun to the Body of Venus in Mundo, Converse Direction..	18 45	19 4
Part of Fortune to the Semiquartile of Venus in Mundo..	19 6	19 8
Sun to the Biquintile of Mars in the Zodiac, Converse Motion....................................	19 49	20 5
Moon to the Parallel of Mars in Mundo, Direct Direction.	20 16	20 10
Moon to the Body of Mars in the Zodiac..............	20 33	21 1
Part of Fortune to the Semiquartile of Mercury in Mundo.	20 46	21 4
Part of Fortune to the Sesquiquadrate of Saturn in Mundo.	21 5	21 8
Ascendant to the Opposition of Mars in Mundo	21 12	21 8
Midheaven to the Square of Mars in Mundo..	21 12	21 9
Ascendant to the Square of Jupiter in Mundo	21 36	22 2
Midheaven to the Body of Jupiter in Mundo	21 36	22 2
Sun to the Square of Saturn in Mundo, Converse Motion.	22 3	22 7
Midheaven to the Pleiades	22 17	22 10
Moon to the Body of Mars in Mundo, Direct Direction ..	22 34	23 1
Moon to the Square of Jupiter in Mundo, Direct Motion.	23 5	23 7
Moon to the Semiquartile of Mars in Mundo, Converse Direction.................................	23 11	23 8
Ascendant to the Semiquartile of Venus in Mundo	23 15	23 9
Sun to the Quintile of Saturn in the Zodiac, Converse Motion.	23 27	23 11
Sun to the Parallel of Jupiter in the Zodiac	24 17	24 10
Moon to the Sesquiquadrate of Venus in Mundo, Direct Direction.................................	24 26	25 0
Ascendant to the Semiquartile of Mercury in Mundo	24 55	25 6
Sun to the Sesquiquadrate of Jupiter in Mundo, Converse Motion..................................	25 21	26 0
Moon to the Square of Mercury in Mundo, Converse Direction...................................	25 36	26 2
Moon to the Sesquiquadrate of Mercury in Mundo, Direct Motion.................................	26 6	26 8
Ascendant to the Semiquartile of Saturn in Mundo	26 30	27 1
Part of Fortune to the Parallel of Jupiter in Mundo......	26 47	27 4
Sun to the Square of the Moon in the Zodiac	27 0	27 7

OR GENETHLIACAL ASTRONOMY.

	ARC.		TIME.	
THE DIRECTIONS CONTINUED.	D.	M.	YRS.	MO.
Ascendant to the Sextile of the Sun in Mundo	27	32	28	1
Sun to the Semiquartile of Venus in the Zodiac	27	33	28	1
Moon to the Square of Venus in Mundo, Converse Direction	27	40	28	2
Moon to the Parallel of Mars in the Zodiac	27	50	28	4
Moon to the Trine of Jupiter in the Zodiac, Converse Motion	27	52	28	4
Moon to the Sesquiquadrate of Saturn in the Zodiac	27	57	28	5
Moon to the Sesquiquadrate of the Sun in the Zodiac	28	0	28	5
Moon to the Sesquiquadrate of Saturn in Mundo, Direct Direction	28	3	28	6
Sun to the Square of Mars in Mundo, Direct Motion	28	24	28	10
Sun to the Parallel of the Moon in the Zodiac	28	49	29	3
Moon to the Trine of the Sun in Mundo, Direct Direction	28	52	29	3
Sun to the Semiquartile of Mercury in the Zodiac	29	6	29	6
Sun to the Opposition of Jupiter in the Zodiac	29	10	29	7
Sun to the Opposition of Jupiter in Mundo, Direct Motion	29	23	29	9
Sun to the Quintile of the Moon in Mundo, Direct Direction	29	56	30	3
Sun to the Trine of Saturn in the Zodiac	30	27	30	9
Moon to the Quintile of Jupiter in the Zodiac	30	39	30	11
Sun to the Trine of Jupiter in the Zodiac, Converse Motion	31	15	31	6
Moon to the Opposition of Saturn in Mundo, Converse Direction	31	24	31	8
Part of Fortune to the Sextile of the Moon in Mundo	32	20	32	7
Moon to the Parallel of Mars in Mundo, Converse Motion	32	26	32	8

When this Native was in the most perfect state of Health, I was requested by her Father, to make some observations on her Geniture; and from the Estimate time of Birth, (as it was recorded in an Ancient family document,) which is inserted in the preceding Figure, *I was perfectly satisfied, that the Moon was Hyleg*, and as the Native had not been exposed to any violent Indisposition, to put Life in danger, I was confident, that the Directions of the Moon to the Parallel of Mars in Mundo, Direct Motion; Semiquartile of Mars in the World, Converse Direction; Quartile of Mercury in Mundo, Converse Motion; Sesquiquadrate of that Star in the World Direct Direction; Parallel of Mars in the Zodiac; Sesquiquadrate of Saturn in Mundo, and Zodiac; and Sesquiquadrate of the Sun in the Zodiac, had not shewed their Effects, and as they were not twelve Months distant at the time I finished the Computations; the Judgment which I delivered in few words, was, that before the end of her twenty-first Year, she would leave this World for a better, however her Father believed in nothing I had said, and passed several *absurd*, and *unhandsome* observations on my Calculations, and Judgment; but Alas!

> The destin'd Victim did resign her Breath,
> By that due Summons from relentless Death.

The Mortal disease according to the positions, and Directions preceding, was a *disorder of the Lungs*, which occasioned a *rapid wasting of the Flesh*, accompanied with a slow nervous Fever. There are some who will probably ask, why the rays of Jupiter did not save Life, as the Moon to his Square in Mundo, was united with those Directions, which I allowed for Death; it is true the Direction of Jupiter follows, but as he was *at that time deprived of his benevolent qualities,* he could not render sufficient assistance to the giver of Life; his subsequent Directions *being void of relief,* were of no avail, though they certainly specified the nature, and original cause of the Native's dissolution.

By Secondary Direction, the Luminaries were in Conjunction in a subterranean position; and both the Malefics were in Mundane

Quartile, from the Eastern, and Southern Angles; and in violent configuration with the Moon in the Nativity; the giver of Life was also in Square to her place in the Geniture. In the Native's last Revolutional Figure, the Hyleg was in Mundane, and Zodiacal Quartile with Saturn; and the Sun was making application to the Body of Mars; the greater Malefic was likewise on the place of Mars in the Radix: and in the Progression, the Luminaries were surrounded by hostile rays, as they approached the superior Angles, and could receive no assistance from benevolent irradiations. At the time of Death, the Moon had the Declination of the lesser Malefic, and was applying to the Opposition of the Sun; she was also in Square with Mars in the Revolution. Mars was in Zodiacal Quartile with Mercury, and on his own Mundane position in the Nativity. Those who will take the trouble to make observations of this kind, and reduce them to practice as occasion requires, will find, that such hostile Motions as I have here investigated, will, when compared with the nature, and Effects of the superior primary Directions, augment their operations; and particularly when they are conjoined, and correspond with those Motions, which are productive of Death; therefore from what has been recorded, the young Students will, I have no doubt attend to the foregoing observations, which may soon be understood by all those who are inclined to occupy their leisure Hours in these Calculations.

The next, and last Nativity, is that of a young Gentleman, who is now living, and in good Health; and as this Geniture has been delivered into the hands of some *ignorant impostors*, who impudently affirm, that he is to Marry at the Age of twenty-five Years, and also obtain considerable Wealth at the Age of thirty-eight: I have therefore Published this Nativity, that the community may notice the **deceit,** and *villany* practised by *illiterate pretenders,* who go about the Country for the purpose of *deceiving* the *ignorant*. The time of Birth inserted in the Celestial Figure, was given to me by the Native's Parents, by whom I was requested to Calculate this Geniture. The Figure of Heaven, with the Directions computed from the Astronomical Tables contained in this Work, are as follow.

OR GENETHLIACAL ASTRONOMY.

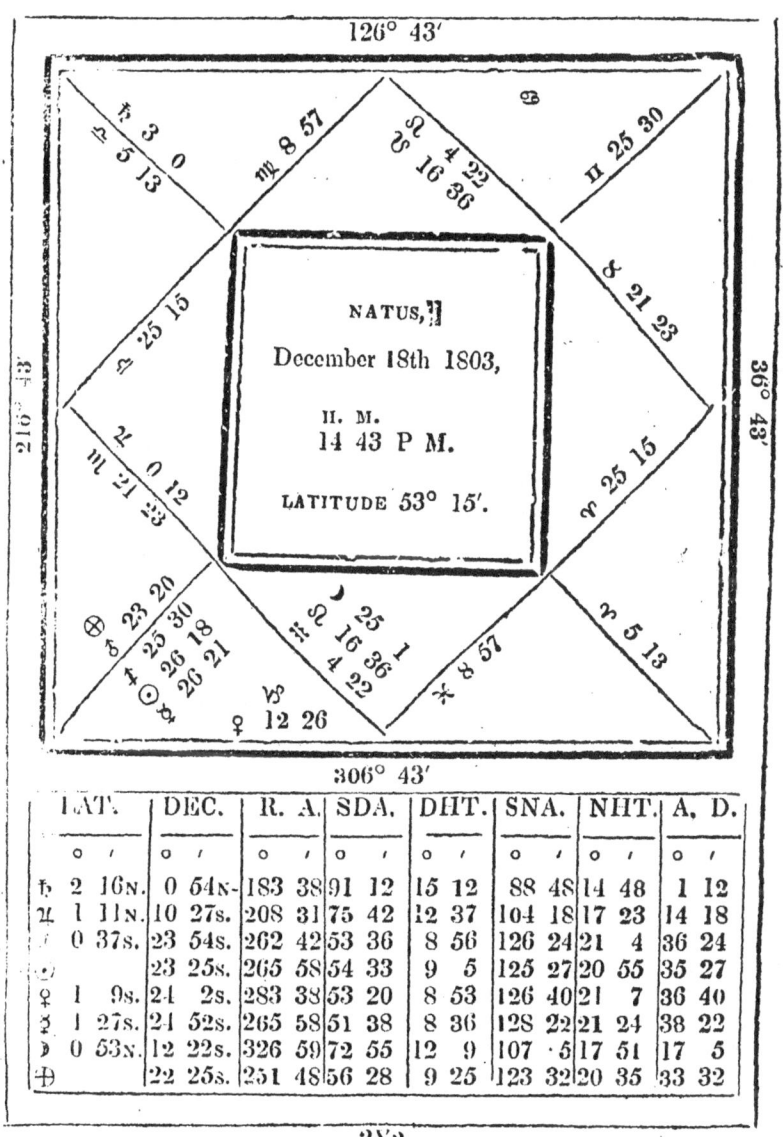

NATUS,
December 18th 1803,
H. M.
14 43 P M.
LATITUDE 53° 15′.

	LAT.	DEC.	R. A.	SDA.	DHT.	SNA.	NHT.	A. D.
	° ′	° ′	° ′	° ′	° ′	° ′	° ′	° ′
♄	2 16 N.	0 54 N.	183 38	91 12	15 12	88 48	14 48	1 12
♃	1 11 N.	10 27 S.	208 31	75 42	12 37	104 18	17 23	14 18
♂	0 37 S.	23 54 S.	262 42	53 36	8 56	126 24	21 4	36 24
☉		23 25 S.	265 58	54 33	9 5	125 27	20 55	35 27
♀	1 9 S.	24 2 S.	283 38	53 20	8 53	126 40	21 7	36 40
☿	1 27 S.	24 52 S.	265 58	51 38	8 36	128 22	21 24	38 22
☽	0 53 N.	12 22 S.	326 59	72 55	12 9	107 5	17 51	17 5
⊕		22 25 S.	251 48	56 28	9 25	123 32	20 35	33 32

CELESTIAL PHILOSOPHY,

A TABLE OF THE DIRECTIONS.	ARC. D. M.	TIME. YRS. MO.
Sun to the Body of Mercury in the Zodiac	0 3	0 1
Jupiter to the Quintile of Venus in the Zodiac	0 21	0 4
Moon to the Semiquartile of Mercury in Mundo, Converse Direction	0 44	0 8
Sun to the Body of Mercury in Mundo, Direct Motion	0 58	0 10
Ascendant to the Sextile of the Sun in Mundo	1 2	0 11
Moon to the Sextile of the Sun in the Zodiac	1 21	1 3
Moon to the Sextile of Mercury in the Zodiac	1 25	1 4
Sun to the Semiquartile of the Moon in Mundo, Direct Direction	1 33	1 6
Moon to the Sextile of Mars in the Zodiac, Converse Motion	1 54	1 10
Ascendant to the Sextile of Mercury in Mundo	2 1	1 11
Moon to the Biquintile of Saturn in the Zodiac	2 6	2 0
Ascendant to the Quintile of Venus in Mundo	2 15	2 1
Moon to the Semiquartile of Venus in the Zodiac	2 33	2 4
Sun to the Body of Mars in Mundo, Converse Direction	2 54	2 8
Moon to the Semiquartile of Mars in Mundo, Converse Motion	4 1	3 7
Sun to the Sextile of Jupiter in the Zodiac	4 17	3 10
Jupiter to the Sextile of Mercury in the Zodiac, Converse Direction	4 22	3 11
Jupiter to the Sextile of Mercury in Mundo, Converse Motion	4 28	4 0
Moon to the Parallel of Jupiter in the Zodiac	4 41	4 3
Sun to the Sextile of Jupiter in Mundo, Direct Direction	5 14	4 9
Moon to the Trine of Jupiter in the Zodiac	5 25	4 11
Jupiter to the Semiquartile of Saturn in Mundo, Direct Motion	5 59	5 5
Ascendant to the Body of Jupiter in Mundo	6 6	5 6
Midheaven to the Square of Jupiter in Mundo	6 6	5 6
Part of Fortune to the Square of Saturn in Mundo	6 16	5 8
Sun to the Square of Saturn in Mundo, Converse Direction	6 23	5 9
Midheaven to the Biquintile of Mars in Mundo	6 33	5 11
Moon to the Biquintile of Saturn in Mundo, Direct Motion	6 44	6 1
Moon to the Sesquiquadrate of Saturn in Mundo, Converse Direction	6 59	6 4
Jupiter to the Sextile of Mars in Mundo, Converse Motion	7 14	6 6
Jupiter to the Parallel of the Moon in the Zodiac	7 18	6 7
Sun to the Square of Saturn in the Zodiac	7 19	6 7
Jupiter to the Sextile of Mars in the Zodiac, Converse Direction	7 41	6 11

OR GENETHLIACAL ASTRONOMY. 315

	ARC.		TIME.	
THE DIRECTIONS CONTINUED.	D.	M.	YRS.	MO.
Sun to his own Parallel in the Zodiac	8	4	7	3
Moon to the Sesquiquadrate of Saturn in the Zodiac, Converse Motion	8	48	7	11
Midheaven to the Biquintile of the Sun in Mundo	9	24	8	5
Midheaven to the Biquintile of Mercury in Mundo	10	35	9	7
Moon to the Quintile of Mars in the Zodiac	10	43	9	9
Ascendant to the Semiquartile of Saturn in Mundo	11	19	10	3
Jupiter to the Sextile of Venus in Mundo, Direct Direction	11	42	10	7
Jupiter to the Semiquartile of Mars in Mundo, Direct Motion	11	48	10	8
Jupiter to the Semiquartile of Mars in the Zodiac	11	51	10	8
Part of Fortune to the Body of Mars in Mundo	12	11	11	0
Moon to the Quintile of the Sun in the Zodiac	13	45	12	5
Moon to the Quintile of Mercury in the Zodiac	13	48	12	5
Jupiter to the Square of the Moon in Mundo, Direct Direction	14	0	12	7
Part of Fortune to the Semiquartile of the Moon in Mundo	14	21	12	10
Part of Fortune to the Sextile of Jupiter in Mundo	14	32	13	0
Jupiter to the Semiquartile of the Sun in Mundo, Direct Motion	14	38	13	1
Sun to the Semiquartile of the Moon in the Zodiac	14	45	13	2
Part of Fortune to the Body of the Sun in Mundo	15	0	13	6
Sun to the Quintile of Saturn in the Zodiac, Converse Direction	15	0	13	6
Jupiter to the Quintile of Mercury in Mundo, Converse Motion	15	1	13	6
Moon to the Semiquartile of Mercury in the Zodiac, Converse Direction	15	12	13	8
Sun to the Quintile of Jupiter in Mundo, Direct Motion	15	35	14	0
Sun to the Parallel of Saturn in Mundo, by the Rapt Motion	15	48	14	3
Jupiter to the Semiquartile of Mercury in Mundo, Direct Direction	15	56	14	5
Jupiter to the Semiquartile of Mercury in the Zodiac	16	7	14	7
Moon to the Semiquartile of Venus in Mundo, Direct Motion	16	15	14	8
Part of Fortune to the Body of Mercury in Mundo	16	19	14	9
Moon to the Sextile of Mars in Mundo, Direct Direction	16	20	14	9
Sun to the Quintile of Jupiter in the Zodiac	17	1	15	4
Moon to the Trine of Jupiter in Mundo, Direct Motion	17	1	15	4
Sun to the Semiquartile of Jupiter in the Zodiac, Converse Direction	17	1	15	4

CELESTIAL PHILOSOPHY,

	ARC.	TIME.
THE DIRECTIONS CONTINUED.	D. M.	YRS. MO.
Sun to the Body of Venus in the Zodiac	17 15	15 7
Jupiter to the Quintile of mars in mundo, Converse motion.	17 2	
Jupiter to the Quintile of Mercury in the Zodiac, Converse Direction	17 3	
Jupiter to the Sextile of Venus in the Zodiac	17 4	
Moon to the Sextile of Venus in the Zodiac	17 5	
Sun to the Body of Venus in Mundo, Direct Motion	18	
Moon to the Semiquartile of Mars in the Zodiac, Converse Direction	18 15	
Jupiter to the Square of Venus in the Zodiac, Converse Motion	18 2	
Ascendant to the Sextile of Venus in Mundo	19	
Moon to the Sextile of the Sun in Mundo, Direct Direction	19	
Ascendant to the Semiquartile of Mars in Mundo	19 1	
Jupiter to the Square of Venus in Mundo, Converse Motion	19 5	
Ascendant to the Square of the Moon in Mundo	20 1	
Midheaven to the Opposition of the Moon in Mundo	20 1	
Moon to the Sextile of Mercury in Mundo, Direct Direction	20 3	
Jupiter to the Quintile of Mars in the Zodiac, Converse Motion	20 3	
Moon to the Sesquiquadrate of Jupiter in the Zodiac	20 45	
Jupiter to the Sextile of Saturn in Mundo, Direct Direction.	21 1	
Midheaven to the Quintile of Jupiter in Mundo	21 1	
Ascendant to the Semiquartile of the Sun in Mundo	21 5	
Midheaven to Cor Leonis	22	
Ascendant to the Semiquartile of Mercury in Mundo	23 25	
Part of Fortune to the Quintile of Jupiter in Mundo	24 38	
Moon to the Trine of Saturn in Mundo, Converse Motion.	24 50	2
Jupiter to the Semiquartile of Saturn in the Zodiac	25 35	2
Sun to the Trine of Saturn in Mundo, Direct Direction	25	
Moon to the Parallel of Saturn in the Zodiac	26	
Ascendant to the Sextile of Saturn in Mundo	26	
Sun to the Parallel of Saturn in Mundo, Direct Motion	27 1	
Moon to the Trine of Saturn in the Zodiac, Converse Direction	27 27	2
Midheaven to the Biquintile of Venus in Mundo	27 34	2
Sun to the Semiquartile of Venus in the Zodiac, Converse Motion	28 8	25 6
Moon to the Square of Mars in the Zodiac	28 57	26 3

Sorry:
The defect on the previous page was that way in the original book we reproduced.

OR GENETHLIACAL ASTRONOMY. 317

	ARC.	TIME.
THE DIRECTIONS CONTINUED.	D. M.	YRS. MO.
Moon to the Sesquiquadrate of Jupiter in Mundo, Direct Direction	29 38	26 11
Moon to the Biquintile of Jupiter in the Zodiac	29 48	27 1
Moon to the Quintile of Venus in the Zodiac	30 3	27 4
Sun to the Sextile of Saturn in the zodiac, Converse Motion	30 6	27 4
Jupiter to the Square of Mercury in Mundo, Converse Direction	30 9	27 5
Moon to the Parallel of Saturn in the zodiac	30 17	27 7
Sun to the Square of Jupiter in Mundo, Direct Motion	30 43	27 11
Midheaven to the Sextile of Jupiter in Mundo	31 20	28 6
Sun to the Quintile of Saturn in Mundo, Converse Direction	31 29	28 8
Moon to the Square of the Sun in the zodiac	31 55	29 0
Moon to the Square of Mercury in the zodiac	31 59	29 1
Jupiter to the Square of Mars in Mundo, Converse Direction	32 28	29 6
Jupiter to the Semiquartile of Venus in Mundo, Direct Motion	32 49	29 10
Moon to the Quintile of Mars in Mundo, Direct Direction	33 11	30 2
Part of Fortune to the Body of Venus in Mundo	33 13	30 2
Jupiter to the Quintile of Saturn in Mundo, Direct Motion	33 21	30 4
Jupiter to the Body of Saturn in the zodiac, Converse Direction	33 58	30 11
Ascendant to the Quintile of the moon in mundo	34 33	31 6
Jupiter to the Body of Saturn in mundo, Converse motion	34 33	31 6
Jupiter to the Square of the Sun in the zodiac, Converse Direction	34 38	31 7
Jupiter to the Parallel of mars in mundo, by the Rapt motion	34 41	31 8
Jupiter to the Square of mercury in the zodiac, Converse Direction	35 20	32 3
Jupiter to the Square of the moon in the zodiac	35 25	32 4
Moon to the Quintile of Jupiter in mundo, Converse motion	35 25	32 4
Jupiter to the Parallel of the Sun in mundo, by the Rapt motion	35 41	32 7
Moon to the Quintile of the Sun in mundo, Direct Direction	35 51	32 9
Jupiter to the Parallel of mercury in mundo, by the Rapt motion	36 20	33 2
Part of Fortune to the Trine of Saturn in mundo	36 40	33 6
Moon to the Biquintile of Jupiter in mundo, Direct Direction	37 12	34 0
Sun to the Trine of Saturn in the zodiac	37 13	34 0
Moon to the Sextile of Venus in mundo, Direct motion	37 22	34 2

THE DIRECTIONS CONTINUED.

	ARC. D. M.	TIME. YRS. MO.
Sun to the Parallel of Saturn in mundo, Converse Direction.	37 32	34 4
Moon to the Quintile of mercury in mundo, Direct motion.	37 38	34 5
Jupiter to the Square of mars in the zodiac, Converse Direction	38 15	35 0
Ascendant to the Quintile of Saturn in mundo	38 41	35 5
Moon to the Opposition of Saturn in the zodiac	38 43	35 5
Jupiter to the Semiquartile of Venus in the zodiac	38 51	35 7
Jupiter to his own Semiquartile in mundo	39 31	36 2
Part of Fortune to the Square of Jupiter in Mundo	39 46	36 5
Moon to the Body of Venus in mundo, Converse motion	39 47	36 5
Moon to the Parallel of Saturn in mundo, by the Rapt motion	40 4	36 8
Ascendant to the Semiquartile of Venus in mundo	40 14	36 10
Midheaven to the Trine of mars in mundo	40 15	36 10
Sun to the Sesquiquadrate of Saturn in mundo, Direct Direction	40 58	37 7
Moon to the Body of Venus in the zodiac, Converse motion.	41 29	38 1
Sun to the Sextile of Venus in the zodiac, Converse Direction	41 37	38 3
Sun to the Semiquartile of mars in the zodiac	42 0	38 7
Jupiter to the Parallel of Venus in mundo, by the Rapt motion	42 34	39 2
Midheaven to the Trine of the Sun in mundo	42 52	39 5
Moon to the Opposition of Saturn in mundo Direct Direction	43 13	39 9
Sun to the Semiquartile of mercury in the zodiac, Converse motion	43 49	40 4
Ascendant to the Semiquartile of Jupiter in mundo	43 57	40 5
Sun to his own Semiquartile in the zodiac	44 35	41 0
Sun to the Semiquartile of mercury in the zodiac	44 38	41 1
Midheaven to the Trine of mercury in mundo	44 49	41 3
Sun to the Semiquartile of Venus in mundo, Converse Direction	44 49	41 3
Jupiter to the Trine of Venus in mundo, Converse motion	45 7	41 6
Jupiter to the Trine of Venus in the zodiac, Converse Direction	45 57	42 4
Jupiter to the Sextile of Saturn in the zodiac	46 23	42 10

In this Nativity, the Horoscope is excluded from the Dominion of Hyleg, in consequence of the position of Jupiter, who is in an Aphetical place, and *properly qualified* for that Office: for he is in *Zodiacal Trine with the Moon, and beholds her by a Parallel of Declination*, and is in Mundane, and Zodiacal Sextile with the Sun, and *ruler of the Part of Fortune* in the Radical Constitution; it is therefore *evident*, that Jupiter is the *legal* significator of Life. Now I do assert, that when the Prorogator is directed to the Quartile of the Moon in the Zodiac, and Parallel of the Sun in Mundo, by the Rapt Motion, the true Arcs of those Directions will be completely finished, and it is from *their Effects*, followed by many others of an obnoxious nature, and power, that I predict the dissolution of this Native: the first Direction above mentioned ascertains the period of that solemn Event, to take place, at the Age of thirty-two Years, and four Months. I am an enemy to *long Epistles* being wrought on any Geniture, therefore the best way is always to *come at once to the point*, and deliver an impartial Judgment on every Event of importance through Life without the least evasion: for when Men produce *vague remarks* where few words are sufficient, it only tends to shew their *ignorance*, and establish their *disgrace*. Those *notorious impostors* who have pretended to Calculate this Nativity, and who have predicted considerable Wealth at the Age of thirty-eight Years, may now observe, by my Computations, and Judgment, founded on the genuine principles of ASTRONOMY, that long before that period arrives, the Native will "pass that Bourn from whence no Travellers return".

At the Age of twelve Years, and seven Months, the Hyleg was directed to the Square of the Moon in the World, by a right Motion, the Effect of which, was productive of *a severe Indisposition*; and although several other inimical Directions were subsequently in operation to the Prorogator; the application of the Aphetical point to the Rays of Venus, saved the Life of the Native at that period.

At the time the *Mortal primary Directions to the Hyleg* will shew their Effects, the benevolent Planet Venus, *cannot render any relief to the giver of Life.* The Directions of Jupiter to the Rapt Parallel of Venus; and to the Trine of Venus in Mundo, and in the Zodiac, Converse Motion, *will be of no avail,* in consequence of the presence of the Enemies, with which Venus will be unfavorably conjoined by the *Rapt Motion of the Earth.*

If we *carefully* examine the nature of the *second* Direction in the Mortal train, and *properly regard* the affliction of the lesser Benefic, with the Rays of Saturn in the Radix, and likewise in directional Motion; we may easily foresee, that the Native's Death will be occasioned by a *violent Fever,* preceded, and attended with a rapid Consumption.

I believe it would not be interesting to the Reader, if I was to discuss all those testimonies which forebode advancement according to the Native's station in Life; but as his demise is not many Years distant, it would be of *no importance* to make observations on those subjects; though I shall here notice, that the Direction of the Midheaven to the Sextile of Jupiter in the World, will *most certainly produce Marriage, and Prosperity, &c.* at the Age of twenty eight Years, and a half. Was this Native destined for a longer Life, I should make copious remarks on the various sideral configurations and Directions, &c; but as that is not the case, I shall decline delivering any other occurrences on his few remaining Years; because when the spirit of the dead has abandoned its lifeless Clay which imprisoned it, *all Terrestrial Wealth, and Happiness, vanish like a shadow, and are no more.*

I have now concluded the thirty remarkable Nativities which I promised to give to the Public; and have endeavored to make *every subject as easy as possible*: the Computations of all the Arcs of Directions are made by *true, and natural Motion,* which may be proved by the use of the Celestial Globe, or Spherical Trigonometry. I shall now proceed with the subsequent part of the Celestial Philosophy, according to the announcement previously given to the Public.

THE EFFECTS OF DIRECTIONS.

The Sun, Moon, Ascendant, or Midheaven, directed to the Conjunction, Square, or Opposition of Saturn, indicates loss of Reputation, Office, and Estate: severe Illnesses, and Accidents of various denominations, according to the Signs, and positions of the significator, and promittor; which must be properly attended to in every Nativity.

The Sun, Moon, Ascendant, or Midheaven, directed to the Sextile, or Trine of Saturn, shews advantage by the means of elderly persons, or a legacy is bequeathed; and the Native is successful in every undertaking. This is to be understood when those Aspects are not augmented, or diminished, by Signs of long, or short Ascension.

The Sun, Moon, Ascendant, or Midheaven, directed to the Conjunction, Sextile or Trine of Jupiter, forebodes respectability, advancement, Honor, and Wealth: the Native is fortunate in all affairs, and Marriage is frequently Solemnized.

The Sun, Moon, Ascendant, or Midheaven, directed to the Square, or Opposition of Jupiter, portends troubles, and vexations, quarrels, and contentions; and loss of Estate by the means of ecclesiastical characters.

The Sun, Moon, Ascendant, or Midheaven, directed to the Conjunction, Square, or Opposition of Mars, are malevolent Directions, and denote manifold disputations, and commotions; scandal, disgrace, and loss of substance: Illnesses of various denominations, and sometimes Accidents.

The Sun, Moon, Ascendant, or Midheaven, directed to the Sextile, or Trine of Mars, gives Honor, and Preferment by Chemistry, or martial employment. In a Feminine Geniture, Marriage frequently occurs.

The Moon, or Ascendant, directed to the Conjunction, Square, or Opposition of the Sun, denotes Indisposition, and injury to the Eyes; many perplexities, and losses: the Native is suddenly deprived of Dignity, and Office, and credit, or Reputation is materially injured. The Midheaven to the Body of the Sun is a propitious Direction, and gives any Native Honor, and Promotion, according to the sphere of Life, which must be impartially investigated in all cases.

The Moon, Ascendant, or Midheaven, directed to the Sextile, or Trine of the Sun, will be productive of happiness, Honor, Wealth, popularity, and renown, and sometimes Marriage.

The Moon, Ascendant, or Midheaven, directed to the Square, or Opposition of Venus, are unpropitious Directions; and forebode troubles, and controversies; the Native also obtains disrespect from Females. The Direction of the Sun to the Square of Venus, is indicative of vexations, and difficulties, by various ways, and means.

The Sun, Moon, Ascendant, or Midheaven, directed to the Conjunction, Sextile, or Trine of Venus, foreshews Honor, and Promotion; the Native is very fortunate in every engagement; and the Matrimonial Union is frequently Solemnized, under the operation of any of these Directions.

The Moon, Ascendant, or Midheaven, directed to the Square, or Opposition of Mercury, denotes many accusations, contentions, troubles, disappointments, and losses, as well as Indisposition; the Native's undertakings are unsuccessful on all occasions. The Sun directed to the Square of Mercury, indicates vexations, and difficulties, in every Geniture.

The Sun, Moon, Ascendant, or Midheaven, directed to the Body, Sextile, or Trine of Mercury, gives an inclination to the Study of Arts, and Sciences; the Native is admired for ingenuity, and learning, and is successful in most undertakings; these Directions also indicate

Travelling; but when Mercury is afflicted in the Geniture, the Conjunction of that Planet to any of the above places, is productive of perplexities, and losses on all occasions.

The Sun, or Ascendant, directed to the Conjunction, Square, or Opposition of the Moon, are very inimical Directions, causing many troubles, difficulties, and losses; any of these Directions put the Life of the Native in considerable jeopardy, either by Indisposition, or Accident. The Midheaven to the Body of the Moon frequently produces Travelling, Marriage, and Prosperity.

The Sun, Ascendant, or Midheaven, directed to the Sextile, or Trine of the Moon, denotes Travelling, comfort, and happiness, with an augmentation of Honor, and Wealth: the Matrimonial Union is generally Solemnized, under the Effects of any of these Directions.

The Part of Fortune directed to any benevolent Aspect, produces an augmentation of Honor, and Riches; but to malevolent Rays, troubles, and a considerable diminution of Wealth.

The Sun, Moon, Ascendant, Midheaven, or Part of Fortune directed to the Quintile, or Biquintile of any Planet, denotes the Native to prosper in every undertaking; the Semiquartile, or Sesquiquadrate, is of a malevolent nature, and power.

The Luminaries directed to their own Sextiles, or to *any* Parallel of the Benefics, either in the Zodiac, or in the World, will consequently be productive of good Effects in the affairs of any Native: but the Directions of the Lights to their own Semiquartiles, or Squares, or to *any* Parallel of the Malevolents, denote troubles, and obstacles, and impair Health.

I have briefly explained the Effects of all Directions, which when compared with the remarks on the Nativities given in this Work, in Examples of Life, and Death, the Student may readily comprehend every portion of their influence in all parts of the Heavens, and in all cases whatsoever.

I have allowed malevolent Directions formed to the Sun, Moon, Ascendant, Midheaven, or Part of Fortune, to be productive of troubles, and losses, &c: in addition to which, I shall notice in this place, that the Hyleg directed to a violent train of unpropitious Aspects, (without sufficient aid from the benefics,) will, in every Nativity, produce inevitable dissolution, either natural, or violent; according to the positions, and configurations of the Celestial Bodies, at the time of Birth, combined with the prevalence of the Anaretical places, and Directions, which has been previously observed. From what I have here mentioned, every Student in this Science, will consequently predict the time of all Momentous Events, from the nature, and power of each Direction.

THE ESTABLISHED METHOD OF SELECTING THE TRUE HYLEG, IN ANY GENITURE.

In order to make the Aphetical places easy to be understood, I shall observe, that they commence with five degrees past the Cusp of the Second House, in the Ascendant, and extend as far as five degrees above the Horizon: the Eleventh House, and centre of that House, the whole of the Tenth, Ninth, and five degrees beyond the latter House, are also Aphetical places; and five degrees past the Cusp of the Eighth, in the Seventh, as far as five degrees past the Occidental Horizon, below the Earth, are likewise Prorogatory places. And among these again are preferred, as stronger, and more powerful, first they which are in the Zenith, then they in the East, next to those, they in the succeedant to the Midheaven, then the West, and lastly, they which precede the Midheaven: for whatsoever House of the twelve above the Earth, hath no configuration with the Horoscope is not proper to be taken; and that in a subterranean place, is unqualified for such a Dominion, except what come in to light with the Ascendant.

The Aphetas, or significators of Life, are five; and those are the Sun, Moon, Ascendant, Part of Fortune, and that Planet who hath most Dignities in the place of the Sun, Moon, Horoscope, and Part of Fortune, in the Figure of Birth; and in the place of the

Conjunction, or Opposition of the Luminaries, preceding the Geniture, in which this regularity must be observed.

In a diurnal Nativity, the Sun shall be preferred if he is in an Aphetical place; but if he be not, let the Moon; if she be not, that Planet shall be accepted that hath most titles of Dominion in the place of the Sun, the preceding Conjunction, and the Horoscope; (and in a Prorogatory place also,) that is, when he hath Dominion three ways or more, in one of the mentioned places, for all the ways of Dominion are five; but if there be none such, the Horoscope shall be taken as the true significator of Life.

By night, the Moon shall be preferred if she be in an Aphetical place; but if she be not, the Sun shall, if he be: if neither of the Luminaries should be so qualified, then take that Planet who hath most Dignities in the place of the Moon, the preceding full Moon, and the Part of Fortune, and in an Aphetical place: if there be none such, the Horoscope shall be taken if a Conjunction preceded, but if it was a full Moon, the Part of Fortune shall be allowed that Dominion, when found in an Aphetical place.

ON THE REVOLUTIONS OF KINGDOMS AND STATES, &c.

When any grand Mutations have come to pass, that are *visible to the World*, and in which the unbelievers are more or less involved, they then say, 'God does all these things,' which I by no means deny; but I ask, how does he perform, and bring to pass such EVENTS, which are considered so *miraculous* to the wisdom of Mortal Men? for it is certain, that *all things on Earth, are dependant on the Heavens, and occult power of the Celestial Bodies, which are secondary causes to execute the* DIVINE WILL, AND ETERNAL DECREE OF THE GREAT CREATOR, which I have proved to the most *licentious Infidel*.

All those who at present deny the existence of Stellar power, and who *impiously slander the Works of the Almighty*, will, (should they survive a few revolving Years,) be perfectly convinced of their Error; for in the Years 1820, and 1821, were observed in the Heavens *many appearances of an extraordinary, and formidable nature,* which cannot happen again for many Centuries to come. The Mundane power of such appearances will become manifest for a long period of time, and will be visible in many parts of the World.

But as the CELESTIAL BODIES are the *representatives* of KINGDOMS AND STATES, I must request the ingenious practitioner to pay the strictest attention to those wonderful Celestial Congresses, which were visible on the 17th 18th and 19th of April 1821; *on those days, Saturn, Jupiter, Mars, the Sun, Venus, and Mercury, were all conjoined in the* SIGN ARIES. Now reader pause, and consider these things in solitude, and do not *hastily*, and *wantonly* condemn, what I am certain you can never understand; for I do positively say, that this *great meeting in the Heavens, does most assuredly forebode a succession of* MANY MEMORABLE EVENTS OF THE GREATEST MAGNITUDE IN FOREIGN REALMS. I dare not presume to offer my impartial Judgment on *all* the DIREFUL EFFECTS of those Celestial Congresses: what the influence of such *remarkable* meetings of the Heavenly Bodies, hereafter will be, must be left for Time to determine. If the young Students are inclined to receive some information on this subject, they may read the names of those Kingdoms, Cities, and Countries, which are governed by the *four Cardinal points*, including those seated under *Gemini, and Virgo*, with *the opposite Signs;* and then they may instantly make their Judgment final, and see *every subsequent occurrence before them*, though yet in the womb of time. The Mundane influence of these Celestial appearances, will extend their *irresistible power with unbounded fury to remote realms for many Years*: HORRID WARS, DISSENTIONS, TUMULTS, VIOLENCE, IMPRISONMENTS, ASSASSINATIONS, SUDDEN DEATHS, *with incurable pestilential Fevers, and disorders of the Lungs, will be experienced in Foreign nations, with the Death of Men in high Authority, and power; dreadful Thunder, and Lightnings, will be prevalent in many places, with* AWFUL CONFLAGRATIONS, *and likewise high Winds, Tides, and violent Hurricanes, with many Shipwrecks, and unfortunate Navigations: great alterations in the Weather for a long period of time; the Waters in the Rivers will be diminished at intervals, and Springs dried up, so that Cattle in several places will receive great injury for want of Water; in consequence of which, will follow incurable diseases among them in several Places: these* DROUGHTS *of long continuance, will at certain periods be succeeded, as well as preceded,* BY UNCOMMON WET WEATHER, *which will cause* GREAT INNUNDATIONS; *Frost, Snow, and intense cold will abound in their Seasons, which will frequently prove injurious to the Seeds, and Fruits of the Earth; excessive heat, succeeded by very sudden transitions of immoderate cold, will very often be severely felt in several places, during many subsequent Years:* but as I have no authority to state WHERE THESE DIREFUL CALAMITIES WILL FALL, I must with reluctance remain silent; however I hope, and trust, that from what I have here stated, every industrious Student, will be enabled to form a correct Judgment on the long continued Effects of those *dreadful Celestial appearances*, which were so remarkably posited at the periods beforementioned.

It frequently occurs, that the Congresses of several of the Planets in some predominating Signs, and places, do not immediately shew their ominous Effects, but *many Years elapses before they become manifestly apparent.* In the Month of March 1789, the Sun, Saturn, Mars, Venus, and Mercury, were all conjoined in the Sign Pisces, and in the same Year, the Revolution in France broke out, which circumstance, and *many subsequent hostilities in that Kingdom,* were evidently foreboded from the Effects of the above Conjunction of five Planets in the Constellation of the Watery Triplicity: and whenever similar appearances of the Heavenly Bodies are observed, (the Sun being *properly* united,) they always produce commotions, and Revolutions, or a change of state in those places, governed by the Signs, and their opposites, which has been before observed: but Peace and Plenty, may certainly be predicted when those Congresses of the Planets have completed their formidable efficacy, or become disjoined by the rapidity of the inferior Stars. I might expatiate upon these subjects, but I believe sufficient has been mentioned by which any attentive Student in this Science, may *precisely* comprehend the manifold, and subsequent Effects of *every* extraordinary meeting of the Celestial Bodies.

CORRECT PRECEPTS FOR COMPUTING THE ECLIPSES OF THE SUN, AND MOON,

TO CALCULATE AN ECLIPSE OF THE MOON.

1. Find by Astronomical Tables, the true Time of the Ecliptic opposition, or full Moon, when an Eclipse is expected to happen: and let that Time be reduced to apparent Time, by increasing, or diminishing the same, by the equation of Time, as occasion requires. To which Time, viz. the true Ecliptic opposition of the Sun, and Moon; find the Moon's true Latitude, and her Hourly Motion in Latitude. Also, the Moon's Hourly Motion in Longitude, in order to find the Hourly Motion of the Moon from the Sun in Longitude. Find the Moon's Horizontal Parallax, and her Semidiameter; the Sun's Hourly Motion, and Semidiameter being found before. The Sun's Horizontal Parallax may always be taken at 9″.

2. Find the Angle of Inclination of the Axis of the Moon's way, with the (Northern) Axis of the Ecliptic; which is to the right hand, if the Moon has North Latitude ascending, or South Latitiude descending; otherwise, if the Moon has North Latitude descending, or South Latitude ascending, the Angle lies to the left hand of the Axis of the Ecliptic.

RULE.

To the co-arith. of log. Sine of the Moon's Hourly Motion from the Sun, add the log. Sine of the Moon's Hourly Motion in Latitude, the sum is the Tangent of the Angle required.

3. To find the nearest approach of the Centres of the Moon, and Earth's Shadow.

RULE.

To the co. sine of the Angle of the Moon's Inclination, add the log. sine of the Moon's true Latitude, (at the Ecliptic opposition,) and the sum will be the log. sine of the nearest approach of the Centres of the Moon, and Earth's Shadow.

4. Then from the sum of the Horizontal Parallaxes of the Sun, and Moon, subtract the Semidiameter of the Sun, the remainder is the apparent Semidiameter of the Earth's Shadow, which must be increased by 50″, on account of the Earth's Atmosphere.

To the Semidiameter of the Earth's Shadow, thus found and increased, add the Semidiameter of the Moon; and if that sum is more than the nearest approach of their Centres, the Moon will be Eclipsed at that Time; but if otherwise, she will not be Eclipsed.

5. The Moon being found Eclipsed; then from the sum of the Semidiameters of the Moon, and Earth's Shadow, subtract the nearest approach of their Centres, and the remainder is the part deficient.

Note. If the parts deficient are less than the Moon's apparent diameter, it shews the Eclipse will not be total; but if they be equal, then the Eclipse will be total without continuance; but if the parts deficient be more than the Moon's apparent diameter, then the Eclipse will be total with continuance.

The Analogy to find the Digits Eclipsed.

As the Semidiameter of the Moon : 6 Digits, or 360 : : part deficient : Digits Eclipsed. or

To the co-arith of logistical log. of the Moon's Semidiameter, add the logistical log. of parts deficient; the sum will be the logistical log. of the Digits Eclipsed.

6. With the argument of Latitude (longitude ☽ in Orbit — correct longitude ☊) found at the Time of the true Ecliptic opposition, take out the Moon's reduction from her proper Orbit to the Ecliptic, which equation is to be doubled, and turned into Time, by the Moon's Hourly Motion from the Sun; and you will have the Time between the true Syzygy and the mean Eclipse, or greatest Obscuration; which is to be added to, or subtracted from the Time of the true Ecliptic Opposition, according as the Moon is yet short of, or

past the next Node, and you will have the Time of the greatest Obscuration, or middle of the Eclipse.

7. *To find the Scruples of Incidence, or Motion of half duration.*

From the square of the sum of the Semidiameters, of the Moon, and Earth's Shadow, in seconds, deduct the square of the nearest approach of their Centres in seconds; the square root of what remains, will be the Motion of Semiduration, in seconds of a Degree.

To find the time thereof, say,

As the Hourly Motion of the Moon from the Sun : is to 1 Hour, or 60 Minutes in Time : : so is the Motion of Semiduration : to the Time of Semiduration; which being subtracted from, and added to the Time of the greatest Obscuration, will give the Time of the Beginning, and End of the Moon's Eclipse.

8. *To find the Scruples of half total Darkness in a total Eclipse of the Moon, and thence the continuance, Beginning, and End of total Darkness.*

RULE.

From the square of the difference of the Semidiameters of the Moon and Earth's Shadow, in seconds of a degree, deduct the square of the nearest approach of their Centres, in seconds of a degree; the square root of what remains, will be the Motion of Semiduration, in total Darkness, in seconds of a degree, which turned into Time, by the Hourly Motion of the Moon from the Sun, and subtracted from the middle of the Eclipse, gives the Time of Immersion or beginning of total Darkness; and added to the Time of the middle of the Eclipse, gives the Time of Emersion or End of total Darkness.

N. B. If the Time found is mean Time, it must be reduced to the apparent Time, by the Equation of Time.

And if the given place be not that for which the Tables are made, the allowance must be made for the difference of Meridians,

EXAMPLE.

A Computation of a total Eclipse of the Moon, December 3rd 1797, for the Meridian of the Royal Observatory at Greenwich.

	D.	H.	M.	S.
Equal Time of the true Ecliptic Opposition of the ☉ and ☽, is December	3	16	16	46
The Equation of Time, add................		+	9	18
The Apparent time at Greenwich	3	16	26	4

At which Time,

	S.	°	′	″
Sun's true place is............................	8	12	35	19
Moon's true place in the Ecliptic	2	12	35	19
Moon's true Latitude, South descending			4	55
Hourly Motion of ☽'s Latitude..............			3	15
Angle or Inclination of ☽'s way		5	40	34
Equat. 14th or reduction in Motion............			0	12
Moon's true Hourly Motion..................			35	14
Sun's true Hourly Motion			2	32
Moon's Horizontal Parallax..................			59	9
Sun's Horizontal Parallax			0	9
Sun's Semidiameter			16	17
Semidiameter of the Earth's Shadow			43	1
Semidiameter of the ⊖'s Shadow increased......			43	51
Moon's Semidiameter to be added			16	6
Semidiameter of the ☽ and ⊖'s Shadow......			59	57
Nearest approach of the Centre's of ☽ and Earth's Shadow			4	54
There remains parts deficient			55	3
Hence, Digits Eclipsed are		20	31	0
Time between the true Syzygy, and the middle of the Eclipse, to be added			0	44
Argument of Latitude was	11	29	10	
Hourly Motion of ☽ & ☉			32	42

For the Motion of half duration of this Eclipse.

                                                    °   ′   ″

Semidiameter of ☽ and ☉'s Shadow.. =59 57
Moon's Latitude, or nearest approach ..   4 54
Sum 1   4 51 = Sine 8,27561
Difference.....................   55 3 = Sine 8,20446

                                                                                    2)16,48007

Sine of Motion of half duration........ 59 45 —— 8,240035

                                          H.   ′   ″

Hence, half duration in Time will be.... 1 49 37

For the Motion of half duration in total Darkness.

                                                                            ′   ″

True Semidiameter of the ☉'s Shadow.. 43 51
Semidiameter of the ☽, subtract 16 6

Difference 27 45
Moon's Latitude, or nearest approach....   4 54

Sum .... 32 39 = Sine 7,97760
Difference .... 22 51 = Sine 7,82261

                                                                     2)15,80021

Sine of Motion of half duration .... 27 19 —— 7,900105
Hence, 27′ 19″ in Time is............ 50 7

Hence, the *Times of this Eclipse, December 3rd* 1797, *at Greenwich near London, according to Solar, or Apparent Time.*

                                        D. H. M. S.

Beginning December.......... 3 14 37 11 P. M.
Total darkness begins..........   15 36 41
Ecliptic opposition 16 26   4
Middle of the Eclipse..........   16 26 48

	H. M. S.
Total Darkness ends	17 16 55 P. M.
Eclipse ends	18 16 25

	H. M. S.
Duration of total Darkness	1 40 14
Duration of the whole Eclipse	3 39 14

Digits Eclipsed..20° 31′ 0″.

Note.

	′ ″
Sum of Semidiameter of ☽ and ☉'s Shadow	59 57
Semidiameter of the ☉'s Shadow	43 51
Latitude of the ☽ at the beginning of the Eclipse	10 45 South.
Latitude of the ☽ at the middle of the Eclipse	4 54 South.
Latitude of the ☽ at the end of the Eclipse	0 57 North.

TO COMPUTE ECLIPSES OF THE SUN.

PRECEPTS.

1. By Astronomical Tables find the time of the true Ecliptic Conjunction, or new Moon, when an Eclipse is expected to happen. From the Horizontal Parallax of the Moon, subtract the Horizontal Parallax of the Sun, the remainder will be the Semidiameter of the Earth's Disk. Likewise, to the Semidiameter of the Sun, add the Semidiameter of the Moon, the sum of which, will be the Semidiameter of the Moon's Penumbra.

2. To the Semidiameter of the Earth's Disk, add the Semidiameter of the Moon's Penumbra, and if the sum exceeds the nearest approach of their Centres, (found like the nearest approach of the Centres of the Moon and Earth's Shadow, in an Eclipse of the Moon,) the Sun will be Eclipsed in some part of the Earth: but otherwise no Eclipse of the Sun can happen.

3. The Sun being found Eclipsed in some part of the Earth, the Beginning, Middle, and End of the general and also central Eclipse, (with respect to the whole Earth,) may be found in like manner as is before directed, for finding the Beginning, Middle, and End of an Eclipse of the Moon.

To Calculate an Eclipse of the Sun for any particular place given, by Parallaxes.

1. Having found by Astronomical Tables, the true Ecliptic Conjunction of the Sun and Moon, together with their places in the Ecliptic; compute the Moon's true Latitude, with all the other requisites, adapted to the particular place given.

Find also, the Moon's Horizontal Parallax, her apparent Semidiameter, and Hourly Motion in Longitude and Latitude, as also the Sun's apparent Semidiameter, and Hourly Motion.

2. To the apparent Time of the true Conjunction of the Sun and Moon, compute the Parallax of the Moon from the Sun, in Longitude.

3. To half an Hour, an Hour or more, (as the said Parallax is small or great,) before or after the true Conjunction, according as the Moon is in the *Eastern, or Western* Quadrant of the Ecliptic, compute again the Parallax of the Moon from the Sun in Longitude; by which means, (from the true,) you will have the visible half, Hourly, &c. Motion of the Moon from the Sun.

Note. To Compute the Parallaxes of the Moon in Longitude, and Latitude, in Solar Eclipses.

For the Moon's Parallax in Longitude.

The Equatorial Horizontal Parallax of the Moon, is first to be reduced from the Sphere to the Spheroid for the Latitude of the place.

To the Sine of the Horizontal Parallax, add the Sine of the Altitude of the Nonagesimal degree of the Ecliptic, and the Sine of the distance of the Sun, (or Moon's visible distance,) from the Nonagesimal degree, and their sum will be the Sine of the Moon's Parallax in Longitude.

Note. The Moon's Parallax in Longitude is to be added, or subtracted to the Moon's true place, as the Sun is to the East, or West of the Nonagesimal degree.

For the Moon's Parallax in Latitude.

To the Sine of the Moon's Horizontal Parallax, add the Co-sine of the Altitude of the Nonagesimal degree of the Ecliptic, and the sum will be the Sine of the Moon's Parallax in Latitude.

Note. The Moon's Parallax in Latitude always depress her Southward, in Northern Latitudes without the Tropicks; that is diminish her *true* North Latitude, and increase her *true* South Latitude.

Now say, As the visible Motion of ☽ ☌ ☉ : is to the Time taken : : so is the Parallax of the Moon from the Sun in Longitude at the Time of the true Conjunction: to the Interval of the true and visible Conjunction, which added to, or subtracted from, the Time of the true Conjunction, according as the Moon is to the East, or West of the Nonagesimal degree, will give the Time of the visible Conjunction of the Sun and Moon.

4. To which time, compute again the true places of the Sun and Moon, with the Parallax of the ☽ á ☉ in Longitude and Latitude, and so find the apparent or visible place of the Moon, in respect of the Sun; and also the Moon's visible Latitude.

5. To ten or fifteen Minutes (more or less,) before or after the visible Conjunction, as the Moon's visible Latitude is found to be increasing, or decreasing, compute the visible Longitude of the ☽ á ☉; with her visible Latitude. Now say, As the Sine of the visible Motion of ☽ á ☉ in Longitude, in the Time taken : is to Radius : : so is the Tangent of the difference of visible Latitudes (between the visible Conjunction and Time taken) : to the Tangent of the Angle of the visible way of the Moon with the Ecliptic at the Time of the visible Conjunction. And, as Radius : is to the Sine of the visible Latitude of the Moon at the visible Conjunction : : so is the Sine of the Angle of the visible way of the Moon with the Ecliptic at that Time : to the Sine of the Motion seen from the visible Conjunction, to the greatest Obscuration.

And, : : so is the Co-sine of that Angle : to the Sine of the visible distance of the Centres of the Sun and Moon at the Time of the greatest Obscuration, that is, their nearest visible distance.

Note. If this distance be less than the Semidiameter of the *Moon's* Penumbra, the *Sun* will be Eclipsed at that place; but otherwise not.

Note. If the Moon's place be more than the place of the Nonagesimal degree, according to the order of the Signs, then she is *East* of the Nonagesimal degree, and the Parallax in Longitude adds.

But if it is the contrary, she is to the *West* of the Nonagesimal degree, and the Parallax in Longitude subtracts.

6. The Sun being found Eclipsed; from the Semidiameter of the Penumbra, subtract the nearest visible distance of the Centres of the Sun and Moon, the remainder will be the part deficient; from which the Digits Eclipsed may be found.

7. Now say, As the visible Motion of the Moon from the Sun in the Time before taken, (before or after the visible Conjunction,) : is to that Time : : so is the Motion seen from the visible Conjunction, to the greatest Obscuration : to the Interval in Time, which being added to, or subtracted from the Time of the visible Conjunction (as the *visible* Latitude is decreasing or increasing) gives the Time of the greatest Obscuration, or the middle of the Eclipse.

8. To the Semidiameter of the Penumbra, add and subtract the nearest visible distance of the Centres of the Sun and Moon,

To the Logistical log. of that sum, add the Logistical log. of their difference; divide that sum by two, and you will have the Logistical log. of the visible Motion of Semiduration in Minutes and seconds of a degree.

9. Now say, As the Sine of the visible Motion of the Moon from the Sun in Longitude for an Hour, or more, before the visible Conjunction, : is to Radius : : so is the Tangent of the difference of visible Latitude in that Time : to the Tangent of the Angle of the visible way of the Moon with the Ecliptic, from the Beginning of the Eclipse to the visible Conjunction.

And, as Radius : is to the Sine of the visible Motion of Semiduration : : so is the Co-sine of that Angle : to the Sine of the visible Motion in Longitude from the Beginning of the Eclipse to the greatest Obscuration, or middle of the Eclipse.

10. Likewise, As the visible Motion of the Moon from the Sun, in Longitude in the Hour, (or more,) before the visible Conjunction

OR GENETHLIACAL ASTRONOMY.

: is to 1 hour, (or more,) : : so is the Motion in Longitude seen from the Beginning of the Eclipse to the greatest Obscuration : to the Time of Incidence; which subtract from the Time of the greatest Obscuration, gives the Time of the Beginning of the Eclipse.

By the like proportions, (from the visible Longitude of the Moon from the Sun in consequence with her visible Latitude for an Hour, or more, after the visible Conjunction,) you may find the Time of Emergence, and so the End of the Eclipse.

EXAMPLE.

Computation of the Solar Eclipse, which happened April 1st 1764, from Tables, agreeing very near with Mayer's Tables of 1770.

For the Meridian of Greenwich, and Latitude 51° 30'.

	H.	M.	S.
Equal Time of the Ecliptic Conjunction, at Greenwich Observatory	10	24	52
Equation of Time, subtract		3	50
Apparent Time at Greenwich	10	21	2

	°	′	″
Sun and Moon's Longitude in the Ecliptic ♈	12	9	43
Right Ascension of the Medium Cæli	346	21	23
Culminating point	15	10	36
Place of Nonagesimal Degree ♈	16	25	
Moon's Ecliptic place subtract ♈	12	10	
Distance of ☽ á Nonagesimal Degree	4	15 west.	
Altitude of Nonagesimal Degree	39	3	
Moon's Horizontal Parallax á ☉ (☉'s 9″)	54	4	
Moon's Parallax in Longitude á ☉	2	33	
Moon's Parallax in Latitude á ☉	42	0	
Moon's true Latitude North ascending, subtract	39	31	
Remains ☽'s visible Latitude South	2	29	

340   CELESTIAL PHILOSOPHY,

	′ ″
Moon's true Hourly Motion	29 44
Sun's Hourly Motion, subtract	2 28
Hourly Motion of ☽ á ☉	27 16
Moon's Horizontal Parallax	54 13
Semidiameter of the Sun	16 2
Semidiameter of the Moon	14 47
Hourly increase of the Moon's Latitude	2 43
Hourly increase of the Sun's Right Ascension	2 17
Hourly increase of the Sun's Declination	0 59

An observation.

Instead of the *Sines* in these operations, as there is trouble to obtain them to seconds, (except you have Tables that has them to seconds,) you may use *Shakerly's* Logistical Log. and then remember to make the first Figure the Index: but then the Co-sines and Tangets must be had from their proper Tables.

As the Moon is to the West of the Nonagesimal Degree at the true Ecliptic Conjunction, the visible Conjunction of course must follow; and as her Parallax in Longitude á ☉ is = 2′ 33″, the visible Conjunction must fall about eight, or ten Minutes after the true Conjunction.

The Requisites for Greenwich.

Eight Minutes after Time of the true Conjunction. 10h. 29m. 2s.

	° ′ ″
Right Ascension of the Medium Cæli	318 21 41
Culminating point	♓ 17 20 35
Place of Nonagesimal Degree	♈ 17 58 0
Moon's true Ecliptic place	♈ 12 13 41
Moon's distance from Nonagesimal Degree	5 44 west.
Altitude of Nonagesimal Degree	39 49 0

OR GENETHLIACAL ASTRONOMY.

	′	″
Moon's Parallax in Longitude á ☉	3	30
Moon's Parallax in Latitude á ☉	41	32
Moon's true Latitude North, subtract	39	53
Moon's visible Latitude South descending	1	39

	′	″
True Motion of ☽ á ☉ in eight Minutes.............	3	38
Difference of Parallax in Longitude of ☽ á ☉ in eight Minutes subtract	0	57
Remains visible Motion of ☽ from Sun in eight Minutes..	2	41

Now, as the visible Motion of ☽ from Sun 2′ 41″ to 8 Minutes, so is the Moon's Parallax in Longitude from Sun at the true Conjunction, 2′ 33″, to 7′ 36″, the Interval between the true and visible Conjunction.

Now from the last statement, I shall proceed to find the Time of the greatest Obscuration, or Middle of the Eclipse.

As the Sine of the visible Motion ☽ from Sun in last eight Minutes, 2′ 41″............... ...	6,89240
To Radius, (or 90°.)	10,00000
So Tangent of diff. ☽'s visible Lat. in 8′—0′ 50″..	6,38454
To Tangent ☽'s visible way from Sun..17° 15′..	9,49214

AGAIN,

As Radius, (or 90°)	10,00000
To Sine of Moon's visible Lat. (8′ after true Conj.) 1′ 39″	6,68121
So Co-sine Moon's visible way from Sun . 17° 15′	9,98001
To Sine of nearest approach of Sun and Moon. 1′ 35″	6,66122

AGAIN,

As Radius, (or 90°)	10,00000
To (Sine of 1′ 35″) same	6,66122

So Sine of Moon's visible way from Sun,....17° 15' 9,47208

To Sine of dist. from visible Conjunction to
the greatest Obscuration, or Middle.... } 0' 28"..6,13330

Now 28" is the Motion from visible Conjunction to the greatest Obscuration; and is turned into Time as follows.

Visible Motion of Moon from Sun in last 8' is 2' 41".

SAY,

As 2' 41" : 8' :: 28" : 1' 24" the Time to be added.

$$\begin{array}{r} \text{L L} \\ 8'\ldots\ 8751 \\ 28''\ldots 21091 \\ \hline 29842 \end{array}$$

Logist. log. of 2' 41" sub. 13495

Logist. log. of 1' 24".... 16347 To be addded for the Middle.

For the Scruples of Incidence.

	'	"
Semidiameter of the Sun...................	16	2
The Moon's at the Altitude of 40°.........	14	57
The Penumbra	30	59
Nearest approach.........................	1	34

$$\begin{array}{r} \text{L L} \\ \text{Sum}\ldots\ 32\ 33\ldots 2656 \\ \text{Remains part deficient}\ldots\ldots 29\ 25\ldots 3096 \\ \hline 2)5752 \\ \hline \end{array}$$

Scruples of Incidence...... 30' 56" 2876

The Digits Eclipsed are found as in Lunar Eclipses, only instead of the Moon's Semidiameter, you must use the Sun's, viz. 16' 2". The part deficient being 29' 25", the Digits Eclipsed, come out 11° 0' 0", on the Sun's lower limb; because the Moon's visible Latitude is South.

To find the Time of Incidence, and thence the Beginning of the Eclipse.

Repeat the Computation for 85 Minutes before the last, (being as near the Beginning as can be estimated,) as under.

	H.	M.	S.
85' before visible Conjunction at Greenwich, viz.	9	3	38

		°	'	"
Right Ascension of Medium Cæli then is......		327	3	25
Culminating point	♒	24	45	31
Place of Nonagesimal Degree...........	♈	0	16	0
Moon's place at this Time	♈	11	31	34
Moon's distance from Nonagesimal Degree....		11	15	34 East.
Altitude of Nonagesimal Degree		31	28	0
Moon's Parallax in Longitude á ☉			5	33
True Motion of ☽ á ☉ in 85 Minutes			38	38
Sum of the Parallax in Long. ☽ á ☉ in 85' (☽ being now East of 90°) viz. 3' 30" & 5' 33" = ...			9	3
Remains visible Motion of ☽ á ☉ in 85 Minutes.			29	35
Moon's Parallax in Latitude á ☉ is			46	7
Moon's true Latitude North at this Time, subtract			36	2
Remains the ☽'s visible Latitude South......			10	5

NOW SAY,

As Sine of visible Motion ☽ á ☉, 85' before visible Conjunction..............	29' 35"	7,93476
To Radius, (or 90°).....................		10,00000
So Tangent diff. ☽'s visible Lat. in 85'....	8' 26"	7,38973
To Tangent of Angle ☽'s visible way á ☉ 15° 55'		9,45497

AGAIN,

As Radius, (or 90°,)		10,00000
To Co-sine of ☽'s visible way á ☉, ...	15° 55	9,98302

344   CELESTIAL PHILOSOPHY,

To Sine of Scruples of Incidence, 30′ 56″ 7,95415

To the Motion of Incidence, 29′ 45″ (Sine.) 7,93717

NOW SAY,

                   L L
As visible Motion ☽ á ☉ (29′ 45″ in 85′,) in 1 Hour 21′ 0″ 4559
To 1 Hour, So the Motion of Incidence, 29′ 45″ subtract. 3047

To the *Time* of Incidence, 1H. 25M. 0S. 1512

To find the Time of Repletion, and End of this Eclipse.

Take an Hour and half after the visible Conjunction at Greenwich.
90′ after the visible Conjunction at Greenwich. 11H. 58M. 3Ss.

	°	′	″
Right Ascension of the Medium Cæli, then is	10	55	6
The Culminating point....................... ♈	11	52	38
Place of Nonagesimal Degree .... ♉	4	33	0
Moon's place in the Ecliptic................. ♈	12	58	0
Moon's dist. from Nonagesimal Degree, (but her visible dist. is 21° 50′ for 21° 35′ + 15′)....	21	35	0
Moon's Parallax in Longitude á ☉ (found by her vis. dist. 21° 50′. and Alt. of Nonages. deg. 47° 50′)		14	5
True Motion of ☽ á ☉ in 90 Minutes is		40	54
Increase of ☾'s Parallax in Longitude from ☉ in 90′ last taken		11	24
Visible Motion ☽ á ☉ in 90 Minutes...........		29	30
Moon's true Latitude at this Time is...... (North.)		43	57
Moon's Parallax in Latitude á ☉................		36	17
Remains Moon's visible Latitude North		7	40

NOW SAY.

As Sine of visible Motion ☽ from Sun, 90′ apparent visible Conjunction.......... } 29′ 30″ 7,93354

OR GENETHLIACAL ASTRONOMY.

To Radius, (or 90°) 10,00000
So Tangent diff. of Moon's vis. Lat. in 90', viz. 9' 19" 7,43299

To Tangent Moon's visible way from Sun .. 17° 32' 9,49945

AGAIN,

As Radius, (or 90°)...................... 10,00000
To Co-sine of Moon's visible way from Sun.. 17° 32' 9,97934
So Sine of Scruples of Incidence .... 30' 56" 7,95415

To Sine of Motion of Incidence, or Repletion, or vis. Motion of Moon from Sun in the Ecliptic, 29' 30" 7,93349

NOW SAY,

As visible Motion of Moon from Sun, 29' 30" in 90'. To 90 Minutes. So Motion of Repletion, 29' 30". To the *Time* of Repletion, viz. 1 Hour, 30 Minutes, as required.

HENCE, AT GREENWICH,

	H.	M.	S.	
Apparent Time of the True Conjunction ..	10	21	2	Morning.
Interval of True and visible Conjunction, add.		7	36	
Apparent time of visible Conjunction	10	28	38	
Interval between visible Conjunction, and Middle of the Eclipse, add		1	24	
Middle, or greatest *Obscurity*............	10	30	2	
Time of *Incidence*, subtract	1	25	0	
Apparent Time of the Beginning...........	9	5	2	
Time of Repletion, add to Middle........	1	30	0	
END OF THE ECLIPSE......................	12	0	2	

SOLAR ECLIPSE, April 1st 1764.

	H.	M.	S.	
Beginning	9	5	2	
Visible Conjunction ..	10	28	38	Apparent Time, Morning.
Middle	10	30	2	
End	12	0	2	

Duration .... 2h. 55m. 0s.
Digits Eclipsed ...... 11° 0' 0"

This Eclipse was observed at *London*, to Begin at five Minutes past nine in the Morning; Middle at thirty-one Minutes past ten; and the end to be about one Minute past twelve at Noon.

The end of the Precepts for computing SOLAR AND LUNAR ECLIPSES.

THE ELEMENTS OF THE GREAT ECLIPSE OF THE SUN, on the 15th OF MAY 1836.
For the Meridian and Latitude of Greenwich.

Mean Time of the Ecliptic Conj. May 15th. 2h. 6m. 44s. P. M.

	°	′	″
Longitude of the Sun and Moon, from the true Equinox	54	42	20
Right Ascension of the Sun	52	20	34
Sun's Declination North	18	57	48
Sun's Horary Motion in Longitude		2	24
Sun's Horary Motion in Right Ascension		2	28
Sun's Horary Motion in Declination, increasing			35
Sun's Semidiameter		15	50
Obliquity of the Ecliptic	23	27	44
Moon's Equatorial Horizontal Parallax		54	24
Moon's Latitude North, increasing		25	42
Moon's Horary Motion in Longitude		30	0
Moon's Horary Motion in Latitude		2	46 ·5
Moon's Horizontal Semidiameter		14	50
Angle of the relative Orbit with the Ecliptic	5	44	32
Horary Motion of the Moon from the Sun in the relative Orbit		27	44
The Equation of Time		3	57

Hence, the Apparent Time of Conjunction. 2h. 10m. 41s. P. M.